ENGLISH
THOUGHT

1860–1900

The Theological Aspect

SOME WORKS BY THE SAME AUTHOR

Religion in the Victorian Era (3rd edition 1953)

The Early Evangelicals : A Religious and Social Study (1953)

Erasmus the Reformer (Hulsean Lectures) (2nd edition 1928)

The Story of England's Church (1945)

Divine Providence and Human Destiny (1943)

The Beginnings of Western Christendom (1948)

Jeremiah (Westminster Commentaries) (1919)

Numbers (Westminster Commentaries) (1927)

From Moses to Elisha (Clarendon Bible) (1929)

The Development of English Theology in the Later XIX Century (1952)

ENGLISH THOUGHT

1860 - 1900

The Theological Aspect

by

L. E. ELLIOTT-BINNS

D.D., F.R.Hist.S.

*Hulsean Lecturer in the University
of Cambridge 1921–2; late Canon
Residentiary of Truro Cathedral*

LONGMANS, GREEN AND CO

LONDON · NEW YORK · TORONTO

LONGMANS, GREEN AND CO LTD
6 & 7 CLIFFORD STREET LONDON W1
BOSTON HOUSE STRAND STREET CAPE TOWN
531 LITTLE COLLINS STREET MELBOURNE

LONGMANS, GREEN AND CO INC
55 FIFTH AVENUE NEW YORK 3

LONGMANS, GREEN AND CO
20 CRANFIELD ROAD TORONTO 16

ORIENT LONGMANS LTD
CALCUTTA BOMBAY MADRAS
DELHI VIJAYAWADA DACCA

First Published 1956

Printed in Great Britain by
Jarrold & Sons Limited, Norwich

PREFACE ·

WHEN I was appointed to deliver the Burroughs Memorial Lectures at Leeds University in 1950 the subject given to me was 'The Development of English Theology in the Later Nineteenth Century', the aim of the course being to provide a sequel to Storr's well-known volume which stopped short at 1860—the author's intention of continuing it never having been carried out. After the publication of the lectures several reviewers expressed regret that the subject had had to be treated within the narrow compass of six lectures; the publishers thereupon asked me to undertake a full-length continuation. The present volume, which incorporates some of the original matter, is the result.

The book, it will be observed, bears a title other than that of its predecessor. The reasons for the change were compelling, if a truly accurate description of its scope and contents was to be attained; for I found that, more or less unconsciously, wider sympathies were flooding into my mind. Here two principles stood out: the close and inevitable connexion between theology and religion, and the extent to which both theology and religion were influenced by, and, in turn, exercised influence upon the entire current of life and thought; for though thinkers, or some of them, might repudiate such conceptions, none the less they were unable to avoid their attraction.

Behind the volume lies the greater part of a lifetime of thought and study; often combined with, though never intermitted by, practical activities (I have had charge of three large parishes, including West Ham) and the problems with which it endeavours to cope I have, in a more developed form, myself experienced and sought to face. And so I ask: 'How far can the new order which is emerging, the various clashes in the complex range of ideas, be reduced to a comprehensive harmony of scheme and design; how far, for me personally, can they be incorporated into the evolving tradition of Anglican teaching and worship?'

What matters supremely is not the details, but the general trend; and so in dealing with the subject of biblical studies (part only of my task) I have deliberately abstained from minute discussions. Here perhaps I suffer from 'excess' of knowledge; for my main preoccupation (apart from history, if indeed, they can be separated from it) has been with these very studies, especially as they concerned the Old Testament. To have treated them at length would have required a volume in itself.

The scope of the work, from its very nature, is primarily descriptive rather than expository; but it is more than a bare catalogue of ideas and opinions, for I have endeavoured to account for their rise and diffusion. This has been a task of immense difficulty, for the filiation of ideas is often as hard to trace as are remote genealogical descents. By relating them to the general intellectual, social, and economic background I have sought to explain their emergence at a particular epoch. In my inquiry I have striven to avoid being influenced by my own special point of view, and any lapses have been unconscious. But such lapses cannot entirely be eliminated, for to write without prejudice is only possible for a mind that is either devoid of previous impressions, or is a mere mirror—and even mirrors may give a distorted reflection. For this reason, among others, I have been at pains to quote rather freely the actual words of contemporary writers. In a few cases books which appeared to be of special importance have been summarized, but to have multiplied such summaries would have greatly increased the size of the volume, and perhaps have become tedious.

To pass judgment on the last century is a hazardous matter, even for those of us who knew it in our youth, for every age has its own form of blindness, as G. M. Trevelyan has recently reminded us (*A Layman's Love of Letters*, p. 106), and in any case we are too near it to assess satisfactorily the value of its contribution to theology, though quite clearly it provided a definite and most important stage of development. In attempting to make even a tentative assessment it is, moreover, necessary to be on one's guard against reading back developments which belong to our own day and were beyond the purview of older generations, for men are seldom aware of the remoter consequences of their theories.

In view of this, and of the danger of putting forth premature judgments, I may seem to have been chary of arriving at conclusions; but such an attitude is really unavoidable, for we must bear in mind the warning of George Meredith in *Modern Love*, L., 11 f.

> Ah, what a dusty answer gets the soul
> When hot for certainties in this our life.

It has been suggested to me that 1914 would have formed a better terminus than 1900; but in confining myself to the nineteenth century I have kept to Storr's original scheme, for which much may be said. After all there was such a thing as the Victorian Era, even in theology.

Finally I should like to express my thanks to the publishers for consenting to the change of title, and to their unknown reader who proposed this, and also put forward a number of very helpful suggestions.

Freshwell House,　　　　　　　　　　　L. E. ELLIOTT-BINNS
Saffron Walden
June 1955

ABBREVIATIONS

Enc. Bib.	*The Encyclopaedia Biblica.*
Enc. Brit.	*The Encyclopaedia Britannica.*
E.R.E.	*The Encyclopaedia of Religion and Ethics.*
J.T.S.	*The Journal of Theological Studies.*

CONTENTS

Chapter One

THE POSITION IN 1860

THE subject of our inquiry is the development of theology during a limited period and within a particular area. It will be well to begin by defining what we mean by 'development' and 'theology'.

Storr, in the volume to which this is a sequel, gave the senses in which he used the terms,[1] and though my own usage is similar it will be an advantage to elucidate it. The term 'development' and the idea itself was first brought into connexion with English Theology by Newman;[2] but even if this had not been the case the notion of development was so widely prevalent that it would inevitably have been applied to theology. Newman seems to have identified development with growth, making use of the simile of the acorn and the oak; but this is to narrow its meaning, and so understood it would provide no satisfactory or adequate definition for our purpose.[3] That purpose is to track the origin and subsequent working out of the various trends in theology belonging to our period and, as best we may, to account for them. The term therefore will be employed, without any technical connotation, as a convenient way of describing the unfolding of ideas, both old and new, disregarding, save incidentally, any

[1] *The Development of English Theology*, etc., pp. 12ff. In an earlier work, *Development and Divine Purpose*, p. 210, Storr equated development and evolution, suggesting that if there is any difference between them it is that evolution directs our thoughts rather to the source, development to the goal, of the process.

[2] Cf. Fairbairn, *The Place of Christ in Modern Theology*, pp. 25ff. He suggested that with Newman it was not so much a scientific doctrine as a form of personal apology, exhibiting, as it were, the logic of his conversion.

[3] Loisy used to say that the development the Church most needed was a development of the idea of development itself.

I

distinction between those which were developments in the stricter sense of the term and those which were of freer growth.

Theology was defined by Fairbairn as 'the science of a living God and of His work in and for a living world'.[1] By some scholars the task of Christian theology is confined to the setting forth in a systematic and connected form of the material contained in the Bible. This, however, is too narrow a restriction and for our purposes theology will be taken in its widest sense. Thus approached it is seen, like natural science, to cover a great variety of subjects; no less than twenty-three departments of theology have been distinguished,[2] though all of them standing in close relation to one another. Our main interest is 'historical theology' whose task is to examine the various leading ideas and to trace their rise and later course; thus linking up with Comparative Religion, whose objects and methods it largely shares, and, on the purely intellectual side, having affinities with the Philosophy of Religion and, indeed, through it, with Philosophy in general.

At this point it is necessary to consider the relations of theology and religion and to attempt to distinguish them the one from the other. This is no easy task, for both in popular usage and actual fact they frequently overlap. Religion, it may be said, has a wider range and provides much of the material upon which theology has to work. Theology, indeed, viewed from one aspect, is the science of religion, and stands to it in the same way as aesthetics stand to art, as harmony to music, or prosody to verse; it has to examine religious experiences of one kind or another, to assess their value, to interpret them, and finally to attempt to arrange them in some kind of systematic form. The scientific theologian may therefore be regarded not so much as an explorer, but as a constructor of maps and diagrams based on the reports and accounts of more adventurous voyagers.

It is, however, easy to make too sharp a distinction between religion and theology and in what follows I may seem at times

[1] *Op. cit.*, p. 403. John Smith, the Cambridge Platonist, would hardly have agreed with this. 'Were I indeed to define divinity, I should rather call it a *divine life*, than a *divine science*.' (*Select Discourses*, p. 3.)

[2] See *E.R.E.*, Vol. XII, pp. 293 ff.

to have overstepped the boundary line which divides them. Any such apparent frontier violations, however, have been deliberate and calculated, and that for two reasons. In the first place the history of Christianity shows quite plainly that ideas which now form part of the accepted dogmatic scheme originally arose among the common people and were eventually accepted on account of their supposed spiritual value; and, secondly, those responsible for framing the theological outline are themselves deeply affected by their own early training and religious environment; they may seek to counteract these effects, or they may be unconscious of them; in either case their outlook on life and on the problems which face them as theologians depends greatly upon such impressions.

Theology, then, is no merely academic pursuit, but is closely linked with everyday life, by which it is influenced, and upon which it exercises influence. But theologians, as is the manner of other thinkers, are often tempted to construct a small private world of their own. To do so certainly simplifies their problems, though it may not conduce to the discovery of correct solutions. They, and leaders of religion with them, are for this reason naturally conservative, disliking new notions which disturb their settled ways and may even make their chosen habitation no longer tenable. Hence their opposition to demands for restatement and reconsideration. Some of them may even go so far as to deny the necessity for any modification, and like unscrupulous or ignorant physicians support their diagnosis by deliberately misinterpreting the symptoms.

But if religion is to survive as a living and effective force and not to subsist as the hobby of a few pious and simple souls, sooner or later its theological outline will be compelled to submit to modifications. A study of conditions in the later nineteenth century and of the influences which induced theologians, slowly indeed and often grudgingly, to make concessions, must be of unquestionable value for their present-day successors. For the problems are still much the same, though our method of treatment may carry a different emphasis. Then the primary line of approach was historical and metaphysical, now it has become more biblical and psychological, and even liturgical. In any event a knowledge of the changes and developments which have led up to the present position is essential, for, again to quote Fairbairn, 'We must understand the factors and forces that have moved and shaped the theologies of the past before we can, even in the rudest outlines, draw the groundwork of a theology for the present.'[1] One lesson, at least, such a study should teach us (and this may give us more sympathy with the apparently excessive caution of theologians and ecclesiastics in the nineteenth century), the danger of attempting a premature synthesis. There are, indeed, times when it is the highest wisdom to be silent and let the years revolve.[2] 'If you marry the Spirit of your generation', Dean Inge has warned us, 'you will be a widow in the next.'[3]

In our study we shall be treading ground which is already well worn by the feet of innumerable scholars; but a fresh exploration is still called for, since ideas operate largely in secret and no age is fully aware of those which are at work in its midst; every passing year enables us to see things in truer perspective and proportion, even if the time has not yet arrived for anything in the nature of a final judgment on the achievements of English theology in the later nineteenth century.

The nineteenth century was a period of vast and profound changes in all departments of life and thought, and none was without its effect upon religion and theology. If such effects were frequently only indirect they were none the less considerable, for life and thought inevitably react upon one another. They had one further consequence, for the novel conditions which were their outcome brought to theologians and religious leaders, in so far as they recognized the challenge contained in them, a fresh realization of the scope and potentialities of the Gospel message.

[1] *Op. cit.*, p. ix. Cf. Sanday, *Inspiration*, p. 3: 'In order to determine how much of our present ideas is valid the first thing to be done is to trace them back to their roots.'

[2] Cf. Dante, *Paradiso*, ix, 4, *Taci, e lascia volgar gli anni.*

[3] *The Diary of a Dean*, p. 12.

Two events seem to me to have had special importance for theology and religion—the repeal of the paper duty in 1860, and the beginnings of a national system of education.[1] The full significance of these changes was not immediately realized, nor the consequences which would follow them. It is a striking fact that the most far-reaching changes in the affairs of men are frequently those which are least recognized by contemporaries. In the past the nation might be said to have been divided into two classes—those who could read and those who could not. Once the burden of illiteracy which lay so heavily, albeit unconsciously, on the great bulk of the population was removed, the way was open for profound changes in every department of life.

The repeal of the paper duty and the enormous increase in the number of those who could read brought a new and potent influence to bear upon the minds of men; that influence was the Press, which henceforth acquired a steadily growing importance and became a factor with which the leaders of the nation would constantly have to reckon. Through the newspapers ideas, and not least religious ideas, would have a much freer and more extensive circulation. There thus arose a new and growing interest in theological questions, and as a further consequence, an insistent demand on the part of the more thoughtful laity for guidance, and in some cases, for modifications in the traditional theology to bring it more into line with current ideas. The extent to which theological subjects found a place in newspapers and periodicals is most surprising, especially when compared with the present-day ignoring of religion in the popular Press. Aubrey Moore wrote in the 'eighties: 'No periodical is complete without an article in which Christianity is defended or attacked.'[2] Predominant among such periodicals was *The Fortnightly Review* which for many educated people, particularly among the younger generation, had almost the authority of a 'gospel', and in nearly

---

[1] Our national system of education is difficult for foreigners to understand since it told against rather than for democratic ideas—that is until it had, in more recent times, developed the secondary side. Attendance at a board school involved a kind of social stigma.

[2] *Science and the Faith*, p. 113.

every issue there was some attack on orthodox beliefs. This was no mere accident, but part of a definite policy on the part of those responsible for its management; as was admitted by John Morley when he said, 'Literature was a weapon, an arm, not merely a literary art.'[1]

Popular interest in theology is reflected in the oft-quoted lines from Browning's 'Gold Hair' published in 1864:

> The candid incline to surmise of late
> 　　That the Christian faith proves false, I find:
> For our Essays and Reviews debate
> 　　Begins to tell on the public mind,
> And Colenso's words have weight.

It was in the same year, 1864, as it happened, that Ruskin made a strong appeal for the setting up of Public Libraries in every considerable city. An act giving power to establish them had been passed in 1850, but there had been but a meagre response on the part of local authorities and it was only by slow degrees that the opportunities which they provided were made available to the general public.

The quotation from Browning brings out another remarkable feature connected with the growing interest in theology—the displacement in the popular mind of the official guardians and exponents of the faith by literary guides.[2] That popular ideas on theology should be shaped and moulded by men of letters was not, of course, an entirely novel feature; Milton, for example, had exercised a considerable influence on the religious ideas of the multitude, and even today, so far as men consider such matters, *Paradise Lost* all unconsciously carries more weight than the early narratives of Genesis. But if such influences had been exercised in the past they were now gaining, through the increase of literacy, greater power and a wider currency.

So much for preliminary remarks. We come now to a consideration of the state of affairs as it existed during the early years

---

[1] *Recollections*, Vol. I, p. 100.
[2] This subject will be dealt with at length in Ch. XIV.

of our period. Many of the influences then at work had been operative in the early part of the century, but they now became more manifest and more potent, having acquired sufficient force to burst through the barriers erected in their course. Soon new tides would mingle with them until they rose at last to an overwhelming flood which not all the efforts of obscurantism could keep out.

Many of the influences were personal, for the Victorian Age was an age of prophets,[1] and took much of its tone from great names rather than from systems of thought. In a sermon to Cambridge undergraduates in February 1909 Bishop Percival described life at Oxford as he had known it fifty years earlier. 'Its thought was inspired and dominated by unusually great personalities, Carlyle, Ruskin, Wordsworth, Shelley, Tennyson, Bentham, Mill; these were the names to conjure with. Browning, Spencer, Darwin were just rising above the horizon.'[2] Carlyle was certainly hailed as a prophet, one who, like the prophets of the Old Testament, denounced sin and evil and, above all, anything which he regarded as pretence and humbug. Young men were especially enthralled by him and the talk of the more earnest was apt to be full of his phrases. By his outspoken witness on behalf of the value and importance of the things of the spirit he performed a useful office in an age of growing materialism.[3] Coleridge, too, still appealed to the more select minds (Hort, for instance, was greatly affected by him), and his stand for freedom of thought in religion as against the too-ready acceptance of authority, and his belief that the most trustworthy guide in matters of faith was the spirit of God working in the Church and in the soul of the individual Christian gave strength and comfort to many a perplexed soul. His importance for the growth of theology has not always been recognized, though Farrar, who had been introduced to his writings by F. D. Maurice, could boldly assert that 'If in later days the Church of England has made an immense advance

[1] Inge thought that the influence of 'prophets' with 'their quality of nobleness' began to decline about 1880. (*The Platonic Tradition*, etc., pp. 90f.)

[2] W. Temple, *Life of Bishop Percival*, p. 6.

[3] See further C. C. J. Webb, *Religious Thought in England*, etc., pp. 67ff.

2

(in theology) the progress is perhaps more due to Samuel Taylor Coleridge than to any ordained or professed theologian.'[1]

In studying the effect of the changed situation upon theology we have again to remind ourselves that much of it was indirect. A new atmosphere was being created and in this new atmosphere theology had to acquire the art of breathing and living, or, as contemporary biologists would have put it, it had to learn to adjust itself to a fresh environment if it was to survive. It follows that what is of the greatest importance for us is to understand the position as a whole, and to regard the details mainly as revealing and illustrating its nature. 'What is important for us to know of any age is not its peculiar opinions, but the complex elements of that moral feeling and character, in which, as in their congenial soil, opinions grow.'[2]

Changes in climate, at least in temperate zones, though frequent are seldom violent, and our reactions to them are instinctive rather than deliberate, as when a man buttons up his coat if the wind suddenly grows chilly. So in the climate of thought necessary adjustments are often made gradually and in part unconsciously in response to the silent pressure of the changed environment. This was certainly true, in large measure, of the modifications in theology and religion in the period under review. There was no formal repudiation of outworn notions, save by the few advanced thinkers, but there was a shifting of emphasis, as a result of which they sank into the background until for practical purposes they were virtually ignored.

The influx of novel ideas and the quickening of mental activity was, in the main, a consequence of the vast accumulation of fresh

---

[1] Bampton Lectures, pp. 422f. For Coleridge's influence in an earlier period see Storr, Ch. XVII. There has recently been a somewhat tardy recognition of the greatness of Coleridge as a thinker: see amongst others J. H. Muirhead, *Coleridge*; Kathleen Coburn, *Inquiring Spirit; a New Philosophy and Presentation of Coleridge from his Published and Unpublished Writings*. There is perhaps a tendency to exaggerate some aspects of his influence as when I. A. Richards in *Coleridge on Imagination* claims that his distinction between the Imagination and the Fancy was comparable in importance for the spiritual world with the discoveries of Galileo for the physical.

[2] Morley, *Recollections*, Vol. I, p. 72.

knowledge. Knowledge, indeed, increased so enormously and covered such wide and varied fields, that it was no longer possible for any single scholar to master it. The polymath of earlier times became almost a legendary figure and no one could hope to emulate him. Specialization became the order of the day and research had perforce to be divided up into a number of isolated provinces. This was a double misfortune; for on the one hand the specialist is apt to assume that the group of facts with which he deals constitute an independent whole, and to forget that they have ultimately to be related to other departments of knowledge; and, on the other hand, the specialist, when venturing outside his chosen field, often suffers from a distorted vision and as a result his conclusions are lacking in balance and proportion.

The division of learning into a number of specialized and generally unrelated departments was a serious handicap to the theologian and made his task more arduous. The ideal of theology is to combine all varieties of knowledge into a single whole, and to see them as emanations from the one source of goodness, beauty, and truth, as gifts descending from the Father of Lights with whom is no variableness or mutability. Can the theologian be blamed if he failed to realize his ideal? His failure, however, though it might be excused, was none the less a disaster, leading as it did to a divorce between the faith and other forms of human activity and thought; and so 'there was on all sides a want of solidity and comprehensiveness in the religious contribution and a dangerous readiness to accept unverified formulas'.[1]

There is a widespread assumption that the Victorian Age was an age of confidence and certitude, that it knew little of the perplexities and ambiguities which beset times more recent. It had, of course, its problems, but these were faced in an optimistic spirit based on a firm and unquestioning belief in its ability to solve them, whether they cropped up in politics, industry, philosophy, or religion. In spite of the great names which in the past have given their support to this assumption I find myself unable to accept it. Such confidence and certitude may have been

[1] Westcott, in *The Life of E. W. Benson*, Vol. II, p. 691.

exhibited in practical life—though even here the age had its worries, trifling it may be when compared with the gnawing anxieties with which we are familiar, yet none the less troublesome—but they were by no means discernible in the regions of thought. The Victorian Age was no age of faith,[1] though it undoubtedly witnessed an increased vigour in practical religion; but such a manifestation was a testimony rather to the depth and sincerity with which beliefs were held than to their ultimate truth. Some, indeed, adopting the teaching of Carlyle and his master Goethe that doubt can only be solved by action, devoted themselves to unceasing labours and works of charity; but action can provide no assured path to the resolving of doubts, though for a time it may dull them, and if inspired by such a motive may easily degenerate into febrile busyness. The era cannot be numbered among the ages of faith; it was too full of doubts and conflicts, and, let it be noted, of inconsistencies and compromises, as men sought to retain their inherited or instinctive faith and at the same time to accept the conclusions forced upon them by the advances of natural science.

The findings of natural science, however, as they were generally received, were at odds not only with traditional forms of belief, but also with the popular faith in freedom and progress. There were few, indeed, who realized this seemingly inevitable conclusion; but as so often happens the insight of the poet pierced the veil which hid matters from less favoured mortals. Here is the opinion of James Thomson, the author of *The City of Dreadful Night*:

> I find no hint throughout the Universe
> Of good or ill, of blessing or of curse;
> I find alone Necessity Supreme;
> With infinite Mystery, abysmal, dark,
> Unlighted even by the faintest spark,
> For us, the flitting shadows of a dream.

[1] A so-called age of faith is often no more than an age of non-inquiry, in which a quickening and invigorating of the life of the Church may be accompanied by childish credulity on the intellectual plane.

Because so many were struggling between the traditions of their fathers and what seemed to them the incompatible findings of the new knowledge, religious faith was looked upon as a matter of the gravest importance; it was, indeed, so fundamental that in the absence of agreement upon it true friendship or complete sympathy and confidence were impossible. As this is a factor which may easily be overlooked by those who live in a more tolerant, because more indifferent, age, it will be well to bring evidence to support the statement. A pathetic illustration is provided by the correspondence between R. L. Nettleship and Henry Scott Holland published in Stephen Paget's life of the latter; on which the preface contains the following comment: 'I hope I have not done wrong to make free use of R. L. Nettleship's letters, they belong to a time when differences of belief were taken gravely, as a tragedy, which now are taken lightly, as a comedy.'

A further manifestation of the value and importance still attached to religious faith is to be found in the fact that many of those who felt compelled to reject much that seemed essential to orthodox Christianity continued outwardly to conform. For them, even after lesser articles of belief had been abandoned, there remained an inner kernel of faith which they could not give up. Among them was J. A. Froude the historian, once a disciple of Newman. Froude himself has left an account of his religious struggles, and it is interesting to notice what elements of orthodoxy he felt able to retain; they included the belief in a personal God, the supremacy of the spiritual over the material, the recognition of a purpose in the universe and of the part which man must play in realizing the divine plan for it, and also the need for 'conversion'. Froude refused to accept beliefs of which he was uncertain and was scornful of those who so readily took much for granted; the right attitude was to await further enlightenment.[1] Another prominent figure who took a similar course, though with a much more restricted basis of belief, was Matthew Arnold, who, when he gave up orthodoxy as a fond but beautiful dream,

[1] See H. Paul, *Life of J. A. Froude*, pp. 429 ff.

continued outward conformity and was not without hope that he might bring some churchmen to his own way of thinking.[1]

The biographies of the later nineteenth century contain not a few records of prolonged and indecisive conflicts carried on in the breasts of those who sought to reconcile their spiritual needs with their intellectual principles. Vaguely aware of a supersensual reality which they could neither find nor forget, they became waifs in an alien world, or, to adopt a more modern figure, dispossessed and stateless persons. Examples may be cited in the cases of Henry Sidgwick the philosopher and John Addington Symonds the poet and historian. Both were profoundly convinced of the need for religion as satisfying man's innate longing for the divine and as the only secure basis for morality; yet neither, in spite of ceaseless efforts, could ever attain to a settled belief. It is surely not unreasonable to trust that 'from these ploughed-up souls the spirit brings Harvest at last', but the problem of the devoted yet disappointed searcher after truth raises many difficulties. It is not, however, a new problem, Aquinas himself endeavoured to meet it, placing the blame for the failure on the seekers and exonerating the divine object of their search. 'Nor is it the fault of the Word that all men do not attain to the knowledge of the truth, but some remain in darkness. It is the fault of men who do not turn to the Word and so cannot fully receive Him.'[2] Such a solution, however, cannot really meet the difficulty; it is too easy, and, if one may use the term, too academic. Some at least of these frustrated seekers were utterly sincere, and only too eager to 'turn to the Word' if only they might find Him; nor, so far as we can judge, were they kept back by intellectual pride or conceit. Their failure may have been due to the mistaken conviction that spiritual truths are to be ascertained by purely mental processes; and also to the desire, in matters so significant not only for themselves but also for others, to make assurance doubly sure, a desire which can never receive full satisfaction

---

[1] Matthew Arnold's attitude will be dealt with at greater length in Ch. XIV.
[2] *Contra Gentiles*, Vol. IV, p. 13.

under the conditions of earthly life. So great was their determination to preserve their intellectual integrity that the grounds of
religious belief were examined with relentless severity and to
it they were even ready to sacrifice the satisfaction of their
spiritual needs. There lies the deep pathos of their struggles,
for they involved a conflict, not between good and evil, but
between good and good—and that is the essence of genuine
tragedy.

Many such seekers were doubtless cold by temperament and
slow to respond to emotional appeals such as drive others over
intellectual difficulties. They belonged to that class for whom
Christina Rossetti spoke so feelingly:

> We are of those who tremble at thy word,
> Who faltering walk in darkness towards our close
> Of mortal life, by terrors curbed and spurred—
>   We are of those.
> Not ours the heart thy loftiest love hath stirred,
> Not such as we thy lily and thy rose,
> Yet, Hope of those who hope with hope deferred,
>   We are of those.

Today such conflicts are comparatively rare, though by no
means unknown,[1] for the religious upbringing which these men
enjoyed is no longer common. But for them the struggle was
intense, and when intellectual honesty compelled them to
abandon their faith it left a void which nothing else could fill.
They still made it their endeavour to live the Christian life and to
practise the Christian virtues whose supreme value they gladly
acknowledged; but they did so in their own strength. Some of
them, too, were not without hope of one day being able to return
to the Church; Sidgwick expressed his own feelings in words
adapted from Tennyson's 'Palace of Art':

[1] D. H. Lawrence is an instance, of whom T. S. Eliot has written that his
vision was spiritual, but spiritually sick. Cf. also Violet Markham's *Return
Passage.*

> Yet pull not down my minster towers, that were
> So gravely, gloriously wrought;
> Perchance I may return with others there
> When I have cleared my thought.[1]

Others baffled by the flood of new knowledge and finding it impossible to reconcile it with the older faith, frankly gave up the task, and plunged into other activities which seemed to them to be more rewarding. Typical of them was T. H. Huxley, who asked, 'Why trouble ourselves about matters about which, however important they may be, we know nothing and can know nothing? We live in a world which is full of misery and ignorance, and the plain duty of all of us is to make the little corner he can influence somewhat less miserable and ignorant than it was before he entered it.'

Because religion was regarded so seriously and was so precious to many devout souls, the changing situation aroused in some of them a feeling of panic; they felt that they were living in what Walt Whitman has called 'quicksand years'. One feature of the situation which helps to explain what may seem to us a needless and excessive anxiety was the fact that the crisis with which they were so suddenly confronted was novel and unforeseen; they had forgotten that similar challenges had been frequent in the life of the Church in previous ages. Since the Deist Controversy of the eighteenth century there had been nothing to cast doubt on the fundamental truths of Christianity, for the disputes which followed the rise of the Oxford Movement and what had been termed Papal Aggression were merely domestic quarrels in which both sides accepted the traditional verities. Now it seemed that religion itself was threatened. Today we have become so accustomed to such challenges that they cause little disquiet; but such was not the case in the middle of the last century, there was then for the ordinary believer a clear-cut line between the acceptance of Christianity in its fullness and absolute unbelief. Can we wonder that for many whose faith was largely traditional

---

[1] *Henry Sidgwick, a Memoir*, p. 202.

and unexamined it seemed as if the very foundations were being undermined? Even Handley Moule, who went up to Cambridge from a pious home in 1860, was filled with painful doubts 'under the continual droppings of the controversies and questions of the present day'.[1] Many of the questions which troubled the pious in the middle nineteenth century now seem harmless enough in the light of fuller knowledge and a different perspective; an acquaintance with Oriental literary methods, for example, removes difficulties over Joshua's halting of the course of the sun, over Balaam's donkey, and even over Jonah's whale.

That a serious crisis was facing religion was recognized by many competent observers. In 1860 Disraeli wrote: 'There are few great things left, and the Church is one of them. No doubt its position at this moment is critical, and, indeed, the whole religious sentiment of the country is in a convulsive state.'[2] Similar views were expressed in January 1869 by Henry Sidgwick: 'I feel convinced that English religious society is going through a great crisis just now, and it will probably become impossible soon to conceal from anybody the extent to which rationalistic views are held, and the extent of their deviation from traditional opinion.'[3] Westcott, too, in the preface to the third edition of *The Gospel of the Resurrection* published five years later, referred to the common assumption 'that once again we are approaching a great crisis in the history of human society and human thought'.

But although there was a real crisis in the religious life of the country, it was not, for reasons which I have already indicated, so overwhelming as many supposed. All religious systems must from time to time face such crises, when men, after a period of acquiescence, begin to inquire into the meaning and value of beliefs and practices which have for long been taken for granted. This is particularly the case when new knowledge is almost daily provoking fresh questionings. Whether the crisis will prove

[1] Harford and Macdonald, *Bishop Handley Moule*, p. 33. His contemporary, W. K. Clifford, was already uttering what Myers has called his 'triumphant proclamations of the nothingness of God, the divinity of man'.

[2] Monypenny and Buckle, *Life of Disraeli*, Vol. II, p. 84.

[3] *Op. cit.*, p. 187.

beneficial or otherwise depends upon the spirit in which it is faced. If the new knowledge is accepted as revealing fresh aspects of truth which faith may use, faith itself receives ampler light and may be expanded in both scope and meaning; if, however, it is met by unreasoning condemnation the result can be only decline and stagnation. To 'turn back in dismay from the problems which may be the entrance to higher truth . . . to flee before the gale which, rightly faced, might have carried us far on our way, is not of faith, but of unbelief.'[1] Tradition may enshrine truth, but the shrine may become a tomb.

A crisis is always a challenge, and certainly the position in which the Church was placed in 1860 and the years following was a challenge to Christianity as generally understood and accepted. But, as so often, the challenge called forth a response, or perhaps it would be truer to say, a variety of responses. Where it was recognized as such there was a corresponding determination to meet it, and when in 1871 J. B. Mozley returned to Oxford as Regius Professor of Divinity Pusey wrote to him: 'It is an encouragement that the battle is so desperate. All or nothing; as when the Gospel first broke in upon heathen philosophers; and the fishermen had the victory.'[2]

But when the hour strikes it is not all men who hear the chimes. So it was in the 'sixties. Many, even among the clergy, had but small suspicion of the storm which was rapidly moving up. To them all this talk of new knowledge and the necessity of taking account of it was but a cloud on the horizon which would quickly pass away, and in the meantime it was best to ignore it. The faith as they understood and taught it met the needs of their own people, so why think of making any change in it? It is a subtle temptation to equate what is found convenient to believe with the truth itself,[3] and unknowingly they succumbed to it; forgetting that any system which refuses to adjust itself to new truth

---

[1] Oman, *Vision and Authority*, p. 74.

[2] *Letters of J. B. Mozley*, p. 319.

[3] Hort condemned 'the conventional English ecclesiastical scholar who does not willingly violate truth, but has never discovered that there is such a thing as truth'. (*Life*, Vol. II, p. 102.)

must ultimately decay,[1] even if for a time it seems to continue to flourish, as the trunk of a tree may stand long after any hope of blossom or fruit is past, retaining 'the action and the shape without the grace of life'. To them the faith was an anchor so firm that nothing could disturb it; but if the figure has biblical sanction it must not be overlooked that though anchors may give a feeling of security they are not conducive to movement, and a vessel at anchor may fail to weather a storm.

The resolve of the traditionalists to hold intact the heritage derived from their fathers was doubtless highly commendable: what was not so commendable was their unwillingness or incapacity to distinguish between genuine heirlooms and objects, useful in their day, which had now become only lumber. To preserve the old exactly as it had been handed down from the past was out of the question; the only wise course was to accept the new truths and to incorporate them in the structure of the faith. 'The broad stream of events', as Westcott has said, 'cannot be stayed or turned back, but it can be guided along fertilizing channels.'[2] This the traditionalists could not grasp, and shutting their eyes to any fresh light they declared in effect that they alone could see. Even the most untenable of the outworks of the faith must be defended, and any who showed signs of making the most moderate concessions were denounced as what we now call 'fifth-columnists'. The suggestion was even made that the new knowledge had been sent by God as a means of separating the true believers from the rest (cf. 1 Cor. 11:19). There might be contradictory statements in the Scriptures, but these were looked upon as proofs of its veracity. Had these religious Quixotes prevailed a disastrous cleavage between the Church and the intellectual life of the nation must have followed, and even as things were, since many educated people looked upon them as typical, Christianity was brought into some contempt.

The controversies aroused by these disagreements were marked

---

[1] Cf. Storr, *Spiritual Liberty*, p. 119: 'If theology becomes static, it inevitably dooms itself to sterility in a moving world.'

[2] *The Incarnation and Common Life*, p. 22.

by much bitterness, especially when pious laymen came forward to defend the old ways.[1] On many of the questions which filled the air with strife and tumult there was little possibility of agreement as the combatants had no clear understanding of the position of their opponents or of what was really at stake. It was a period of low ebb in the theological world, and Dale writing in 1864 could lament that the race of theologians seemed almost extinct.[2]

The rigid attitude which regards Christianity as a closed system based on an infallible Bible, reveals a strange lack of trust in the guidance of the Holy Spirit.[3] By clinging obstinately to their preconceived notions men may fail to recognize the signs of His working; they may even seek to erect barriers in its way. So in days long ago Amos had warned his contemporaries that the Day of the Lord might come in a form which they did not expect (5: 18), and Jesus Himself was rejected because He was not the kind of Messiah that the nation desired. To liberal thinkers this type of ultra-orthodoxy was regarded as a sin against the Holy Ghost. Its exponents might keep out the light by drawing down the blinds; but drawn blinds may signify that there has been a death in the house.

Before leaving the subject of obscurantism two further observations must be made. First, the refusal to accept unwelcome conclusions was by no means confined to the defenders of traditional beliefs; John Stuart Mill once remarked that 'The future of mankind will be gravely imperilled if great questions are left to be fought out between ignorant change and ignorant opposition to change.'[4] Secondly, opposition on the part of the traditionalists was by no means confined to the ignorant and unlearned. The Tractarians, for example, were most anxious to avoid anything

---

[1] In 1857 Hort had written: 'Much in the ecclesiastical history of the last few years suggests . . . that a section of the laity are greater enemies to freedom of thought than the clergy.' (*Life*, Vol. I, p. 366.)

[2] Dale, *Life of R. W. Dale*, p. 201.

[3] Cf. Matheson, *Life of Hastings Rashdall*, p. 195: 'To assume that the whole truth is to be found in the decisions of the past is really to disbelieve in the guidance of that Holy Spirit of Whom it was promised that He should lead Christ's disciples to all truth.'

[4] Quoted by Morley, *Recollections*, Vol. I, p. 56.

which suggested that the Church of England was departing in any way from the Catholic Faith, for this might lead to another wave of conversions to Rome; hence their special alarm over the writings of Colenso, who after all was a bishop. But the older Anglo-Catholics, as represented by Dr. Pusey and his disciple Dr. Liddon, were deeply concerned on other grounds as to the effects which would follow the dissemination of the new ideas. As early as 1866 the latter had written to Stanley: 'Is not the practical question this—Whether the Church of Christ is to be viewed as a mere Literary Society, or as a home and mother of dying souls.'[1] Liddon, it may be remarked, condemned Stanley as having no logical faculty by which he would be compelled to realize the outcome of his views.[2] But he himself was hampered in his thinking by too great a trust in logic, as was pointed out by a friendly critic, Francis Paget. Paget speaks of him as following 'a single train of thought or inference, pressing it without regard to the surrounding facts which tell upon it'. To Lightfoot, Oxford thinking as a whole was vitiated by this method.[3]

Many theologians who had become convinced of the truth of many things in the new outlook were reticent about making them widely known; they even tried to conceal from the public the results arrived at by German scholars, a procedure which was exposed and condemned by Bishop Thirlwall,[4] as well as by Benjamin Jowett. The latter recognized that it was impossible to keep knowledge at one level in Germany and at another in England. To him the great danger was 'not lest reason should destroy religion, but lest intellectual persons should reject the truth itself, when stated in grotesque and impossible forms'.[5] It is hard for us to realize the attitude of the devout at this epoch; they seemed determined to preserve 'an immunity from doubt'

[1] Prothero, *Life and Letters of Dean Stanley*, Vol. II, p. 171.
[2] Johnston, *Life and Letters of H. P. Liddon*, p. 274.
[3] Paget, *Francis Paget, Bishop of Oxford*, pp. 318 f.
[4] Thirlwall (Bishop of St. David's, 1840–74) was a Cambridge man and well acquainted with German theology. He was a man of immense learning and of strict impartiality.
[5] Abbot and Campbell, *Life and Letters of Benjamin Jowett*, Vol. I, p. 260.

by 'a resolute ignorance';[1] but as Dr. Johnson said in *Rasselas* 'ignorance when it is voluntary is criminal'. Oman has recorded the shock which he experienced during the Robertson Smith controversy, on being told by a lawyer, who was also an elder of the Church, that even if Robertson Smith was right and what he proclaimed was the truth, 'It is a dangerous truth, and he has no right . . . to upset the Church by declaring it.'[2]

But the English people could not indefinitely be kept behind an iron curtain, and the Press and the opponents of Christianity were not slow to popularize views to which the official teachers were either hostile, or concerning which they were reticent.

The ultra-orthodox might be thrown into a panic—Dean Church, with some severity, could say that many of them were behaving 'more like old ladies than philosophers'—and even grave theologians be disquieted by the changing atmosphere of thought, but for some of the younger generation the situation was brimful of promise and hope. 'We threw everything into the seething pot and wondered what would emerge', wrote Stopford Brooke.[3] The times needed strong medicine, and they were only too ready to administer it. With the prevalence of such a spirit it is not surprising that they despised the past and showed little gratitude to those who had gone before them and the work which they had done, preserving many things which were valued even by the Liberals. The eyes of such enthusiasts were all on the future, and with undue optimism they seemed to expect the harvest before spring itself was at an end. Much of this was but the ebullition of youth, and with more experience of life and deeper study many of them recovered their balance and a saner view of the relative values of the new and the old. They were going through a condition of 'yeast', to adopt a term made current by Charles Kingsley's novel of that name, and were apt, like the young and inexperienced in every age, to be scornful of the old

---

[1] Cf. Coleridge, *Aids to Reflection*, Aphor. XIII, comment.

[2] *Vision and Authority*, p. 9. For an exactly similar attitude on the part of a scientist see p. 42 below.

[3] Jacks, *Life and Letters of Stopford Brooke*, p. 628.

merely because it was old. This rough method of dealing with what had gone before did not a little to add to the difficulties of the situation and to stiffen orthodox opposition.

In both of the universities liberal views were spreading with great rapidity mainly owing to the influence of J. S. Mill. Mill had denounced the insincerity of those who accepted traditional views without careful examination. This standpoint was shared by many laymen who were forthright in condemning those who took Orders though unable to accept in a literal sense the formularies to which they subscribed. So widespread was this feeling that when Creighton was ordained in 1870 there was much adverse comment. Later he told his wife that 'it was the habit in Oxford to assume that a man who took Orders must be either a fool or a knave, and that as people could not call him a fool, they concluded that he must be a knave'.[1] Creighton, however, was perhaps exaggerating a little, for the same year saw the ordination of E. L. Hicks, the future Bishop of Lincoln, a man already known as an ardent reformer and an exponent of liberal ideas in both politics and theology. As he held a lay fellowship at Corpus Christi there was no necessity for ordination in his case. Even by 1870 a reaction against the barrenness and poverty of a stark rationalism was already gathering force, and religion, with the support of idealistic philosophy, not to mention the growing influence of the poetry of the romantics, was again venturing to raise its head.

Many of the most bitter attacks on Christianity came from those who had once been its adherents. Among the most active was Leslie Stephen. He had been ordained priest six months before the publication of *The Origin of Species*, but that event does not seem to have affected his beliefs, for in the following year he urged Ainger to take Orders.[2] It was not, indeed, until 1875 that he ceased to be a clergyman. John Morley, another doughty opponent of orthodoxy, had gone up to Oxford with the intention of being ordained.[3] Sidgwick had had the same

---

[1] *Life and Letters of Mandell Creighton*, Vol. I, pp. 75f.
[2] Sichel, *Life of Canon Ainger*, p. 76.   [3] *Recollections*, Vol. I, p. 31.

intention and did not finally abandon it until he was twenty-two.[1] Lecky, who produced his *History of Rationalism* when only twenty-seven, had studied for Orders so as to qualify for a family living. One of the most extraordinary cases was that of Walter Pater.[2] Having lost his faith—it is said through the influence of Stanley and the writings of F. D. Maurice—and having openly scoffed at Christianity and those who still persisted in holding it, he actually sought ordination from Bishop Tait of London and, but for warnings sent to the bishop, might have succeeded in his wish. Pater's interest in religion was purely aesthetic and his desire for Orders was inspired solely by the opportunities which they would open to his taking part in beautiful ceremonial. He was in fact an extreme example of what is known as the 'acolyte' type of ordinand, a type which is often an embarrassment to examining chaplains.

These were perhaps extreme cases, for, as we have seen, many of the laity who gave up Christianity in its orthodox form still conformed outwardly. But for members of the clergy who adopted liberal views the matter was more difficult. In actual fact very few relinquished their Orders. There was, of course, Leslie Stephen, others included Stopford Brooke, who continued his ministry at Bedford Chapel on an undenominational basis, W. G. Clarke, the public orator at Cambridge, and C. Kegan Paul.[3] In 1862 F. D. Maurice knew of several cases of clergymen surrendering their livings because unable to conform to 'such antiquated books as the Bible and the Common Prayer-Book'.[4]

There was one notorious case of expulsion, that of Charles Voysey, rector of Healaugh in Yorkshire. In 1868 he published a volume entitled *The Sling and the Stone* in which he apparently denied the efficacy of the Atonement and the true nature of the Incarnation, and also condemned any worship of Christ as idolatry.

[1] *Henry Sidgwick, a Memoir*, pp. 47, 62.
[2] T. Wright, *Life of Walter Pater*, Vol. I, pp. 136 ff., 207.
[3] Leslie Stephen professed to find Paul the prosperous publisher much less interesting than Paul the heretical clergyman: see *Henry Sidgwick, a Memoir*, p. 487.
[4] *Life of F. D. Maurice*, Vol. II, p. 427.

When called upon to resign Voysey defended himself on the ground that since all theological terms were ambiguous and inadequate they could no longer be taken in their literal sense. None the less the Privy Council ordered his ejection in 1871. Later he became the founder of the Ethical Church.[1]

Those Liberal clergymen who retained their Orders had no enviable position; but though frowned upon by the authorities and objects of suspicion to their brethren, they held on their course; Canon Fremantle of Canterbury (later Dean of Ripon) even contributed to *The Fortnightly Review*. Their position was made less difficult by the passing of the Clerical Subscription Act in 1865 by which the clergy were to give only a general assent to the Prayer Book and the Thirty-nine Articles and to promise to use the prescribed forms in Public Worship unless otherwise authorized by the proper authority. The subsequent Clerical Disabilities Act of 1870 allowed clergymen for the first time to relinquish their Orders. Before the passing of the Act, although they might resign their livings and cease to exercise their ministry, they still ranked as clerics. Thus the right to hold liberal views, so long as no fundamental article of the faith was denied, was gradually established.

An important manifesto of liberal Christianity appeared in 1865 with the publication of *The Life and Letters of F. W. Robertson*. The author was Stopford Brooke, an unexpected choice, for he was then a little-known Irishman who had only recently left college. In the same year E. A. Abbott, with his Cambridge honours thick upon him—he had been senior classic in 1861—returned to the City of London School as headmaster, where he would not only exhibit his genius as a teacher, but also produce numerous learned theological works of a definitely liberal character.

If liberal views were spreading in the universities, and if scholars,

---

[1] Jowett had warned Voysey against the danger of too candid an expression of his views as likely to interfere with his 'real usefulness'. (*Life of Jowett*, Vol. I, p. 402.) Mrs. Humphry Ward condemned them as 'mere arbitrary remoulding and petulant upsetting': see Janet Trevelyan, *Life of Mrs. Humphry Ward*, p. 33.

or some of them, were becoming acquainted with the work being done in Germany, the general public, as we have seen, was, so far as possible, being kept in ignorance of what was taking place. But just before 1860 there had been an attempt on the part of a few theologians to break down this conspiracy of silence by the publication of *Essays and Reviews*.

What concerns us here is not the contents of this famous volume,[1] but its reception and consequences. It may, however, be pointed out that it had no great intrinsic worth—the only really valuable essay being that of Mark Pattison on 'Tendencies of Religious Thought in England, 1688–1750'—and contained little that was new, at least to scholars, whilst its whole tone and outlook was too negative to make it a real contribution to theology. None the less its consequences were enormous, and it may well be said to have precipitated a crisis, for the views it set forth were regarded in most quarters as alarmingly new and dangerous. J. B. Mozley considered that such views if taken up by the mass could only result in 'simple infidelity and indeed atheism',[2] and suggested that the writers themselves would have shrunk from publishing their essays had they foreseen the effect they would have upon simple folk. Stanley had declined to contribute to the volume, for though he was in sympathy with its objects he felt that the time was not yet ripe for widely disseminating ideas which would only be misunderstood by the ordinary churchgoer. Another who refused to take part was Hort.

The objects and motives of the writers, however, were misunderstood and even misrepresented, and the extensive publicity attained by the volume was something which they had not anticipated. They regarded their venture as merely a collection of personal utterances and any kind of joint responsibility had been deliberately disclaimed. How far they aimed at any serious contribution to thought is not at all clear; Temple, at least, who gave only ten hours to his essay (hence no doubt some unguarded

[1] See *Religion in the Victorian Era*, pp. 146 ff. and Storr, pp. 429 ff.
[2] *Letters of J. B. Mozley*, p. 250.

expressions) can scarcely have thought that he was taking part in a weighty manifesto.[1]

But whatever may have been the intentions and anticipations of the writers, when once the contents of the volume became known there was immediate and widespread alarm and denunciation. Evangelicals and Tractarians, forgetting their differences, joined in protest and condemnation; some bishops denounced it; two of the authors were prosecuted, though unsuccessfully; a whole series of replies was made; and in general there was an attempt to crush it by the exercise of authority. The excitement persisted for a considerable time and when in 1869 Temple was appointed to the bishopric of Exeter a High Church journal described the event as 'the darkest crime which had been perpetrated in the English Church'.[2] But not all orthodox churchmen were carried away into crude condemnation. The saintly G. H. Wilkinson, later to follow E. W. Benson at Truro, welcomed the increased and more intelligent interest in theological questions aroused by it among the laity who had mainly what he described as 'a sort of stupid historical faith, very vague and seldom strengthened by reflection'.[3] Westcott, while not approving of the volume as a whole, felt that the chief danger was 'a reaction more perilous than scepticism'; he also thought that those who attacked the writers, from bishops downward, were likely to do much harm to the Church and to truth, for such opponents showed themselves 'profoundly ignorant of the elements of the difficulties out of which the Essays have sprung'.[4] Hort expressed his opinion that the essayists seemed 'to *believe* very much more of truth than their so-called orthodox opponents', though he feared that one effect of the volume would be to fling back 'into mere orthodox assertion many who were feeling their way onwards'.[5]

Volumes issued to combat *Essays and Reviews* served for the

[1] E. G. Sandford, *Frederick Temple: an Appreciation*, p. 205.
[2] Prothero, *Life and Letters of Dean Stanley*, Vol. II, p. 372.
[3] Mason, *Memoir of G. H. Wilkinson*, Vol. I, p. 82.
[4] *Life and Letters*, Vol. I, pp. 214f.
[5] *Life*, Vol. I, pp. 428, 436f.

time to reassure simple believers and the strictly orthodox among the clergy, but it cannot be said that they had any lasting effect in stemming the flood of enlightened opinion. Liberty to apply critical methods to the Bible and to accept the findings of scientists would never again be denied to competent and devout scholars.

Among new influences which were telling in a liberal direction one of the most powerful was a growing contact with scholarship in Germany. Before 1860, though German work on the classics was fairly well known, few English theologians were at all familiar with what was being done on their special subject. Pusey, as a young man, had studied Semitic languages in Germany and in 1825 Thirlwall had translated Schleiermacher's *Critical Essay on St. Luke*. Coleridge, through the generosity of the Wedgwoods, the potters, had spent a year of study in Germany, and Carlyle had brought some German notions to the attention of English readers. All this, however, did not amount to much, especially where theology was concerned. There was, in addition, the habit of Nonconformist students, who were debarred from English universities, of continuing their studies on the Continent.

One reason for the tardy interest of English scholars in German theology may have been the shock produced by Strauss's *Life of Jesus* published in 1835.[1] If this was typical not much help was to be expected from Germany. But this was too hasty a judgment and German theologians had much to teach English scholars, and that not only by way of the methods to be employed. For in Germany there was a unity and consistency in theological study which was lacking over here; a great advantage, even though it might occasionally lead to that specially German fault of forcing the facts into a preconceived scheme, what they themselves call *Tendenzschriften*.

During our period German influences came in with increasing volume, and by its close,[2] or least by the early years of the present

---

[1] A revised and less offensive edition was later produced and translated into English in 1865.

[2] Even then knowledge of German methods and results was not too widely held and Sidgwick used to say that it was a trade secret at Cambridge that 'originality' in lecturing could be attained through a knowledge of German.

century, they were regarded with a veneration which, looking back, was undoubtedly excessive; a compensation, it may be, for the previous neglect.

Other influences which would have a profound effect on English theology were topical, rather than national or territorial, and will receive detailed treatment in subsequent chapters. It will, however, be useful at this point briefly to glance at them and to discuss their relations with one another.

These influences can most conveniently be grouped under three heads, and as it happened each of them was represented by an outstanding publication in the years immediately before 1860. Darwin's *Origin of Species* and Mill's *On Liberty* came out in 1859 and in the previous year Buckle's *History of Civilization*. Thus we get our three divisions of science, philosophy, and history. Although Buckle's volumes are now almost entirely forgotten, perhaps a little undeservedly,[1] it was the last influence which in the long run proved most disturbing, and not as is popularly imagined the impact of natural science. The latter would, indeed, at first seem the most menacing, but it was the rigid application of historical methods to the records of Christianity which above all would revolutionize theology.

Behind these three separate influences, as we can now see, a single tendency was at work; they might flow in by different creeks and inlets, but they were impelled by the same rising tide of thought. So close, indeed, was their inter-relation and inter-action that it is not always easy to distinguish them; none the less 'if they are to be properly understood, they must be isolated and severally analyzed'.[2] United, their effect was to make a breach with the past wider even than that made by the Renaissance of the fifteenth and sixteenth centuries. The latter, after all, was a rebirth, or claimed to be, a return to Latin studies and to a much

---

[1] Gooch, *History and Historians in the Nineteenth Century*, p. 585, writes: 'though he shares the confident dogmatism of his age, his book has marked an epoch in the life of readers all over the world and gave an impetus to the sociological investigation of the past'.

[2] E. Troeltsch in *E.R.E.*, Vol. VI, p. 716.

smaller extent to Greek.[1] But the new knowledge and the new methods, as they penetrated the life and thought of mankind, involved a complete change of outlook.[2]

The acceptance of the theory of evolution gave to existence a sense of continuity which it had hitherto lacked, and brought in order and lucidity; at the same time it aroused a new interest in the past as an important factor in explaining the present, whilst both past and present were regarded as giving promise for the future. That future, in view of man's achievements during the period of his known history, was conceived of as full of unlimited possibilities of further advance. For the Greeks the golden age had lain in the past, and even the Jews spoke of a time when the first ancestors of the race dwelt in an earthly paradise; Christianity, however, had always looked to the future, but in so far as it located that future in another world, or made it dependent on the work of Providence, its teaching was repudiated by the ardent minds of the new scientific era. The golden age which they foresaw was to be realized here on earth, and it would owe nothing to any supernatural guidance or help; man's own efforts, wisely directed by reason and informed by the new knowledge, would suffice eventually to bring it into being.

One effect of the doctrine of human progress was to subordinate the good of the individual to that of the race. Men were not ends in themselves but only means to an end beyond them. They must, therefore, gladly sacrifice themselves, or if need be, and this has a sinister ring, allow themselves to be sacrificed, for the welfare of the whole. This notion incidentally was in direct contradiction to the prevailing Utilitarianism which saw in society but a means for promoting the well-being and happiness of the individual.

But if such an outlook has for us a sinister note it was not

[1] The influence of the latter has been greatly exaggerated; see my Hulsean Lectures *Erasmus the Reformer*, pp. 4f.

[2] Cf. Illingworth in *Lux Mundi*, p. 132 where he wrote: 'great scientific discoveries, like the heliocentric astronomy, are not merely new facts to be assimilated; they involve new ways of looking at things'.

without valuable teaching for an era which had become excessively individualistic, and that not least in religion. 'History and science, rather than our religion', wrote Clutton-Brock, 'have taught us that our fate is not private and individual, but common.'[1]

Turning to the relations of science, philosophy, and history, it may be said that science, for its part, was a giver rather than a receiver, supplying new facts upon which the others would work, and also more exact methods of dealing with facts in general. There grew up, indeed, a school of historians which delighted to call itself scientific. In regard to the relations of science and philosophy it is hazardous to venture upon generalizations, since different philosophical schools adopted different attitudes towards both science and history. The Positivists, for example, looked upon the discoveries of natural science as providing the only reliable form of knowledge, thus basing philosophy on science, as medieval philosophers had based philosophy and science upon theology. So far as this attitude was accepted philosophy unwittingly imposed a form of tyranny upon both itself and upon history; for even those who repudiated Positivism were often unconsciously affected by its presuppositions. But most philosophers, even those who lauded natural science, lacked any adequate knowledge of its ever-changing outlook or of the real implications which this would involve for their own studies. The laws of causation, for example, were taking on new forms, the theory of relativity was already foreshadowed, and the concept of mass was being displaced by that of energy. Scientists, for their part, were too busy observing phenomena to have leisure or inclination to philosophize about them; none the less their labours were helping to provide additional material for those with greater aptitude and opportunity for speculation. One fundamental difference between science and philosophy must not be ignored—that is the different object of their endeavours. 'In modern times science and philosophy are separated from each other. Science reaches certain results. It tests

[1] *What is the Kingdom of Heaven?*, p. 80.

them. We can act upon them. Philosophy has been occupied with the question of meanings.'[1]

Turning to the relations of philosophy and history we find that many philosophers despised history as merely, in Bosanquet's phrase, 'the doubtful story of successive events';[2] in their view history could only provide what Plato had called 'opinion' and not absolute knowledge. Philosophy seeks for what is universal and tends to belittle happenings in time and space, but it is liable to forget that if such happenings fail to furnish any clue to the nature of the universe (and, for many, evidence of providential guidance) at least they exhibit humanity in action, and thus supply material which the philosopher can only neglect to his own hurt.

The historian, for his part, is not greatly concerned with the universal; and even the doctrines of rival philosophical systems are valued mainly as illustrating the movement of thought; he desires to know when they emerged, and what was their fate, but the precise content of their teaching has for him but small significance.

Although evolution is popularly associated with science alone, the cognate idea of development was permeating both history and philosophy. Truth thus came to be regarded, not as something fixed and absolute, but as in a state of constant growth as fresh knowledge rose above the horizon. Such a view seemed difficult to reconcile with the orthodox idea of revelation as being, not the result of the discoveries of man, but the voluntary disclosure of God.[3] The conception of development was none the less an advantage to the theologian, for it could be used to explain the growth of religion and to account for the very different levels of attainment in the Old and New Testaments. The theory of natural selection, which was Darwin's explanation of the way in

---

[1] G. H. Mead, *Movements of Thought in the Nineteenth Century*, p. 343.

[2] *The Principle of Individuality* etc., p. 79. Sidgwick could also write: 'History always fascinates me, though I am repelled from it by a conviction of its comparative uselessness.' (*Henry Sidgwick, a Memoir*, p. 435.) Some historians were equally repelled by philosophy; Freeman once threw a volume of Plato across the room in disgust.

[3] The subject will be fully discussed later: see pp. 180 ff.

which evolution worked, could also be used by the theologian to meet the criticism that the choice of the Jewish people as recipients of special divine favour was unjust to other nations; the Jews were 'chosen' because of their unique aptitude for apprehending spiritual realities. Thus science, in the words of A. J. Balfour, 'adopted an idea which has always been an essential part of the Christian view of the Divine economy, and has returned it again to theology, enriched, strengthened, and developed'.[1]

From these influences which pressed upon it theology was able to acquire other gains. They provided it with new facts concerning both man and the universe; and once these facts had been established beyond reasonable doubt, those who held that God Himself was the creator and sustainer of all things could not fail to regard them as constituting a fresh revelation of Himself. Much of this rich, new knowledge might seem to conflict with the biblical records; but this did not involve their rejection, it was rather a call to a fresh examination of the Scriptures in the light which they brought, and, it might be, to the realization that the records, though suited to the requirements of humanity in a lower state of development, stood in need of reinterpretation.

If these influences seemed at first to be largely destructive, further consideration showed that this was not really the case; they were a purifying medium, straining out what was unworthy and misleading. So in ancient Israel the prophets had endeavoured to free the traditional faith from the gross features, fruits of primitive religious ideas, which still survived in it.

Science, philosophy, and history were thus the purgatory of religion and theology, and when the things that were shaken had been removed the structure was seen to be more secure. As my revered teacher, Professor Gwatkin, said in his Gifford Lectures 'Science has been a destroying spirit, and has filled the temple of truth with ruins. But the things she has destroyed were only idols. Religion—the highest ideal—she has placed on a firmer throne than ever.'[2]

[1] *The Foundations of Belief*, p. 320.
[2] *The Knowledge of God*, Vol. II, p. 278.

Chapter Two

THE IMPACT
OF NATURAL SCIENCE:
MIRACLES

IN England as elsewhere the later years of the nineteenth century were characterized by an enormous expansion of scientific knowledge. There was not only an immense accumulation of new material, but also the promulgation of many novel theories. The discoveries of scientists were due in a large measure to vast improvements in the available apparatus and to the introduction of new and more effective instruments, such as the spectroscope used by Stokes and others in astronomy; but above all to an intense application to the solution of problems which had so far baffled them and the conducting of fresh experiments.

In physics the most important development was the abandonment of the purely mechanical outlook which went back to Newton, mainly as the result of experiments, conducted by Faraday and continued by Clerk Maxwell, in connexion with the phenomena of electro-magnetics and the diffraction of light. In biology the new cell theory was of outstanding importance, and even more the work of Charles Darwin. In geology the realization that changes had taken place over a vast era of time had immense repercussions in other departments of science for it provided an infinitely longer period during which evolution had been at work in place of the few thousand years which earlier biologists, accepting the biblical chronology, had had at their disposal. This may be illustrated by Lyell's *Evidence of the Antiquity of Man* published in 1863. Towards the close of the century great attention was paid to the study of the effects of heredity, following the work of Galton and Weissmann, and culminating in Bateson's revival of the theories of Mendel. The last decade saw also the beginnings of discoveries which were big with consequences for the future; such as Oliver Lodge's experiments with wireless waves, the work of William Crookes on X-rays, and that of J. J. Thomson on electrons.

Discoveries followed one another in such rapid succession and in such varied fields that it was difficult to grasp their implications or to estimate their possible effects. Somewhat later Bishop Burroughs of Ripon made the whimsical suggestion that all research should be abandoned for a time in order that what was already discovered might be assimilated. This reminds one of Cotter Morison's reaction to the problem of over-population: 'If only the devastating torrent of children could be arrested for a few years, it would bring untold relief.'

Such a course, it need hardly be said, was quite out of the question, scientists could not possibly be expected to hold their hands; none the less it might have been well for them and for their studies if they had had more time for reflection before arriving at conclusions based on the new discoveries. Many 'articles of faith' accepted by scientists in the nineteenth century have now been discarded or greatly modified. No one now believes in a universal aether,[1] nor accepts the nineteenth-century idea of space; the doctrine that matter can neither be created nor destroyed seems to be contradicted by the observations of modern astronomers; and the dualism of matter and force is no longer recognized; whilst the quantum theory has brought in a new era in physics.

The conception of evolution had long been current before the days of Darwin. It was a leading idea with the Hegelians, and even earlier it had been applied by Goethe and Schelling to the physical world, whilst, in England, Coleridge had declared that 'Nature is a line in constant and continuous evolution.'[2] The

[1] The use of Greek seemed to give an air of respectability and even of ancientry to scientific terms as a bogus pedigree to an upstart family.
[2] *Aids to Reflection* note to comment on Aphor. CIX.

publication of *The Vestiges of Creation* in 1844 had also made it widely known;[1] and Newman's *Development of Doctrine*, which also appeared in that year, is 'full of biological colour and analyses with great insight the conception of growth'.[2]

Darwin's contribution to the theory of evolution was to suggest a method by which it worked, what he called natural selection. Evolution, as he conceived it, was the result of the struggle for existence; those organisms which proved capable of adapting themselves to their environment survived, those who lacked this ability went under. Darwin, however, though he gave the highest place to natural selection did not consider that it was the only factor in the working out of evolution, and though he maintained that it worked 'solely by and for the good of each being',[3] the impression which it left on the mind of the general public was that of 'nature red in tooth and claw'. It was also open to the criticism that those best fitted to survive might not necessarily be the highest types, the rather unfair example of a man meeting a tiger in a jungle was given as an instance—a better example was the existence of parasites.[4] That evolution worked by way of a steady and continuous process was repudiated by some scientists; Bateson in *Materials for the Study of Variation* brought evidence to show that Nature sometimes worked by 'leaps'.

When *The Origin of Species* was published in 1859 it did not immediately arouse alarm in religious circles.[5] It was, indeed, welcomed by some churchmen. R. W. Church, for example, found in Darwin a greater gravity and literary power than in the author of *The Vestiges of Creation*, and thought that the outcry against *The Origin of Species* was not so great as in the case of the

[1] This volume, published anonymously, was the work of Robert Chambers, 'a devout theist (who) held that the doctrine of evolution was a support to the argument from design'. (Storr, pp. 364f.)

[2] Storr, p. 295.   [3] *The Origin of Species*, p. 428.

[4] Huxley, it may be noted, definitely repudiated the idea that all adaptations made for progress. (*Darwiniana*, Vol. II, pp. 90f.)

[5] *The Descent of Man* published in 1871 was in many ways calculated to give a greater shock to the traditionalists.

former volume, 'partly from ... a little more wisdom in the public'. He himself regarded it as '*the* book of science which has produced most impression here of any that has appeared for many years'. In March 1861 he wrote: 'The book, I have no doubt, would be the subject still of a great row, if there were not a much greater row going on about Essays and Reviews.'[1] Two years later Kingsley wrote to F. D. Maurice that 'Darwin is conquering everywhere ... by the mere force of truth and fact.'[2] Wider publicity was given to the theories of Darwin and their supposed inconsistency with traditional religion at the famous Oxford Conference in November 1864 when Bishop Wilberforce, who had already demolished Darwin's arguments to his own satisfaction in an article in *The Quarterly Review*, made a sweeping attack upon them.

One reason for the immense popularity of *The Origin of Species*, when once attention had been drawn to it, was the style in which it was written, a style which avoided the undue use of technical terms and so could be understood by any intelligent reader. This, of course, made it all the more dangerous in the eyes of the defenders of orthodoxy, and a bitter controversy soon got under way. It is this religious aspect of the controversy alone which is now remembered, and it is often cited, sometimes by those who might have been expected to know better, as a classic example of theological obscurantism. In actual fact the main opposition, as Darwin himself had anticipated, came from his fellow scientists,[3] including the great anatomist Richard Owen (1804–92). The permanence of species was a doctrine held by all leading naturalists and geologists and Darwin recorded that none with whom he discussed the matter had any doubts about it.[4] No blame therefore, can reasonably be attached to churchmen,

---

[1] *Life of Dean Church*, pp. 183 f., 188.
[2] *Charles Kingsley*, Vol. II, p. 155.
[3] See Raven, *Science, Religion and the Future*, pp. 35 ff. and cf. Morley, *Recollections*, Vol. I, p. 13: 'One group of scientific men fought another group over the origin of species.' Lyell's views on geology had met with similar opposition from scientists.
[4] *Life of Charles Darwin*, Vol. I, p. 87.

from Bishop Wilberforce downwards, if they accepted the prevailing judgment of men of science and joined with them in the condemnation of a novel and doubtful theory. In 1860 Huxley stated that 'the supporters of Mr. Darwin's views . . . were numerically extremely insignificant'.[1]

It is interesting to observe the various arguments, apart from those advanced by scientists and religious leaders, put forth by critics of Darwin. Max Müller urged that man's use of language was decisive evidence that he could not be descended from the brutes.[2] Another who attacked the Darwinian theory was Samuel Butler. Butler came of clerical stock, his grandfather had been Bishop of Lichfield and his father was a parson, but he had reacted strongly against religion, as readers of that rather painful book *The Way of All Flesh* need not be reminded. Butler's theory was that evolution depended, not on natural selection, but on what he called 'unconscious memory' working in individuals. His idea attracted little attention at the time but has received more serious notice in the present century.

The teaching of Darwin was regarded by many, even among serious and sober thinkers, as having definitely undermined Christianity; religious views might persist in pious circles, but could hardly be maintained by those who possessed reasoned judgment. This notion was eagerly welcomed by the more extreme liberals as freeing man at last from an age-long tyranny, and it was hoped that the very idea of God would soon disappear; so Swinburne proclaimed in 'Hertha':

> Thought made him and breaks him,
>   Truth slays and forgives;
> But to you as time takes him,
>   This new thing it gives,
> Even love . . . that feeds upon freedom and lives.

---

[1] *Op. cit.*, Vol. II, p. 186.
[2] *Life of Max Müller*, Vol. I, p. 452. His controversy with Darwin, it is refreshing to note, was carried on in a very friendly spirit.

Little did they realize what would be the outcome of that 'liberation', or imagine the harsher tyrannies that would be imposed upon mankind.[1]

That Darwin's theories should have aroused such extravagant expectations is somewhat surprising; Darwin himself was no sharer in them, and when asked by Tennyson whether his conclusions told against Christianity, replied: 'No, certainly not.'[2] Evolution merely attempted to explain a process; 'why there has been any evolution at all, and why it has taken a spiritual direction, evolutionary science is not competent to say'.[3] All that Darwin's theories really did was to destroy the old teleology, as it had been taught by Paley for example, with its special contrivances and the notion that the wisdom and goodness of God could be demonstrated from Nature regarded as a kind of machine.[4] When Nature was viewed no longer as a machine, but as an organism, the argument from design based on its utility no doubt lost cogency, but the idea of purpose in the universe was really deepened and widened. Darwin wrote in 1873: 'The impossibility of conceiving that this great and wondrous universe arose through chance seems to me the chief argument for the existence of God.' Even earlier J. S. Mill had written: 'I think it must be allowed that, in the present state of our knowledge, the adaptations of Nature afford a large balance of probability in favour of creation by intelligence.'[5]

Some of the wiser and more thoughtful Christian leaders recognized the truth and usefulness of Darwin's doctrine. To the opinions of Charles Kingsley and Dean Church already

[1] There was something to be said for this attitude since it cannot be denied that religion was being used to bolster up the prevailing social system. This is why Socialism on the Continent and present-day Communism are anti-religious.

[2] *Memoir of Alfred, Lord Tennyson*, Vol. II, p. 57. Liddon acknowledged the debt owed to Darwin for his courageous adherence to theistic views. (*Life and Letters*, p. 276.)

[3] Storr, *The Living God*, p. 60.

[4] For a discussion of Paley's views and a restatement of the argument from design see Storr, *Development and Divine Purpose*, pp. 21 ff. and 122 ff.

[5] *Theism*, p. 175.

quoted we may add the conclusion of Frederick Temple that it was an aid to religion as tending 'to make the Creation more wonderful than ever. For it shows not a number of isolated creations, but all creation knit together into a complete whole.'[1]

One apparent effect of the teaching of Darwin and of evolution in general was not, as Swinburne imagined, to exalt humanity, but to degrade it. Copernicus had dethroned the dwelling-place of mankind from being the centre of the universe,[2] now man himself was shown to be, at least so far as his body was concerned, only a part of the natural process and akin to the beasts by which he was surrounded. The statement in Genesis that he was a special creation could no longer be maintained and individual men now came 'to be envisaged rather as transitory embodiments of relatively abiding types than as themselves the supremely important realities for the sake of which the whole process exists'.[3] If Galton, who had been led to the study of heredity under the influence of *The Origin of Species,* had had his way it might seem that man was further to be degraded by being subjected to the methods and procedure of a stud farm.

If it can be proved that the spiritual nature of man is of the same character as his physical nature, or merely imaginary, then he does, indeed, suffer a great and final degradation. This had been argued long before by Francis Bacon when he said of man: 'If he be not kin to God by his spirit he is an ignoble creature.'[4] Liberal thinkers, however, and quite rightly, found nothing to worry them in this exposure of man's very humble origins; what mattered was his present exaltation. 'We have little to learn of apes', wrote George Meredith with lofty scorn, 'and they may be left.'[5]

But the change in man's status is not perhaps so great after all,

---

[1] Sandford, *Frederick Temple: an Appreciation,* p. 301.

[2] On the question as to whether there are other inhabited worlds than ours see James Ward, *Pluralism and Theism.*

[3] Webb, *Religious Thought in England,* etc., p. 13.

[4] Essay, 'On Atheism'.

[5] *The Egoist,* p. 2. In *Diana of the Crossways,* p. 15, however, he refers to the 'unfailing aboriginal democratic old monster that waits to pull us down'.

for as the latest product of evolution he is still the crown of creation, so far as it is known to him; and even if the earth can no longer be regarded as the centre of the universe the practical difference it makes is of little consequence; Westcott, indeed, could argue that it had been 'brought back again to be the true centre in a deeper sense than of local position'.[1] The real significance of things depends, not on bulk or station, but on intellectual and spiritual qualities. 'We attribute an absolute worth and dignity to spirit, simply because it possesses the power of purpose, purposeful thought, purposeful action, purposeful love.'[2] The truth of this contention is not always easy to grasp, and still more to maintain, for the magnitude of material things is ever pressing upon us, the magnitude of mind we are unable to perceive. Man must ever be on his guard against what has been called 'astronomical intimidation'. Some, indeed, may react against it with scorn, as Coventry Patmore, for example, when he wrote:

Not greatly moved with awe am I
To learn that we may spy
Five thousand firmaments beyond our own.
The best that's known
Of the heavenly bodies does them credit small.

The fact that man can comprehend with ever-growing knowledge the nature of the physical universe shows beyond doubt that he surpasses it, and even if, as Pascal once said, 'the entire physical universe conspired to crush a man, the man would still be nobler than the entire physical universe, for he would know that he was crushed'.

Science undoubtedly had great achievements to its credit, for it was a creator, as well as a discoverer, and in a comparatively short time had not only revolutionized social and economic life, but also the entire outlook of educated men and women. It is no marvel therefore if some scientists, in striking contrast to those

[1] *The Gospel of Life*, p. 12.
[2] Illingworth, *Divine Immanence*, p. 14.

4

of our own day,[1] calmly assumed that its findings would never
be challenged, or that W. K. Clifford could even identify the
advancement of scientific thought with human progress itself.[2]
We escaped by a very narrow margin the setting up of a new
orthodoxy based on science, having as its Aquinas the venerable
figure of Mr. Herbert Spencer.

It is very remarkable that scientists, who would have been
appalled at the thought of dogmatizing on scientific matters
lying outside their special province, did not hesitate to utter
pontifical pronouncements upon metaphysics and theology where
such knowledge as they might possess was even more scanty.[3]
In his presidential address to the British Association in 1871
Tyndall made an attack on orthodoxy which exposed him to
considerable ridicule. In referring to primitive religions he
explained that his knowledge of them was derived from a few
popular text-books, and his antiquated notions of history doubtless emanated from a similar source. Such floundering provoked
Robertson Smith to write a highly satirical article; but a more
sober reply was produced by two eminent scientists, Professors
Tait and Balfour Smith, in a volume entitled *The Unseen Universe*.
They there argued that religion and science, far from being
opposed, were really upholding identical conclusions—the
existence of a transcendental universe and the immortality of the
soul.[4]

Undeterred by this exposure Tyndall in 1874 produced what
he was pleased to call an *Eirenicon*, a patronizing, not to say
contemptuous, volume 'in which he offered to religion the shells

---

[1] 'Few more remarkable changes have taken place in the history of scientific
thought than the movement of self-criticism, which, during the last fifty years,
has revolutionised the scientific outlook and completely changed the relation of
natural science with theology and philosophy.' (A. Wood, *In Pursuit of Truth*,
p. 19.)

[2] Huxley in an essay on 'Science and Culture' (*Selected Works*, Vol. III)
prophesied that a time was coming when education would be based on science,
not on literature and the humanities.

[3] See some trenchant remarks by A. L. Moore in *Lux Mundi*, p. 144.

[4] This volume, though now quite forgotten, had great influence at the time:
see Black and Chrystal, *William Robertson Smith*, pp. 161 ff.

of the oyster—as much fancy and poetry as ever it liked—and complacently retained for mathematics and Natural Science and for Agnosticism . . . all the succulent food of truth and reality.'[1]

Thus whilst science was exalted as a living light among 'the watch-fires of the world', some of its exponents, exasperated by what they regarded as merely perverse opposition, were not content to 'lift the torch of reason in the dusky cave of life', but thrust their smoking brands in the faces of their opponents. This, however, could not be said of the greater men, although they too might resent the refusal to accept views which to them seemed so obvious and incontrovertible.

Too great an absorption in the study of physical nature may have blinded scientists to the value of things spiritual and to much that gives to life its real significance,[2] but they did not confine reality to the material world. 'God and spirit I know', said Tyndall, 'and matter I know, and I believe in both.'[3] Even Huxley, regarded by many as the chief protagonist of the scientific view of life, declared that 'The antagonism of Science is not to Religion, but to the heathen survivals and bad philosophy under which Religion herself is well-nigh crushed.' In his Romanes Lecture for 1893 he proclaimed the view that the higher life of man was in no way due to natural evolution, but on the contrary the result of his struggle against it. Even Herbert Spencer recognized the need for some kind of religion as a corrective of Naturalism.

Scientists might denounce their opponents for basing their conclusions on hypotheses which were incapable of proof and the ordinary man might contrast the need for 'faith' in religion (for him any truth should be self-evident) with the confident assertions of science; in reality, however, science worked largely by 'faith', faith in the order and harmony of the universe, and many of its discoveries were equally based on assumptions which could

[1] Von Hügel, *The Reality of God*, pp. 196f.
[2] This was admitted and regretted by Darwin: see *Life*, Vol. I, pp. 102f.
[3] *Memoir of Alfred, Lord Tennyson*, Vol. II, p. 380.

not be proved.[1] The claim, for example, that like causes will always produce like effects may be true of the past, but who can guarantee that it will be true of the future? The whole conception of Nature as a unity must be accepted on faith, for our cosmos might conceivably be a chaos.

Science, moreover, was not entirely free from obscurantism, and some of its practitioners showed nervousness when confronted with claims that seemed to conflict with their preconceived ideas. Telepathy is an instance of this, for a prominent biologist once said to William James that even if it were true, 'scientists ought to band together to keep it suppressed and concealed. It would undo the uniformity of nature, and all sorts of things without which scientists cannot carry on their pursuits.'[2]

Furthermore, although science had made wonderful discoveries it had no answer to give to the riddle of the universe. None the less its prestige ranked very high with the multitude, who were not greatly interested in such high matters, and were impressed by the ability of science to provide means for material betterment. There was as yet no suspicion of the immense harm which would follow scientific discoveries and the destructive use which might be made of them—the atom-bomb and chemical and biological warfare lay in the hidden future. But even if this darker, malevolent side had been absent and all inventions had been beneficent, evil might have come from them, because of their emphasis on the material aspects of life.

It is often the fate of scientific hypotheses to become popular superstitions long before they have been either proved or disproved, and the general attitude to science partook of superstition, for few had any adequate knowledge of its aims and methods, or realized its limitations. People talked glibly of 'science' as if it were a single entity, and did not realize its immense complexity

---

[1] Cf. A. Wood, *The Pursuit of Truth*, p. 39, who writes: 'the more one thinks about the outstanding general theories of science and the method of their discovery, the less important does the part played by any logical process seem to be. The discoverer has used imagination, insight, and intuition.' Tyndall, it may be noted, once wrote a paper 'On the Scientific Use of the Imagination.'

[2] *The Will to Believe*, p. 10; cf. above, p. 20.

and innumerable ramifications, nor the difficulty of obtaining even a working knowledge of its various branches. They accepted the world as perceived by their senses with its apparent stability and compactness as 'real'; being entirely ignorant of the fact, now established by physicists, that it is 'no more solid than a snow-storm'.[1] Well might Illingworth complain that 'so many people are shaken by scientific doubts only because they don't know enough science'.[2]

It would be interesting to know how far the popular belief in science was inspired by that very deceptive phrase 'the laws of Nature'. A law is something imposed by authority[3] and must be obeyed, a 'law of nature' is merely the formulated explanation of phenomena so far as they have been observed and classified.[4] The statement that objects 'obey' laws (e.g., of gravitation), almost as if in so doing they exhibited a commendable virtue, is entirely misleading, for a natural law cannot be 'disobeyed'; if a law is apparently broken it means that it was not a 'law', but an erroneous or inadequate description.

Because scientific statements are mainly descriptive and not explanatory they are less open to disproof than statements in other departments of learning. Improved methods may make the descriptions more accurate, and even where the explanatory element has been superseded the 'law' may still be 'true' in practice. If, for example, gravitation is a property of space and not of matter, as scientists now suspect, Newton's law of gravitation would still hold good.

But science was not everywhere so highly regarded. In the academic world it was looked upon as an upstart—the public schools and universities were still largely under clerical influence

---

[1] Evelyn Underhill, *Mysticism*, p. 11.   [2] *Life*, p. 49.

[3] The Duke of Argyle wrote a learned volume with the title *The Reign of Law*. (It may be pointed out that it is rulers, and not laws, that reign.)

[4] Cf. Huxley: 'A law of nature, in the scientific sense, is the product of a mental operation upon the facts of nature which come under observation, and has no more existence outside the mind than colour has. . . . The tenacity of the wonderful fallacy that the laws of nature are agents, instead of being, as they really are, a mere record of experience . . . is an interesting psychological fact.'

—and scholars knew, as the general public did not, the limitations of science and also that it spoke with a divided voice. Science, too, had its critics among those who were by no means orthodox Christians. Carlyle once said that 'if Adam had remained in Paradise there had been no anatomy and no metaphysics'.

In attempting to assess the effects of scientific discoveries and theories upon religion and theology it is necessary to bear constantly in mind these different attitudes towards science, and to observe that their impact upon popular religion was very different from their impact upon theology.

The progress of science and the diffusion of the scientific point of view raised many problems for the theologian; though if he were sufficiently wise he would not fail to recognize that even if much in the Bible could no longer be taken literally yet its real value as concerned with the relations of God to man and man to man, was unaffected, it might even be said that it had been enhanced. But his task was heavy and arduous, for not only had he to attempt to assimilate a multitude of new facts, he had also to adjust his ideas to an entirely new way of looking at things. Christian beliefs had been formulated in an age which held a geocentric theory of the universe, and certain of them, such as our Lord's visible Ascension and the conception of a local heaven 'above the bright blue sky', were clearly incompatible with the new point of view. But, on the other hand, science was useful to genuine theology in a variety of ways for it helped to place in truer perspective many pagan ideas which survived in the Old Testament, ideas which represented God as capricious, open to cajolery and flattery, in fact a counterpart of a typical Oriental despot. Science showed that Nature worked uniformly and could be relied upon, so far as man had knowledge of her ways; that disaster and disease were not wayward inflictions on a people because of some, possibly quite unconscious, offence on their part or neglect to provide the requisite offerings, but were due to causes which could be definitely traced. If Nature punishes ignorance as severely as deliberate breaches of her 'laws', yet this is but a call to study her ways with greater diligence. Physical science in its outlook was much more akin to Jesus in His attitude to the Father than to much in the Old Testament.

A benefit of another kind was conferred by science in so far as it served to correct any over-emphasis on the transcendence of God, to which theology had been prone,[1] by showing that He was still active in the world. For 'a belief in natural law is essentially a belief in a present God'.[2]

But if those competent to judge the situation saw in science no necessary threat to religion its effects on those less instructed were disastrous. In their eyes the discoveries of science had demonstrated that the Bible was not all that had been claimed for it, and this added to the general uncertainty of the times. The better educated were led to a magnification of the importance of the natural order, and even some of the orthodox were tempted to see in it the only source from which man might derive any reliable knowledge of the deity. Hitherto science had been regarded by the man in the street as a means of instruction of a mild kind or as providing a diverting recreation for those who took an interest in such matters; now it was hailed as a new gospel promising a course of endless progress, the trusty guide to an earthly paradise. Thus the ground was made ready for a sort of religion of Nature which in a few generations entirely displaced Christianity for a large portion of mankind. Such was the opinion of William James.[3]

In contrast with the uncertainties which were beginning to surround religion science seemed so confident and assured. After all the scientist could demonstrate the truth of his theories, or so it was fondly imagined,[4] whilst religion when challenged to perform

---

[1] It is, of course, equally dangerous to over-emphasize the immanence of God for that may lead to pantheism. God must not be identified with the universe which He has created.

[2] Westcott, *Christus Consummator*, p. 60. Some apologists, by a kind of argument *ad hominem*, pointed out that a law implies a legislator, a somewhat specious line to take.

[3] *Varieties of Religious Experience*, p. 91.

[4] The truth is that in the 'most exact of the exact sciences we have no infallible criterion of truth and no infallibly true theories'. (A. Wood, *In Pursuit of Truth*, p. 66.)

a similar feat was obviously at a loss. Men in their ignorance had forgotten that 'nothing worthy of proving can be proved' and well merited the caustic condemnation uttered years before by Coleridge: 'The man who will believe nothing but by force of demonstrative evidence . . . is not in a state of mind to be reasoned with on any subject.'[1] There were even scientists who shared this point of view and rejected religion 'as something unverified and unverifiable by the only methods which were generally regarded as rational and scientific'.[2] It is also to be noted that orthodox Christians who clung to miracles as demonstrating the truth of the Gospel actually held much the same position.

Many not unthoughtful people surmised, though few scientists would have agreed with them, that science furnished a perfectly rational and plausible account of the origin and development of the universe and of the origin and development of man himself; believing that all things would sooner or later find a place in some scientific category as parts of a vast mechanical process. But this, of course, was a starkly materialist point of view and very disquieting in the eyes of those who, whether orthodox Christians or not, still clung to a spiritual interpretation of the universe. It was not only Whitman who heard

the o'erweening, mocking voice,
Matter is conqueror—matter triumphant only, continues onward.

Materialism may be regarded under two distinct aspects. On the one hand it signifies an attitude to reality, what may be called philosophical materialism; on the other it denotes a way of life, a trust in material things. Each helps the other; for concentration on material things cannot but fail to deaden the spiritual faculties, and the abandonment of spiritual values drives men to seek solace or forgetfulness in the things of the senses.

The age was one which saw in the multiplication of comforts and luxuries a palpable sign of progress and the ultimate way to

---

[1] *Aids to Reflection*, Aphor. XCVIII, §19 (note).
[2] Webb, *Religious Thought in England*, etc., p. 7.

happiness. It failed to realize that material benefits could provide but fleeting satisfaction, since they were incapable of contenting the deeper cravings of the soul. Such an attitude was in part a reaction against religion as popularly taught and understood, and the Church must take its share of the blame. It had 'over-spiritualized' religion, and seemed to have forgotten that the good things of the earth were gifts of God to His children, and to be enjoyed as such. This was really an inexcusable lapse in a faith which placed the Word become flesh at the centre of its creed. For Jesus, at least as depicted in the first three gospels, God was the God of nature as well as the God of grace, and life was looked upon as a single whole.

As a philosophy, materialism can offer no satisfactory solution of the problems which beset mankind; it is, indeed, not so much an attempt at a philosophy as a denial that any philosophy is possible.[1] Materialism as a system has the appearance of completeness only because it ignores those facts which are incompatible with it,[2] and dismisses whole tracts of experience as irrelevant or illusory. In its blindness it gives to the universe a greater dignity and importance than the mind which is able to discover, in part at least, its supposed significance. Materialism, moreover, hovers precariously on the verge of absolute scepticism; for we are dependent for our knowledge of physical objects upon the impressions they make upon our senses, and we have no guarantee that such impressions can be relied upon.[3]

Even in practical life materialism fails to provide the satisfaction which it promises. Far from having fulfilled Bacon's high dream

[1] 'The fundamental doctrines of materialism . . . lie outside the limits of philosophical enquiry . . . it is of little moment whether we express the phenomena of matter in terms of spirit, or the phenomena of spirit in terms of matter.' (T. H. Huxley, *Collected Essays*, Vol I, pp. 162, 164.)

[2] 'We accomplish the apparently miraculous feat of reducing a chaotic world to order, because we carefully confine our attention and our efforts to those portions which we find can be ordered.' (N. R. Campbell, *Elements of Physics*, p. 87.)

[3] 'If sensation is all that is given us, then we can never know anything but our own ideas . . . of the outward world we know and can know absolutely nothing, except the sensations which we experience from it.' (J. S. Mill, *Logic*, p. 39.)

of achieving dominion over matter, man, as a result of his efforts, finds himself the slave of his own creation, the servant of the machine.

Some ten years before our period began Browning in the opening lines of 'Easter Day' had exclaimed 'How very hard it is to be a Christian!', referring not to intellectual difficulties, but to the realization of Christian ideals in actual life. In regard to materialism the case is different, for men succeed only too well in living life on a material plane; but anyone who tries to defend materialism on intellectual grounds, or even to formulate it, soon finds himself in difficulties. We do not know what matter is, for 'matter in the sense of the materialist—is something which nobody has ever seen, touched or even handled'.[1]

As science is concerned with but a part, though a highly important part, of reality, so its findings make their appeal, not to the whole man, but only to certain sides of his multifarious being—to the intellectual, and to some degree, it may be, to the moral; but the emotional and spiritual it leaves untouched. By its too facile explanation of things a mechanical age robs life of mystery and grace, and takes away all sense of drama and romance.

> There was an awful rainbow once in heaven:
> We know her woof, her texture; she is given
> In the dull catalogue of common things.[2]

If, however, it is easy to pick holes in the materialistic fabric and to underline the limitations of science, it cannot be ignored that scientific discoveries brought about a revolution in the outlook of mankind. Owing to the difficulties raised by science as to its contents the reading of the Bible came to be neglected and its terms and phrases largely passed out of general use. On the other hand the notions of science and even its terminology were widely disseminated, and gradually displaced religious categories.

---

[1] Hastings Rashdall, *Philosophy and Religion*, p. 7.
[2] Keats, *Lamia*, Pt. 2, ll. 231 ff.

Progress was substituted for providence in the popular mind, and causation took the place of purpose and divine judgment.

The difficulties for religion which the spread of science aroused were met in various ways. The Church of Rome naturally had its cut and dried methods and the Vatican Council of 1870, (the famous council which recognized papal infallibility) anathematized all who said that 'the doctrines of the Church can ever receive a sense in accordance with the progress of science other than that which the Church has understood and still understands'. Among the ultra-pious of other denominations there were also attempts to belittle the worth of scientific discoveries, and when genuine science seemed to contradict the Bible refuge was found in pseudo-science. Sometimes the evidence of both the Bible and of science was twisted so as to bring them into supposed agreement; a notorious example of this endeavour was Sir J. W. Dawson's *Modern Science and Bible Lands* of which a third edition appeared in 1895. It received a well-deserved denunciation from Driver.[1]

Those who were more favourably disposed towards scientific discoveries made much of the gaps in our knowledge which science had so far failed to bridge, and, by a kind of inverted agnosticism, tried to buttress the faith by ignorance rather than by knowledge. This was, in any case, a very forlorn hope, for science as it advances gradually fills in the gaps and illuminates the surviving obscurities. Moreover, such an attitude of mind, if logically pressed, would dread rather than welcome any fresh discoveries and is entirely unworthy of those who professed to be followers of One who declared that He was not only the Way and the Life, but also the Truth. The whole standpoint showed a very inadequate idea of God and by limiting the range of His activity impoverished religious thought. 'The real God', as someone has said, 'does not reside in the interstices left by science. He is not to be found in the sandbank of diminishing mystery.' The whole argument was based on a wrong conception of the relations of the natural and the supernatural. These are not alien

[1] *Genesis* (Westminster Commentaries), p. 23, note 3.

to each other, and to use the term 'supernatural' as implying that 'the higher spiritual levels of life are *not* natural' is to be greatly deceived.[1]

At the same time Christian thinkers were justified in maintaining a certain reserve towards the discoveries and theories of natural science (as further experience has abundantly proved); for they were founded 'on inquiries which left vast areas of life unexplored'.[2] Modern science is mainly research science and as such it is concerned with specific problems and 'does not undertake to give a systematic account of the world as a whole in any specific field'.[3] Science, moreover, finds supreme significance in the cosmic and the general and takes little account of the experiences of the individual. Yet these too are 'facts' in the fullest meaning of the term. Illingworth cited the effect of a sunset or a piece of music as examples of 'impressions which profoundly touch the feelings and modify the conduct of innumerable men'; and argued that such impressions 'may even be called more real . . . than their mechanical causes'.[4] There was also a growing suspicion that scientific discoveries, which in their early days had given men a sense of freedom and expansion, would in the long run tell against them. The uniformity of nature might prove a severe restriction, and man find himself trapped in a scheme of things which had no mercy and no pity, a scheme of things in which events were entirely determined by their temporal antecedents. To Christians there seemed to be something especially revolting in the apparent deification of natural law and causal uniformity.

The conflict between religion and science which waged so fiercely during the latter part of the nineteenth century, a conflict which seems now hardly comprehensible, was due to a great

---

[1] The word is to be used only by way of contrast with 'the partial and conventional use of "nature" as a term under which we sum up all that constitutes this present and visible system of things'. (H. Scott Holland in *Lux Mundi*, p. 10, note 1.)

[2] Major, *Life of W. Boyd Carpenter*, p. 149.

[3] G. H. Mead, *Movements of Thought in the Nineteenth Century*, p. 264.

[4] *Divine Immanence*, pp. 55 f.

variety of causes, and perhaps above all to the failure of both sets of combatants to understand the aims and objects of the other. Bitterness was greatly increased by the exaggerated claims put forward on behalf of one side and the other, though not as a rule by those who had the best right to speak on its behalf; many claims advanced on the side of science would have been discountenanced by its leading exponents, as the attacks on science by some of the ultra-orthodox would have been repudiated by the better instructed and more balanced leaders of religion. In the heat of the struggle, however, there was an understandable tendency to take such extreme utterances as typical and representative. If to religious men the claims of science seemed over-ambitious, ill-founded, and aggressive, the claims of religion appeared equally so to scientists. But in the contemporary state of things some kind of conflict was inevitable, for 'if it is true, as most theologians have believed, that religious truth is essentially final, absolute and therefore unprogressive, there will arise . . . an irreconcilable divergence between science and religion'.[1] This was the real crux, and if it is now difficult for us to comprehend the vehemence which was called forth it is simply because our attitude towards the Bible and its authority has been so radically changed; for there was a time when the extent of its authority, regarded by many as verbally inspired, was unlimited, and no one could deny that there was a clash between its statements and the conclusions of natural science.

Between genuine science and genuine theology there can be no permanent opposition, for both have to do with the world which God has made, and fresh discoveries, are literally discoveries, and not something which man has effected or created. The facts have been there all the time, and their discovery has the nature of a new revelation to man by God. Farrar, in this as in other respects, far in advance of his age, had already recognized this truth, and in his Bampton Lectures for 1885 boldly proclaimed that 'true science and true religion are twin sisters, each studying her own sacred book of God, and nothing but disaster

[1] Schiller, *Problems of Belief*, p. 20.

has arisen from the petulant scorn of the one and the false fear and cruel tyrannies of the other'.[1] The discoveries of science, once they are established—and this is often a less certain process than is sometimes imagined—cannot be ignored by the theologian; whilst the scientist for his part has no justification in contemptuously dismissing the religious sentiments of the human heart as unworthy of consideration, or even as 'survivals' which will ultimately disappear. Science, furthermore, must be willing to recognize its own limitations. It seeks for truth with unselfish and ardent endeavour, but such truth as it succeeds in grasping is incomplete and partial only and must be carefully distinguished from the reality which is the goal of the theologian.

The solution of the conflict is for both religion and science to recognize their different spheres. But this is not always an easy matter, for as in the conflicts between the Empire and the Papacy in the Middle Ages, such spheres undoubtedly overlap. To define their exact limits is beyond human ingenuity.

There were in our period numerous attempts to reconcile religion and science, and of most of them it may be said that they were either premature or delusive. As with many so-called understandings in politics, both domestic and international, they largely depended for their acceptance on the use of formulas which the two sides interpreted in different senses.

In this connexion mention must be made of the writings of Henry Drummond. These had an immense popularity, the best known of them, *Natural Law in the Spiritual World*, went through thirty editions between 1883 and 1890. Drummond's object was to demonstrate that the scientific principle of continuity applied in the spiritual as well as in the physical world, and that the same laws from the same God were equally operative in both. But the analogy, though attractive, was misleading; for it is hazardous to apply scientific principles outside their proper sphere, a circumstance which scientists themselves seem often to forget. If Drummond's volume did much to reassure simple believers and seemed to promise a hope of reconciliation between religion

[1] *The History of Interpretation*, p. 428.

and science, scholars regarded it in a very different light. To them its underlying fallacies and forced parallels were but too clearly apparent; Hort condemned it as 'a quite singularly muddle-headed book' which gave a fresh illustration of 'the powerlessness of the mere love of natural science to teach men to think'.[1] In 1894 Drummond published *The Ascent of Man* in which he pointed out that man's struggle is not entirely for his own survival, but also for that of others; this he considered to be 'the Further Evolution . . . the closing act in the drama of Man'.[2]

Before leaving the subject of the reconciliation of religion and science it will be useful to recall Jowett's forecast that this would only be finally accomplished when religion was 'enlightened, extended and purified, and philosophy and science inspired and elevated, and both allied together in the service of God'.[3]

One subject upon which science and religion seemed especially to be opposed calls for some notice—the question of miracles. There had been a time when men had grown tired of discussing the matter and preferred to turn to other more profitable subjects; but by the beginning of the nineteenth century it had again aroused interest,[4] an interest which in our period became acute. Increased attention was focused on miracles by J. B. Mozley's Bampton Lectures for 1865, and R. W. Church, reviewing them in *The Times* for 5 June 1866,[5] could go so far as to write that 'The way in which the subject of Miracles has been treated, and the place which they have had in our discussions, will remain a characteristic feature of both the religious and philosophical tendencies of thought among us.' Mozley's lectures are a grave discussion of a grave matter in which no attempt is made to evade the difficulties. His arguments, though they acquire fresh weight from his characteristic force and grace of style, are merely those which had become traditional. The discussion centres round two questions: 'Are miracles possible?' and 'If so, can any of them be proved?' In other words he deals first with the scientific and

---

[1] *Life*, Vol. II, p. 340.   [2] *Op. cit.*, p. 443.
[3] *Sermons on the Faith of Darwin*, pp. 20 f.   [4] Cf. Storr, pp. 198, 370 f.
[5] Reprinted in *Occasional Papers*, Vol. II, pp. 82 ff.

philosophical aspects, and then proceeds to the historical. Like Bishop Butler, whose manner of treatment he recalls, Mozley believed that the miraculous was a necessary element in revelation, and he could not conceal his amazement, an amazement shared by other orthodox theologians, at the attitude of men like Stanley who did not seem to recognize the immeasurable difference that miracle or no miracle made in our idea of religion.[1]

Mozley's approach to the controversy was calm and dignified; but others did not always exhibit a similar restraint and serenity, for here, as in the wider field of conflict between religion and science, there was much misunderstanding and refusal to consider the opposing point of view. The narrowly orthodox shut their ears to any criticism of any miracle recorded in the Bible; though many, of less rigid outlook, drew the line at those miracles which were parts of the gospels. Scientists retorted that since miracles did not happen there was no point in discussing the evidence for them; an attitude of mind unworthy of the seriousness of the question, and as we now realize one which was based on false assumptions; for present-day scientists admit that they possess no criterion by which to decide whether any specific event is according to the laws of Nature or not.[2]

As the knowledge of Nature was extended into ever fresh fields, anything like a violation of her laws became more and more repugnant to contemporary ideas. Long before, indeed, Pope had described a God who would interfere with the course of Nature as resembling 'some weak prince . . . prone for his favourites to reverse his laws'.[3] In any case to seek for evidence of the divine working solely in the irregular is to liken the doings of God 'to the spasmodic incalculable action of a capricious man'.[4] Henry Drummond thought it a monstrous limitation 'to single out a few specific wonders authenticated by ancient documents,

[1] *Letters of J. B. Mozley*, p. 260.
[2] Cf. A. Wood, *op. cit.*, p. 74: 'the pseudo-scientific attack on miracles delivered in the nineteenth century . . . involved . . . a complete misconception, namely, that an unexplained event necessarily meant a breach of a law which admitted no exceptions'.
[3] *Essay on Man*, IV, 121 f.   [4] Sanday, *Inspiration*, p. 444.

and to attach to them the epithet miracle'.[1] Those theologians who had a knowledge of natural science rejected any thought of arbitrary interferences; such interpositions would be, as Aubrey Moore told the Reading Church Congress in 1883, 'as fatal to theology as to science'.[2] The renewed emphasis on the immanence of God turned the thoughts of theologians to seek for evidence of divine providence not in supernatural interferences, such as might befit a purely transcendent deity, but in the constant and regular ordering of Nature.[3]

Those scientists who were especially critical of orthodox religion decried any kind of miracle as an unworthy piece of magic, forgetting that 'behind a miracle there is an intelligible purpose'. It must, however, be admitted that some apologists for Christianity had given them an excuse for such a dismissal of the miraculous, for there had been an appeal to miracles as, with the detailed fulfilment of prophecy, among the strongest proofs of the truth of the Gospel. The appeal to miracles, however, had not in the past been so common or so extensive as is often supposed, it had, indeed, been rejected by Jesus (Mt. 4:5 f., Lk. 4:9 ff.) and by St. Paul (1 Cor. 1:22 f.); while the Alexandrian Fathers had attached little value to it, as also to the appeal to prophecy, and Luther had roundly said that 'external miracles are the apples and nuts which God gave to the childish world as playthings; we no longer have need of them'.[4]

To attempt to bring in miracles as evidence for a revelation, or as substantiating certain ideas, can never be satisfactory. Portents might compel belief, but it would be but a poor form of belief, and the observer would be apt to be bewildered rather than impressed. Such a method is coercive in its nature and over-rides the free spirit of man, and as Emerson has said, 'to aim

---

[1] *The New Evangelism*, p. 107.

[2] *Science and the Faith*, p. 225. Gore, *The Incarnation*, p. 42, pointed out that the Greek Fathers 'often teach us that even miracles must not be lawless, but in harmony with nature's fundamental law'.

[3] For a consideration of the relation of miracles and the divine immanence see Illingworth, *Divine Immanence*, pp. 101 ff.

[4] Quoted Allen, *The Continuity of Christian Thought*, p. 286.

to convert a man by miracles is a profanation of the soul'.[1] Acceptance must come through the eager devotion of heart and will, not by means of compelling signs.[2]

Christians were coming to see that though a belief in miracles might be part of the traditional faith, that faith was quite independent of them, and therefore that attacks upon them ought not to be taken too seriously.[3] Westcott urged that they should be regarded, not so much as evidence of the truth of Christianity, but as an integral part of the divine revelation. The Gospel miracles at least were a witness to the impression produced by Jesus on His contemporaries, and moreover were always a vehicle for spiritual lessons; they were, indeed, acted parables.[4]

> Miracles may have been attributed to those who have promulgated creeds at various times, but these miracles did not form a constituent part of the teaching; they were not blended with it as those of our Lord were. They were introduced only to serve as credentials, so that an appeal to them may silence incredulity; they convey no lesson, they only serve as proof.[5]

Historical criticism naturally regarded all stories of miracles as of doubtful value and ascribed them to untrained observation or unverified inference. Baden Powell in *Essays and Reviews* had allowed that such stories might be true, but not as miracles. It was the fashion to attempt to explain their origin by rationalizing them. Of such attempts it may be said that they now seem more difficult to believe than the miracles themselves.[6] In *Ecce Homo*

---

[1] *Works*, Vol. I, p. 131.

[2] See Westcott, *The Gospel of Life*, Ch. VIII 'Signs as a Vehicle of Revelation.'

[3] Cf. Illingworth, *Personality: Human and Divine*, p. 203.

[4] Cf. Gore's definition of a miracle as 'an event in physical nature which makes unmistakably plain the presence and direct action of God working for a moral end'. (*The Incarnation*, p. 45.)

[5] Latham, *Pastor Pastorum*, p. 74.

[6] This method was already discredited before the end of our period and Sir William Ramsay in 1895 could say of the miracles in Acts: 'Twenty years ago I found it easy to dispose of them; but now-a-days probably not even the youngest among us finds himself able to maintain that we have mastered the secrets of nature, and determined the limits which divide the unknown and the impossible.' (*St. Paul the Traveller and the Roman Citizen*, p. 87.)

Seeley accepted the performance of miracles by Jesus, for otherwise the history of the Church was inexplicable, but he pointed out that Jesus used His miraculous powers with great restraint. There was a tendency even amongst the strictly orthodox to make a distinction between the various narratives, including those recorded in the gospels; some were better attested and more congruous with the character of Jesus than others. One fact which emerged was a cause of concern; the discovery that the evidence for miracles outside the Christian tradition could be as strong as that for those of the Bible.[1]

Thus a complete change of point of view came about; miracles, instead of being relied upon as evidence for the truth of Christianity, were now to be accepted because of their connexion with it. They were, moreover, no longer regarded as violations of law, or as a kind of running repairs by the Creator to a machine which threatened to go wrong. It was man's sin and the disorder which it had occasioned which made them necessary; an idea suggested long before by Leibniz who had said: 'I hold that when God works miracles, He does not do it in order to supply the wants of Nature, but those of grace.' Such a view, however, was not without its difficulties, for it might seem to lay too great stress on the needs of man at the expense of the providence of God. This objection had been noticed by Hort as early as 1859 when he wrote of miracles that they might be considered 'solely with reference to the present needs of men, and as conditioned solely by man's capacity for them at the time. I think they are at least as much connected with crises of God's eternal plans of revelation, education, and government which cannot be set aside by man's unbelief'.[2]

By the end of the nineteenth century most orthodox scholars, as we have seen, were prepared to admit that there was a distinction between the various miracles, and there was a tendency, justified on the grounds of historical criticism, to reject many of

[1] Cf. Streeter, *Restatement and Reunion*, p. xii. 'It is less the weakness of the evidence for the biblical miracles than the strength of the evidences for others, that constitutes the main difficulty at the present time.'

[2] *Life*, Vol. I, p. 404.

the miracles of the Old Testament, though this was extended but sparingly to those of the New. Some theologians made a further distinction between miracles in general, and those which were articles of the creed, above all the Virgin Birth and the Resurrection. These, although their importance and the evidence in their favour were very different, were considered as equally sacrosanct.

The doctrine of the Virgin Birth had become a matter for controversy, though Gore thought that it was mainly in conversation and not in literature,[1] and there were liberal scholars who insisted that its acceptance should no longer be required of Christians. They pointed out that although found in early Western Creeds it was absent from the original Creed of Nicaea. The New Testament evidence is confined to the accounts in Mt. 1:18ff. and Lk. 2:1ff., accounts which some scholars regarded as of dubious value. There is no reference to it in Mark, John, or in St. Paul, and it is never appealed to in support of the doctrine of the Incarnation. It was suggested that the real reason for the idea of the Virgin Birth was a desire to break the entail of original sin which was supposed to be transmitted through the father alone. One further objection was that an abnormal birth would destroy the true manhood of Jesus. The defence of the doctrine was undertaken by Gore in his *Dissertations*, pp. 3 ff. He sought to show that 'the Virgin Birth has in Christian tradition from the first been held inseparable from the truth of the Incarnation' and that 'the doctrine of the person of Christ is in reality inseparable from the fact of His birth of a virgin'; at the same time he was prepared to admit that 'in the beginning of Christianity the belief in Jesus as the Son of God was . . . prior to the knowledge of His Virgin Birth', and that some of those who doubted or disparaged the doctrine were orthodox in other respects.

The doctrine of the Resurrection stands in a very different category whether for the evidence in its favour,[2] or for its

[1] *Dissertations*, p. 3.
[2] Gwatkin considered that 'few events are so well attested'. (*The Sacrifice of Thankfulness*, p. 35.)

importance. From the first it had been amongst the central doctrines of Christianity,[1] and as the supreme miracle of revelation, its successful defence is a step towards the acceptance of the historic worth of the lesser miracles.

During our period it had to bear much criticism, but this was no novel experience, nor can it be said that anything new, on the side of either attack or defence, emerged.[2] There was, however, an increasing tendency to 'spiritualize' the events connected with it; to admit the appearances, but to reject the empty tomb. This argument was even put forward by some of orthodox belief who hoped thus to retain the 'kernel' of the traditional doctrine whilst discarding the 'husk'. But others could find no such distinction and rejected the whole story; for them even the 'kernel' was shrivelled and unpalatable. The defenders of the truth of the doctrine received some support, not perhaps very welcome in view of its origin and implications, from spiritualists. Myers ventured to predict that 'in consequence of the new evidence, all reasonable men, a century hence, will believe the Resurrection of Christ, whereas, in default of the new evidence, no reasonable man, a century hence, would have believed it'.[3]

---

[1] Cf. Westcott, *The Gospel of the Resurrection*. St. Paul was prepared to stake the whole Christian position on its truth. (1 Cor. 15:14.)

[2] The various stock arguments, for and against, are summarized in *E.R.E.*, Vol. I, p. 617.

[3] *Human Personality and Its Survival of Bodily Death*, Vol. II, p. 288.

Chapter Three

THE IMPACT OF PHILOSOPHY:
PHILOSOPHY AND RELIGION

Jowett had seen in the alliance of science and philosophy the supreme hope for the elevation of religion.[1] But the signs that such an alliance was possible were but scanty; in fact science and philosophy were drifting apart and both were tending to become more self-sufficient. This was largely a consequence of over-specialization and the habit of multiplying technical terms, a process which rendered each more incomprehensible to the other. Philosophers seemed to take a delight, as someone has said, in 'stating a self-evident truth in language nobody can understand', and, to add to the general obscurity, the various schools had their own special terms which were not only unintelligible to non-philosophers, but might be equally obscure to the adherents of other schools. The Hegelian members of the Synthetic Society led by R. B. Haldane, for example, were in the habit of making long harangues that were quite incomprehensible to the rest of the society.[2] This recalls the story of a bewildered examiner during an Oxford *viva* in philosophy who turned to a colleague and whispered, 'Of course the man's talking nonsense, but is it the right kind of nonsense?'

Though some philosophers welcomed the results and methods

[1] See above, p. 53.

[2] Arthur Balfour wrote to Wilfrid Ward in May 1896: 'The Hegelians are no doubt a perturbing element in our debates. For some reason which I have never yet been able to fathom, they not only insist in talking a foreign language, but invariably assume that their hearers understand it.' (Quoted Maisie Ward, *The Wilfrid Wards and the Transition*, p. 364.) Haldane, though he appreciated the social side of the meetings, thought that otherwise they were a waste of time. 'Half of those present do not understand what the other half are talking about'. (*Op. cit.*, p. 371.)

of natural science, even to an excessive degree, others more or less ignored it as incapable of throwing light on ultimate reality. Science dealt with phenomena and took no interest in matters which were vital for philosophy. This was unfortunate for 'it cannot be a matter of unconcern whether reality . . . is something which justifies and backs up those interests which we recognize as highest in human life or whether the latter are but the unessential incident upon the surface of a universe which, at its heart, is quite indifferent to them'.[1] Science, in a word, offered no intelligible explanation of the universe as a whole and could contribute nothing towards the solution of the problem 'of how in a world governed by mechanical forces alone there can arise a being who frames for himself moral and spiritual ideals'.[2] The idea of evolution might seem to provide a clue to processes, but had nothing to say about ends, and the new ideas taken as a whole were so complex and manifold that their effect was to add to the prevailing confusion rather than to diminish it.

Science for its part ignored or despised metaphysics, and in doing so had the support of philosophers of the Utilitarian and Positivist schools, and also the Ritschlians. Metaphysics had, indeed, been somewhat neglected since Kant's day, but the publication of F. D. Maurice's *Moral and Metaphysical Philosophy* in 1861 did something to revive interest in the subject. Those who affected to belittle metaphysics thereby revealed their lack of insight, for such speculations, even if they achieve no very definite results produce valuable by-products and help to illuminate 'other subjects that are commonly and conveniently regarded as distinct. The debt of the special sciences to metaphysical discussions could not easily be over-estimated.'[3]

The differences between science and philosophy and the desire to inquire more deeply into them moved a number of thoughtful men to establish the Metaphysical Society in 1869.[4] It had a varied

---

[1] A. K. Rogers, *Modern Philosophy*, p. 229.
[2] Storr, p. 228.   [3] *E.R.E.*, Vol. VIII, p. 598.
[4] See further R. H. Hutton 'The Metaphysical Society: a Reunion' in *The Nineteenth Century* for August 1885 and A.W. Brown, *The Metaphysical Society: Victorian Minds in Crisis, 1869–80.*

and comprehensive membership and Archbishop Magee wrote: 'We only wanted a Jew and a Mahomedan to make our religious Museum complete.'[1] Among the members were philosophers like Sidgwick, W. G. Ward, and James Martineau; scientists such as Huxley, Tyndall, and Clifford; a number of ecclesiastical leaders, among them Cardinal Manning and Archbishops Thomson and Magee; nor were there lacking men of letters in the persons of Tennyson, Ruskin, R. H. Hutton,[2] and Leslie Stephen; nor politicians like Gladstone and Morley.

The meetings of the society do not seem to have brought the various problems discussed any nearer to a solution, nor do the members appear to have shifted their original positions in consequence of them, but the personal intercourse of men of differing views helped to remove bitterness and misunderstanding. When the society was started there was a natural fear that it might arouse some acrimony, but this was far from being the case, and in the end it 'died of too much love', so Huxley is reported to have said.[3] The meetings certainly enabled men of different views to explore their different positions and to define them, even if no bridges were established to span the dividing gaps. They also served to promote a new interest in metaphysics, and, incidentally, to reveal to those who could no longer accept the Christian scheme the need for seeking a new and stable foundation for ethics.

The object of the Metaphysical Society had been sufficiently ambitious, nothing less than co-operation in the quest of ultimate truth and reality. Some years after its demise a similar association called the Synthetic Society,[4] was founded; but with a more limited objective—the discovery of a working philosophy of religious belief. The Synthetic Society was started in 1896 by

---

[1] J. C. Macdonald, *Life and Correspondence of W. C. Magee*, Vol. 1, p. 284.

[2] R. H. Hutton was editor of *The Spectator* and had been a Unitarian and a disciple of Martineau, but under the influence of F. D. Maurice he became an orthodox Christian.

[3] *The Wilfrid Wards and the Transition*, p. 351.

[4] See further *op. cit.*, pp. 354 ff. and 417 ff. where the rules of the society and a list of members will be found.

A. J. Balfour and Wilfrid Ward and included among its members survivors from the earlier society, such as James Martineau, R. H. Hutton and Henry Sidgwick. Amongst newcomers were Charles Gore, R. B. Haldane, Baron von Hügel, Bishop Talbot, Sir Oliver Lodge, and Sir Alfred Lyall. Sidgwick took a leading part in the conduct of the society and after his death in 1900 the meetings were suspended for a year and finally came to an end in 1908.

We come now to a consideration of the various systems of philosophy which flourished during our period, viewing them primarily as they influenced theologians and the development of theological thought.

Ideas may be held over a wide area and for long periods without necessarily originating any special system of philosophy or religious belief, but unless they are drawn within the orbit of some previously existing system they tend sooner or later to become articulate in a system of their own. Philosophical systems arise 'through some element in the totality of our experience being regarded as of supreme significance for the interpretation of the whole'.[1] Systems of philosophy may be undermined by the discovery of supposed defects in their fundamental ideas;[2] none the less the rejection of such ideas and the systems based on them does not mean, even for those who disagree, that all value has been lost. 'Even those of us who do not believe in the philosophical soundness of Kant's *Kritik* profess great respect for its educational value.'[3] The prevailing conception of development tended to support this procedure, for as Edward Caird said: 'We have learned to look on the speculations of earlier times, not as dogmatic systems to be accepted or rejected, but rather as the first stage in the progressive evolution of a thought, of which, in a further stage, we ourselves are the organs and interpreters.'[4]

---

[1] L. Hodgson, *The Doctrine of the Trinity*, p. 21.
[2] Cf. Henry Jones, *Browning as a Philosophical and Religious Teacher*, p. 232: 'The superstructure of philosophical edifices is usually put together in a sufficiently solid manner—it is the foundation that gives way.'
[3] *Henry Sidgwick*, p. 159
[4] *The Critical Philosophy of Kant*, Vol. I, p. 68.

The most influential system of philosophy when our period opened was Utilitarianism.[1] This system had already a long history behind it but was destined before many years had passed to suffer at least a partial eclipse. Kant had dealt it a shrewd blow when he had insisted 'that duty lost its high significance if it was reduced to the pursuit of pleasure, or to any self-interested calculation of consequence'.[2] In any case Utilitarianism was a somewhat bleak and uninspiring system doing little to foster the loftier aspirations of humanity. It had no absolute values, since everything existed for the sake of something else, knowledge for use, art for edification; nor did it find any joy in the passing moment,[3] and this in spite of its expressed anxiety to promote the happiness, harmony, and comfort of the race. In practice, it may be remarked, this was largely a negative process which consisted in freeing mankind from the restraints of tradition, especially as it was enshrined in religious beliefs.

J. S. Mill, who had been one of the chief exponents of Utilitarianism, came in later life to realize its limitations, and its lack of any satisfactory philosophy of either society or history. The publication of his *Theism*, written between 1868 and 1870, but not published until 1874 the year after his death, aroused considerable dismay among his followers and made 'a sort of intellectual scandal'.[4]

Mill's progress towards the position taken up in *Theism* had been slow and gradual. That man needed some kind of religion he had long realized, and in *The Utility of Religion*, written between 1850 and 1858, he had commended, though with no great enthusiasm, the 'religion of humanity'. This type of religion had doubtless been suggested by the ideas of Comte,[5] which he

---

[1] See further Leslie Stephen, *English Utilitarianism*, E. Albee, *A History of English Utilitarianism* and *E.R.E.*, Vol. xii, pp. 562 ff.

[2] Storr, p. 144. Mill in a defence of Utilitarianism in 1863 (reprinted from articles in *Fraser's Magazine*) maintained 'that the happiness which forms the utilitarian standard of what is right in conduct, is not the agent's own happiness, but that of all concerned'.

[3] Cf. Jacks, *Life and Letters of Stopford Brooke*, p. 582.

[4] Morley, *Recollections*, Vol. i., p. 106. See further Storr, pp. 392 ff.

[5] See further Storr, pp. 394 ff.

helped to make more widely known in *Comte and Positivism* (1865), although he had no sympathy with Comte's later notions. These were set forth in *Politique Positive* which the author designed to supersede his earlier *Philosophie Politique*. The main effect of his endeavour was to split up his followers in both France, where it was rejected by Littré,[1] and England.

Although Comte had died in 1857 he had a small, but influential, body of disciples in England, including Frederic Harrison, E. S. Beesly, and J. H. Bridges. They were in the habit of holding meetings in Fetter Lane for the worship of humanity, where it was said there were three persons and no God. His teaching continued to attract wide attention and in October 1868 Kingsley could write: 'The very air seems full of Comtism.'[2] But Positivism, although its social teaching was taken up by Westcott and others, was too artificial a system to retain its influence indefinitely. Comte himself in formulating his system had undertaken a task for which he had no really adequate equipment and his 'limited knowledge of history discounts the value of his survey of development'.[3] Huxley delivered Comtism a lethal blow when, in a damning phrase, he summed it up as 'Catholicism minus Christianity.'[4]

From a Christian point of view the chief value of Comtism was to be found in the testimony which it bore to man's innate need of some form of religion, even if it denied the possibility of metaphysics; but like Utilitarianism its only service to theology was the negative one of challenging its exponents to re-examine their fundamental beliefs and presuppositions. Incidentally it was Frederic Harrison who first brought *Essays and Reviews* to the notice of the educated public by an article on what he called 'Neo-Christianity' in the *Westminster Review*.

[1] Littré was baptized shortly before his death. See the moving account (in which Littré is not actually named) in Von Hügel, *Essays and Addresses*, Vol. I, pp. 3 f.

[2] *Life*, Vol. II, p. 214.

[3] Gooch, *History and Historians*, etc., p. 585.

[4] Renan said of Comte that he repeated in bad French what all scientific thinkers for two centuries had seen as clearly as himself.

One philosopher who exercised great influence throughout most of our period was Herbert Spencer, though his doing so is a little difficult to explain. Max Müller described him as 'a writer without any background—I say on almost every page, "There he has discovered London again."'[1] Sidgwick, who as a young man had been attracted by Spencer and always retained admiration for the breadth of his knowledge and his power of combination and induction, became 'appalled by the grotesque and chaotic confusion of his metaphysics' and dismissed his *Data of Ethics* as 'crude and superficial'.[2]

The explanation of his popularity is probably to be found in the appeal which he made to thoughtful people who were not trained philosophers and by his offering them a system which had an ordered set of beliefs capable of being applied directly to life and taking account of the changed intellectual climate. He may be said to have supplemented the biological theories of Darwin, which concerned the individual, by extending evolution to organic life in all its departments.[3] His ideas, too, of political and social freedom were in a line with the progressive thought of his day, and he may be said to have been their spokesman. But his dogmatism and other limitations told against him.[4]

In later life Spencer lost some of the buoyancy which had marked his earlier years and the decay of his popularity saddened him and caused a loss of confidence in himself. This was increased by the change in the mental atmosphere of the times, for scientific discoveries were not working out in accordance with his optimistic forecasts. By the close of the century his system was as good as dead and his teaching no longer attracted much attention. C. C. J. Webb has noted that a list of lectures in philosophy at

---

[1] *Life*, Vol. II, p. 188. In this he anticipated the line taken by G. K. Chesterton in *Orthodoxy*.

[2] *Henry Sidgwick*, pp. 76, 277, 344.

[3] He even had the notion that the development of English law and political institutions could be used to illustrate his 'evolutionary philosophy' and enlisted the help of the youthful Asquith in collecting material to support it. See *Life of Lord Oxford and Asquith*, Vol. I, p. 46.

[4] See further *Religion in the Victorian Era*, p. 275.

Oxford about this time contained a number on Kant, but not a single one on Spencer.[1]

Like the philosophies already noticed the most useful service rendered by that of Herbert Spencer was in the main negative; above all in the emphasis which he placed on the limitations of the range of human knowledge. This, however, did not lead him to take the further step of recognizing the need for a divine revelation.

The systems we have so far considered were too critical and destructive, too narrowly intellectual, to provide for the deeper needs of humanity. It is not therefore surprising that they provoked a reaction towards Idealism.[2] Such a reaction had been promoted some time before by the teaching of Hegel and had profoundly affected theological thought; Storr, indeed, could claim that 'Our theological outlook today is what it is, largely because this philosophical development took place.'[3] Hegel died in 1831 and his influence had already declined in Germany by the time our period opened, although elsewhere it was still growing.[4]

From the point of view of this study the great services which Hegel rendered were first, to introduce the historical element into the philosophy of religion (his notion of the 'world spirit' means that God is ever realizing Himself in the story of mankind), and secondly, to apply the idea of development to theology itself. He sought for the real not 'as is popularly imagined, from logical forms, but from human experience';[5] but at the same time he was not content to base the truth of religion solely on feeling or even upon the moral consciousness. His chief influence was exerted in the realm of dogmatic theology, above all in Christology, for it was because his theories proved unacceptable that

[1] *Religious Thought in England*, etc., p. 97.

[2] Storr defined Idealism as 'signifying, in contradistinction to materialism, the priority and supremacy of the spiritual in man and in the universe around him.' (p. 143.) See further *E.R.E.*, Vol. IX, pp. 300 ff.   [3] Storr, p. 199.

[4] Sidgwick wrote in 1870: 'There is no doubt that Hegelianism is on the increase—everywhere except in Germany.' (*Henry Sidgwick*, p. 230.)

[5] R. B. Haldane, *Autobiography*, p. 347.

others were stimulated to work on the problem of the relation between the Jesus of history and the Christ of dogma. Hegel, who was a Lutheran, regarded his ideas as a defence of orthodox Christianity; but many took a very different view.[1]

In England the move towards Idealism,[2] which was also a return to the teaching of Kant, may be said to have had its rise in 1865 or even earlier.[3] In that year J. H. Stirling published *The Secret of Hegel* and about the same time T. H. Green finally settled in Oxford. The movement was later reinforced and strengthened by Green's *Introduction to Hume's Treatise on Human Nature* (1874) and by two studies on Kant by Edward Caird (1878 and 1889). Oxford was the chief centre of the reaction, and in the words of Quiller-Couch, 'The young tenants of the Home of Movements, turning from Mill and Mansel to Kant and Hegel, pursued the evasive Absolute far into the night.' But Mill still had his followers, though the move from him continued. Sidgwick wrote in 1885 'the reaction against him [Mill] is still active in my own mind as well as in that of others'.[4]

The most influential exponent of Idealism in England was T. H. Green.[5] 'He it was,' wrote Scott Holland, 'who shook us all free from the bondage of cramping philosophies and sent us out once again on the high pilgrimage towards Ideal Truth.'[6] Green is sometimes regarded as a disciple of Hegel, whom he had studied in his younger days, but this was by no means the case. R. G. Collingwood considered that his philosophy and that of

[1] J. K. Mozley pointed out that there is 'no agreed interpretation of Hegel's doctrine, particularly in relation to Christian theology'. (*Some Tendencies in British Theology*, p. 117.)

[2] For Idealism in England see Webb, *op. cit.*, pp. 99 ff.

[3] 'Although Neo-Kantism may be taken as having its rise about 1865, yet the cry for a return to the epoch-making Kant had been raised long before.' (*E.R.E.*, Vol. IX, p. 905.)

[4] *Henry Sidgwick*, p. 420. Sidgwick was in a sense a Utilitarian and E. Albee, *Hist. of English Utilitarianism*, declared that his *Methods of Ethics* was 'the last authoritative utterance of the traditional utilitarianism', but he differed from the earlier Utilitarians by basing his system on a number of fundamental 'intuitions'.

[5] See further R. L. Nettleship, *Thomas Hill Green: a Memoir*.

[6] *A Bundle of Memories*, p. 145.

his followers 'so far as they had one single philosophy, was a continuation and criticism of the indigenous English and Scottish philosophies of the middle nineteenth century. It is true, that unlike most of their compatriots, they had some knowledge of Hegel, and a good deal more of Kant.'[1] It was through the influence of Lotze that Green became dissatisfied with Hegel.[2] Lotze attached great importance to the idea of personality in God and it was he who rescued Haldane from the materialistic phase which followed the abandonment of his early faith.[3] Hastings Rashdall has described him as 'the one philosopher of our time who is at once a thinker of the highest rank and wholly and unexceptionably Christian in his thoughts'.[4] Lotze's views first became well known in England through the translation of his *Microcosmos* in 1887.

Green was a stern critic of the shallow agnosticism which flourished in his day, and was also insistent on the self-sufficiency of the moral ideal, which for him required no bolstering up by the offer of rewards or the threat of punishments. At the same time he recognized to the full the part which religion must play in upholding morality. It may, indeed, be said of him that he was more interested in ethical than in metaphysical problems.

Green exercised a very wide influence in Oxford, and Asquith going up in 1870 found him regarded as undoubtedly the greatest personal force in the real life of the university.[5] Bryce, who had been Green's contemporary, looked upon him as 'the most powerful ethical and most stimulating intellectual influence upon the minds of the ablest youth of the university'. Although far removed from orthodoxy he 'exerted over orthodox Christians a potent and inspiring religious influence'.[6]

Green was the first layman to become a tutor at Balliol, and

---

[1] *Autobiography*, p. 16.   [2] See Nettleship, *op. cit.*, p. 192: cf. p. 126 note.
[3] *Autobiography*, pp. 12 f., 30, 344 f.   [4] In *Contentio Veritatis*, p. 43.
[5] Cf. the interesting testimony of Chavasse who was an Evangelical. He wrote, 'the man who made the deepest impression upon me was the late Professor Green, who seemed to have more of the prophet about him than any man I have had the honour of meeting'. (Lancelot, F. J. *Chavasse*, p. 26.)
[6] *Studies in Contemporary Biography*, p. 99.

he made it his custom, following the example of his clerical predecessors, to address his pupils on the evening before the administration of Holy Communion. One of his sermons, delivered in a lecture-room soon after his appointment in 1870, *The Witness of God*, and another on *Faith* preached eight years later, not on this occasion to his pupils alone but to the senior members of the college as well, were published after his death by Arnold Toynbee to whom he entrusted the MS.

Although Green exercised such great influence in Oxford it never equalled that of Mill, being neither so extensive nor so persistent. Bryce thought that it tended to decline after his appointment as professor in 1878 when he was no longer in a position to establish or maintain so many personal links with the growing generation of students.[1] Another cause, no doubt was his comparatively early death, and that of his chief disciple, R. L. Nettleship. Moreover his teaching met with a good deal of criticism, even on its ethical side; Sidgwick, after two careful readings of the posthumous *Prolegomena to Ethics*, concluded that 'it would not do'.[2] But if Green's influence on philosophical thought did not go unchallenged, his influence on theological thought was profound. This came about through the impact of his teaching on the little group of Oxford Anglicans who would one day produce *Lux Mundi*.

Idealism in England was maintained by Bernard Bosanquet and F. H. Bradley—but with a difference. Both came to deny that '*personality* can be regarded, from the point of view of metaphysics as ultimately real', and Bosanquet exhibited 'a distinct advance . . . in the direction of that immanentism which is the note of the whole tendency'.[3] Although Bradley lived in Oxford he had few personal contacts with either teachers or students; none the less he 'was extremely influential in the years which saw the publication of his *Principles of Logic* and (ten years later) of his *Appearance and Reality* although his views met with a good deal of criticism'.[4]

[1] *Op. cit.*, p. 95.   [2] *Henry Sidgwick*, p. 380.   [3] Webb, *op. cit.*, p. 100.
[4] Webb in a review of my Burroughs Memorial Lectures in *J.T.S.* Oct. 1952, pp. 296 f. There is an interesting study of Bradley by T. S. Eliot *For Lancelot Andrewes*, pp. 67 ff.

Edward Caird looked upon *Appearance and Reality* as 'the greatest thing since Kant', and John Buchan, no mean student of philosophy, said that it was one of the few books of his day 'which our descendants will regard as a philosophical classic'.[1]

Opposition to Idealism began from the moment of its revival. As early as 1866 Sidgwick had concluded that it was 'a monstrous mistake', adding 'we must go back to Kant and begin again from him'.[2] In Oxford the opposition was led by Thomas Case and later by John Cook Wilson, who were especially critical of the more advanced form which it had taken in the writings of Bradley.[3] In Scotland, too, criticism had been voiced by A. Seth (Pringle-Pattison) in his lectures on *Hegelianism and Personality* (1886), especially for its potential threat to the conception of religion as the personal communion of man with God. The opposition gathered force during our period, though it was not until the beginning of the present century that it became fully active with the appearance of *The Refutation of Idealism* by the Cambridge philosopher G. E. Moore.

The main criticisms of Idealism were, first, that it was too speculative and intellectual, too ambitious and daring, in that it was attempting a premature synthesis before all the necessary facts were available; and, secondly, that it tended to belittle the personality of the individual.

It is to be noted that both Idealists and Realists accepted the theory of evolution, though they took up a different attitude towards it. The Realists were only interested in the process as explaining man's development in terms of nature; the Idealists laid emphasis on the supposed end towards which evolution was working, an end which they regarded as spiritual.

The *Lux Mundi* group was almost unique in English theology

[1] *Memory Hold-the-Door*, p. 203.

[2] *Op. cit.*, p. 151.

[3] E. L. Hicks, looking back in 1903, reported that 'Bentham gave way to Kant and Mill to Hegel, a change came over Oxford which has been among the reactionary influences—religious, speculative and political—of the last thirty years.' (Fowler, *Life*, p. 40.)

6

in giving it a philosophical basis; England here differed materially from Germany where theology and philosophy went hand in hand, as in the case of the Tübingen school and Hegel. Another German philosopher who influenced theology, at first in his own land and then elsewhere, was Ritschl who died in 1889 at the age of 67.[1] In early life he had been a disciple of Hegel, but like most of his contemporaries in Germany had reacted towards Kant. He was also greatly influenced by Schleiermacher.[2]

One of the leading features in Ritschlianism, here going beyond Schleiermacher, was a profound distrust of metaphysics, a distrust also extended to dogma which was regarded as an amalgam of theology and metaphysics. The Ritschlians disliked dogma, 'not because it may be at times a misdevelopment, but because it is a development; not because some of it may be antiquated Philosophy, but simply because it is Philosophy'.[3] The Ritschlians also tended to see in the contents of the religious consciousness the only fruitful field for theological investigation. In making this limitation they were apt to deny to the intellect its legitimate rights and so helped to prepare the way for the 'irrational' trend which has been characteristic of much Protestant theology in recent times. Thus they endeavoured to release theology from the dead-weight of dogma and to bring it into closer relation with religious experience. A praiseworthy object, but one whose limitations they did not fully perceive; for unless the implications of religious experience are thought out and find expression in dogmatic statements, religion may degenerate into a mere sentiment divorced from all definite beliefs.

Religion for the Ritschlians was predominantly a practical affair, and following Kant they linked it closely with ethics; it could in fact be looked upon as the divine response to the moral needs of mankind. Hence they laid immense stress on the

---

[1] On Ritschlianism see *E.R.E.*, Vol. x, pp. 812 ff., J. K. Mozley, *Ritschlianism* (1909) and E. A. Edghill, *Faith and Fact* (1910).

[2] On the great influence exercised by Schleiermacher see Storr, Ch. XIII. He affirmed that 'The Ritschlian school looks to Schleiermacher as its direct inspirer.' (p. 248.)

[3] Hastings Rashdall, *Philosophy and Religion*, pp. 163 f.

Kingdom of God, not in any mystical[1] or eschatological sense, but as something to be realized 'in and through the events of the world of everyday experience'. The conception of the Kingdom was to regulate all attempts at Christian dogmatics.[2]

Ritschl strongly insisted on the historicity of Jesus and the importance of His teaching; it was through Christ alone that God was revealed to man. Hastings Rashdall, whilst commending him for 'putting the personal and historic Christ and not any doctrine about Him in the centre of the religious life', drew attention to his limitations, for 'we must first believe there is a God to be revealed before we can be led to believe in Christ as the supreme revealer'.[3] What must be called Ritschl's over-emphasis on the unique character of the revelation through Christ led not only to a rejection of natural religion, but also to a depreciation of the Old Testament,[4] and the denial of any contribution from the non-Christian religions. But though Ritschl laid this strong emphasis on the idea of a divine revelation, even if he limited its scope, he refused to recognize any supernatural character in the records of the revelation, a position which in this country was maintained by Robertson Smith.

The fundamental weakness in Ritschl's position was that he had no adequate conception of Christianity as a historical religion, and though he gave so high a place to the historical Christ, from the standpoint of orthodox Christianity, he had no effective belief in His pre-existence or in His present sovereignty.

A well-known principle of Ritschl and his followers was the distinction they made between judgments of existence and judgments of value. They denied 'that the propositions of theology could claim to be *judgments of existence*, which might conflict with those of natural science or of history as statements of purely objective facts. They were rather to be classed as *judgments of value*

---

[1] The Ritschlians condemned all mysticism as belonging to a metaphysical type of piety: cf. Inge's protest in *Personal Idealism and Mysticism* (1907).

[2] *E.R.E.*, Vol. x, p. 818.   [3] *Op. cit.*, p. 162.

[4] It is interesting to notice that Ritschl's first published work was *Das Evangelium Marcions und das kanon. Evang. des Lukas* (1846). Was it from Marcion that he had imbibed his low idea of the Old Testament?

and ranked with moral judgments which affirm, as Kant had insisted, not what *is* but what *ought to be.*'[1] Such value judgments, however, cannot give more than a presumption of existence, and for those who have a high regard for history and historical events are clearly defective. But it would be unjust to condemn the Ritschlians too harshly when we recall the circumstances of their day. They had to confront

> materialistic science which seemed to many to be destined to take all knowledge for its province and to make any kind of idealistic or theistic philosophy out of date. When we detect, as we surely must, inconsistency and ambiguity in their theology, we must bear in mind that they were desperately defending the right of Christian faith to exist. They chose to retire into the fortress of value. Perhaps they were right. At any rate it is clear that Christian faith begins as a value-judgment and that the scientific method cannot tell us what is either good or beautiful.[2]

The followers of Ritschl diverged considerably from the teaching of their master, and in diverse directions.[3] The best known of them, at least to English theologians was, of course, Harnack. He, however, was by no means typical, and stood on the left wing of the school.

Although some of the works of Ritschl had been translated as early as 1872 by John Black, it was not until the last decade of the nineteenth century, by which time the Ritschlians had acquired a predominant position in German Protestant theology, that his views began to attract much attention in Great Britain, and then mainly across the border in Scotland. At first his somewhat novel ideas aroused hostility, but fuller knowledge and consideration gradually modified this. Denney in his *Studies in Theology* (1895) criticized the rejection of metaphysics and the evidence of natural religion, and Orr in *The Ritschlian Theology*

[1] C. C. J. Webb, *Religious Thought in England*, etc., p. 129.

[2] W. R. Matthews addressing the Modern Churchmen's Conference at Oxford: printed in *The Modern Churchman*, 1953, p. 184.

[3] Those who are interested in these divergences may consult *E.R.E.*, Vol. x, p. 817.

and the Evangelical Faith (1897) condemned the restriction of revelation to Christ alone. A greater sympathy, which stopped short of full agreement, can be seen in Garvie, *The Ritschlian Theology* (1899).

The Ritschlians, whilst emphasizing the subjective elements in religion and distrusting philosophy and metaphysics, had clung tenaciously to the historic Christ as the medium of revelation. This could hardly be affirmed of a movement which owed something of the ready welcome it received in certain quarters to the Ritschlian notion of value-judgments. This was Pragmatism which first emerged towards the close of the nineteenth century. The term itself became known through William James's pamphlet *Philosophical Conceptions and Practical Results* (1898), though he himself seems to have borrowed it from C. S. Pierce. In *The Will to Believe* (1897) James had already set forth the doctrine which, in fact, he had long been expounding. It became popular in England through F. C. S. Schiller's essay 'Axioms as Postulates' contributed to *Personal Idealism* (1902), and through James's own *Varieties of Religious Experience* which was published in the same year.

Pragmatism is rather a tendency in thought than a body of philosophical principles and behind its various forms 'lies the common assumption of the testing of the truth of an idea, of a hypothesis, by its actual working'.[1] Even the existence of the deity is brought to this test: 'God is real since He produces real effects.'[2] In its extreme form it regards Truth not as 'an immutable reality, but merely [as] that idea which happens to work out as true and useful in any given experience. There is no reality behind appearance . . . all faiths, all figments, are equally true, provided they be comfortable and good to live by.'[3] Since the test of any idea was its capacity to 'work' in the present, Pragmatists were disdainful of historic facts. Thus the mainspring of the movement was the desire to achieve practical results. 'Beliefs . . .

[1] Mead, *Movements of Thought*, etc., p. 344.
[2] James, *Varieties of Religious Experience*, p. 517.
[3] Underhill, *Mysticism*, p. 17.

are rules for action; and the whole function of thinking is but one step in the production of active habits.'[1]

Somewhat similar notions were held by the French Roman Catholic Modernists who accepted the Church as an effective organization, but regarded the truth or falsehood of the events upon which it based its claims as a matter of little consequence.[2]

A striking feature in the thought of the closing years of the nineteenth century was the emergence of what is comprehensively called Humanism. The term was first used as an equivalent of 'anthropocentric', as distinguished from 'naturalistic' by A. Seth (Pringle-Pattison).[3] Its technical use to denote a system of philosophy goes back to F. C. S. Schiller, *Humanism* (1903), and thus falls just outside our period; but the ideas for which it stands were already in circulation.

Humanism as a theory of existence was avowedly a revival of the critical relativism of Protagoras,[4] and makes man the measure of all things. It follows that the real concern of philosophy is the interpretation of human experience and for this task, so it is claimed, man has all the necessary powers. He must trust for the salvation of the race to science and the growth of knowledge; evil has no real existence, and for the Christian doctrine of the fallen state of man there must be substituted the notion of human perfectability.

The emergence of Humanism may not be unconnected with the abandonment of the old notions which had given so exalted a position to man and his little earth. In other words it was man's assertion of his continued significance. Since man, it is held, is capable of working out his own destiny and even of exercising an increasing measure of control over nature, there is no need to bring in the idea of God or Providence; in fact, such an idea is only a delusion and where encouraged may be a hindrance to progress. Such was the teaching of Karl Marx, and today it is

[1] James, *op. cit.*, p. 444. Cf. Browning, *Sordello*: 'Thought is the soul of act.'
[2] On this movement see below, pp. 309f.
[3] *Man's Place in the Cosmos* (1897), p. 61.
[4] See Plato, *Theaetetus*, 152 A. Aristotle condemned the notion as suicidal and as leading to indifference in conduct.

largely the unconscious belief of much of Western civilization, even when opposed to Communism.

Humanism is fundamentally antagonistic to Christianity, for the Christian, in Browning's words, must affirm that 'Man is not God, but hath God's end to serve.' The Christian also believes that 'Christ came to liberate human thought from systems of morality having their centre and source in man (cf. 1 Pet. 1:21) . . . and that the moral universe tends to a more comprehensive end than the perfection of humanity.'[1]

What the future of Humanism will be is difficult to forecast. It certainly suffers from a number of obvious weaknesses. It robs man of God and in His place offers the conception of Humanity; a conception too vast and too impersonal to melt the hearts or steel the wills of those who are themselves persons. Moreover it also takes away man's worth as an individual and is at bottom an attempt at self-deception on a gigantic scale. Modern man, standing abashed and cowering in the machine world which he has himself made, has lost any true sense of his own ultimate value, which is spiritual. But he doubts whether he possesses a soul, and in any case he can seldom call his soul his own. Furthermore Humanism seems to be a view of life best fitted for an age of prosperity and may find it difficult to survive in less happy days. The most damaging criticism, however, is that many of its fundamental assumptions are open to question. Problems of sociology and economics cannot be solved as simply as those of physics, nor can the same methods be usefully applied to them. At bottom they are spiritual problems and can only be met by spiritual remedies. Man may have made tremendous strides in controlling the natural world; but what is disquieting, as recent experience abundantly demonstrates, is that the extension of his control over nature is accompanied by the diminution of his control over mental and moral forces.

An extreme example of the same general point of view represented by Humanism, although not technically connected with it and having striking differences from it, may be found in the

[1] R. L. Ottley in *Lux Mundi*, pp. 341, 343.

teaching of Nietzsche (1844–1900). Nietzsche regarded the progress of the race as bound up with the elimination of the weak and unfit; he could even glorify war as a means to this end, for he held that 'a good war hallows every cause; war and courage have done greater things than love of your neighbour'.[1] Nietzsche looked forward to the emergence of a race of supermen, a term which he adopted from Goethe; but unlike Goethe he was notoriously scornful of the common folk, they were only slaves and so well fitted to follow the moral teaching of Christ.[2] Nietzsche's influence in England was of tardy growth, but with the dawn of the twentieth century it came in with surprising force.[3]

We come now to the consideration of the relations between philosophy in general and that aspect of it which has been named the philosophy of religion. It is not easy to differentiate between them, for from the earliest times philosophy has had a theological side, 'and it has often been from the side of religion that great thinkers have received their first impulse toward philosophy'.[4] For some thinkers the two are almost identical. Hegel, for example, insisted that 'religion and philosophy coincide: in fact philosophy is itself a divine service',[5] whilst Max Müller referred to them as 'two dialects of the same language', both of which he could speak in all honesty.[6]

Both religion and philosophy have the same general objective, which is to combine all experience into a single, all-comprehensive system, a system, moreover, which will provide the ultimate ground and unity of all being and all knowledge; in other words

[1] *Thus Spake Zarathustra*, Vol. I, p. 10.
[2] Oscar Wilde used to say that Christian morality was fit only for the middle classes.
[3] Houston Stewart Chamberlain's *Foundations of the Nineteenth Century* (1895) was not translated until 1910.
[4] F. R. Tennant in *Enc. Brit.*, Vol. XXIII, p. 62. Hastings Rashdall looked upon the philosophy of religion as 'not so much a special and sharply distinguished branch or department of Philosophy, as a particular aspect of Philosophy in general'. (*Philosophy and Religion*, pp. 3f.)
[5] Wallace, *Prolegomena to the Study of Hegel's Philosophy*, p. 24.
[6] *Life*, Vol. II, p. 40.

a description of reality as a whole, of truth, 'not in one region but in all; Truth apprehended, if it may be, in its highest unity'.[1]

But if they have a common goal there are certain definite differences between them. These may be considered under three heads: (*a*) a difference in the object of speculation; (*b*) a difference in the final end of their search; and (*c*) a difference in the method of approach.

(*a*) *The Object of Speculation*

The philosophy of religion is no merely theoretical department of learning, but has a practical aim. The secular philosopher may pursue his study in a spirit of complete detachment regarding it as an end in itself, and the ideas with which he is concerned as so many counters in a game, or pieces on a chess board, which he manipulates according to his will. If he has been stimulated to speculate merely to satisfy intellectual curiosity (in itself a quite admirable motive) he may be content with lifeless abstractions, and the nature of such fresh knowledge as he acquires and its practical effects will concern him but little. He may even be a professional student or a pedant (such as Wagner satirized by Goethe in *Faust*) with no genuine desire to discover truth.[2] Like the imaginary Hegelian he would be prepared to say: 'Even if (the world) were a thousand times worse than it is, it could be arranged in categories and explained by philosophers. And what more do you want?'[3] The religious philosopher, however, can never be content with bare abstractions, and for him the search for knowledge is a solemn duty leading, so he hopes, to a practical outcome, a better life, a greater love for God and His fellows, and a worthier adoration.

[1] Westcott, *Religious Thought in the West*, p. 251.
[2] John Buchan confessed that for him philosophy was 'always an intellectual exercise, like mathematics, not the quest for a faith'. It interested him to 'study the different patterns which different thinkers made out of the universe'. (*Memory Hold-the-Door*, pp. 37f.)
[3] See Jowett, *Sophist*, Vol. IV, p. 329. A passion for arranging life may be an excuse for not experiencing it, or evidence of an incapacity to do so.

(b) The End of the Search

For both religion and philosophy the end is an all-containing unity; religion, however, demands that the 'end' shall be personal, whereas philosophy in its effort to unify knowledge is unconcerned as to whether the basis of such unity is personal or not. For those who cannot accept any explanation of the universe which does not include the possibility of relationship between God and man philosophy can never be enough. This was the attitude of T. H. Green who in 1872 wrote to Scott Holland: 'I never dreamt of philosophy doing instead of religion. My own interest in it, I believe, is wholly religious; in the sense that it is to me . . . the reasoned intellectual expression of the effort to get to God.'[1]

It will be useful here to draw attention to the different attitudes of science, of philosophy, and of religion towards the universe as it is known to them. They may be summarized in the form of three questions which each is supposed to put. That of science is 'How?', that of philosophy is 'Why?', but that of religion is 'Who?'. In other words science is interested in the way in which the universe works, philosophy seeks for a cause[2] and a goal, as does religion; but the latter can only be satisfied if that goal can be shown to be a Person.

(c) The Method of Approach

In his attempt to systematize all knowledge and to give a complete account of all experience the religious philosopher attaches greater importance to the emotions and the imagination than does the general philosopher who tends to rely on the intellect alone. The philosopher adds stone to stone in an edifice which has its basis on the earth; the theologian leaps away from the earth in response to a divine vision, and then endeavours to construct a ladder to bring it down to earth. For the theologian the mind alone can never bring knowledge of God, it must act

---

[1] Quoted, Paget, *Henry Scott Holland*, p. 65.

[2] Inge, it may be noticed, doubted the ability of philosophy to account for the existence of the universe. 'No philosophy, as far as I know, can really explain *why* there is a world.' (*Vale*, p. 49.)

in conjunction with other faculties. Reality is not purely intellectual[1] and the search for it demands the activity of man's personality as a whole. A religion based on pure thought could never bring permanent satisfaction, nor, for that matter, could a religion based solely on feeling; thought and feeling must be blended or even fused, if stability and balance are to be attained. Otherwise any religious system will be a house divided against itself, or, in more modern terms, a split personality.

There had been a time when over-critical minds had seen in any claim to special religious experiences evidence of conscious imposture; but this was a thing of the past and serious students no longer held it. In some cases no doubt deceit or hypocrisy were present, but these had ceased to be brought up against religious experience as a whole. There were, however, still those who attempted to account for it as due to reflex actions not fully understood, or even to sheer hallucination. The fact that some mystics, to whom appeal was made, were definitely pathological subjects was apt to arouse suspicion. One reason for prejudice against 'religious experience' was that those who claimed to have undergone it were different from ordinary folk (an argument which would also discredit the poet or the artist), being what the eighteenth century would have called 'enthusiasts', and it cannot be denied that in some extreme cases the manifestations claimed were entirely divorced from moral values. But such an attitude ignored the vast number of men and women who were obviously as sane and as practical as their neighbours; moreover, the appeal to religious experience cannot be confined to that of the individual, in whom it must necessarily be incomplete and lacking in balance, it has a much wider connotation.

Those philosophers who refuse to consider religious insight are in reality as obscurantist as the ultra-orthodox who reject inconvenient facts. Religious experience, the communion of the devout soul with its God is a *fact* which cannot be set aside or

[1] Cf. Illingworth, *Personality, Human and Divine*, p. 128: 'the assumption that the knowledge of God is primarily intellectual involves . . . an undervaluing of His attribute of holiness'.

ignored, in spite of attempts to explain it, or even to explain it away, as a delusion. This negative attitude is often found in those who have but slight acquaintance with practical life, whose own experience, as a consequence, is sadly limited; for there are notions which seem sound enough in the study or the lecture room but which break down when exposed to the rough and tumble of the market place.

For the religious philosopher religious experience is a fact, and, indeed, experience must precede any attempt at formulation of theories. He must start 'with the presupposition that religion and religious ideas can be taken out of the domain of feeling or practical experience and made objects of scientific reflection'.[1]

This brings us to another difference of approach. Philosophy accepts no authority but that of reason; or in other words it relies on the rationality of the universe and the power of the human mind to fathom its secrets. Such results as it obtains are the reward of man's efforts after fuller knowledge. Theology, however, claims to have as its foundation a divine revelation and assumes the authority of the Bible and of the creeds as containing a summary of its teaching. For most modern theologians, however, as for Bishop Butler,[2] this revelation is not above reason, but must be tested, and if need be, modified by it.[3]

The modern point of view might seem to bring philosophy and theology, as represented by the philosophy of religion, very close together, and so it does; but there still remains a fundamental cleavage. If philosophy reaches any kind of belief in God, that God is the conclusion of an inferential process, and such a deity can hardly be regarded as satisfactory to the Christian. 'God, if

---

[1] Caird, *Introduction to the Philosophy of Religion*, p. 1.

[2] Cf. *Analogy*, Pt. II, Ch. III, 'Reason . . . is . . . the only faculty we have wherewith to judge concerning anything, even revelation itself.'

[3] Cf. Storr, *Development and Divine Purpose*, p. 9. 'We can no longer adopt the medieval *dictum* that philosophy is the handmaid of theology. . . . The principle of authority cannot be, for a reasoning being, an ultimate principle. In so far as the dogmatic utterances of any theological system represent the summed up reflection of the thoughtful minds of the past, the Philosophy of Religion will treat them with the uttermost reverence; but she will hold herself free to criticize them, and, if need be, to restate them.'

He exists, is not the conclusion of an argument, but the most stupendous of facts.'[1]

The acceptance of the authority of the revelation contained in the Bible, even though it might be subject to the scrutiny of reason, probably accounts for the slight interest in philosophy and its problems taken by the bulk of English theologians. It thus constituted a danger, for it might lead to theology cutting itself off too sharply from secular studies and thus becoming artificial and unnatural.

Too great a dependence on a supposed revelation might also lead to a rigid attitude of mind and the conservation of obsolete traditions. It is not to be wondered at if many philosophers regarded theologians not as disinterested seekers after truth, but as the apologists of a dogmatic system who deliberately ignored fresh facts and refused to admit the need for modifications rendered necessary in the light of the growth of knowledge.[2]

Such an attitude of condemnation, however, was unjust to many theologians who freely accepted the need for a restatement and vindication of their faith. They were not content to find the sole basis for Christianity in the emotions, or even in the pronouncements of an authoritative Church; in their view it was not enough for a Christian to have 'a blind faith for which he can give no better reason than that it makes him comfortable to hold it, or that he has been ordered to hold it by some authority into whose trustworthiness it is forbidden to inquire'.[3]

There was thus a lack of full accord between philosophy and theology, though both might seek a goal which was practically identical. Theology with its conviction of the truth of a divine revelation was working outwards from a fixed centre; philosophy was working inwards from the circumference. They might seem to draw nearer to one another in their different processes, but

[1] Figgis, *The Gospel and Human Needs*, p. 36.
[2] Cf. R. G. Collingwood, *Speculum Mentis*, p. 145. 'Religion is not the highest form of truth, even though the truth which it reveals is substantially the highest and final truth. Its message is formally imperfect, tainted by the displacement of assertion from the truth to the symbol.'
[3] A. E. Taylor, in *Essays Catholic and Critical*, p. 31.

they had not yet met, nor was there any real promise that such a culmination of their efforts was at all likely.

Meanwhile if complete or even approximate agreement could not be attained, each had to be prepared to respect the labours of the other, and to admit its right to adopt its own methods. The philosopher was called upon to give a fuller recognition to religious experience as part of the material with which he had to do; the theologian to abandon any over-emphasis on authority and to recognize the need for the full and free use of reason.

Theology, in so far as it claimed to be the science of religion, was bound to come to some kind of terms with philosophy, for 'thoughtful men, in proportion as they are in earnest with their religion, must ask themselves what general theory of the world it involves, what attitude towards contemporary thought it obliges them to take'.[1] McTaggart used to say that 'No man is justified in a religious attitude except as the result of metaphysical study',[2] and in the earlier part of the century the traditional theology had 'found itself powerless, for it had no religious philosophy worthy of the name. The last forty years ... saw theologians forced out of their attitude of isolation, and driven to hold commerce with the wider thought around them.'[3]

There is thus a need for a philosophy of religion, of a system in which due place is found for religious experience, for imagination and intuition, and for tradition. But all these before being incorporated must justify themselves at the bar of reason.[4] This, as Hastings Rashdall has observed, was 'the spirit of that noble band, the Cambridge Platonists',[5] and he added, 'is the spirit

---

[1] Illingworth, *Reason and Revelation*, p. 112.

[2] James Adam wrote to T. R. Glover: 'You really must devote a year or two to the exclusive study of (Plato), if you mean to do anything useful for the interpretation of religious thought.' (*The Religious Teachers of Greece*, p. xlvii.)

[3] Storr, p. 5.

[4] Cf. Haldane, *The Pathway to Reality*, p. 6 (The Gifford Lectures for 1902–3): 'Feeling would appear to become valuable only after it has been justified by thought.'

[5] It was Culverwell, one of them, who wrote that 'We prefer reason, a daughter of eternity, before antiquity, which is the offspring of time.' (*Discourse of the Light of Nature*, p. 212.)

which we want to see rekindled in our schools of theology'.[1]
It had, also, been the spirit of Coleridge when he affirmed that
our Lord has 'been graciously pleased to forbid our receiving as
the *King's* Mandates aught that is not stamped with the Great Seal
of the Conscience, and countersigned by the Reason'.[2]

The faith then, if it is to be entirely worthy of the name, must
be a union of feeling and thought, of heart and mind. But these
are not always happy in their marital relations, and as is usual
in such cases the fault is not exclusively on one side. Upholders
of reason may decry the place of the emotions, and those who
depend upon intuition and the feelings for evidence of the truth
of their religion may well seek to escape the tests of reason by
refusing to accept its jurisdiction. But to refuse to recognize the
validity of reason is to question the rationality of the universe.

Those who were critical of reason had much to justify their
objections to it, for reason is often applied in regions where it is
out of place. 'There are a thousand familiar disputes which
reason can never decide, questions that elude investigation and
make logic ridiculous,' wrote Dr. Johnson in *Rasselas*; and those
thinkers who rely upon it exclusively seldom escape some form
of scepticism. 'It is not the reasoning power which, of itself, is
noble, but the reasoning power occupied with its proper objects.
Half of the mistakes of metaphysicians have arisen from their not
observing this.'[3] Reason, if over-emphasized, tends to identify the
intellect with the self; but man is more than a mind, he is also a
heart and a will, and these, too, have their legitimate demands.

Reason, then, however much we value it and however much
we may shrink from appearing to go against it (lest we be
dubbed obscurantists) must be recognized as subject to definite
limitations, and these must be acknowledged if real progress is
to be made. It is, for one thing, incapable of taking those flights
into the sublime which are possible to insight and intuition, for
the 'finite intellect cannot transcend the conditions of finitude'.
Reason needs to be supplemented by imagination, and the two

---

[1] *Principles and Precepts*, p. 211.   [2] *Aids to Reflection*, Aph. XCII.
[3] Ruskin, *The Stones of Venice*, Vol. III, ch. iv, §7.

are often opposed. Matthew Arnold tried to combine them by inventing the phrase 'the imaginative reason',[1] but though happy and giving promise of usefulness the phrase is really deceptive, and too slender to bear the volume of traffic to which it may be subjected.

Reason cannot create faith, which is the result of an act of the whole moral being, the response to the challenge 'Lovest thou Me?' The beneficial functions of reason are, indeed, largely negative, it is 'critical and formative, not creative';[2] and as such it may do good work in rejecting fanciful and unworthy ideas concerning religion. But applied too drastically it is apt to provoke a reaction towards superstition; for if religion becomes too logical and intellectual it will fail to provide for the spiritual needs of the mass of believers; offered stones when they demand bread, they may turn to the husks on which the swine are fed. It is undoubtedly possible to over-exalt reason—Herbert Spencer complained that it had become a kind of idol—but to neglect or depreciate it can only lead to disaster; the attempt to exclude reason, moreover, may be nothing more than a cowardly device by which problems are avoided rather than honestly faced.

Theology, then, is defective unless the religious experiences which underlie it are tested by reason. But reason is a somewhat elusive term and in practice it often means no more than the philosophical outlook which is predominant at any particular time. If theology, therefore, becomes unduly subservient to reason it may find itself, as in Germany, too closely attached to a single philosophical system. But if theology is to express itself in a form which will appeal to contemporary thought this cannot entirely be avoided.

> Theology must sometimes [as Dr. Tennant has said] deliberately take over ready-fashioned concepts from philosophy . . . and the theology of any particular generation can hardly avoid using, unconsciously if not with full awareness, the ideas and beliefs of contemporary science, and allowing them to mould its exegesis and its doctrine.

[1] *Essays in Criticism*, Vol. I, p. 220.   [2] Westcott, *The Gospel of Life*, p. 290.

To be really satisfactory theology must have philosophical outworks and be willing to submit itself to philosophical criticism; just as a really sound metaphysic must have a firm theological centre.[1] But every religion, it may be urged, even the most primitive, has already some kind of metaphysic, whether conscious or unconscious. That may be true; but something more is here in question, a formal expression of a metaphysic. Religion, even when based on a revelation, cannot achieve this unassisted.[2]

> Christian theology cannot satisfactorily create its own metaphysic. It must call in the aid of philosophy for the task. A theology which seeks its material only in the revelation contained in the Bible will both fail to understand that material itself and will make the part a standard for interpreting the whole.[3]

If theology, however, realized its need for a metaphysic and for restatement on philosophical lines the time had not yet come for this to be successfully achieved. The vast expansion of knowledge, the general state of flux and uncertainty, put this out of the question, and any such statement, had it been attempted, would have been both premature and tentative; 'new truth must be solidified by time before it can be built into the eternal truth of Christianity'.[4] The *Lux Mundi* group might play with the idea of producing a new *Summa* and as late as 1916 William Temple could write: 'We need very urgently some one who will do for our day the work that St. Thomas Aquinas did for his',[5] but such an achievement, even if anyone capable of accomplishing it could have been found, was impossible in the late nineteenth century, and one might venture to prophesy, will remain

---

[1] Illingworth as a young man deplored the habit of rushing straight into theology without any consideration of the philosophical outworks; and later he saw that there could be no new metaphysic unless there was a firm grasp of the theological core. (*Life*, pp. 36 and 160.)

[2] Cf. Whitehead, *Religion in the Making*, pp. 39f. 'Buddhism is a metaphysic which gave birth to a religion—Christianity is a religion vainly seeking a metaphysic.'

[3] Storr, p. 14.

[4] H. Drummond, *The New Evangelism*, p. 153.

[5] *Mens Creatrix*, p. vii.

7

impossible within any foreseeable future. R. G. Collingwood might attempt to bring Hobbes up to date in *The New Leviathan*, but conditions are so different from those of the thirteenth century that no new Aquinas can now arise.

There were not lacking in our period a number of philosophers who, accepting the Christian point of view, endeavoured to work out a philosophy of religion which would be in accord with the thought of the day. Like other philosophers they held different opinions on a number of questions; Hastings Rashdall, not the least able of them, was, for example, a determinist. Some of them were amateurs, such as A. J. Balfour whose *Foundations of Belief* was published in 1895.[1]

Mention may here be made of F. D. Maurice, although his best work had been done before our period.[2] His return to Cambridge in 1866 as Professor of Moral Theology[3] was welcomed by Sidgwick as bringing fresh life to the study; but he would have exercised more influence if he had not insisted on retaining Vere Street Chapel in London (until his health compelled him to give it up) and the principalship of the Working Men's College. At first his lectures were well attended, but when the novelty had worn off numbers declined sharply and Hort in 1868 described them as 'full of good matter and brilliantly written, but miserably attended'.[4] C. C. J. Webb regarded Maurice as 'one of the most influential figures in the religious world of his generation', and added, 'there is a danger that his importance in his own day compared with men of greater gifts of expression, may be underrated'.[5] There has recently been a praiseworthy return to the study of his ideas and teaching.[6]

[1] C. C. J. Webb, *Religious Thought in England* etc., p. 156, said that his writings had 'all of them but one theme: the importance of attending not only to the *rational grounds* but to the *non-rational causes* of belief'.

[2] See Storr, pp. 340 ff. He had influenced T. H. Green in his younger days: see Nettleship, *T. H. Green*, p. xxv.

[3] Kingsley, as Regius Professor of Modern History, was one of the electors.

[4] *Life*, Vol. II, p. 89.   [5] *Op. cit.*, pp. 85 f.

[6] E.g. A. R. Vidler, *The Theology of F. D. Maurice* and A. M. Ramsey, *F. D. Maurice*. One of the best short books on Maurice is still that by C. F. G. Masterman.

At Cambridge there was also James Ward, a pupil of Lotze, who had the distinction of defeating F. W. Maitland in a contest for a Trinity fellowship in 1872. Ward first became well known in 1899 through his Gifford Lectures, *Naturalism and Agnosticism*.

The most influential group of Christian philosophers, however, was that already referred to as disciples of T. H. Green.[1] The alliance of this group with Idealism was undoubtedly useful in its beginnings as offering resistance to sheer Naturalism; but by the end of the century the utility of the connexion was open to question. Alliances, we know, can be profitable up to a point, but if the ultimate, as distinguished from the immediate, aims of the allies are divergent, they lose their meaning.[2] The urgent problem for these Christian Idealists was the exact relation of God and the Absolute,[3] and some of them were inclined to accept too readily a philosophy which was predominantly immanentist. Gore was here an exception owing to his vivid awareness of moral distinctions. This emphasis on immanence, of course, fitted in well with the Logos theology, and seemed to provide for the recognition of the divine purpose in history; but it passed over much that was fundamental in Christian tradition as contained in the Bible, in earlier thinkers, and in the liturgy.

Outstanding in his group, and, indeed, among Christian philosophers of his day was J. R. Illingworth. He had an extraordinary ability for making himself popularly understood and his works had an immense circulation, appearing in paper-backed editions and being translated into many languages, including

---

[1] James Martineau, who agreed with Schopenhauer that any form of Hegelianism was a *reductio ad absurdum* of philosophy, was much puzzled to explain its popularity, especially among the young High Churchmen at Oxford: see J. Estlin Carpenter, *James Martineau*, pp. 535 ff.

[2] Cobden said of nations going to war that they know who is their partner in the first dance; but they cannot tell with whom they may be dancing at the end of the ball. (F. W. Hirst, *Early Life and Letters of John Morley*, Vol. II, p. 41.)

[3] Both Bradley and Bosanquet denied personality in the Absolute (see above p. 70). Cf. Ottley, *Lux Mundi*, p. 349: 'It is characteristic of the Christian spirit frankly to recognize the natural world in its due subordination to personality, in its subserviency to ethical ends. An absolute idealism is not less alien to this standpoint than a crude materialism.'

Chinese and Japanese. Most of them appeared after 1900; but during our period, in addition to two essays in *Lux Mundi*, he published his Bampton Lectures on *Personality: Human and Divine* and also *Divine Immanence*. Illingworth's contribution to thought, however, was hampered by the retired life he was compelled to lead and by a lack of means which prevented his obtaining the newest books. This kept him ignorant of modern developments. But apart from this, like other members of the *Lux Mundi* school, having made considerable progress in a liberal direction he refused, in later life, to advance any further.

One admirable characteristic of these Christian philosophers was their attitude to reason. They were genuine rationalists, giving to reason its due and proper place, and neither despising what lay below it, nor being reluctant to go beyond it where necessary. Reason to them was precious because they believed that the divine Logos was ever at work in the world, guiding and co-operating with, though never superseding, the spirit of man. They could even trace its operations in secular thought which they held had 'often corrected and counteracted the evil of a Christianity grown professional, and false, and foul'.[1]

We may close this chapter by briefly summarizing the services, both positive and negative, which philosophy may be said to have rendered to theology. As we have already noticed philosophy and theology did not work closely together in England as they did in Germany. There the Tübingen school had definitely tried to fit Christianity into a Hegelian mould; and it is not without interest to notice that some of its leading exponents, Baur and Strauss for example, had been philosophers before ever they turned their thoughts to the study of theology and Church History. To them it was philosophy which furnished the only real clue to the development of Christianity.[2] There was nothing comparable to this in England, not even in the *Lux Mundi* school, and we must seek for the effects of philosophy in less direct ways.

[1] Illingworth in *Lux Mundi*, pp. 143, 155 f.
[2] Baur once wrote: '*Ohne Philosophie bleibt mir die Geschichte ewig tod und stumm.*'

In the first place philosophy was an aid to theology through the part it played in that unification and systematizing of knowledge which was their common aim. It also provided theology with new categories or conceptions for the work of interpretation; as well as systems devised by human thought which could be set alongside dogmas based on revelation. By bringing their conclusions to the test of such systems theologians were often enabled to discard elements which were merely local or accidental. By its researches in the field of epistemology it made available new means of assessing the value of methods of thought, and by its insistence on the necessity of bringing all things to the bar of reason (a principle which was widely adopted by theologians of a liberal outlook) it helped to purify popular religion, and even theology itself, of notions that were unworthy and fanciful.

On the other hand philosophy might have a deterrent effect on the study of theology and by its over-emphasis on criticism add to the general unsettlement. In 1868 Liddon went so far as to state that the prevalence of the views of Mill, Bain, and Spencer, since they denied the first and highest theistic truth, had made all serious theology impossible in Oxford.[1]

The greatest service, which philosophy rendered to theology lay, probably, in the exposure of the limitations of the human mind to discover reality, and the consequent need for some assured basis such as, for those who were able to accept its teaching, religion claimed to provide. Men may seek to satisfy their craving for a knowledge of ultimate truth by means of philosophy and feel that they have made progress towards that end; but the satisfaction which this may afford them has to be tempered by the realization that there are further desires which philosophy cannot assuage. Having scaled the foot-hills of knowledge they find themselves face to face with range after range of higher peaks.

The logical outcome of philosophy is to lose itself in religion, for 'philosophy is thought, and thought always involves finitude and opposition. . . . Its business therefore is to show the finitude of all that is finite, and through reason to demand its complement

[1] Johnston, *Life of H. P. Liddon*, p. 113.

and completion in the infinite.'[1] Even those philosophers who attain to a belief in God, or as they might call Him, the Absolute, have but a limited notion of the deity, for as the result of an intellectual process He may be little more than an abstraction and lack anything which can fairly be called personality. Such a belief may provide light and comfort for a few cultivated and select souls, but it is hardly a compelling motive for the lives of ordinary men and women, nor can it furnish that unifying force which will bind them into a community. R. W. Church spoke of the highest philosophy current in the Roman Empire as 'often very noble and true in its language, able . . . in evil days to elevate and comfort and often purify its better disciples—but unable to overawe, to heal, to charm a diseased society: which could never breathe life and energy into words for the people'.[2] To this opinion may be added what E. S. Talbot said of the same age, and it may be applied to philosophy in every age, 'It lacked a foundation upon a Rock. It had the certainty, if certainty at all, which belongs to profound intuitions and to a wide interpretation, not that which makes a definite, settled, and above all, communicable conviction.'[3]

[1] Rosenkrantz quoted by Edward Caird, *Hegel*, p. 40.
[2] *The Gifts of Civilisation*, p. 174. Cf. Réville, *History of Religion*, p. 2: 'A religion may become philosophical, but no philosophy has ever founded a religion possessing real historical power.'
[3] In *Lux Mundi*, pp. 104f.

Chapter Four

THE IMPACT OF HISTORICAL STUDIES: ARCHAEOLOGY

THE second half of the nineteenth century saw a revival on a noteworthy scale of interest in historical studies in this country.[1] During the Restoration period and the early years of the eighteenth century England had possessed a remarkable school of medieval historians;[2] then for more than a hundred years history, in spite of a few great names such as Gibbon and Macaulay, fell into neglect and even into something akin to contempt. The revival of interest came about, at least in part, through the theories of Darwin which revealed Nature at work in time. Earlier the accepted view that organisms were permanently divided into different species had led Hegel and others to deny that Nature had any history at all. The new scientific influence, however, was not without its drawbacks, for it led to the extension of the idea of 'evolution' to departments of knowledge to which strictly speaking it did not apply. The crude transference of the hypothesis to the conduct of human affairs, for example, did much harm,[3] for 'evolution' in history is a very different thing from 'evolution' in Nature, since the human element takes a conscious part, exhibiting will and purpose. Furthermore, the notion began to prevail that to have traced out the development of an idea or an institution was fully to have accounted for it.[4]

[1] For historical studies in the earlier part of the century see Storr, pp. 115ff., 201f. [2] See D. C. Douglas, *English Scholars.*
[3] Cf. *Life and Letters of Mandell Creighton*, Vol. II, p. 469.
[4] Storr protested against the reckless use of the term, which for many seemed by its bare utterance to bring 'a lucid explanation of all difficulties'. (*Development and Divine Purpose*, p. 13.)

History in the past had been the work of amateurs and had formed part of general literature or *belles lettres*, a phase which may be said to have ended with Froude, a brilliant though at times a careless writer.[1] The motives inspiring those who pursued it had been various; some were moved by antiquarian curiosity or by the desire to unearth matter useful for propaganda and so to demonstrate that 'their opinions or policies [were] those of venerated personalities in the past';[2] some had artistic or aesthetic interests and were attracted by 'the teeming wealth of incident and the suggestive action and charm of individuals';[3] the ultra-romantic wished to live imaginatively in former ages or to find a way of 'escape' from the present.

Such motives, although they did not disappear entirely, fell into the background.[4] History began to be studied for its own sake, and scholars made it their primary aim to discover what actually had happened. This did not, of course, reduce history to a 'pure' science, but the investigation of the past was helpful in accounting for the present,[5] and provided some guidance for the future. At Cambridge Seeley quite openly regarded history as a school for training statesmen and diplomats.

When Stubbs was appointed Regius Professor of Modern History at Oxford in 1866 he was the first trained historian to occupy the post. But he had not learned his methods in the university, but in his country living at Navestock in Essex. His successors, Freeman and Froude, had likewise worked away from Oxford. Creighton too had begun his historical studies at Oxford,

---

[1] Froude has been unduly criticized for his occasional lapses; it must be remembered that he was a pioneer in the study of archives and based his work on original documents.

[2] C. C. J. Webb, *Religious Thought in England*, p. 19.

[3] *E.R.E.*, Vol. vi, p. 718.

[4] History was still invoked to provide evidence for certain sociological and economic theories; and theologians appealed to it as the working out of the divine plan and even extended its scope into eternity.

[5] Cf. Storr, *Development and Divine Purpose*, p. 213: 'The sense of the continuity of human life impressed itself upon men's minds, and they began to understand how every age was vitally linked with and obeyed its predecessors, and how even reaction was a form of obedience.'

but had worked out his methods mainly in the isolation of his Northumbrian parish of Embleton. Henceforward, however, history would more and more be studied in the universities and more and more become the virtual monopoly of dons and their pupils; in fact, the study would become a vast co-operative enterprise. Stubbs, Freeman, and J. R. Green, had worked in conjunction, but there had not been anything resembling the co-operation which would later exist. The new methods had been largely derived from Germany and German scholars, and under the leadership of Stubbs a new school of historians began to grow up in Oxford; they were introduced into Cambridge by Creighton when he became the first Dixie Professor of Ecclesiastical History in 1884.

Historical studies were greatly helped in England by the establishment of *The English Historical Review* in 1866 with Creighton as editor. One of those chiefly responsible for its foundation was Lord Acton. Acton as a young man had wanted to go up to Cambridge, but was prevented by his being a Roman Catholic, and so he studied history under Döllinger at Munich. In 1895 he became Regius Professor of Modern History at Cambridge in succession to Seeley, and it was he who planned the *Cambridge Modern History*.

The new school of historians, following the maxim of Ranke that the facts are all important, tended to concentrate on the study of details. The older historians, whose primary object was to produce a narrative which was at once enlightening and picturesque, would have scoffed at this concentration as mere pedantic trifling. They themselves, however, had been deficient in critical ability and the authorities, especially original documents, which they were able to consult were restricted in range. The result was that they had been too ready to accept as true much that was mere legend or propaganda. The defects in their representations of what had happened in the past were soon exposed and denounced when a closer scrutiny and a more intensive research were applied to them. Such exposure was inevitable, but it created the impression that the new historians were bent only on destruction. The

American humorist, Artemus Ward, put this opinion in his quaint way when he wrote: 'The researches of many eminent antiquarians have already thrown much darkness on the subject; and it is possible, if they continue their labours, that we shall soon know nothing at all.' But such a process was necessary if firm foundations were to be laid for further advance.

Freeman is supposed to have said that a manuscript was only valuable when it had been printed, and, unlike Froude, he himself worked almost entirely on printed sources. But the adoption of the new methods changed all this, and it might even be held that historical research, unless it resulted in the discovery and publication of fresh material, had missed its mark. An insistence on the importance of discovering fresh material is, of course, praiseworthy; but it can be exaggerated, for it may culminate in the production of numerous elaborate and carefully documented essays which no one, except a few specialists, will read or care to read. When Lord Acton made his famous attack on Creighton's standpoint and methods he warned him, in words which had almost a sinister ring,[1] that 'Studious men who [had] grown grey with the dust of papal archives [were] on the track behind him.' But these pallid scholars are often content with the mere accumulation of material and descend to the grave leaving behind them (as Acton himself did) only a reputation for vast learning and a few thin volumes of collected essays and reviews.

In the present age of specialization no single scholar can hope to master more than a restricted period, and historians are more and more being compelled to imitate the methods of the laboratory and to entrust much of the detail of their work to pupils and assistants. It is possible that two distinct types of historical student will eventually emerge—the type which will give itself up entirely to research pure and simple, and that which will correlate and present the results of the labours of others. It is hardly necessary

---

[1] G. M. Trevelyan has assured us that Acton dearly liked 'to make your flesh creep'. (*Clio, a Muse*, p. 51.)

to insist, however, that scholars of the latter type must themselves have served an apprenticeship as 'hewers of wood and drawers of water'.[1]

A too exclusive concentration on the collection of facts was a definite weakness in the historical studies of the later nineteenth century, for it was not adequately balanced by the use of the imagination,[2] and without imagination the most learned historian will produce only dull, dry as dust, chronicles, without life or fire, mere skeleton maps of events. Facts became almost an end in themselves. But if facts are the necessary basis for an exact assessment of any situation or development, even more necessary is the ability to judge which of them are really significant. Facts are not history, but the raw material for history. R. G. Collingwood, a redoubtable critic of the Victorian conception of the writing of history, affirmed that, 'Nothing capable of being memorized is history.'

Anticipations of this attitude are to be found in *The New Republic*, that amazing *tour de force* of W. H. Mallock, then an Oxford undergraduate, published in 1877. In it he said: 'The least important of all the world's events are those that you can localize exactly, and put an exact date to; those alone which most historians see, . . . events . . . I call *illustrations* of history; but I do not call them history.' And again, 'Our past must be an extension of the present, or it is no real past.'[3]

If history owed some of its restored prestige to the work of scientists, it was also indebted to them for improved methods. In some respects history and science run in parallel lines, for history 'collects and sifts facts, gets them down as correctly as it can, classifies them, and then, making hypotheses, tests and tries them

---

[1] 'Brickmakers are well enough,' wrote Philip Guedalla, but 'the edifice of history calls for an architect as well.'

[2] It is, of course, necessary to keep the imagination under control and to realize its proper function. This recalls the witty accusation once brought by Sheridan against Dundas, that he was indebted to his imagination for his facts, whilst his memory only supplied him with jests. (T. Moore, *Life of Sheridan*, Vol. II, p. 471.)

[3] *Op. cit.*, Bk. III, Ch. II, (1908 edn., p. 131).

till it arrives at conclusions that stand every test and trial it can apply'.[1]

The historian, like the scientist, has a standpoint from which he starts and an end towards which he is working; but there is a real difference between them, for though the historian may take up a purely scientific attitude to facts and seek to explain and interpret them through their causal relations, personal judgment must come in. Ideally the historian may be unswayed by 'passion and prejudice', but no one is without prejudices, although these may be unconscious. An absolutely impartial mind would be a mind without any content.

Schopenhauer rejected the claim of history to be a science on the ground that it was ever concerned with the particular and not the universal. But this is to exaggerate the difference between them. The scientist must concern himself with the particular, and the historian does not shrink from making generalizations; though the latter may not be so certain as those of the scientist, especially in the sense that they are less available as a basis for predicting the future course of events.

In adopting scientific rules for weighing evidence historians did not always realize the immense difference between their own studies and those of scientists. The scientist can either reproduce the objects he studies, as in chemistry, or observe them afresh, as in astronomy; this the historian cannot do, save only in his own consciousness. There is a further difference which cannot be ignored. Events in Nature are events and nothing more; events in history are the product, at least in part, of human agency, planned by man and carried out in accordance with his planning, so far, that is, as he has the necessary ability.

In his quest for certainty there is a distinct danger that the scientific historian may demand more than the evidence can possibly afford him, until he arrives at the stage which provoked Anatole France's playful jibe and be incapable of accepting anything as true unless it took place in a laboratory. Furthermore the amount of certainty obtained by the scientist was greatly

[1] Elton, *Frederick York Powell*, Vol. II, p. 4.

exaggerated in the nineteenth century, and especially by those who had no first-hand knowledge of his methods. After all it is in mathematics alone that complete certitude is possible, and then only because mathematics deals with abstractions. None the less 'our ability to interpret human history by the light of present experience is far inferior to our power of similarly interpreting physical phenomena'.[1] The scientific historian may garner an immense harvest of facts, but he has often only a vague conception of the mysterious workings of the human mind.

In their desire to demonstrate that history is a science some historians, though by no means all, seemed to think it necessary to banish from their pages that literary charm which might suggest that it was a branch of letters. The debate as to whether history is a science or a branch of letters is entirely futile,[2] in spite of the immense excitement it once aroused, for it obviously belongs to both and from both the historian must be prepared to learn their lessons. In the collection of his material he must be a scientist; but in the arrangement and presentation of his results he must, so far as in him lies, be a literary artist. Profundity of research must be crowned by lucidity and precision of style.[3]

History may be a department of letters but it has its own characteristics. The novelist or the poet may rely on inspiration and on his own imagination fortified and tested by experience; the historian must have as a basis all the necessary facts, so far as he can lay hands on them. Thus history became avid of additional materials upon which it could work. Libraries were ransacked for hidden documents and the earth itself for the remnants of lost civilizations; the researches, too, of the anthropologist were brought into service. Alongside this search for new material there was a recognition of the utility of existing sources of information. This was especially true of architecture, which was no longer regarded merely as a technical subject but as an expression of the

[1] Illingworth, *The Doctrine of the Trinity*, p. 222.
[2] Lord Bryce once remarked that one might just as well argue whether the sea was blue or green, since it is sometimes one, sometimes the other.
[3] On the changes in the study and teaching of history see G. M. Trevelyan's delightful essay 'Clio, a Muse' in the volume to which it gives the title.

culture and tendencies of the era in which it arose and developed, and as providing a perpetual memorial of the greatness and genius of peoples. Here Ruskin had much to teach.[1]

Archaeological research had already been very active before the beginning of our period, now it was pursued with greater vigour and skill and the results were astounding. Discoveries followed one another in an almost breathless succession,[2] and forgotten peoples and lost civilizations sprang suddenly to light. In 1874 Schliemann revealed the antiquities of Troy; then came the discovery of the Minoan civilization; and from Egyptian dustheaps came fragments of lost dramatists and Aristotle's *Constitution of Athens*. The well-worked fields of Assyria and Babylonia were yielding new treasures to the enriching of Old Testament studies; it was in 1876 that George Smith published the Creation and Deluge tablets from Nineveh. Behind Babylonian and Assyrian civilization it was now discovered that there lay an older Sumerian culture,[3] a culture which itself stood in some relation to that of the Indus valley as later researches have since revealed. The Hittites were also recognized as a greater people than had hitherto been suspected.

One effect of these and other like discoveries was to reveal how much closer had been the connexion between the East and the West;[4] another, and even more important, effect was to give a new idea of the vastness and extent of human achievement over a long period of centuries. This tended at first to reinforce the optimistic outlook of the times; but by the close of the century it was beginning to be realized that since progress had been neither uniform nor uninterrupted the fate which had come upon great civilizations in the past might perchance befall our own. Writing

---

[1] Freeman in his first considerable published work *A History of Architecture* (1849) had drawn attention to its neglect as a 'document'.

[2] See further *Authority and Archaeology, Sacred and Profane* (ed. D. G. Hogarth).

[3] Cf. C. L. Woolley, *The Sumerians* (1928), p. 183: 'Three generations ago the existence of the Sumerians was unknown to the scientific world; today their history can be written and their art illustrated more fully than that of many ancient peoples.'

[4] The recent discoveries at Ras Shamra and Mari further illustrate the connexion.

in 1905 Gertrude Bell, as a result of her travels and explorations in the Ancient East, could say: 'We in Europe are accustomed to think that civilization is an advancing flood that has gone steadily forward since the beginning of time. I believe we are wrong. It is a tide that ebbs and flows, reaches a high water mark and turns back again.'[1] The extension of the horizon of history and the immensely increased span of human life upon this planet which it postulated was of importance to theologians, for it confirmed the findings of geology and ruled out once and for all the accepted biblical chronology.

Archaeology thus provided abundant new material upon which the historian could work, and what is important to remember, much of it was different in kind from that previously available. Hitherto historians had had to rely mainly on written authorities, now the spade had come in to supplement and, in some cases, to correct the pen; material coming down from the remote past could be handled and examined. But here a warning is necessary, for it is easy to give an exaggerated importance to archaeological material and to imagine that because it comes from contemporaries and is graven in rock or moulded in clay it cannot be disputed. This is by no means the case, for some inscriptions have been tampered with, as by the substitution of later names. Nor can we ignore the very human tendency to magnify triumphs and minimize failures. Kings and cities, as Hogarth has pointed out, deliberately tried to deceive contemporaries and posterity, and their inscriptions may need correction from literary sources.[2] It is also necessary to realize that archaeological material is often only fragmentary and that much of it has survived by accident. It cannot therefore be accepted as giving a complete view of things, and may, indeed, be definitely misleading.[3]

Speaking of Greece Jowett in the preface to his translation of *Thucydides* (1881) opined that archaeology could add little to our

---

[1] Lady Bell, *The Letters of Gertrude Bell*, p. 176.

[2] In *Authority and Archaeology*, p. ix.

[3] The availability of material may give a false importance to an era or a country. Toynbee thinks that the Ptolemaic monarchs have been thus favoured at the expense of the Seleucid; see *A Study of History*, Vol. I, pp. 6f.

knowledge beyond 'a few facts'. There is, of course, a sense in which that was true if we think of Greece in the classical age only, but regarded from a wider point of view we now know that Greece (and Rome also)

> far from standing near the beginning of recorded history, were the heirs of a long series of brilliant civilizations. Our whole perspective has been changed. The ancient world ceases to be merely the vestibule to Christian Europe, and becomes in point of duration the larger part of human history.[1]

For our purposes archaeology is mainly of service in so far as it is concerned directly with the Bible, and a brief survey of the new discoveries in that field is now called for. Their chief value does not consist, as the Fundamentalists vainly imagine, in their confirmation of statements in the Bible, but on the contrary in their correction or supplementing of such statements.

It will be convenient to begin with Palestine since most of the events recorded in the Bible took place there. Palestine, it may be said, was rediscovered by Edward Robinson in 1841. He, like Schliemann in regard to Troy, had from boyhood nourished a desire to explore it; and like Schliemann his desire was fulfilled. After Robinson came his disciple Titus Tobler and soon a number of surveys and a whole spate of travel volumes followed.[2] In 1852 Victor Guérin had begun single-handed to provide a map, but it was not until 1863 that it was published. By that time a better map had already appeared, that of Van de Velde which came out in 1858 and held its place up to the publication of the ordnance map of the Palestine Exploration Fund. This society had been established in 1865 and it was not until 1877 that the corresponding German society was founded. The results of

---

[1] Gooch, *History and Historians*, etc., p. 496. Cf. Sir Arthur Evans in the preface to Hawes, *Crete the Forerunner of Greece*: 'This revelation from the past has . . . more than an archaeological interest. It concerns all history and must affect the mental attitude of our own and future generations in many departments of knowledge.'

[2] The most popular travel volume was still Stanley's *Sinai and Palestine*, published in 1856.

exploration were summed up in 1894 by George Adam Smith in his *Historical Geography of the Holy Land*, a fine piece of pioneer work, though not without its defects. But even after much work had been done no less than 290 Old Testament and eight New Testament sites were still unidentified, and many of the proposed identifications were far from certain.

The scientific excavation of Palestine can hardly be said to have begun before the arrival of Flinders Petrie from Egypt in 1890.[1] Palestine has not furnished as much evidence as might have been expected; there were, of course, no remains of splendid buildings or sculptures as in Egypt or Babylonia, and but few inscriptions, and those of no great length, have been discovered. Some religious objects from early times may have been destroyed by the Jews, especially after the return from the Exile; but many such have been discovered in excavations on sites which have been occupied by many cities.[2] Amongst the most valuable finds were potsherds. No trace has been found of the presence of foreign monarchs on the soil of Palestine and the standard of material civilization revealed is comparatively low,[3] which makes the emergence of the prophets and other religious teachers of the Hebrews and of the whole Hebrew literature a remarkable phenomenon.[4]

Most of the discoveries referred to belong especially to Old Testament studies,[5] and in addition to them was the mass of material coming from Babylonia and Assyria, as well as from Egypt where the discovery of the Tell el-Amarna Letters in 1887

---

[1] See further R. A. S. Macalister, *A Century of Excavation in Palestine* (1925), F. J. Bliss, *The Development of Palestinian Exploration* (1906) and Vincent, *Canaan d'après l'Exploration récente* (1907).

[2] Flinders Petrie and Bliss found traces of eleven, dating from 1700 to 400 B.C., at Lachish, and Macalister seven at Gezer.

[3] See Macalister, *op. cit.*, p. 146. His low opinion of the state of civilization has been rejected by later archaeologists as 'based on erroneous dating of an inferior settlement': see *The Old Testament and Modern Study*, p. 16.

[4] Macalister, *op. cit.*, p. 295 says: 'That men gifted with a philosophical instinct so clear, and with a literary skill so marvellous, should have arisen in a soil so sordid is hardly to be explained otherwise than as a miracle.'

[5] See further Driver, Schweich Lectures for 1908.

8

was outstanding. Flinders Petrie began work in Egypt in 1880 and when three years later The Egyptian Exploration Society was founded he became its chief agent.

Many of the discoveries were valuable mainly for philological studies and of these the Moabite Stone was perhaps the most interesting. It was found in 1868 and showed not only that the Moabite language was closely akin to Hebrew—it might rank almost as a dialect of Hebrew—but that the religious outlook of the Moabites was so similar to that of the Hebrews that the inscription, if the names were altered, would read like an extract from the Book of Kings.[1] In 1880 a short inscription was discovered at Siloam which may probably be dated *c.* 700 B.C.;[2] until the Gezer inscription was found in 1908 it ranked as the oldest known inscription in Hebrew. Then in 1896 Mrs. Lewis and Mrs. Gibson came across the first fragments of the original Hebrew of Ecclesiasticus which had come from a genizah at Cairo.[3]

Turning to Semitic languages in general mention may be made of the publication by De Vogüé in 1868 of a large number of inscriptions from Palmyra. Then in 1890 and the year following came what G. A. Cooke has called 'The most important discovery since the finding of the Moabite Stone'[4] in the shape of three inscriptions from Zingirli, a small village not far from Aleppo in north-west Syria. They are written in archaic characters not unlike those of the Moabite Stone. The first two were inscribed on a colossal statue of the god Hadad; the third, discovered in 1891, was on the wall of a palace.[5] Much fresh material also came from Arabia; Nabataean inscriptions from the north-west in 1884–5 and Sabaean and Minaean from both the north-west and the south between 1869 and 1894. It may be asserted that in the last three decades of the century the outline of early Arab civilization in the

---

[1] For a reproduction and translation see G. A. Cooke, *North Semitic Inscriptions*, No. 1 or Driver, *Samuel*, pp. lxxxiv ff.

[2] See Cooke, *op. cit.*, No. 2, or Driver, *op. cit.*, pp. viii ff.

[3] For further details see Charles, *Apocrypha and Pseudepigrapha of the Old Testament*, Vol. 1, p. 271.

[4] *Op. cit.*, p. ix.

[5] See Cooke, *op. cit.*, Nos. 61–3.

south was revealed for the first time through the work of Halévy and Glaser.[1]

For the New Testament, archaeology, from the nature of the case, was not quite so fruitful. Mention, however, may be made of the excavations of J. T. Wood at Ephesus of which he published an account in 1877, supplemented later by the expert knowledge of E. L. Hicks in *Ancient Greek Inscriptions in the British Museum*, Vol. III, no. 2 (1890), and of the better known discoveries of W. M. Ramsay in Asia Minor. The greatest service rendered by archaeologists to New Testament studies came with the unearthing of the Egyptian papyri. These showed that the Greek of the New Testament and of the Septuagint was no unique dialect.[2] The service rendered by the papyri had, with noteworthy insight, been anticipated by Lightfoot when in a lecture as early as 1863, he remarked in reference to a New Testament word found elsewhere only in Herodotus:

> You are not to suppose that this word . . . had fallen out of use in the interval, only that it had not been used in the books that remain to us: probably it had been part of the common speech all along. I will go further, and say that if we could recover letters that ordinary people wrote to each other without any thought of being literary, we should have the greatest possible help for the understanding of the language of the New Testament generally.[3]

John Wordsworth, a friend of Lightfoot, when Grinfield Lecturer on the Septuagint at Oxford, made a similar suggestion in 1877.

The discovery of the papyri followed the British occupation of Egypt in 1882, but really systematic work did not begin until 1889. Six years later Grenfell and Hunt made their sensational discovery of words said to have been spoken by Jesus Himself, as well as a third-century MS. of Matthew I. The first to make full

---

[1] See further Glaser, *The History and Geography of Arabia before Mohammed* (1890) and D. G. Hogarth, *The Penetration of Arabia* (1904).

[2] It was thought at one time that this dialect was peculiar to Egypt, but this has been disproved by the discovery of its use elsewhere.

[3] Quoted by Milligan, *Selections from the Greek Papyri*, p. xx.

use of the new material made available by the discovery of the papyri was Adolf Deissmann whose *Bibelstudien* was published in 1896. The new light on the Greek of the Bible which came from papyri suggested that Modern Greek might also be of value; the possibilities of this source of information had already been recognized by W. F. Moulton in his edition of Winer published *c*. 1870.[1]

Another line of research which brought fresh light was the renewed study of Aramic, presumably the original language spoken by Jesus and His disciples. Here the outstanding work was Dalman's *Die Worte Jesu* which appeared in 1898 and was soon afterwards translated into English. Work on the text of the New Testament was also assisted by the discovery of a new Syriac version of the gospels by Mrs. Lewis at Mount Sinai. This was published in 1894.

Among other discoveries helpful for the study of the gospels was the recovery of the text of Tatian's *Diatessaron*, which was made available for English readers in Samuel Hemphill's edition (1888). Strangely enough the necessary material had been in existence long before, but had been neglected or unknown. It went back to the publication of an Armenian edition of the works of Ephraem Syrus prepared by the monks of San Lazarro in Venice in 1836 which included a commentary on the *Diatessaron*. A Latin translation was published by Mösinger in 1876 which Ezra Abbot brought to the notice of scholars in his *Authorship of the Fourth Gospel* (1880). An edition of the *Diatessaron* in Arabic from a forgotten MS. in the Vatican Library was produced by A. Ciasca in 1888.[2]

Other discoveries which illuminated, if not the New Testament itself, yet the early days of Christianity included *The Teaching of the Twelve Apostles* (*The Didache*) in 1875, the *Apology of Aristides* in 1891, and Syriac and Latin versions of I Clement. Mention may also be made of the finding in 1884 in a tomb at

[1] See further Thumb, *Greek in the Hellenistic Period*.
[2] I owe much of these particulars to Lawlor and Oulton, *Eusebius*, Vol. II, pp. 151f.

Akhmim of fragments of the so-called *Gospel of Peter* and of the related *Apocalypse of Peter*.

The Didache, which was discovered by Bryennios in the Patriarchal Library at Jerusalem was one of the most important finds in our period, but unfortunately there is no consensus of opinion as to its date and place of origin. Some scholars regard it, in any case, as the production of a remote and backward church whose evidence must be received with caution.[1]

Although the so-called Church Orders were known in our period, *The Apostolic Constitutions* had, indeed, been much used in post-Reformation controversies, not much attention was paid to them until the present century.[2] Other existing sources which had hitherto been neglected now came to be used by theologians; of these the most important were the Jewish apocryphal writings. Before our period the only works of this character which had been at all well known were *The Testaments of the Twelve Patriarchs* and *IV Ezra*. Until the publication of the Oxford *Apocrypha and Pseudepigrapha of the Old Testament* under the editorship of R. H. Charles in 1913 students had had to rely on editions of the separate writings. Many of these had been produced, especially by Charles and M. R. James, and in Germany Dillmann had been very active, above all in work on Ethiopic versions and writings.[3]

Christianity is a historic religion and bases its claims on the truth of certain happenings in the past. Modernists may assert that it is the idea which is important, quite apart from whether it is supported by history or not, but that has never been the traditional attitude. 'Whatever else the event in history may carry with it . . . it must stand its ground as a mere historical event. The mere fact may be but a part of it; yet all will be overthrown if the fact be not a fact.'[4] This being so Christianity

---

[1] An interesting study of the document is C. Taylor, *The Teaching of the Twelve Apostles with Illustrations from the Talmud* (1886).

[2] See further my *Beginnings of Western Christendom*, pp. 248 ff. and J. V. Bartlet, *Church-Life and Church-Order*.

[3] See further articles in *Enc. Bib.* by R. H. Charles (pp. 213 ff.) and M. R. James (pp. 249 ff.). [4] R. C. Moberly in *Lux Mundi*, p. 172.

could not remain immune when new methods of historical criticism were being applied on every hand.

Furthermore the Church as we know it today is the result of a long period of development and this is a factor of immense importance; Hort indeed has affirmed that 'The History of the Church from its foundation to the present hour is hardly less necessary to the Church at large than the Gospel itself, whatever it may be to the individual disciple.'[1] Interest in this aspect of the subject had been revived in England through the rise of the Oxford Movement with its appeal to the past and the reaction aroused by it in other schools of thought. There had also been a noteworthy renewal of interest in the subject among Protestant theologians on quite other grounds; for they were coming to value the Church, not so much as the guardian of tradition, as the continuous embodiment of the faith.

The history of the Church, especially in its early, formative stages, is an important department of theology and a vast amount of work was done upon it during our period, so vast, indeed, that space forbids more than a mere glance at what was accomplished. The outstanding name was, of course, that of Harnack. The *Texte und Untersuchungen* which he edited from 1882 onwards illuminated every corner of the first three centuries, whilst his *Dogmengeschichte*, an abbreviated translation of which appeared in 1892, set forth his views on the development of Christian doctrine.[2] In this country the greatest contribution to the subject was Lightfoot's *Apostolic Fathers*. Mention must also be made of H. M. Gwatkin's *Studies in Arianism* (1882) and of Hatch's two volumes *On the Organization of the Christian Church* and *The Influence of Greek Ideas and Usages upon the Christian Church*.[3]

In the seventeenth century English theologians had given much attention to the works of the Fathers, but during the eighteenth century and the early part of the nineteenth, they had been largely

[1] *The Way, the Truth, the Life*, p. 35.

[2] He also produced between 1893 and 1904 his *Geschichte der alt-christlichen Literatur bis Eusebius*. *Die Mission und Ausbreitung des Christentums i. d. ersten drei Jahrhunderten* was not translated until 1904.

[3] See below, pp. 128 f., 261, 266.

ignored, and only a few scholars were half-apologetically pursuing such antiquarian studies. There came a revival with the Oxford Movement and the publication of The Ante-Nicene Library which made many of them available to those whose knowledge of the original Greek and Latin was inadequate; there was also The Library of the Fathers to which Pusey contributed a volume on Justin Martyr (1861).[1] During our period special attention was again directed towards them and there was a renewed interest in their expository work; Swete edited *Theodore of Mopsuestia on St. Paul* (1880) and A. E. Brooke *Origen on St. John* (1896).[2]

The renewed study of the Fathers was inevitably accompanied by the application to their writings of the new historical methods, and they were no longer regarded with a reverence which fell short only of that accorded to the Bible. One very important result of this fresh turning to Patristics was a revived appreciation of Greek theology; an appreciation which would have most important consequences, especially for the doctrine of the Incarnation.[3]

As long ago as 1844 S. R. Maitland's *The Dark Ages* had brought fresh light on a little known and greatly misrepresented period, and he exposed the erroneous nature of a number of constantly repeated opinions concerning it.[4] The later part of the nineteenth century also saw a great revival of interest in this and other parts of the Middle Ages. It was especially active in Germany where political motives were at work, for the establishment of the new German Empire turned men's thoughts back to the Holy Roman Empire and the connexion with Italy—a subject which aroused many acrimonious discussions.

In England good work had been done in this, as in other fields, by Dean Milman who died in 1865. His pioneer, if defective, *History of Latin Christianity*, appeared shortly before our period, three volumes in 1854 and three in 1855. It was Milman, who,

---

[1] Mention must also be made of Harvey's edition of the works of Irenaeus (1857).

[2] See further Swete, *Patristic Study* (1901).   [3] See below, p. 244.

[4] Maitland had been trained as a lawyer and later became Lambeth librarian. He was the grandfather of a still more famous historian, F. W. Maitland.

in the phrase of Gooch, relieved England from Newman's reproach that she possessed no ecclesiastical historian save Gibbon. Milman's history goes down to 1455, but in its treatment of the later years it is thin and superficial. R. W. Church once thought of filling the gap, but he gave himself up to a number of short studies and it was not until just before he became Dean of St. Paul's in 1871 (he was then fifty-six) that he produced *St. Anselm*, his main contribution to ecclesiastical history apart from *The Oxford Movement* (1891).[1] It was left to Mandell Creighton to cover these later years from the great Schism onwards.

Creighton had hoped to bring his *History of the Papacy* down to the Council of Trent, but other calls prevented his doing more than reach the beginnings of the Reformation. The first two volumes appeared in 1882, then came two more dealing with the Renaissance popes in 1887, and a final volume in 1894 which brought the work to 1527. Creighton had been made a bishop in 1891 and his last volume was completed in the few leisure hours which fall to the lot of a diocesan. His work is recognized, even by Roman Catholics, as fair and impartial, but it suffered from the restricted range of material which was available to him.[2] Creighton was a true disciple of Ranke and desired above all to state the facts, with no desire to prove anything, nor had he any philosophy of history. His work is therefore cool and detached. The most attractive parts of it are those concerned with the Renaissance and the growth of art and culture in which Creighton took an especial interest, his first idea, indeed, had been to write a history of Italian Art; the rest deal too much with the surface of things, and for this reason among others he failed to give any convincing explanation of the rise of the Reformation. Creighton refused to

[1] C. C. J. Webb has said of Church that his 'influence . . . upon many contemporaries better known to the public than himself entitles him to a more important place in the history of religious thought in this country than his comparatively small output of theological and religious literature might suggest'. (*Religious Thought in England* etc., p. 101.)

[2] The Vatican archives were not open when he began his work. The first volume of the monumental work of Pastor, the Roman Catholic scholar, which covers the same period and has since gone far beyond it, appeared in 1885 and was translated in 1891.

pass judgment, even on errant popes, a circumstance which aroused the anger of Lord Acton who openly attacked him for what he regarded as a dereliction; to Acton the moral shortcomings of the popes was a tragedy which ought not to be glossed over.

In pursuing the work of ecclesiastical historians down to the Reformation I have perhaps strayed away from our strict subject; to follow it further would involve still more straying and in any case lack of space would prevent it. It may be said of English ecclesiastical historians that, with the exception of Lightfoot (and even he was greater as a historian than as a theologian), they were not interested in theology in the narrower conception of the term.[1] Their main concern was with outward events and spectacles and they exhibited but small desire to trace out the unseen currents of thought or doctrine which lay beneath them and by which they were influenced. This defect does something to justify Newman's charge against Englishmen as a whole, that it is difficult to wind them up to a dogmatic level. One historian there was who possessed the necessary theological qualifications, William Bright, a pupil of Arnold, though of very different views. Bright, who held the chair of Ecclesiastical History at Oxford from 1868 until his death in 1901, was a profound scholar, who, in spite of the extent and exactness of his knowledge, never received the recognition to which he was entitled, probably because he published so little. His greatest work *The Age of the Fathers*, a monument of learning and erudition yet written in an attractive style, was not published until after his death.

Two fields of study, subsidiary to ecclesiastical history, Liturgiology and Canon Law, did not attract much attention until the later part of the period, though Hatch had lectured on both of them at Oxford. Bright had already shown an interest in liturgies, his *Ancient Collects* having appeared in 1857;[2] then in 1881 F. E. Warren published *The Liturgy and Ritual of the Celtic*

---

[1] Their ignorance of theology might occasionally lead them astray. Sanday once wrote that 'Even eminent historians may sometimes err through imperfect knowledge of Greek' (in *J.T.S.*, ii, p. 293).

[2] There are many allusions to the subject in his letters: see B. J. Kidd and P. G. Medd, *Letters and Memoir of W. Bright*, pp. 138 ff.

Church and two years later edited the *Leofric Missal.* Interest in the subject was stimulated by Duchesne's *Origines du Culte Chrétien* (1889) which was translated in 1895, to be followed in 1896 by Brightman's *Liturgies.* About the same time W. H. Frere was turning from general ecclesiastical history to specialize in liturgiology, editing the *Winchester Troper* for the Henry Bradshaw Society in 1894 and in 1898 publishing the first volume of *The Sarum Consuetudinary.* Interest in Canon Law was fostered by the work of Stubbs who advanced the theory that although Roman Canon Law was honoured in the English Church in pre-Reformation days it was not held to be binding. This conclusion was eagerly welcomed by the supporters of the Oxford Movement, so much so that it aroused the comment that they seemed anxious to prove that the Church of England was 'Protestant before the Reformation and Catholic afterwards.' This witticism came from F. W. Maitland. Maitland was not interested in squabbles between rival factions in the Church and had moreover a great admiration for Stubbs; none the less his study of the subject convinced him that the bishop had been mistaken, Roman Canon Law had been fully received in England, although like other legislation it might not always be observed, especially where there was royal interference. Maitland had taken as a basis for his researches Lyndwood's *Provinciale* of 1430.[1]

As in the case of science and philosophy, and, indeed, in conjunction with them, the impact of history with its new methods and point of view created much unsettlement. No longer was history willing to be regarded, as in medieval times, as the handmaid of metaphysics; and many historians, whatever their personal convictions might be, repudiated all theological presuppositions in their work. Others went still further and urged that man must look forward and not backward, and that the modern world demanded an entirely fresh outlook. History

[1] His conclusions first appeared in *The English Historical Review* during 1896 and 1897. They were republished together with other essays in *Roman Canon Law in the Church of England* (1898).

for them was the record of man's progress in time and space, and by it truth was gradually being unveiled. There was no denial that Christianity had introduced fresh spiritual forces into the world, but there was a danger (so it was said) that men might allow their minds to be too greatly influenced by events which had taken place, if, indeed, they had taken place at all, in a distant past and in a simpler and less complex state of society. Here it may be noted that Gore admitted that there was a tendency 'to exaggerate the extent to which the mere evidence of remote facts can compel belief'.[1]

Ideas of this nature, could hardly fail to change, and change drastically, the outlook of those who accepted them, or were influenced by them. For many they seemed to degrade existence to a purely material plane and to deprive it of any underlying spiritual significance. There was a loss of the sense of purpose and meaning in life, and also of the notion that man formed part of an ordered system of things directed by Providence and had his part to play in the realization of the divine plan for the world. This was utterly opposed to the Christian conception of the philosophy of history which saw a gradual development, beginning in the Old Testament and continuing down to the present. Its dominant belief was that 'through time and in the seeming maze of human history a divine, eternal purpose, is being gradually worked out'.[2] This purpose, however, was essentially spiritual, and did not necessarily involve material improvement.

Those who rejected the Christian explanation of history were faced by the problem as to whether the process had any meaning at all, and if it had, whether it was within man's power to discern it. In the ancient world Plato and others had thought that the world went through a perpetual cycle of changes; but such a theory could not satisfy the modern mind. There are historians who claim to be able to discern a pattern behind events; but others confess that they are completely baffled and can trace no evidence

[1] In *Lux Mundi*, p. 247.
[2] Storr, *Development and Divine Purpose*, p. 17. See also my *Divine Providence and Human Destiny*.

of any guiding hand and no principles which might supply a basis
for a philosophy of history.

Connected closely with the notion of the providential guidance
of history is the question as to whether its course reveals any
demonstration of the value of moral ideals, and whether it has
any lessons at all to teach in the sphere of ethics. This is a matter
beset with almost insuperable difficulties. If history is thought to
provide information on the subject it has 'to be interpreted and
evaluated by comparison with a system of values which it is the
task of ethics to construct. But ethics itself must derive its
knowledge of values from the facts of history. . . . We are thus
confronted with a logical circle.'[1]

This question as to the ability of history to provide guidance
on questions of ethics brings up the related question as to whether
it is the right and the duty of the historian to pass moral judgments,
a matter upon which Acton and Creighton, as we have already
noticed, were in sharp disagreement. Perhaps the wisest comment
on the dispute was that of Sidgwick who wrote in a letter to
Creighton in August 1898:

> As regards Acton's view of the historian's duty to pronounce moral
> judgments I am inclined to say that it is not the historian's business
> to be either judge or advocate, but merely to give the reader the
> means of judging . . . but certainly the contemporary moral code,
> so far as this is ascertainable, is a historical fact . . . and it is a part of
> the historian's business to ascertain whatever can be known about
> this.[2]

The general unsettlement produced by the application of the
new historical methods was heightened by the fact that the
results which they claimed to achieve were themselves uncertain
and tentative. Historians might reach conclusions; but these
were always liable to be upset by the discovery of fresh material,
or by a different approach, or by the application of a different
standard of values. Knowledge of the past can never be complete
and all attempts to delineate it are subject to revision. In this

---

[1] E. Troeltsch in *E.R.E.*, Vol. VI, p. 722.   [2] *Henry Sidgwick*, pp. 569 f.

respect history seems to compare very unfavourably with natural science which reveals an ordered and harmonious system, a system, moreover, having every appearance of reliability, though for us it is nothing like so stable as it was for the nineteenth century.

The study of history, although it has illuminated much of the past and provided solutions for some of its problems, must on the whole be regarded as having had negative and even destructive effects. It led to the challenging of traditional theories, such as providential guidance; it exposed the spurious nature of many of the sources upon which earlier conclusions had been based; and in general may not unjustly be described as 'a school for scepticism and caution [which] yields but little real information, and more than anything else brings home to man the limitations of his knowledge'.[1] The application of its methods to theology has been followed by consequences as serious as those in any other sphere, and not least in the matter of biblical studies.

[1] Troeltsch in *op. cit.*, Vol. vi, p. 718.

Chapter Five

BIBLICAL STUDIES:
THE UNIVERSITIES

To apply the new methods of historical criticism to the biblical records was for the theologian a matter of urgency, since the gap between theology and the outlook made necessary by the growth of knowledge could never be spanned so long as untenable theories of the inspiration and authority of the Bible continued to prevail. Theology must be built up afresh on a solid basis of ascertained facts. Hence the true Fundamentalist is not he who refuses to allow any examination of the foundations of the faith, but he who strives to make those foundations as secure and sound as possible, even if the process involves the abandonment of some cherished beliefs.

Before going further it will be well to recall that the Bible itself makes no claim to be 'history'. In spite of the common usage the Old Testament has no 'historical' books, for the Jews ranked Samuel and Kings among the 'prophets'; thus declaring that their purpose was primarily religious, to tell of God's dealings with the forefathers of the race—as a consequence they were apt, like the medieval chroniclers, to include anything that went for edifying, without too strict an inquiry into its genuineness. Hence, too, their neglect of the political and secular activities of the various monarchs; the outstanding illustration of this is the case of Omri, one of the most important of Israelite kings, whose reign is dismissed with only a brief mention. The same principle is to be found in the writers of the gospels, for though they are presented in a historical form, their primary function is to declare a message.

But if the Bible did not claim to be history yet like every other ancient record or collection of records it had perforce to submit to an intense scrutiny; and it may be noted that in no other field of study have the sources been so thoroughly investigated, even the labours of classical scholars on their texts are hardly comparable. It was only by undergoing such treatment that the Bible could preserve its influence, and even its right to respect and continued veneration. The scholars who undertook the task were, it need scarcely be pointed out, inspired by no hostile or destructive spirit, save in a few instances; on the contrary many of them, especially in England, were sincere believers. In Germany Dr. Schechter thought that much of the criticism of the Old Testament was a product of anti-Semitism,[1] but this is surely an exaggeration.

What, it may be asked, were the principles which underlay the application of critical methods to the Bible? In the first place, I would suggest, scholars endeavoured to discover what the records actually said, and what they meant to the original hearers or readers. The application of this principle involved the rejection of much traditional interpretation, because all too frequently it was out of relation to the real meaning of the passages expounded. This was especially the case with the various allegorical and fanciful expositions which had been read into the text. The record must be permitted to speak for itself. But in listening to its voice allowance had to be made for the very different methods of thought and utterance current at the time and in the place of origin of the various documents. Even today the mind of the Oriental works in ways which are very diverse from those usual among Europeans, being uninterested in exactness of detail, and framing statements which are not intended to be taken literally. So had it been with the biblical writers and with those who later attempted to interpret them. Their standard of historical accuracy, like their science, was that of the age and country in which the documents were composed.

In spite of many merits and real sincerity of purpose the work

[1] Quoted in *The People and the Book*, p. 406.

of critics in our period suffered from a number of defects, some
of them of a grave nature. As with other contemporary historians
they were prone to lose themselves in the study of details and the
establishment of minute facts. Their whole line of approach was
too analytical, for they forgot that the Scriptures constituted
'a whole which had been felt as a whole by innumerable minds
for many centuries'.[1] They were, moreover, often blind to the
deeper, underlying meaning of much of the literature with which
they dealt. Some critics, especially in Germany, showed a lack
of reverence in their attitude and seemed unaware that they were
concerned with sacred matters. The wise dictum of Bengel, that
before attempting to interpret the New Testament a man must
ask himself if he had the right to do so, was forgotten or ignored.
This accounts for the numerous facile, and often self-contradictory,
theories which were put forward, and for the ready and rationalizing explanations of apparent difficulties.

The critical study of the Bible in England, although much
valuable work was done by scholars elsewhere, was mainly
carried on in the universities, and above all at Oxford and
Cambridge. The Universities Act of 1877 had left the official
teaching of theology in both them and their component colleges
as a monopoly of the Church of England; but the admission of
Nonconformists soon led to the foundation of theological
colleges in university cities,[2] and from them as well as from
Nonconformists resident in the universities a new and not
unimportant stream of scholarship, which had hitherto often
been separate, was drawn into the general flow.

The chief credit for the advance of biblical studies in England,
especially as regards the New Testament, must be given to what
is sometimes called the Cambridge school.[3] This is generously

---

[1] F. D. Maurice, *The Kingdom of Christ*, Vol. II, p. 145. (Everyman ed.)

[2] Mansfield College was transferred from Spring Hill to Oxford in 1886 and
Manchester College in 1893. At Cambridge things were more delayed and
Westminster College was not founded until 1899.

[3] It must not, however, be forgotten that the tentative beginnings of New
Testament criticism on modern lines go back to Stanley and Jowett whose
commentaries were published in 1855.

admitted by Hastings Rashdall, an Oxford man, who says that
its members 'raised English theology . . . from a condition of
intellectual nullity up to the level of the best German work,
while they infused into it a characteristic English spirit of caution
and sobriety'.[1] But to speak of a Cambridge school is perhaps a
misnomer, for Cambridge, as Inge has said, 'had generally
produced men rather than movements'.[2]

It is interesting to notice that it was the theologians who first
made use of the new historical methods in Cambridge, and in his
inaugural lecture in 1884 it was to them, rather than to the
professed historians, that Creighton turned for examples of the
way in which history should be studied.[3]

Theological studies in Cambridge during our period were
dominated by three great figures: Lightfoot, who after having
previously taught theology there, held professorships from 1861
to 1879; Westcott, who was Regius Professor from 1870 to 1890
when he succeeded Lightfoot, who had been his pupil, as Bishop
of Durham; and Hort, who held professorships from 1878 until
his death in 1892.

Lightfoot has been declared to be 'the greatest interpreter of
the New Testament in our day'.[4] Handley Moule, who worked
under him, specified as his greatest merits 'unfailing thoroughness
of knowledge and unsurpassable clearness of exposition and
instruction'.[5] But in spite of these opinions and of his numerous
and excellent commentaries Lightfoot was fundamentally a
historian[6] rather than a theologian in the more restricted sense.

[1] *Principles and Precepts*, p. 164.

[2] *The Platonic Tradition in English Religious Thought*, p. 40. Cf. Warre Cornish,
The History of the English Church in the Nineteenth Century, Vol. II, p. 209. 'The
temper of Cambridge is cooler than that of Oxford, and unfavourable to hero-
worship. The tone of thought is that which is bred of study, not emotion.'

[3] See *Historical Lectures and Addresses*, p. 2. 'The traditions of theological
learning have been thoroughly leavened by the historical spirit. . . . Theology
has become historical, and does not demand that history should become
theological.'   [4] W. Temple, *Life of Bishop Percival*, p. 155.

[5] Harford and Macdonald, *Bishop Handley Moule*, p. 19.

[6] Acton once spoke of 'our three Cambridge historians, Maine, Lightfoot,
Maitland', each a pioneer in his own special department of research and each a
name of significance for universal history. See Fisher, *F. W. Maitland*, p. 174.

9

Speculation as such only interested him from the historical angle and his knowledge of philosophy was limited; even doctrine, although he was acquainted with what had been written on the subject, did not greatly attract him. Hort considered that his doctrinal comments in *Galatians* belonged 'far too much to the mere Protestant version of St. Paul's thoughts, however Christianized and rationalized', and concluded that his 'mental interests lay almost exclusively in concrete facts and written words. He never seemed to care for any generalization.' 'No one', he added, 'can with advantage be everything; and he gained much by what was surely a limitation.'[1] Lightfoot's finest achievement was his edition of *The Apostolic Fathers* which Cuthbert Turner declared to be 'the greatest contribution to patristic learning in the last two centuries'. Harnack, it may be noted, was equally impressed by the work.

In 1868 Lightfoot was offered the bishopric of Lichfield, and though urged by those whom he consulted to accept it he felt that his work in Cambridge was too important to be given up. Then, eleven years later, came the offer of Durham, and after long consideration he finally accepted it. Hort concurred with this decision; but others regretted it. Dean Church had urged upon him 'the interests, not so much of knowledge, but of study, and for the value in such days as ours of a life professedly devoted to these ends, contented to fulfil them with the enthusiasm, the conscientiousness, the unselfish independence with which all great ends must be followed'.[2] In spite of the great work which Lightfoot did at Durham, and he himself did not doubt that his choice had been right,[3] the cause of learning suffered grievously, and it might have been well had he allowed Church to persuade him to remain at Cambridge and St. Paul's. Lightfoot, however, continued to carry on his theological and historical work, often in his early days at Durham putting in two or three hours before breakfast. This habit he was compelled to abandon when it became obvious that the strain was more than his health could

[1] *Life*, Vol. II, pp. 79 and 410f.   [2] *Life*, p. 326.
[3] *Ordination Addresses*, pp. 194–6.

bear, and there can be but little doubt that his life was shortened by such labours. In any case his output was severely restricted by his other and more pressing duties.[1]

As a pure scholar Westcott was probably the least great of the three, and the long years he had spent at Harrow, before his return to Cambridge, had perhaps made his approach to Greek too classical. His work will scarcely endure as will that of Lightfoot, and he lacked the comprehensive learning and philosophical breadth of mind which distinguished Hort. At the same time it is probable that had he given himself more to philosophical studies he might have developed that side of his teaching. The essays collected in *The Religious Thought of the West* reveal a genuine gift for that line of inquiry and much in them still has living worth. In critical ability Westcott was also a little deficient, being apt to be influenced by subjective considerations and to embark on over-subtle explanations.[2] Dale, who held him in much reverence, thought that he was reluctant to give any exact definition of his ideas.[3]

In spite of these defects, Westcott in his day exercised a much more widespread influence than either Lightfoot or Hort. This was a consequence of his numerous interests apart from scholarship; for he was deeply concerned over the social problem and over the expansion of the Church in other lands. Westcott must be regarded primarily as a religious teacher and guide, rather than as an investigator of truth, and in his studies he always seemed to see the past by the light of the present and its needs; but by his emphasis on the teaching of the fourth gospel and his knowledge of the Greek Fathers he helped to change the direction of theological thought in this country. Westcott was the mystic and prophet of the little band, and though men might fail to

[1] R. W. Dale, writing in 1883, said, 'If he had not been made a bishop we should have had two or three great books from him by this time. His silence gives us Congregationalists another argument against Episcopacy.' (*Life*, p. 524.)

[2] Sanday described Westcott's early volume *An Introduction to the Study of the Gospels* as 'calling for criticism all the more because it is so full of ingenuities'.

[3] *Life*, p. 673.

understand many of his utterances they could not fail to be impressed by his spirituality and Christian zeal. The essence of his teaching is to be found in sermons delivered in Westminster Abbey during August 1885 and January 1886, later published under the title of *Christus Consummator*.

Hort was more liberal and more 'sacerdotal' in his views than the other two; and he outranged them in the extent of his knowledge, for he was a competent student of natural science and had a philosophical mind. Hence he was more daring in speculation and less bound by tradition. 'To identify [truth and orthodoxy]', he said, 'seems to me to involve the practical loss of either . . . most orthodox criticism in England is reckless of truth and unjust to the authors of other criticism.'[1] Above all else he regarded himself as a seeker, and even hesitated to accept the Hulsean Lectureship because of 'a growing dislike of the position of a professed advocate'.[2] New truth, even if it seemed to 'be acting to the injury of the faith' was to be welcomed.[3] It would be a grave mistake, however, to imagine that he had any doubts concerning the truth of Christianity. When, after his death, *The Way, the Truth, the Life* was at last published it demonstrated 'how openness of mind could co-exist with an unshaken grasp of central truths', and in it he presented a 'large and progressive faith which seemed as far removed from ordinary dogmatism as dogmatism itself from religion'.[4] Although much of the work done by Hort was 'concerned with settling details of linguistic or historical accuracy . . . his thoughts were ever set on the deeper questions which lay behind them'.[5]

If Hort did not possess those gifts of organization and administration which enabled his colleagues to oversee in succession the great diocese of Durham his devotion to scholarship was even greater than theirs. He looked upon 'the steadfast and persistent pursuit of truth (as) a moral and spiritual discipline', involving 'a life of

[1] *Life*, Vol. II, p. 147.
[2] *Op. cit.*, Vol. II, pp. 52 f.
[3] *Op. cit.*, Vol. II, p. 156.
[4] *Op. cit.*, Vol. II, pp. 371 and 373.
[5] *Op. cit.*, Vol. II, p. 53 (the opinion of Westcott).

vanities abased and ambitions foresworn'.[1] Unfortunately his work as a teacher was handicapped by a shyness which made personal intercourse difficult, as well as by a temperament which shrank from putting his thoughts into written form. Those thoughts lay very deep and could be brought to the surface only with difficulty, if at all. When they emerged their value was in proportion to the profundity of their source.

Although the three friends worked together in perfect harmony they were not entirely of the same outlook in matters ecclesiastical. Lightfoot and Westcott would nowadays, I suppose, be classed as Liberal Evangelicals, though Westcott was critical of the Evangelicalism of his own day; Hort, however, was a 'staunch sacerdotalist' and shocked his friends by expressing his conviction that Protestantism was only 'parenthetical and temporary'.[2] This difference of standpoint may have been among the reasons why they produced no systematic theology, though it had been the earnest desire of Westcott to crown his own work by a treatise on Christian doctrine for which he collected voluminous notes. *The Gospel of Life* was, however, a partial fulfilment of his ambition.

When Westcott resigned the Regius Professorship in 1890 on his appointment to Durham he was succeeded rather unexpectedly by H. B. Swete. Commenting on the appointment W. Bright wrote in 1893:

> while Westcott was the dominant Cambridge teacher, I never... could help feeling that he was an Alexandrian Father revived under modern conditions...Westcott, like Clement of Alexandria, seemed to me to take his reader through a golden Platonic mist. The present Regius Professor of Divinity ... will revive doctrinal theology where its place has been too much occupied by historical criticism.[3]

Although Swete, like Benaiah, the son of Jehoiada, 'attained not to the three' (2 Sam. 23:23), he accomplished a very important

---

[1] *The Way, the Truth, the Life*, pp. 93 f.
[2] *Life*, Vol. II, p. 86 (cf. Vol. I, p. 400 and Vol. II, p. 31).   [3] *Letters*, pp. 347 f.

work by steering Cambridge theology through a perilous time of transition. By temperament and experience he was well fitted for this task, for though in his younger days he had been a bigoted opponent of the new views and had said of Colenso: 'The axe raised by episcopal hands to fell the Pentateuch is seen to be laid at the root of Christianity',[1] by a gradual and almost unconscious process he had come to hold a more critical position. Thus he was able to preserve Cambridge theology from indulging in too hazardous ventures. Swete himself wrote many volumes, and did valuable pioneer work on the text of the Septuagint of which he produced an edition (1887–94); but his most striking contribution is to be found in a gift for organizing and encouraging the work of others. It was he who was largely responsible for the foundation of *The Journal of Theological Studies*, as well as for the Central Society for Sacred Study.

Westcott once wrote to Dr. Dale 'I am not a patient reader of commentaries',[2] a surprising statement in view of the large number of commentaries produced by him and his friends. Sanday, addressing a Cambridge audience, described it as 'the home of commentaries'.[3] This form of scholarship is more liable than most others to become obsolete with the growth of new methods and the discovery of fresh material, none the less a great deal of their work is still of considerable value when the necessary modifications have been made. It is often thought that the Cambridge school was prone to become over-absorbed in details of language and style; but though its adherents gave close attention to such matters they never lost sight of the real end of theological study, or forgot that spiritual things are spiritually discerned. For Hort 'the attainment of truth in matters of historical or linguistic fact was . . . always not an end but a means', and he was especially anxious 'not to drown literature and history in a textual flood'.[4] Westcott, writing from Harrow

---

[1] *Henry Barclay Swete: A Remembrance*, p. 103. This volume contains an appreciation of Dr. Swete's contribution to theological learning from the pen of Dr. Bethune-Baker.

[2] *Life of Dale*, p. 683.

[3] *The Life of Christ in Recent Research*, p. 40.   [4] *Life*, Vol. II, pp. 53 f., 421.

in 1864, could declare that '"Grammar" I simply hate.'[1] The deeply reverent and dependent spirit in which they approached their work provides an admirable example, and perhaps one that is needed, to their successors. Lightfoot held that the only effective way of knowing the Greek Testament was by prayer, and Scott Holland said of Westcott, 'He cannot venture to criticize a verse without a prayer.'[2] But their fundamental principle was to insist that all criticism must be based upon the best available text and that words must be given their proper meaning and value. This aspect of their work has been well summed up by Warre Cornish: 'If the Cambridge school of theology has helped both religion and science by honest dealing with words, by inquiring, that is, what words mean, not what they may be made to mean, Westcott, Lightfoot and Hort deserve grateful mention in the history of the Church of England.'[3]

Turning to the sister university we find an Oxford which no longer breathed the last enchantments of the Middle Ages, an Oxford which had, indeed, been reformed, but not without loss in the process; so at least the older generation thought. A spirit of pessimism seemed to prevail, and Frederick Temple, on a visit in 1870, was struck 'by the pervading melancholy of the older men'.[4] Max Müller writing in 1875, felt that the university had sadly deteriorated in the twenty-five years he had known it; though he was not without hope for the future as he found much good material among the younger men.[5] A similar unfavourable judgment was passed by another resident, a distinguished Balliol man, who in 1879 was reported to Hort as saying 'What would I give to have Lightfoot and Westcott at Oxford! And yet no, for they would not find the material to work on; they can only speak to patient workers, while we have only brilliant talkers.' He also declared that many were giving up Christianity altogether in a reaction from the sacerdotal tone of the dominant school.[6]

One of the outstanding figures at Oxford during the greater

[1] *Life*, Vol. I, p. 285.   [2] *Henry Scott Holland*, p. 59.
[3] *History of the English Church in the Nineteenth Century*, Vol. II, p. 210.
[4] *Memoirs*, p. 187.   [5] *Life*, Vol. I, p. 487.   [6] *Life of Hort*, Vol. II, pp. 276f.

part of our period was Benjamin Jowett whose long and influential life came to an end in 1893. Jowett, in spite of much outward success, is rather a pathetic figure, for he was cramped by his peculiar temperament and limited outlook. He seems never to have resolved the conflict between his critical instincts and his religious feeling. Leslie Stephen, with his incisive wit, said of him, 'He stood at the parting of many ways and wrote "No thoroughfare" upon them all.' Asquith who was at Balliol from 1870 to 1874 considered that he 'never at any time had anything definite to teach, being always an eclectic with a horror of one-sidedness'. He also said that in his time Jowett 'was already looked upon by the more advanced spirits, as an extinct volcano, and even a bit of a reactionary. He certainly viewed with uneasiness Green's militant and contagious propaganda.'[1]

If the more advanced liberals regarded Jowett as behind the times he himself was deeply disappointed by the effects of the spread of liberal views. At the end of his life, when trying to persuade Cosmo Gordon Lang to undertake theological teaching at Balliol, he confessed, 'We don't seem able now to inspire the young men. *We may have truth . . . but we have no fire.*'[2] These factors, however, must not lead to a disparagement of Jowett and the influence which he exercised in Oxford and elsewhere through his pupils. He certainly had a gift for discerning the significance of things and anticipated many later developments. In one matter, however, he was unfortunate in his forecast, for he doubted whether any considerable light would ever be thrown on the New Testament from inquiry into language.[3] But this judgment was made before 1860, and no one then imagined the treasures which awaited discovery in the sands of Egypt; so there was some excuse. As many regard Jowett as a kind of iconoclast it must not be forgotten that he had a profound realization of the needs of ordinary Christians and was ever anxious to avoid causing offence to 'Christ's little ones.'

[1] Spender and Asquith, *Life of Lord Oxford and Asquith*, Vol. I, p. 37.
[2] J. G. Lockhart, *Cosmo Gordon Lang*, p. 101.
[3] *Essays and Reviews*, p. 477.

Jowett's work as a theologian was handicapped by an inadequate knowledge of what had been done by previous writers and his learning was somewhat superficial. His methods of translation were criticized by both Lightfoot and Hort, but when this was brought up against him during the controversy over the Greek Professorship, Hort with the full concurrence of Lightfoot hastened to explain that what they had criticized was not ignorance, but what they regarded as erroneous opinions.[1]

To Jowett's credit must be placed the fact that he was a stimulating force urging men to think freely and fearlessly for themselves, and that he stood determinedly for complete freedom in research and interpretation when such a stand involved risk and unpopularity. At the same time he was ever insistent that theories should not be allowed to outrun facts. Gore, who had been his pupil, always kept a portrait of Jowett in his study; 'When I feel I am stressing an argument too far,' he once wrote, 'I look at Jowett and he pulls me up.'[2]

The departure of Stanley to the deanery of Westminster in 1864 removed from Oxford another stimulating and inspiring force. Stanley had an amazingly rich fund of information and wrote on many different subjects, the Old and New Testaments, and various epochs of Church History among others, and had a tenacious if not always quite accurate memory. His weakness was that he skimmed over the surface of things and never went really deep. 'He lacked the resolute, determined concentration on the mastery of a single branch of knowledge, the sustained attention to any one line of thought, which are essential to intellectual leaders.'[3] But Stanley inspired others to venture along paths which he pointed out, even if by temperament and

---

[1] *Life of Hort*, Vol. I, p. 375. His translations of Plato have not escaped criticism. Ingram Bywater records that Swinburne on a visit to Jowett was asked by the latter to look through his first version of the *Symposium*. Swinburne managed to detect several errors which he announced by crying out 'Another howler, Master!' Jowett with the patience which he always exhibited to Swinburne, merely replied 'Thank you, Algernon, thank you!' See Edmund Gosse, *Algernon Charles Swinburne*, pp. 212 f.

[2] *Life*, pp. 38 f.

[3] R. E. Prothero, *Life and Letters of Dean Stanley*, Vol. II, p. 20.

circumstances he was prevented in sharing their journey. It was his influence which inspired J. R. Green, who wrote to him in 1863, 'I have often longed, in the midst of my work, historical and clerical, to tell you how wholly that work and the happiness that comes of it, is owing to you.'[1] In addition to stimulating others to undertake research, Stanley made widely known the conclusions of scholars and popularized knowledge in all kinds of quarters. It has been said that he did more than anyone else to make the Bible a reality in English homes.

Theology at Oxford, however, was probably much more alive than some of the older men, whose faces still turned in longing to a vanished past, were willing to recognize. At any rate an honours school was established at Oxford in 1868, with the first examination in 1870; whereas the first Cambridge theological tripos examination was not held until four years later.

It was in 1867 that Edwin Hatch, after a period of teaching in Canada, returned to Oxford as Vice-Principal of St. Mary's Hall. Like Westcott, Lightfoot and Benson he had been a pupil of Prince Lee at King Edward's School, Birmingham. Hatch was a man of decided character and originality of thought; he insisted on making up his own mind on any question quite apart from what had been held by his predecessors, and Sanday judged rightly when he said that he was 'bolder and more disinterested than even the great Cambridge trio'.[2] Hatch was the author of many writings; his *Essays in Biblical Greek* appeared in 1889, but the *Concordance on the Septuagint* (in conjunction with Redpath) not until after his death. His fame, however, at least for his own day, rested on his two series of Lectures, the Bamptons in 1880 and the Hibberts in 1888. The Bampton Lectures *On the Organization of the Christian Church* provoked much discussion and roused considerable controversy; but it was the Hibbert Lectures on *The Influence of Greek Ideas and Usages upon the Christian Church*

---

[1] *Letters of J. R. Green*, p. 17.

[2] In a paper read at a conference of Modern Churchmen. See *The Modern Churchman*, Vol. x, pp. 378 ff.

(published after his death and edited by A. M. Fairbairn) which had the greatest influence and received the widest notice. His thesis was that the original Gospel, which for him was the Sermon on the Mount, had been changed from a way of life into a creed under the pressure of Greek philosophical and theological conceptions. He put forth two alternative ways of regarding these modifications. If Greek elements are alien to primitive Christianity they should be eliminated; if, however, they are a rightful development it follows that they themselves cannot be regarded as immune from modification in the light of subsequent developments. The weak points in Hatch's thesis were that he rather oddly took no account of the actual theological developments within the New Testament itself, and that he laid far too great an emphasis on the influence of Greek ideas. 'What the Church borrowed from Greek thought was her terminology, not the substance of her creed',[1] and even so the Church infused her own meaning into the terms which she borrowed.

Hatch's breadth of learning and complete fairness were acknowledged, even by those who could not agree with his conclusions, and his comparatively early death, brought on by overwork, was widely lamented. As Hort has said: 'So much remained for him to do, that no one else can do so well.'[2] Incidentally he had the distinction of being one of the few English theologians who exercised influence in Germany. In the preface to the English translation of the third edition of *The History of Dogma* (1894) Harnack referred to his work as providing 'the most ample proof for the conception of the early history of dogma which is set forth in the following pages'.[3]

When the Oriel Professorship was established in 1883 its first holder was John Wordsworth. Wordsworth had thought of going to Cambridge, in accordance with family tradition, and seemed never quite at home in the atmosphere of Oxford. While teaching at Harrow he came under the influence of Westcott; but though he admired Westcott's scholarship he was critical of his

---

[1] Gore, *The Incarnation*, p. 101.   [2] *Life of Hort*, Vol. II, p. 408.
[3] Harnack translated the Bampton Lectures into German in 1883.

exegesis. He found in Lightfoot a more congenial teacher and established a life-long friendship with him. After his return to Oxford he tried to get the Cambridge school better appreciated there, but he himself gradually drew away from them, though in the earlier stages of his work on the Vulgate he was glad of Westcott's assistance. Wordsworth was an able classical scholar and as a young man had a knowledge of early Latin which was unrivalled in this country. He might have become another Casaubon, but instead he chose to dedicate his powers to biblical studies, and in conjunction with H. J. White he undertook the great edition of the text of the Vulgate New Testament which is known by their names.[1]

The outstanding figure in Oxford theology during the closing years of our period was William Sanday, who was appointed to the Dean Ireland Professorship in 1882, moving on to the Lady Margaret chair in 1895. Sanday had a wide knowledge of the work of German and American scholars, but was less informed of what was being done in France. Philosophy and dogmatics lay rather outside his interests, which may account for his being occasionally led away by new ideas whose implications he had not fully realized. Cautious by nature his advance in critical views, or perhaps in their proclamation, was very gradual; at one time, for example, he had accepted the truth of miracles which he would later deny.[2] One of his great merits, as with Swete in Cambridge, was the encouragement of younger men whom he gathered round him in seminars, a method not then very common in England. Most of his writings appeared in the twentieth century, but the Bampton Lectures on *Inspiration* in 1893 made him well known, whilst the article on the life of Christ which he contributed to Hastings's *Dictionary of the Bible* (later republished as a separate volume) is still one of the best attempts to deal with the subject.

The most important contribution to theology, however,

[1] See E. W. Watson, *The Life of Bishop John Wordsworth*, Ch. VII.
[2] He gave an interesting and enlightening account of his progress in *Divine Overruling* (1920).

which came from Oxford, was the production of the *Lux Mundi* group, of which Gore was the leader. As a boy at Harrow he had been greatly inspired by Westcott, though this influence affected his practical work, such as social reform, rather than his theology. His training under Jowett, to which reference has been made, caused him to be suspicious of anything like mere conjecture, none the less he ever aimed at achieving definite results, even if they were incomplete.

Lux Mundi owed much of its importance and influence to the unity of outlook of the various contributors; for it was the outcome of a much longer preparation and of a closer consultation than is common in such joint enterprises; and each essay illustrated, from a different angle, the underlying theme of the whole volume. The essayists were a band of earnest thinkers who had long been striving to reconcile the claims of reason and of revelation; thinkers who had a strongly dogmatic faith and were entirely loyal to the creeds. Their object was to demonstrate that the new knowledge was capable of being combined with the essentials of traditional Christianity, and so to interpret the faith as to make it acceptable to their contemporaries. The volume had an immense success and went through fourteen editions before the end of the century; the tenth edition, which appeared in 1890, contained a new and important preface.

In spite of the avowed aims of its contributors when *Lux Mundi* appeared in 1889 it met with a very varied reception. To the older generation, of whom Liddon was typical, it came as a grievous shock. Liddon ought to have been prepared to meet it, for he had written to Scott Holland in 1884: 'I have feared sometimes that the younger Churchmanship of Oxford was undergoing a silent but very serious change through its eagerness to meet modern difficulties and its facile adoption of new intellectual methods, without fully considering the uses to which they might be put by others.'[1] The outcry, however, was

---

[1] S. Paget, *Henry Scott Holland*, p. 112. Liddon spoke of it with scorn, as proclaiming 'the inspiration of inveracity'. He never recovered from the shock, which probably hastened his end, for he died on 9 September 1890.

nothing like so vehement as that which had greeted *Essays and Reviews* a generation earlier; but even so there were those who demanded that the contributors should resign their Orders. The latter, it may be remarked, were equally surprised at the outbreak of hostility.[1] Scott Holland wrote: 'We seemed to ourselves to have been saying these things for years; and to have heard everybody else saying them. Now suddenly we find it all spoken of as a bomb.'[2] Though naturally distressed by the pain which they were causing to men to whom they had owed so much and whom they respected so highly, the contributors felt that no withdrawal from the position they had taken up was possible. The outcry, fierce as it was for a time, soon passed, and the coming century saw many of the so-called heretics occupying high places in the Church and university.

If the older Anglo-Catholics were alarmed by *Lux Mundi*, to liberal theologians it was a disappointment. 'It has a more friendly and Christian tone', wrote Jowett, 'than High Church theology used to have, but it is the same old haze and maze—no nearer approach of religion whether to morality or to historical truth.'[3] In spite of this and similar criticisms *Lux Mundi* undoubtedly did much to spread moderately critical views among Churchmen, especially among those of the Anglo-Catholic school, and to give them countenance and a certain respectability. It also helped some of the younger generation to whom the Christianity of Liddon was 'impossible to believe', and that of Jowett 'not worth believing',[4] to consider once again the claims of the historic faith; and that was no small achievement.

The growth of interest in biblical studies during our period is reflected in the immense production of literature dealing with the subject. Smith's *Dictionary of the Bible* had begun to appear in 1859, but the end of the century saw the publication of similar works of a more adequate nature. The first volume of Hastings's

[1] Before publishing his essay Gore had consulted Dean Church who advised him to go ahead, though in a review in *The Guardian* he later criticized it for overstatement. *Life of Gore*, pp. 104 f.
[2] S. Paget, *op. cit.*, p. 281.   [3] *Life*, Vol. II, p. 377.   [4] *Life of Gore*, p. 119.

Dictionary of the Bible came out in 1898, to be completed six years later. It represents a somewhat cautious and conservative point of view, which cannot be said of its contemporary, *The Encyclopaedia Biblica* (1899–1903).[1] The Old Testament articles in the latter were many of them marred by the eccentricities of Cheyne, who was one of the editors, and those on the New by the drastic criticism of certain continental scholars, such as Schmiedel and Van Manen. Their theories, it may be stated, have since been decisively rejected by later critics.

The two older universities inaugurated series of special studies; the *Studia Biblica* at Oxford in 1885, and the more ambitious Cambridge *Texts and Studies* six years later. Periodicals dealing with theological subjects also began to appear such as *The Expositor*, *The Expository Times*, and in 1899 *The Journal of Theological Studies*. Biblical scholars could no longer be content with the space allocated to their studies in classical and other journals.

The most striking evidence for the renewed interest in the study of the Bible, however, is to be found in the numerous series of commentaries which began to be poured forth. One of the earliest was undertaken at the suggestion of the Speaker, and to it Westcott contributed the volume on *St. John* which came out in 1880. Dr. Pusey had projected a series in defence of traditional views, in which he hoped Liddon would co-operate; but nothing came of it save his own *Minor Prophets* (1860–77) which though exhibiting wide learning and spiritual insight are quite devoid of critical judgment.

Dr. Smith had intended supplementing his *Dictionary of the Bible* by a series of commentaries, but the project was abandoned in 1863. In the meantime Macmillans had already approached Westcott, who was to have taken part in Smith's proposed venture, suggesting the publication of commentaries on the books of the Greek New Testament. Eventually he, with Lightfoot

---

[1] Dedicated to W. Robertson Smith who had discussed the scheme with J. B. Black but did not live to see it get under way. His place was taken by Cheyne.

and Hort, agreed to take part in the scheme.[1] The Johannine literature, including the *Revelation* was assigned to Westcott, the Pauline epistles and Hebrews to Lightfoot; the Synoptic gospels, *Acts*, and the catholic epistles (except those of John) to Hort. The full scheme was never carried out, though Westcott did his share and *Hebrews* in addition, and Lightfoot wrote on most of the Pauline epistles; Hort, however, failed to make any contribution; though incomplete, but valuable, comments on part of *James*, 1 *Peter*, and *Rev.* 1–3 were published after his death. Benson, who had not been among those originally selected, wrote on the *Revelation*.

Less elaborate series were the *Cambridge Greek Testament* and the *Cambridge Bible for Schools and Colleges*. A *New Testament Commentary for English Readers* edited by Ellicott was published in three volumes in 1878–9 and was followed by another on the Old Testament in five volumes during 1882 to 1884. These were combined into *The Complete Bible Commentary for English Readers* in seven volumes (1897). A very popular series was the *Expositor's Bible* which, as the title suggests, was homiletic rather than critical; it included four outstanding volumes by G. Adam Smith, two on *Isaiah* (1888–90) and two on *The Twelve Prophets* (1896–8). *The Expositor* was also responsible for a commentary on the Greek Testament in four volumes. Towards the end of our period the International Critical Commentary with a very high standard of scholarship began to appear. Two notable volumes from English scholars were published in 1895: Driver's *Deuteronomy* and *Romans* by Sanday and Headlam. Another series based on the Revised Version and intended to bring the results of modern criticism to the notice of the general reader was the Westminster Commentaries edited by Walter Lock. Gibson's *Job* appeared in 1899 and Rackham's *Acts* in 1901.

For Introductions to the Bible English scholars had mainly to rely on the works of French and German writers, some of which were translated. Then came Driver's *Introduction to the Literature*

[1] See *Life of Hort*, Vol. 1, pp. 371f., 417f., and *Life of Westcott*, Vol. 1, pp. 205ff.

of the Old Testament (1891) to which nothing quite comparable on the New was produced in our period, though Samuel Davidson was useful and there was also, from Dublin, the valuable work of Salmon. Concordances were also making an appearance. Hatch and Redpath to the Septuagint, and Moulton and Geden to the Greek New Testament both came out in 1897. Thayer-Grimm's *Lexicon of the New Testament* had appeared in 1888; but students of Hebrew had still to be content with translations of Gesenius, though a new lexicon based on Gesenius, the well-known Brown, Driver and Briggs, was already in hand; the first part was published in 1891, but it was not completed until 1906.

Chapter Six

THE OLD TESTAMENT

TURNING to a more detailed examination of the work done in biblical studies we naturally begin with the Old Testament.[1] At the opening of the period the state of the study was one of much confusion, as the new theories, introduced from the Continent, and their implications had not yet been fully grasped; but gradually, as these won considerable acceptance, a more stable position was attained though much difference of opinion on details still remained.

Alarm amongst the upholders of traditional views went back to the publication in 1830 of Milman's *History of the Jews* in which he treated the subject as he would have treated the history of any other Oriental people; his calling Abraham a 'sheikh' seems to have been particularly a cause of offence. It was not, however, until 1862 when the first of Bishop Colenso's studies on *The Pentateuch and Joshua* appeared that alarm became acute. Colenso was a mathematician, and he was worried by the many inconsistencies which he found in the figures of the Pentateuch; he confessed that while he was prepared to accept a miracle, he could not accept a false arithmetical statement. Colenso unfortunately adopted a very unconciliatory attitude and the extreme novelty of his ideas, to those at least who were in ignorance of what was being done by continental scholars, naturally aroused much opposition and even some derision. Samuel Wilberforce, with his ready wit, explained that, of course, the mathematical bishop

[1] See Cheyne, *Founders of Old Testament Criticism*, Pfleiderer, *Development of Theology in the Nineteenth Century*, pp. 252 ff., Gooch, *History and Historians in the Nineteenth Century*, pp. 522–34, and S. A. Cook, 'The Present State of Old Testament Research' in *Cambridge Biblical Essays*, pp. 53 ff.

could not forgive Moses for having ventured to write the Book of Numbers. Some of his criticisms have been accepted by later scholars, but much of his work was fanciful and lacking in positive value. None the less it served to draw attention to difficulties, obvious as they now seem, which had been passed over or explained away.

It was also in 1862 that Stanley published the first volume of his *History of the Jewish Church*, a work which 'contained little that was original and nothing that was profound', though good use was made of his knowledge of the Holy Land. Stanley's point of view was very similar to that of Ewald whose *History of Israel* he later translated (1869–80). The influence which Ewald exerted on Stanley was typical of the general development of Old Testament studies in England, and in view of the great importance of the work done in Germany and elsewhere it will be an advantage briefly to review it before continuing further.

By later standards Ewald was conservative in his views, and the long dominance which he exercised tended to check further progress, especially in regard to Pentateuchal criticism. Wellhausen, who had been his pupil, termed him *der grosse Aufhälter* who by his authority retarded the growth of a true interpretation of Jewish history. Ewald's understanding of the prophets was more profound than that of any of his contemporaries, but he made no attempt to compare the different documents of the Pentateuch and the laws contained in them with the data available in the historical and prophetic books. It would be just to say that he was primarily a student of languages (his contributions to philology were weighty) rather than a theologian or a historian. The motives which inspired his writings were largely apologetic and he attached great value to the conception of the Jews as the chosen people. Accordingly his history was derived almost entirely from the Old Testament narratives and took little notice of either the history or the religions of other peoples of the Ancient East. But in spite of these limitations, by his enthusiasm and powers of narration he aroused fresh interest in the Old Testament and in the story of the Hebrew race.

New views as to the composition and dating of the books of the
Old Testament had been slowly spreading. Hupfield, for example,
had divided the Pentateuch into various sources, but had made
no attempt to date them. The merit of amalgamating the different
theories into a consistent scheme belongs to Graf, though he owed
a good deal to the influence of Reuss whose pupil he had been.
In *The Historical Books of the Old Testament* (1866) he took
Deuteronomy, which he identified with the law book discovered
in the temple in 621 B.C., as a centre and from it worked out the
relation of the other sources. One theory which was but slowly
accepted, somewhat strangely to us, was the post-exilic date of
P. Graf's scheme was eagerly welcomed by Kuenen whose
Religion of Israel appeared in 1869. Kuenen's influence would
have been more widespread but for his dull style and clumsy
methods. His volume contained long appendices and voluminous
notes and its chief value lay in its being a collection of material.
Kuenen was severely critical of the earlier narratives of the Old
Testament and considered that little before 800 was reliable. He
differed from Ewald in denying the unique position of the Jewish
people and this helped to confirm prejudice against his writings
and ideas; neither *The Religion of Israel* nor his later volume
Prophets and Prophecy in Israel (1877) awoke much interest in
England at the time.

Wellhausen has told us that as a young man he had been puzzled
by the fact that in the developed Law and in the prophets he
seemed to find himself in two different worlds. The notion that
the prophets were in reality earlier in date than the Law and the
Levitical system was suggested by Vatke at Berlin and by Reuss
at Strassburg, but it did not become prominent until the appearance of Duhm's *Die Theologie der Propheten* in 1875.

Three years later the publication of Wellhausen's *History of
Israel*[1] drew the attention of the educated world to the importance
of the new critical ideas and in fact 'aroused the greatest excitement among historians and theologians all over the world'.[2]

[1] An English edition did not appear until 1885; later he contributed the article
on 'The History of Judah and Israel' to the *Enc. Brit.*   [2] Gooch, *op. cit.*, p. 526.

The title of the work is a little misleading and in later editions Wellhausen called it *Prolegomena*. A much fuller attempt to present the whole history from the critical point of view came with Stade's *History of Israel* (1881–8). Stade's work, however, was marred by its controversial tone, for he delighted to expose what he regarded as the falsity of the traditional views.

Although Wellhausen's theories created such great excitement and were adopted by many Old Testament scholars, some remained aloof or became antagonistic. Hommel, for example, after agreeing with them later reverted to the traditional position, whilst Kittel's acceptance was subject to considerable reservations.

According to Gooch 'the most fascinating history of the Jewish people ever written'[1] was that of Renan. Renan as a young man earned fame as a Semitic scholar, but later he turned for a time to Christian origins; then at the age of sixty he took up the *History of Israel*, the various volumes of which appeared between 1887 and 1891. Like his New Testament work it is spoilt by too great subjectivism and the use of an unbridled imagination; Kuenen complained that his acceptance or rejection of material was equally governed by caprice. Renan attached great value to the early traditions of the Old Testament, but only in the sense that they created an atmosphere, the actual narratives he regarded with some suspicion. One queer feature of his book is that he seems to go out of his way to reverse the judgments of the canonical writers; condemning David, Solomon, and Elijah, but praising Ahab as a tolerant and enlightened monarch. The written prophets fare little better at his hands, though he gives them credit for transforming Jehovah from a tribal into a universal deity. He also praises them for defending the rights of the poor and oppressed. For the writer of the later chapters of Isaiah, however, he has a great admiration and hails him as the forerunner of Jesus Himself.

Such in brief outline was the development of Old Testament studies on the Continent. We return now to trace their progress in this country. The introduction of the new views was mainly

[1] *Op. cit.*, p. 528.

the work of W. Robertson Smith.[1] Robertson Smith, after studying under Lagarde at Göttingen, returned to Scotland in 1870 to become Professor of Oriental Languages and the Old Testament in the Free Church College at Aberdeen. Five years after his appointment articles which he contributed to the *Encyclopaedia Britannica* caused him to be accused of heresy; and although he was cleared of the charge he had to resign his post. The trial attracted wide attention and aroused interest in the views for which condemnation had been sought. This interest was increased through the popular lectures which he then proceeded to deliver and afterwards to publish in volumes entitled *The Old Testament and the Jewish Church* and *The Prophets of Israel*. When Cheyne wrote the introduction to the second edition of the latter in 1895 (the year after Robertson Smith's death) he claimed that it had 'achieved one of the greatest known literary successes in the department of theology'. He also expressed the opinion that had the author himself been able to revise his book he would have been much more drastic in his criticisms.

At Oxford the Regius Professor of Hebrew was E. B. Pusey, who as a young man had studied Semitic languages in Germany with painstaking diligence. There for a time he fell under the influence of a very mild form of criticism from which he later reacted, and for the remainder of his life he was a vigorous defender of the traditional position, as can be seen in his commentary on *Daniel* (1863). He also published a commentary on *The Minor Prophets* of a less controversial character and marked by devotional insight and fervour.[2] That Pusey possessed vast learning cannot be denied, but he was so obsessed by traditional views that any critical faculty was completely silenced. As an Old Testament scholar Pusey seems to have exercised but little influence in Oxford. John Wordsworth, who cannot be regarded as a hostile witness, said that in his own early days in the university,

[1] See further Black and Chrystal, *William Robertson Smith*.
[2] Newman wrote to Pusey congratulating him on this work, considering that such volumes were the most effective way of meeting the scepticism of the day. See *Letters of J. B. Mozley*, p. 259.

in the 'sixties, he had but few pupils. It was as a preacher and a spiritual director that he was mainly valued.

When Pusey's long tenure of the professorship was ended by his death in 1882 he was succeeded by S. R. Driver. Just before his appointment Driver had become convinced of the truth of the Graf-Wellhausen position and did much to commend it. His *Introduction to the Literature of the Old Testament* forms a landmark and demonstrates the extent to which modern views had made their way in England.[1] There can be no question that Driver (1846–1914) did more for Old Testament studies in England than any other scholar. This was due, not only to his immense fund of knowledge, but also to the deeply religious tone of all his writings. He never tried to press his views, partly from a desire not to disturb less courageous and less informed believers, and partly because he felt that he himself needed time to develop and mature them. Another leading Old Testament scholar in Oxford, T. K. Cheyne (1841–1915), was not characterized by the same reserve, at least in his later years. In 1885 Westcott had thought of him as one who had done and would do the most useful work in Old Testament exegesis.[2] Cheyne's *The Prophecies of Isaiah* (1880–1) is cautious and reserved, but in his Bampton Lectures for 1891 on *The Historical Origin and Religious Ideas of the Psalter* he adopted an extreme critical position, bringing down most of the psalms to the Persian period and many even to Maccabean times. His latest work during our period was *Jewish Life after the Exile* (1898). Cheyne held the Oriel professorship from 1885 to 1908, and at one time had been loosely connected with the *Lux Mundi* group.

In Cambridge the introduction of critical views, though in a comparatively mild form, goes back to J. J. S. Perowne's *Commentary on the Psalms* (1864). Later the presence there of W. Robertson Smith[3] from 1883 to 1894 did much to stimulate

[1] A sixth revised edition appeared in 1897. In the previous year it had been translated into German by Rothstein.

[2] *Life*, Vol. II, p. 45.

[3] He succeeded E. H. Palmer who had been murdered in the Sinai peninsula in October 1882.

Semitic studies in general and through them to throw light on the Old Testament. During these years he produced *Kinship and Marriage in Early Arabia* (1885) and *The Religion of the Semites* (1889). In 1882, the year of Driver's appointment at Oxford, A. F. Kirkpatrick became Regius Professor of Hebrew and did much to encourage Old Testament studies on modern lines, though his principal writing, a commentary on *The Psalms*, was not completed until 1902. Before that he had published *The Divine Library of the Old Testament* (1891) and *The Doctrine of the Prophets* (1892).

A great step forward followed the return to Cambridge of H. E. Ryle as successor to Hort as Hulsean Professor in 1887. It was his avowed object to make the Old Testament the chief subject of his teaching, and above all to remove unreasoning prejudice against critical views. In this he was very successful and his lectures were attended by large numbers, sometimes as many as two hundred being present. He had also a considerable literary output. His *Introduction to the Canon of the Old Testament* and *The Early Narratives of Genesis* both appeared in 1892. Like Driver his teaching was characterized by reverence and restraint, none the less he once informed his pupil, A. H. McNeile, that he expected a stake in the market place. One of his ambitions was to write a history of Israel, but this and other projects had to be abandoned on his appointment to the bishopric of Exeter in 1901.

Jewish scholars were naturally a little suspicious of the new approach to their sacred book, but among the more liberal many of the theories put forward by critics of other faiths were accepted, as can be seen, for instance, in C. G. Montefiore's valuable Hibbert Lectures for 1892 on *The Religion of the Ancient Hebrews*.

What, it may be asked, were the chief contentions of the new criticism? The most revolutionary was that the prophets came before the Law. As this theory is often misunderstood it will be well to point out that by the Law was meant the developed priestly system as seen in P, for 'no critic doubts that the laws of JE (Ex. 21-3, etc.) are earlier than the prophets'.[1]

[1] Driver, *Introduction to the Literature of the Old Testament*, p. xix.

The writings of the prophets, apart from additions and insertions, were regarded as units, with the exception of Isaiah where 40–55 and 56–66 were held to be later (and also 13:1–14, 23, 21:1–10, 24, 27, 34–36). It was Duhm who in 1892 first made a distinction between 40–55 and 56–66, placing the latter chapters shortly after the earlier ones. His theory was accepted by some English scholars, including Cheyne and G. Adam Smith. Another book which was thought to be a combination of two authors was Zechariah where chapters 9–14 were separated from the rest. Ezekiel had so far escaped analysis into different sources and was accepted as the work of a prophet of the sixth century living in Babylon. All these conclusions as to unity, date and location, have since been challenged. Many critics looked upon the earlier prophets, or some of them, as being antagonistic to the priestly cult, and as emphasizing the moral requirements of religion and deprecating its sacrificial aspects. (Cf. Am. 5:21–4, Hos. 6:6, 8:13, Is. 1:10–12, Mic. 6:6–8, Jer. 6:20, 7:22f., 11:15, 14:12.)

Criticism of the Pentateuch (to which many scholars added Joshua to form the Hexateuch) was mainly devoted to an endeavour to distinguish the various sources from which it had been compiled. At one time P had been thought to be the oldest source, but this was gradually abandoned and it was recognized as the latest. It could be clearly distinguished from the other sources, as could also D. The oldest sources of all J and E were less easy to separate, as was admitted by such critics as Wellhausen, Kuenen and Driver. The questions of the unity and the dates of the different documents found critics at some variance.[1]

As to the so-called historic books, Joshua as we have seen was linked up with the Pentateuch, and its account of the conquest, so far as it was represented as rapid and complete, was rejected. The accounts in Judges were also questioned; the judges were none of them rulers over all Israel, nor did they follow in succession, some were probably contemporaries.[2] Behind the

---

[1] See further W. E. Addis, *The Documents of the Hexateuch* (1892, 1898) and Carpenter and Harford Battersby, *The Hexateuch* (1900).

[2] See further G. F. Moore, *Judges* (1895).

books of Samuel and Kings lay a number of sources and traditions which were often in conflict; the older material had been fitted into a framework by a later compiler with a strongly Deuteronomic point of view, though this is not so marked in the case of Samuel as in Judges and Kings.[1]

In an article in *The North American Review* in 1892 C. A. Briggs claimed that the Psalms, which he regarded as the hymnbook of the second temple, formed the 'key to the Old Testament'. Much work was done on them in our period and the result of it was to reject the Davidic authorship of the whole, and even to question whether any of the psalms came from him. It was seen that previous collections had been incorporated in the book and the possibility of earlier psalms having been adapted to later conditions was accepted. There was much difference of opinion over the dates of the various psalms; the headings, though not without their use, were rejected. Some extreme critics held that the later psalms came from the Maccabean period and that possibly most of them, at least in their present form, should be assigned to that era. The rejection of the headings, which gave the psalms a historic setting, seemed to rob them of much interest; but it may be pointed out that it in no way impaired their spiritual value, indeed it may be argued that this was really deepened by being divorced from supposed temporal and local circumstances.

Of the other books in the Writings, as the Jews called the third division of their Canon, the Wisdom literature was ranked as exilic or post-exilic, Daniel was placed in the Maccabean age, whilst Chronicles was seen to be a late rewriting of the older books in the times of Ezra-Nehemiah.

Sanday summed up the results of Old Testament criticism as having shown the untrustworthy character of Jewish traditions concerning authorship, the composite character of many of the books, the presence in the Pentateuch of matter which in its present shape is not earlier than the Exile, and the composition of Deuteronomy not long before its discovery under Josiah.[2]

---

[1] See further Driver, *Notes on the Hebrew Text of Samuel* (1890), and Burney, *Notes on the Hebrew Text of Kings* (1903). [2] *Inspiration*, pp. 129 f.

These 'results' were often spoken of as 'assured' though their extent was often exaggerated, and even misrepresented by opponents of the new views. At the end of the century the critical position as then expounded seemed unassailable as a whole, though it was admitted that many details still remained to be settled or to be left uncertain owing to the lack of sufficient criteria for reaching any final decision.[1]

In recent years the Graf-Wellhausen position has come under strong challenge from critics who reject it in whole or in part, and various and diverse hypotheses have been advanced to supersede it. But the new suggestions are far from convincing and in my opinion the older critical position may still be said to stand in its broad outline.[2] The prevailing acceptance of evolution as an explanation of any and every kind of development during our period undoubtedly had its effect on Old Testament criticism, and it cannot be denied that the process by which the Old Testament grew up was made much too simple and orderly; no sufficient allowance was made for differences in both time and locality. It is possible that the criticism of recent scholars has been equally influenced, perhaps unconsciously, by the general reaction in thought.

The views of critics by their apparent inconsistency with the traditional belief in the Bible, and even by their novelty, caused many to regard them with disquiet and even with horror. But further examination and the passing away of the feeling of novelty led gradually to a saner and more tolerant outlook. This,

[1] Robertson Smith took a very optimistic view of the work done by critics and in the preface to *The Religion of the Semites* he referred to Kuenen and Wellhausen as 'the men whose acumen and research had thrown so much light on the historical order of the Old Testament documents, and especially of the documents of which the Pentateuch is made up, that nothing of vital importance for the study of Old Testament religion still remains uncertain'. Cheyne, however, a little later realized that there were still many problems which remained unsolved and that the results of literary criticism would have to be modified in view of increasing knowledge derived from archaeology and the comparative study of social customs. Fresh light would also come from comparative philology. Amongst other things he saw that the question of Deuteronomy had not been finally settled. See *Enc. Bib.* 2056f.

[2] See further H. H. Rowley, *The Growth of the Old Testament* (1950).

however, took time. In 1866 Kingsley could write to F. D. Maurice: 'All this talk about the Pentateuch is making me feel its unique value and divineness so much more than ever I did, that I burn to say something worth hearing about it.'[1] Such an utterance seems to come strangely from one so open-minded, so possessed by the scientific outlook, as Kingsley. It must be remembered, however, that he was referring to the crudities of Colenso and not to the theories of later Old Testament scholars. The progress of critical views was certainly handicapped by the extreme and even fanciful theories put forward by certain scholars, Cheyne was in this an especial offender, which provoked derision rather than alarm. But the work of sober scholars, and above all, of Driver, slowly made its way and conciliated much of the opposition; though even Driver's *Introduction* called forth a protest which was signed by many of the clergy.

Many, however, who realized the strength of the critical position and the weight of evidence behind it were held back from accepting it owing to their belief that it challenged the authority of Jesus. He had referred to Moses, to David, and to Daniel (Mark 13:14) and therefore the authorship of the Law, of the Psalms, and of the book of Daniel, could not be questioned by those who acknowledged His lordship. Such an attitude, of course, raised deeper problems, and involved the question as to how far our Lord's knowledge of matters of scholarship and of history was merely that of the men of His day; it could also be argued that even if He possessed superior knowledge He would naturally use the names then current, for no other reference was reasonably possible. It is difficult to suppose that His use was intended to make any express declaration on the subject. 'That our Lord . . . designed to pronounce a verdict on the authorship and age of its (i.e. the Old Testament) different parts, and to foreclose all future inquiry into these subjects, is an assumption for which no sufficient ground can be alleged.'[2] Sanday, after a very careful examination of the question, came to the conclusion that 'the procedure of Christ and His Apostles in reference to the

[1] *Life*, Vol. II, p. 160.   [2] Driver, *Introduction*, p. xii.

Law was more revolutionary than anything that is involved in accepting the lessons of criticism'.[1]

Many of those who attacked the new views were really unqualified to express any opinion, at least so far as scholarship was involved, and their main weapons were abuse and ridicule. They waxed facetious over Pentateuchal criticism, pointing out that although the critics denied the Mosaic authorship they had at any rate made the Law into a 'mosaic'. They failed to realize that a work might be a 'mosaic' and still retain its own pattern, and that skilful borrowing is often a sign of genius. Others, whose learning cannot be questioned, also took up the challenge. Pusey produced an impressive volume in 1865 in defence of the traditional date of Daniel, and others of real scholarship also wrote in support of the traditional position. The chief result of such works was to reassure the pious, though if they had actually read them, which one imagines was seldom the case, they could not have failed to be horrified and alarmed by the considerable concessions made to the critical position even when it was rejected as a whole. This applies to Hommel's *Ancient Hebrew Tradition*, translated in 1897, and the various writings of that eccentric archaeologist, Professor Sayce, including *The Higher Criticism and the Monuments* (1893).[2] By way of illustration we may take Sayce's admission that the biblical chronology must be adapted to that of the Assyrians with their accurate and careful records,[3] and his criticisms of the compiler of Chronicles.[4] Such concessions cannot be reconciled with any theory of 'verbal inspiration' and give away the whole position of the narrow conservatives

[1] *Inspiration*, pp. 407 ff.

[2] Orr, *The Problem of the Old Testament*, though it did not appear until 1905, represents the conclusions of the best conservative scholars. It, too, makes a number of concessions.

[3] *The Higher Criticism and the Monuments*, pp. 318 and 406.

[4] Cf. *op. cit.*, p. 462 where he said that 'archaeology makes it clear that his statements are not always exact. We cannot follow him with the same confidence as that with which we should follow the author of the Book of Kings. His use of the documents which lay before him was uncritical, the inferences he drew from his materials were not always sound, and he makes them subserve the theory on which his work is based.'

who refuse to recognize the possibility of any errors in the biblical records.

In their attempts to refute the critics many defenders of traditional views appealed to archaeological discoveries. It is true that the Tell el-Amarna Tablets revealed the existence of writing in Palestine and its neighbourhood before the period of the Exodus; but it was only extreme critics who had denied its possibility. This fact discloses one of the unfair methods adopted by the traditionalists, that of taking some extreme and highly vulnerable theory as typical of criticism as a whole and using it as evidence of the weakness of the entire fabric. Sayce was especially optimistic in his claims, saying amongst other things that 'wherever archaeology has been able to test the negative conclusions of criticism, they have dissolved like a bubble into the air', and that Assyriology 'has for ever shattered the "critical" theory which would put the prophets before the Law'.[1] Driver dealt faithfully with Sayce and his one-sided assertions when he wrote: 'his statements are very often inexact, and the defeats which he represents critics as constantly sustaining at the hands of archaeology are purely imaginary, being obtained either by attributing to them opinions which they do not hold, or by basing upon the monuments more than they legitimately prove'.[2] Hommel was more cautious and restrained, but critics of standing are all agreed that though he had collected much interesting materials from the inscriptions he had entirely failed to refute the critical position.[3]

Archaeology had certainly not refuted the critical position as a whole, though it might have demonstrated the inaccuracy of some extreme theories. On the other hand it had rendered notable service, above all by rescuing the Hebrews from that state of isolation which a study of the Old Testament alone must inevitably suggest, and by drawing them into the stream of general history. The Hebrews can no longer be regarded as

[1] *Monument Facts and Higher Critical Fancies*, pp. 25 and 87.
[2] *Introduction to the Old Testament*, p. 3.
[3] Cf. Driver, *op. cit.*, pp. 158f.

distinct from their neighbours whom they resembled not only in race and language, but even in religion; we now see them not as living in a kind of vacuum, but as moving against the vast background of the ancient Oriental world. All this is pure gain; the records lose nothing of their religious value, whilst the Hebrews become more human, and in consequence, of greater help to us who live in modern times.

In details also, archaeology has done extraordinarily useful service. Not only has it confirmed many statements in the Old Testament, but what is of still greater value it has supplemented or corrected them where they were imperfect or inaccurate. Amongst other things it has provided, what had been previously lacking, an assured basis for biblical chronology, and has thrown light on sites which had not hitherto been identified, and even given reality to historical persons, such as Sargon, who had not been known from records outside the Old Testament.

Towards the end of our period a subject which aroused much interest and fierce controversy was the question as to how far the Jews had been influenced by Babylon. This did not really come to a head before the publication of Delitzsch's lectures in Berlin in 1902 on *Babel and Bible* but it was already being discussed. The pan-Babylonian school exaggerated Babylonian influence and through scholars like Winckler and Jeremias carried it to sensational lengths, but this must not be allowed to blind us to its reality and extent. This was clearly demonstrated by the Tell el-Amarna Tablets which revealed Babylonian culture as stretching from the Euphrates to the Nile. There were also numerous parallels between Hebrew narratives, customs, and laws which could not be denied. The close connexion of laws received fresh illustration and more detailed evidence by the discovery of the Code of Hammurabi in 1901.[1] If at the close of the nineteenth century it was too early to decide the exact nature of 'the debt to Babylonia . . . its recognition has sufficed to revolutionize

---

[1] See Rogers, *Cuneiform Parallels to the Old Testament* (1912) and S. A. Cook, *The Laws of Moses and the Code of Hammurabi* (1903).

the study of early Israel and to provide a new background for the religious history of the world'.[1]

In the earliest attempts to decipher inscriptions much help had been received from the recognition in them of proper names. In our period they came to have a further function and received intensive study; for such names gave a clue to the ideas of those who made use of them, and also threw fresh light on philological problems; in Hebrew, for example, certain roots found in other Semitic languages have survived only in proper names. The pioneer in this line of study was Nestle whose *Die israel, Eigennamen nach ihrer religionsgeschicht Bedeutung* appeared in 1876. Meanwhile there was a steady stream of new names coming in from fresh discoveries of Assyrian-Babylonian lists and inscriptions which were of growing assistance and many of them were incorporated by M. Grünwald in *Die Eigennamen des Alt. Test.* (1895). In the year following, the results of the study became more readily accessible in England with the publication of G. B. Gray's *Hebrew Proper Names*.

The study of proper names was but one branch of that comparative study of Semitic languages in general which was being perseveringly pursued in different lands. By it not only did Hebrew words come to be better understood, but also grammatical usages and forms; though in the first flush of enthusiasm there was a tendency to press analogies too far and in general to handle the material with a lack of discretion. Good pioneer work was done by Robertson Smith, and by Wright whose *Comparative Grammar of the Semitic Languages* was published in 1890, the year after his death. The introduction to Driver's *Notes to the Hebrew Text of Samuel* (1889) was also helpful. It was, however, in France and Germany that most progress was made, and one of the first attempts to deal with the subject in a systematic way was Lidzbarski's *Handbuch der nordsemitischen Epigraphik* (1898).

The attempt to place the Old Testament in the setting of Semitic religion in general will always be associated with the name of Robertson Smith and his *Religion of the Semites*. He himself

---

[1] Gooch, *History and Historians in the Nineteenth Century*, p. 534.

paid a well deserved tribute to the work of Dr. John Spencer, Master of Corpus Christi College, Cambridge, who in the latter half of the seventeenth century laid the foundations of the study in his *Ritual Laws of the Hebrews*, written in Latin. Although the writings of Robertson Smith seem to show that the religion of the Old Testament was the outcome of a process similar to that undergone by other Semitic religions, he himself always refused to accept such a conclusion and condemned the views of 'those who are compelled by a false Philosophy of Revelation to see in the Old Testament nothing more than the highest point of the general tendencies of Semitic religion'.[1] He was justified in as much as though religion among the Hebrews may have had the same lowly origins, it rose to spiritual heights which went far beyond the reach of the rest.[2]

The more closely the religion of the Old Testament is compared with that of the other Semitic peoples the greater are seen to be the differences between them. No doubt there are many similarities, and here and there we can find traces of primitive myths of a not very elevated character and of the survival of heathen customs or even their reintroduction in times of peculiar stress, but the tone as a whole is infinitely more reverent and one might almost say more sane. In other records the emphasis seems to be patriotic rather than religious, though it is hazardous to make any such distinction as the fortunes of the nation and its deity were so closely bound up together. The object of all such records is, of course, to stimulate devotion and loyalty; but in the Jewish records (at least in their present form) there is not found the same desire to glorify the monarch as in those of other peoples. It is true that the glory and empire of Solomon are extolled in

[1] Black and Chrystal, *W. Robertson Smith*, pp. 536f. Many scholars found it impossible to understand Robertson Smith's position and complained that 'he pursued the methods of rationalistic literary analysis while holding the faith of Bibliolatrous superstition'. (*Op. cit.*, p. 571.)

[2] Cf. Driver, Schweich Lectures, p. 90: 'Archaeology demonstrates . . . that though the religion of Israel was built upon the same material foundations . . . it rose immeasurably above them; it assumed . . . a unique character, and in the hands of its inspired teachers became the expression of great spiritual realities such as has been without parallel in any other nation of the earth.'

Kings, but even there the primary object is to glorify the God of Israel. Moreover kings are subject to the judgment of the messengers of Jehovah and their importance is assessed, not by their political or military achievements, but by their services to religion. It may also be pointed out that the parallels with the religions of other peoples are largely matters concerning the cult, and are to be found in the priestly elements of the Old Testament. What differentiates the religion of Israel most clearly from that of the neighbouring peoples is the prophetic element.[1]

The supreme value of the Old Testament for today, even apart from its spiritual and moral teaching,[2] is that it gives us 'that clear and all-sided insight into the meaning and practical worth of the perfect scheme of divine grace which can only be attained by tracing its growth'.[3] But in tracing out that growth much caution is demanded. The religious development of any people is seldom or never uniform; different sections will at any given period have reached very different levels of attainment, and we must be on our guard against attributing to the nation as a whole ideas and aspirations which are in fact the possession of a few only of the higher minds. Furthermore we must not imagine that progress was constant and uninterrupted. The Old Testament reveals that even in the earliest period to which its records go back there were singularly noble conceptions of the character of Jehovah (one need but cite Exodus 34:6f., which comes from JE), whilst in some much later passages He is set forth in a quite unworthy manner, resembling a modern dictator with his methods of 'frightfulness'.

As in the construction of Solomon's temple use was made of components derived from different regions and the help of foreign workmen was invoked, so Israelite religion was built up

[1] Robertson Smith always maintained that 'all purely "naturalistic" explanations of the development of Hebrew prophecy were doomed to failure, and that the uniqueness of the revelation recorded in the canonical scriptures must be recognized'. (*Op. cit.*, p. 527.)

[2] See C. F. Burney, 'The Permanent Religious Value of the Old Testament' in *Contentio Veritatis*, pp. 167 ff.

[3] W. Robertson Smith, *The Prophets of Israel*, p. 6.

of diverse and apparently conflicting elements—Canaanite, Babylonian, Persian and Greek among others—but in the end attained a certain unity. The different ideas of Jehovah and of religion itself—from the spirituality of the prophets to the aridity of parts of the Wisdom literature—which the records reveal, mark stages in a prolonged and uneven process.

Chapter Seven

THE NEW TESTAMENT

WE come now to the New Testament,[1] and here the general tendency towards the end of the period was on the whole in a conservative direction, especially as regards the authorship of the Acts and the Pauline epistles; criticism had been too harsh, for as Dr. Lock pointed out in his inaugural lecture as Dean Ireland's professor at Oxford in 1896 classical writings—he gave Aristotle's *Poetics* as an instance—are accepted as genuine on evidence which is much more slender than that demanded for New Testament writings.[2]

New Testament criticism may be said to have three branches— historical, literary, and textual. The last stands a little apart and will receive separate treatment; the other two are largely inter- dependent, for the criticism of documents and the attempt to place them in their historical setting form a sort of combined operation in which each may help the other. It was one of the merits of Baur that he saw the need for treating the various books no longer as isolated works but as belonging to the general historical environment of primitive Christianity. This line of approach, incidentally, was in accord with modern scientific method where the organism is studied in connexion with its environment, and the more that is known of the latter, the more readily can the development of the former be examined.

The minute and detailed study of the environment of primitive Christianity, of the age in which the books of the New Testament

---

[1] See further W. C. Allen, 'Modern Criticism and the New Testament' in *Contentio Veritatis*, pp. 206 ff. and Pfleiderer, *Development of Theology*, pp. 209 ff.
[2] *The Bible and Christian Life*, p. 70.

were composed, was greatly helped by the discoveries of archaeologists and the researches of secular historians. More and more it
was realized how much the prevailing ideas of the period, both
Jewish and Hellenistic, had influenced the mind of the early
Church. Furthermore it was recognized that doctrinal considerations were already at work in the New Testament itself;
even in the Synoptic gospels theological presuppositions may
be discerned, and this is much more so in the fourth gospel. These
theological conceptions were the outcome of the religious
experiences of the primitive community and it was therefore
necessary to view the New Testament in their light so far as they
could be ascertained. Among the first to recognize the importance
of this line of approach was T. H. Green who wrote 'The habit
of regarding the writings of the New Testament as a body of
doctrine pitched into the world all at once' has led men astray,
for 'an examination of these writings themselves might satisfy us
that they came into being as successive assertions of the fulness of
Christian life against a contemporaneous stiffening of it either
into Jewish ordinance or gentile philosophy'.[1]

So too in regard to the Canon. The fact that certain books
were incorporated into it is to be explained, at least in part, by
their doctrinal fitness,[2] to which also their survival itself may
have been due. Although the reception of the Canonical scriptures
shows the unique importance which they held in the eyes of the
early Church, an examination of the process by which they were
ultimately received also shows, in certain cases, how narrow was
the margin between acceptance and rejection. For the theologian
the fact that certain books ultimately found a place in the Canon
does not exempt them from examination and testing, along with
his other authorities they must be submitted to criticism.

Although there was a growing realization of the part taken by
the community in shaping the form of the various New Testament
writings and in selecting those considered worthy of inclusion

[1] *Works*, Vol III, p. 170.
[2] Cf. Moffatt, *Introduction to the Literature of the New Testament*, p. 9. 'The
New Testament Canon represents a dogmatic selection from the literature of
primitive Christianity.'

in it, the extent to which common tradition rather than literary dependence might account for resemblances between them had not yet been grasped. On the other hand, by a kind of reaction from the traditional view which had denied the possibility of disagreement among 'inspired' writers, there was in some quarters, as Gore complained, 'too much interest in discussing and emphasizing differences between the writers'.[1]

The varied attitudes adopted by scholars towards the material at their disposal and their different methods of approaching it naturally led to a wide divergence in the conclusions reached by them. As a consequence there was much confusion and controversy. This was above all the case in considering the picture of Jesus and of His teaching presented in the gospels, a subject which formed the chief interest of New Testament scholars in our period. The more radical critics regarded Him merely as a man who grew as other men, and sought to explain Him from this standpoint; statements in the gospels which conflicted with their presupposition were to be rejected as due to superstitious additions or interpretations. The weakness of this method was that by it the critic could make the evidence square with any preconceived idea of Jesus which might satisfy him. But such reconstructions seldom satisfied others, and certainly failed to provide any adequate account of the devotion shown to Jesus from the earliest days for which records are available, nor for the subsequent development and growth of the Church. The more orthodox in their approach gave full weight to later developments and sought to discover a conception of Jesus which would account for them. There might be gaps and difficulties in the gospel narratives, but taken as a whole they could be accepted as presenting One who was what the Church had always claimed Him to be— truly human, yet also something more than human.

Fairbairn has said that the 'most distinctive and determinative element in modern theology is what we may term a new feeling for Christ'.[2] The amount of literature produced directly on this

---

[1] *The Holy Spirit and the Church*, p. 116.
[2] *The Place of Christ in Modern Theology*, p. 3.

subject, both in England and elsewhere, was enormous, and it has been skilfully summarized by Schweitzer in his well-known volume, the English translation of which received the very appropriate title of *The Quest of the Historical Jesus*. To discuss these various attempts is beyond the scope of the present inquiry, but two works deserve special notice on account of their appearance early in our period and the wide popularity which they acquired—Renan's *Life of Jesus* and *Ecce Homo*.

Renan had at first been influenced by Strauss but reacted from his mythical theories. His residence in Syria had given him an intimate knowledge of the background of the gospel story and a very vivid imagination was brought in to supplement the known facts. The result was what someone has called a 'gospel in Dresden china', an emotional and even sentimental account of the life of Jesus which, though it may be admirable as literature, cannot be taken very seriously as history. Renan's book was translated soon after its publication in 1863 and served a very useful purpose as a challenge to thought and also as showing that Jesus had been an actual man who lived a life very like that of other men; He was no mere abstraction. Thus in spite of its many and obvious weaknesses

> the book was symptomatic; it was the first volume in a series that increased in wisdom as it grew in number, recognizing throughout this truth—that Christianity was to be explained not through abstract principles, tendencies, differences, conciliations, but through its most creative Personality.[1]

Ecce Homo was the work of Seeley, the Cambridge historian, but when it appeared in 1865 the name of the author was not disclosed. This aroused considerable speculation as to his identity which probably drew attention to the book; J. B. Mozley wrote to R. W. Church in March 1866 saying that everybody was talking about it.[2] Church had already reviewed the book at considerable length in *The Guardian* for 7 February and welcomed it as 'a protest against the stiffness of all cast-iron systems, and a

---

[1] Fairbairn, *op. cit.*, p. 279.   [2] *Letters of J. B. Mozley*, p. 268.

warning against trusting what is worn out'.[1] It had also been reviewed, favourably on the whole, by Mr. Gladstone, and this served to increase popular interest. Rather strangely it found little approval from Jowett and his circle, so Church informed Mozley, 'though whether . . . from opposition or rivalry is not clear'.[2] Seeley's volume was regarded by many as an attack on the orthodox doctrine of the person of Christ, but the author himself had had no such intention; he desired to approach the study of Jesus by dealing first with the human side. He published a sequel entitled *Natural Religion* in 1882 which, however, attracted but small notice; many who had hoped that in it Seeley would advance to a consideration of the divine side of Christ were disappointed, and it is probable that dogmatic questions were alien to his temperament.

Many attempts to write the life of Christ appeared in England and came from a great variety of points of view; there is an immense gap between imaginative works such as that of Farrar (the first of numerous editions came out in 1874) and, say, Sanday's *Outlines* reprinted from Hastings's *Dictionary of the Bible*.

Towards the close of our period New Testament scholars were agitated by the emergence of a very novel conception of the significance of Jesus, the advocates of which looked upon Him solely as a prophet who proclaimed the speedy end of all things, 'the ecstatic herald of the Kingdom of God'. This eschatological interpretation was mainly due to a reaction from the view, predominant in Liberal Protestant circles in Germany, that He was little more than a teacher of lofty morals and the example of a perfect life. This latter conception failed to take account of certain aspects of the gospel narratives for it could not be denied that in them the thought of the return of Jesus, the final judgment, and the establishment of His rule on earth, were given great prominence. Certain scholars, the most prominent being Johannes Weiss and Schweitzer, now insisted that these should

---

[1] Reprinted in *Occasional Papers*, Vol. II, pp. 133 ff.
[2] *Letters of J. B. Mozley*, p. 284.

be given due weight. But as so often happens, the reaction was carried too far and the moral teaching and the earthly life came, in their turn, to be disparaged; nor did the advocates of the new standpoint in their enthusiasm sufficiently consider the possibility of the two strands being combined. In England the eschatological position was accepted by a number of leading theologians, especially by those who held the view that the divine immanence had been over-emphasized, as also the importance of the picture of Jesus presented in the fourth gospel where eschatology is given but a subordinate place.[1]

Fresh interest in the subject of eschatology had already been aroused and additional matter for its study provided through the publication of editions of the Jewish and early Christian apocalyptic writings. Unfortunately Schweitzer, the chief exponent of eschatological views, had little first-hand knowledge of this literature, as Charles, in the second edition of his *Eschatology* (1913), took care to point out.[2]

Attempts to recover a picture of Jesus as He actually lived and taught seemed to Fairbairn to have been successful, and he could affirm, with what now seems undue optimism, that 'for the Christian theologian, the most significant and assured result of the critical process is, that he can now stand face to face with the historical Christ, and conceive God as He conceived Him'.[3]

But even if such attempts had been as successful as Fairbairn imagined, they would still have had serious limitations. Westcott has pointed out that 'By no effort could the spectator in a later age place himself in the position of the disciples before the Passion and Ascension. The exact reproduction . . . of what met their eyes would not produce on him the effect they experienced. The scene would require artistic interpretation in order that the idea might be preserved.'[4] Many, indeed, had no great desire to

[1] The common notion that eschatology is absent from the fourth gospel needs considerable modification: see Howard, *Christianity According to St. John*, pp. 106ff.

[2] Dalman, *The Words of Jesus*, pp. 132 and 248, had already protested against fanciful ideas of Jewish messianic hopes in the time of our Lord.

[3] *Op. cit.*, p. viii.   [4] *Religious Thought in the West*, p. 337.

recover the historical Jesus; for to them the most significant thing and the most helpful for faith, was not Jesus as He had appeared in time and space, but Jesus as spiritually arisen within the hearts of men in their own day.

In view of the intense interest in the life of Jesus in our period it necessarily followed that renewed and concentrated study would be devoted to the gospels.[1] Here two great problems awaited solution: (*a*) the origins and mutual relations of the first three gospels, generally known as the Synoptic; and (*b*) the authorship of the fourth gospel and its relation to the other three. It might almost seem that these problems received too much attention and that the contents suffered neglect in consequence. There was certainly a danger that the historical and literary aspects of the gospels might be regarded as, in Burkitt's words, 'the beginning and the end of serious Gospel study, rather than as questions that must be settled because on other grounds we have to study the Gospels'.[2]

What is now known as Form criticism had not yet been utilized, though there had been some anticipation of it; Schleiermacher, for instance, considered that detached passages about Christ had been written out and incorporated in the gospels, whilst Newman at times seemed to see in the gospels 'not a regular history, but biographical anecdotes strung together'.[3]

It is to be regretted that the great Cambridge scholars did not devote more attention to the problems connected with the gospels.[4] Westcott published his *Introduction to the Study of the Gospels* in 1860, a not very satisfactory piece of work, and thereafter concentrated on St. John. It had been intended that Hort should take up the study of the Synoptics, but he never found

---

[1] See further Armitage Robinson, *The Study of the Gospels* (1902).

[2] In *Cambridge Biblical Essays*, pp. 195 f.

[3] *Life and Letters of Dean Stanley*, Vol. II, p. 341. It had also been anticipated by the so-called 'fragment' hypothesis for the Pentateuch put forth in the early years of the century.

[4] Salmon suggested that a greater interest in the genesis of the gospels would have helped Westcott and Hort in their textual studies: see *Some Criticisms of the Text of the New Testament*, p. 117.

time or opportunity to pursue it. Swete followed the same course and in his commentary on *St. Mark* (1898) practically ignored the Synoptic problem.

In older days the numerous likenesses between the first three gospels had been easily explained as due, not to any kind of dependence upon one another, but to their common inspiration. But this did not account for their diversities. In our period three suggested lines of explanation were put forward: (a) dependence on a common oral tradition; (b) direct borrowings from each other; and (c) the use of common sources.

The oral theory was held by Westcott and A. Wright in England, but did not find much favour elsewhere. It suggested that some kind of 'official' gospel in an oral form had been formulated in the earliest days of the Church, perhaps in both Aramaic and Greek, and that it was handed on by word of mouth as part of the teaching of converts. No documentary source was postulated. At a later date this gospel took written form in Mark, of which Luke was a still later development. Matthew was thought to represent a Hebrew recension of the common tradition. The weakness of this theory is that it takes too much for granted and makes assumptions which are unsupported by evidence, nor does it account for the differences between the gospels, and especially the absence from Mark of material found in Matthew and Luke.

Those who wished to study the problem were greatly helped by the publication in 1880 of Rushbrooke and Abbott's *Synopticon* in which the texts of the three gospels were printed in parallel columns. Special attention was called to those passages which were common to all three or to two of them only.

Although Lessing had reached the conclusion that Mark was the earliest of the gospels the Tübingen school accepted the traditional view that Matthew was the oldest.[1] It soon came to be seen, however, that this would not work, and a general consensus of opinion gave Mark the priority, holding that it had

[1] They took it as representing the Ebionite point of view, with Luke as Pauline, and Mark an attempt to reconcile the two.

been used by Matthew and Luke.[1] Some scholars, however, made the suggestion that behind Mark there was a still older document, an Ur-Marcus, and if this had been used by Matthew and Luke it would explain passages in which they agree against Mark.

Another factor demanding explanation was the presence in Matthew and Luke of passages, mainly of teaching, which are not found in Mark. To account for them the use of another source was suggested, to which the name Q was given for convenience, since it seemed unlikely that there had been borrowing between Matthew and Luke. Attempts to reconstruct this supposed document have been made, but none of them is entirely convincing, for it may be taken as most probable, in view of the manner in which Mark is used by Matthew and Luke, that not all of it appears in either of them.

By the close of the century a considerable measure of agreement on the problems had been attained. Mark was accepted as the earliest gospel, and it was assumed that it, and at least one other source, had been used by the other two evangelists. But there was still much unagreed or unexplained, in particular the exact nature and contents of Q, and the origin of matter peculiar to Matthew and Luke respectively. There was also uncertainty as to the dates of the various gospels. But behind these lesser problems lay one much more fundamental; that is, how far the gospels present an entirely reliable picture of the earthly life and teaching of Jesus, in view of possible modifications of the materials through dogmatic bias by the early Church. Some such modifications can be seen in the way in which Mark has been used by Matthew and Luke. Did they also antedate Mark itself? Thus there was a tendency to a kind of stalemate, for behind Mark and Q there seemed to be a period about which nothing definite was known.

Sanday in summing up work on the Synoptic problem expressed the view that no completely acceptable result had been

[1] As late as 1884, however, E. A. Abbot, *The Common Tradition of the Synoptic Gospels*, rejected the use of Mark by the others.

arrived at, though he considered that 'the great mass of the narrative [of the gospels] took its shape before the Destruction of Jerusalem, *i.e.* within less than forty years of the events'.[1]

In the matter of the several gospels there was in England a considerable amount of agreement. The traditional authorship of Mark was accepted, and also the probability of Petrine influence, even by those who questioned his having had any share in its composition.[2] Rome was favoured as the place of writing and a date between 65 and 70. The so-called little apocalypse (ch. 13) was regarded by many as a separate document, and there was also difference of opinion as to the original ending of the gospel.

The authorship of Matthew and its place of origin were felt to be insoluble problems. The date also was uncertain; it was obviously later than Mark and might even be later than Luke.

Since the great majority of English theologians were agreed that Luke came from the author of Acts questions concerning it could not be considered in isolation. Some scholars were inclined to place Luke rather late in view of its possible dependence on Josephus; but as both may have used a common source, this was by no means necessary. The statement in Luke 1:1 that many had already taken in hand the writing of gospels was also taken as a sign of a late date, though here again quite needlessly. There was, however, a general agreement that Luke was later than the Fall of Jerusalem in A.D. 70.

We come now to problems connected with the fourth gospel.[3] Hitherto, in spite of attacks by Strauss and others, the traditional view had in general prevailed; Schleiermacher had attached great value to it, and later still Renan had made it the basis of his *Life of Jesus*. But now it began to be the subject of hot debate. In his Bampton Lectures for 1866 Liddon declared that it had become the battlefield of the New Testament, just as Daniel was the battlefield of the Old. The traditional authorship was

---

[1] *Inspiration*, pp. 281 and 283.

[2] Salmon, *The Human Element in the Gospels*, p. 21.

[3] See further Howard, *The Fourth Gospel in Recent Criticism and Interpretation*; Sanday, *The Criticism of the Fourth Gospel*, and Edwyn Hoskyns, *The Fourth Gospel*, pp. 17 ff.

strenuously maintained by Westcott, Hort and other English scholars; but there remained the difficulty that there is no evidence to show that the apostle John was ever in Ephesus or its neighbourhood, which was generally accepted as the place of the gospel's origin. There was equal difficulty over the supposed 'John the Elder'. Taking the gospel as it stands many scholars saw in it an attempt to readjust the Christian message to a new age and new conditions; some of them, however, exaggerated its Hellenistic character.

The relation of the fourth gospel to the other three was a problem upon which much work was done. It was often assumed that John was acquainted with the Synoptics, and that he was even at pains to correct some of their statements. Much weight was given to his historical allusions; Sanday, for example, considered that the narrative bore stronger marks of originality and nearness to the facts than that of the Synoptic gospels.[1] Fairbairn's opinion was that

> a cycle of tradition that helps to explain it is slowly being recovered, and a clearer and more literary conception of the relation of the speeches to the speaker and the reporter is being formed, whilst a broader notion of its method and function is filling it with new historical content.[2]

In Germany Wellhausen and Ed. Schwartz suggested that behind the gospel there was an original document which had been worked over by a later hand, an idea which received little favour in England where the tendency was to regard it as representing the outcome of the meditations of St. John in old age. But even if this were the case the question remains as to what were actual facts and what were the fruits of the apostle's pious imaginings.

The vindication of the early date and genuineness of Acts[3] was a striking feature of our period. The Tübingen school had seen in it a late document designed to conciliate the various

[1] *Inspiration*, p. 287 and *The Expositor*, 1892, pp. 293–6.
[2] *The Place of Christ in Modern Theology*, p. 291.
[3] See further J. W. Hunkin in Foakes Jackson and Lake, *The Beginnings of Christianity*, Vol. II, pp. 396 ff.

warring elements which they professed to have discovered in the early Church, and in Germany many still clung obstinately to some such hypothesis, as Harnack observed as late as 1906.[1] Those who accepted the authenticity of the work received welcome and unexpected support from Sir William Ramsay, the archaeologist and classical scholar, who, having approached the Acts as a forgery of the mid-second century, was compelled to change his opinion owing to the accurate knowledge which the author evidently possessed of places in Asia Minor which he mentioned.[2] At first Ramsay limited his recognition of Lucan authorship to the 'we passages', but later he extended it to the whole. His two volumes, *The Church in the Roman Empire* (1893) and *St. Paul the Traveller and the Roman Citizen* (1895) made an impressive contribution to the subject.

The problem of the authorship of Acts divides itself into two parts; the relation of the so-called 'we passages' to the remainder of the book, and the connexion between it and the third gospel. Renan, it may be remarked, had accepted the Lucan authorship before 1883. As early as 1892 Harnack became convinced that the 'we passages' were by the same writer as the other parts of Acts, and, tentatively, that that author was St. Luke.[3] In England a vigorous plea for the early date of Acts was made by R. B. Rackham in the first volume of *The Journal of Theological Studies* (1899), which he followed up by the well-known commentary in the Westminster series.[4]

As in the case of Acts criticism of the Pauline epistles, towards the close of the century, was moving in a conservative direction. Baur had accepted only Galatians, Corinthians and Romans as fully genuine, but the opinion that, with the exception of the

---

[1] *Luke the Physician*, p. 7.

[2] Lightfoot in *Essays on 'Supernatural Religion'*, pp. 291 ff. had already drawn attention to the accuracy of the references to the geographical, political and social background.

[3] *Texte und Untersuchungen*, Vol. VIII, iv, pp. 37 ff. His chief writings on the subject did not appear until after the close of our period.

[4] In 1893 Sanday had deplored the lack of a good commentary in English on the Acts. (*Inspiration*, p. 319.) Rackham's work filled the gap for the time being.

Pastorals and Ephesians, they all came from St. Paul gradually began to prevail.[1] Many scholars were prepared to accept Ephesians also.[2] Objections to this epistle arose from its likeness to Colossians, the suggestion that the readers were unknown to the writer (1:15, 3:2, 4:21), and the lack of any reference to St. Paul's long sojourn there. But these difficulties are removed if, as the textual evidence suggests, the original letter was a circular sent to different churches with a special heading inserted in each several case. The position of the Pastoral epistles was more doubtful; though most of those who rejected them were prepared to admit that they contained Pauline matter. There were, however, scholars who accepted them. Hort believed that even in their present form they were by St. Paul;[3] as did Godet in his *Introduction to the Pauline Epistles* (1893) and Ramsay; whilst Sanday found the external evidence remarkably good and early.[4]

By way of reaction from the theories of the Tübingen school the writings of St. Paul were approached in a new spirit, and there was a tendency to emphasize their agreements with rather than their divergencies from other Christian documents. Somewhat later than our period Kirsopp Lake put this point of view very strongly.

> Treat the Epistles as letters; recognise that in letters the subjects discussed are not those on which all parties are agreed, but those on which there is difference of opinion, so that the really central points are not those which are supported by argument, but those which are assumed as generally believed, and it will appear that the Christianity of St. Paul did not really differ from that of the Catholic Church as we find it at the beginning of Christian history.[5]

Kirsopp Lake's comment draws attention to one weakness in the criticism of the epistles during much of our period, a

---

[1] The Dutch scholar Van Manen had rejected them all; but found few to share his views.

[2] Fairbairn did not consider that any case had been made against those generally accepted, including Ephesians (*op. cit.*, p. 303).

[3] *The Christian Ecclesia*, p. 171. [4] *Inspiration*, p. 364.

[5] *The Earlier Epistles of St. Paul* (1911), p. 424.

weakness inherited from earlier times and not yet, it may be said, entirely eliminated; that of treating St. Paul as the framer of a theological system, and of regarding his epistles, in consequence, not as occasional letters, but as careful and elaborate statements of doctrine. One result of this treatment was to distract attention from the man himself and his experiences and to ignore his historical setting.[1]

The growth of a more critical attitude towards the gospels and the questioning of the extent to which they had been influenced by later ideas made scholars turn the more eagerly to the writings of St. Paul, which were admittedly among the earliest Christian documents we possess, earlier even than the gospels in their present form. Some, indeed, exaggerated the influence of St. Paul and set him up as the real founder of Christianity as it developed in the second century. The relation of the teaching of St. Paul to that of the original Gospel proclaimed by Jesus, however, did not in England arouse nearly as much attention as it did in Germany, and to a slighter extent in France.

The most important contribution of English scholarship came from Lightfoot. His commentary on *Galatians*, which appeared in 1865, set a new standard for such productions. It was followed by *Philippians* (1868) and *Colossians* (1875); whilst notes on othe: epistles were published in 1895 soon after his death. Scholars in England were pretty well agreed in their views of the Pauline epistles, save in the case of the recipients of the epistle to the Galatians. In 1867 Perrot in *De Galatia prov. Romana*, pp. 43 f. had suggested that they were not some otherwise unknown Christians in the north of the province, but those whose evangelization is recorded in the first missionary journey in Acts.[2] This so-called South Galatian theory did not attract much notice in England until it was taken up by Ramsay in *The Historical Geography of Asia Minor* (1890) and later in his commentary (1899). Thereafter it was accepted by a number of scholars,

[1] One interesting attempt to restore the balance was H. St. John Thackeray, *The Relation of St. Paul to Contemporary Jewish Thought* (1900).

[2] This was also the opinion of Renan and most French critics.

including Askwith *Date and Destination of Galatians* (1899), though it did not receive entire agreement. Some critics who accepted the South Galatian theory felt that it involved a much earlier date for the epistle and therefore made it the first of all the Pauline writings.

Of the remaining books of the New Testament not much calls for notice. Westcott brought out a commentary on *Hebrews* in 1889. Hebrews had originally been assigned to Hort, and had he undertaken it his commentary would probably have been very different from that of Westcott whose knowledge of the Old Testament and of Judaism in the Christian era was not so profound. Westcott also published a commentary on the *Johannine Epistles* in 1883. The other General epistles failed to find scholars in agreement. Most English scholars, led by J. B. Mayor, held James to have been written by the brother of the Lord, and to be early; but on the Continent it was generally put much later, perhaps as late as the middle of the second century. There was much the same divergence of views over 1 Peter. As to 2 Peter and Jude, which are closely linked, there was a tendency to regard them both as late documents, though some critics accepted the genuineness of Jude.

The book of Revelation[1] produced no outstanding volume from English scholars; Benson, indeed, published a commentary in 1900, but it was, from the standpoint of scholarship, very inadequate as the writer lacked any adequate knowledge of the Jewish background. Hort had lectured on the first three chapters in 1889 and his notes were published in 1908. He placed the composition of the book under Nero, rejecting the prevailing idea that it came from the reign of Domitian, and Sanday in the preface to Hort's posthumous volume was inclined to take the suggestion seriously, though he recognized its difficulties, as Hort himself had done.[2] The early date made it easier to attribute both Revelation and the gospel to St. John, for difference of style

[1] See further Milligan, *Discussions on the Apocalypse* (1893).

[2] Earlier still Sanday had expressed the view that the arguments for the earlier date were still unanswered (*Inspiration*, p. 373).

and ideas might then be explained as due to lapse of time. The Tübingen school had accepted the Johannine authorship of Revelation, but not of the gospel. Conservative scholars in England were inclined to recognize his authorship of both books; a more advanced group, however, suggested that they came from the same circle in Asia Minor, though composed by different writers. In 1886 Harnack and Vischer had put forward the notion that Revelation consisted of two parts, the earlier written by a Jew in the time of Nero, and the later a kind of supplement added by a Jewish Christian in the time of Domitian. This view did not find much acceptance. In the general approach to the book and its contents there had been a noteworthy change, for it

> ceased to be read and interpreted as a mysterious prophecy which conceals even more than it reveals all the destinies of all the empires that rule the Christian centuries, and has become one of our most significant documents for the interpretation of the mind of the parties within the primitive Church.[1]

Having given a brief account of the historical and literary criticism of the New Testament we come now to consider the criticism of the text.[2] The importance of establishing the true text cannot be exaggerated, for the interpretation of a passage may depend on a single word. The Received text, which underlies the Authorized English Version is unsatisfactory, for it was the product of an age when the principles of the science were but little understood, and in any case it is based on what are now known to have been inferior MSS. Attempts to arrive at a more satisfactory text had been made before 1860 by Lachmann, Tregelles, and Tischendorf; but their suggested emendations did not go very far. When, however, Tischendorf discovered the Codex Sinaiticus in 1859 he proceeded to construct a much more radical text. Still further changes followed the publication by the papal authorities of an edition of the Codex Vaticanus in 1867.

The main credit for the great advance in textual criticism

---

[1] Fairbairn, *op. cit.*, p. 19.
[2] See further Kenyon, *The Textual Criticism of the New Testament* (1901).

which was a feature of New Testament scholarship in our period belongs to the English scholars Westcott and Hort, and above all to the latter.[1] They may not, indeed, have made discoveries of fresh MSS., but they made full use of the materials collected by others. Their text did not appear until 1881 and in the introduction Hort laid down the principles which must underlie all adequate textual criticism. The theory of Westcott and Hort, which was based on the division of MSS. into families, was not entirely novel, having already been employed by Griesbach, but they applied it in a new manner. The available MSS. were arranged by them in four groups. The Received text, which they called Syrian, was placed later than the rest, and the greatest weight was given to the Neutral group which depended on the two ancient codices, Vaticanus and Sinaiticus. Related to this latter group was the Alexandrian which differed from it mainly in a careful regard for correctness of style and language. Finally there was the so-called Western text which had been widely current in the second century and was to be found chiefly in Codex Bezae, the Old Latin, and other versions.

When Westcott and Hort finally published their text it met with fierce criticism in some ultra-orthodox quarters. Dean Burgon, the principal defender of the Received text, was no mean scholar, but his knowledge of the subject was clearly inadequate, for such knowledge could come only after long years of toil and reflection. If, however, his knowledge was defective he made up for it by his immense controversial powers. The attack was delivered in three articles in *The Quarterly Review*, later republished in a volume entitled *The Revision Revised* (1883). Burgon poured much ridicule on the notion that the true text had been lost for fifteen hundred years and that it was to be found in only two MSS.—Vaticanus and Sinaiticus.[2] These he likened to the 'two false witnesses' of Matt. 26:60. He also drew

[1] Each worked independently and then compared their results. See *Life of Hort*, Vol. II, pp. 243 ff.

[2] Ramsay, it may be noted, considered that there were cases in *Acts* 'in which over-estimate of the the two great MSS. . . . has led to the adoption of a reading which obscures history'. (*St. Paul the Traveller and the Roman Citizen*, p. 24.)

attention to some weak points in the theories underlying the text which would later be developed. Hort himself took no notice of such onslaughts, but Sanday made a reply in *The Contemporary Review*. Less prejudiced and better qualified scholars, however, welcomed the results of Hort's labours; some even went so far as to consider that the last word had been spoken on the subject. This, however, was too optimistic a conclusion, for the discovery of fresh material and more recent work suggest that Westcott and Hort undervalued the Western text which they regarded as a corruption of the Neutral. Another conclusion has also undergone criticism. Hort had affirmed that 'even among the numerous unquestionably spurious readings of the New Testament there are no signs of deliberate falsification of the text for dogmatic reasons'.[1] This is hardly the view of present-day critics who consider that the text was more freely handled in the early days than Hort realized,[2] though Sanday had discerned its possibilities.[3]

Criticisms of Westcott and Hort which have been made since the appearance of their text, however, affect but a few passages, and we may still be assured that it, or something very like it, gives us a more solid foundation for the text of the New Testament than exists for any other ancient writing.[4]

In addition to the textual criticism of the Greek New Testament much work was also done on the text of the versions and above all on the Latin. Rönsch's *Itala und Vulgata* appeared in 1868 and a second edition in 1875, but in England it was John Wordsworth,[5] with the help of H. J. White, who bore the burden of this inquiry. He began work in 1878, but spent much time over preliminary explorations and it was not until 1882 that he issued a detailed prospectus, *The Oxford Critical Edition of the Vulgate New Testament*. The first part did not appear until 1889,

[1] *Introduction*, p. 282.
[2] See C. S. C. Williams, *Alterations to the Text of the Synoptic Gospels and Acts*.
[3] See *Inspiration*, pp. 295 and 297 where he said that 'the functions of copyist and editor were apt to run into each other', and 'at first freedom was the rule, scrupulous accuracy the exception, in propagating the text of the Gospels'.
[4] For later developments see Kenyon, Schweich Lectures for 1932.
[5] See E. W. Watson, *John Wordsworth*, pp. 140ff.

and the second which completed the gospels in 1898. The work is still incomplete though additional parts have been published at regular intervals.

The disclosure of the unreliability of the Received text led the Canterbury Convocation to appoint a committee in 1870 for the purpose of revising the Authorised Version of the Bible. Scholars who were not Anglicans were invited to take part in the work of the committee. The New Testament came out in 1881, the year of the publication of the text of Westcott and Hort, and was followed by the Old Testament in 1885; the Apocrypha had to wait for another eleven years. The Revised Version met with a varied reception; it was certainly more accurate than the Authorized, but unfamiliarity told against it; it had also undoubtedly suffered from a literary standpoint and can hardly be said to have carried out the expressed intention of the promoters to produce a rendering which would be both 'literal and idiomatic, faithful to each thought of the original, and yet in the expression harmonious and free'. Many of the changes were slight and unimportant, there were 36,000 in the New Testament alone, and caused irritation and at the same time often marred the familiar cadence of the older version. Some of the defects of the Revision were due to its having had too many 'cooks' and the impossibility of getting complete agreement, and as many of them were orthodox and not a little timid, what was really the better reading often found no place in the text,[1] but was consigned to the margin. There can be no doubt that the whole scheme was premature, and as Armitage Robinson has said: 'It is one of the tragedies of Scholarship that the version was made a generation too soon.'[2]

[1] Timidity and a sentimental conservatism no doubt were also responsible for the retention of erroneous renderings (as distinct from changes demanded by better readings). An example is Ps. 23: 2 'he leadeth me beside the still waters', an operation which no Palestinian shepherd could have carried out; what the Hebrew really says is 'he leadeth me *to* refreshing waters'.

[2] In *Lightfoot of Durham*, p. 126. Hort had written in 1870 that 'the criticism of both Testaments, in text and interpretation alike appears to me to be just now in that chaotic state . . . that the results of immediate revision would be peculiarly unsatisfactory'. (*Life*, Vol. II, p. 128.)

Westcott and Hort's text of the New Testament was perhaps the greatest single contribution to biblical studies made by English scholars in our period; but there was much else of which we may be proud. If the whole contribution was not on so vast and comprehensive a scale as that of the Germans, it represented much solid work, though in the light of further progress it now seems a trifle over-cautious. But the fact that it was less spectacular and experimental was really an advantage; for a slow growth is not subject to those reactions which so often follow more revolutionary changes. English theology has ever been 'determined to make good the lesser steps before it attempts the greater'.[1] It has also to be remembered that English theology had behind it, what German theology lacked, a long and honourable tradition of sober achievement, and that its very maturity made it hesitant over embarking too readily on new ventures. England certainly possessed scholars of the first rank, though not in such numbers as did Germany. Acton in his inaugural lecture as Professor of Modern History in Cambridge could affirm that Lightfoot and Hort 'were critical scholars whom neither Frenchman nor German has surpassed'.[2] If they lacked some of the merits of the Germans they also avoided some of the defects and limitations which so often rendered the work of the latter less fruitful than otherwise it might have been. We watch with amazement their diligence and persistency, as with Teutonic thoroughness they unwaveringly pursue the 'infinitely little', and we admire their courage and veracity, their literary and historic sense. But at the same time we deplore their lack of imagination and their tendency to judge authorities as if they were German professors writing in their studies and surrounded by works of reference. As a result of their ignorance of life as it is lived outside a lecture room, they failed to give vitality or even coherence to the facts which they accumulated with such laboriousness. Westcott said, 'they never look through the records to what lies beyond them', whilst Fairbairn found them wanting in

[1] Sanday, *op. cit.*, p. xvii.
[2] *Lectures in Modern History*, p. 17.

'reverence, love of the beautiful and the sense of the holy'.[1] Perhaps as good a summing up as any was that which came from Frederick Temple who had some familiarity with their writings: 'They did admirable service: for there are no other investigators like them for patience and thoroughness. But I was long ago convinced that the last word can never come from Germany.'[2]

[1] *The Place of Christ in Modern Theology*, p. 192.

[2] Sandford, *F. Temple: an Appreciation*, p. 198. These drawbacks were not confined to theologians, for Conington, the Professor of Latin at Oxford, found the same kind of failure to understand the classics. This he put down to the absence in German education of the high place given to composition which in England taught men to appreciate the spirit of the writers whom they attempted to imitate. See E. W. Watson, *Life of John Wordsworth*, p. 51, note 1.

Chapter Eight

THE BIBLE:
INSPIRATION: REVELATION

DURING our period various factors were at work to change men's views of the Bible; natural science had clearly demonstrated that its statements concerning the physical world could not be made to square with what had come to be known of that world;[1] whilst biblical studies had shown with almost equal clarity that many of the accounts contained in it could no longer be taken in a literal sense.

In consequence of biblical studies, which are here our main concern, a number of conclusions had gradually been established, at least for thoughtful people. It was recognized, for example, that the Bible was not all of a piece, but the outcome of a long process; even the New Testament was seen to consist of different layers, for ideas and doctrines are found in the Pauline epistles and in the fourth gospel which are absent from the earlier records of the Synoptists. In the past both orthodox and sceptics had regarded the Bible as a single whole; now both alike could agree that its contents were diverse, and that a more discriminating approach to them was necessary.

Another conclusion was that allegorical interpretation was no safe or sufficient guide, and as a result many passages in the Old Testament which had been regarded as Messianic forecasts were rejected. Again, comparative philology had shown that the

[1] The realization of this had come earlier, at least to educated people. Ruskin had written in 1851: 'If only the Geologists would let me alone, I could do very well, but those dreadful hammers! I hear the clink of them at the end of every cadence of the Bible verses.' (Cook, *Life of Ruskin*, Vol. II, pp. 19f.)

175

languages in which the Bible was written were not unique. Hebrew was merely one member of a group of Semitic languages, and not, as some had supposed, the speech of the heavenly courts;[1] whilst the Greek of the Septuagint and of the New Testament was largely that used in the contemporary world.

Theologians in applying to the Bible the methods of historical criticism had to treat it like any other book,[2] and it was this process, perhaps more than any other, that caused the greatest unsettlement. Renan tells us that he gave up orthodox Christianity, not on account of difficulties about miracles or the supernatural, but solely in consequence of biblical criticism. 'If I could have believed that theology and the Bible were true, none of the doctrines would have given me any trouble. My reasons were entirely of a philological and critical order.'[3] To many, quite apart from any results that scholars might claim to have reached, the attempt itself savoured of blasphemy. So men had condemned Erasmus because, as they said, by correcting errors in the text of the New Testament he was making the Holy Ghost conform to the rules of grammar.

Upholders of the traditional view of the Bible might scoff at the variety and contradictory nature of many of the new theories, none the less they had a kind of cumulative effect and aroused much alarm. This was made more terrifying by the fact that since critical inquiries were possible only for the few they constituted a vague and mysterious threat; and also by the failure of the conservatives to make any distinction between the reverent scholarship of those who sincerely accepted the Christian faith

---

[1] There is a story told of an elderly lady who began the study of Hebrew in order to fit herself for the converse of the life to come.

[2] The Bible, of course, can never be treated exactly like any other book, for it is wrapped up in the history of the society which produced it—the People of God. Moreover, its contents make it different from any other collection of literature. What scholars claimed was that similar methods should be employed. Davidson in the preface to his commentary on *Job* (1862) complained that the usual approach was defective, for by it exegesis and grammar were deduced from dogmatic, instead of dogmatic being deduced from grammar.

[3] *Recollections of my Youth*, p. 260.

and the wildest of rationalists.[1] Indeed it was the use of such methods and the acceptance of such views by some of the clergy, and their prevalence in the universities, which was the most potent cause of distress and irritation. The alarm of the tradition-alists was further increased by the declaration of the Lambeth Conference of 1897 that it was the right and the duty of Christian theologians and teachers to apply critical methods to every part of the Bible, and by its confident anticipation that the results of such a process would be 'an increased and more vivid sense of the Divine revelation'.

But even some of those whose standpoint was less rigid shared in the prevailing alarm, and the question was naturally asked 'If once you begin to tamper with the Bible where will you stop?' Carlyle, in spite of his genuine admiration for Dean Stanley, is said to have remarked: 'There's that Dean, down in the hold; bore, bore, boring, and some day he will bore through and let all the water in.'

Christian scholars did not look upon their views as a rejection of the belief that a revelation was contained in the Bible, all that they affected was the form which the revelation had taken. Nor did they deny the presence in it of inspiration, but sought by an examination of the various parts of the Bible to determine the manner of its operation. Here it is necessary to distinguish clearly between the different elements in the record and to limit the function of inspiration to what may be called the spiritual aspect. The biblical writers nowhere claim to have received information on historical matters from supernatural sources; like other historians they simply made use of whatever material was available to them. This is clearly demonstrated by Luke 1:1-4. As Driver has said, 'the function of inspiration was to guide them in the disposal and arrangement of their materials, and in the use to which they applied them'. None the less criticism of any and every kind seemed a direct challenge to the

[1] Cf. Davidson, *Life of A. C. Tait*, Vol. 1, p. 276: 'The science of reverent Biblical criticism was, to most people, absolutely unknown ... and it is difficult to realize the vague terror with which much of what is today the general belief of Christian men was lumped together as "Rationalism".'

traditional view, a view which was held by Evangelicals and Tractarians alike.

But the traditional view rested on very insecure foundations and had no justification in the Bible itself. It had arisen partly from an erroneous interpretation of the phrase 'the Word of God', which was identified with the Bible, and partly from the Jewish attitude to the Old Testament, which was taken over and extended to the New. At the time of the Reformation stress had been laid on the witness of the Scriptures, and unjustifiable ideas of the manner of their inspiration (a matter which the Church has never defined) began gradually to impose themselves on later Protestant thought. This had not been the case in the earliest days of the movement; for Luther had been somewhat of an iconoclast in his views of the Bible. Not only did he reject James 'as an epistle of straw', but also Revelation, and declared that he found more of a Gospel in St. Paul's epistles than in the Synoptics. He could even make merry over the childishness of the book of Jonah and deny the Mosaic authorship of parts of the Pentateuch.

The popular view of inspiration was possible only because of complete ignorance of the manner in which the Bible, and in particular the New Testament, had come into being. Nothing was known of the long process by which certain books were eventually accepted as canonical, and others rejected. Men spoke as if the Bible in its present form had dropped straight from Heaven. In practice most Englishmen believed in the inspiration of the Authorized Version (hence the alarm over textual criticism and revision) and there is a story of a mythical working man who gave up Christianity on being assured that the Bible was not originally written in English.

The idea of an inspired book is difficult to grasp, though not the notion of inspired writers. The prevalent view was that in the case of the Bible these had been mere scribes who wrote from divine dictation. A more seemly idea of God and of His ways with man would have exposed the unworthiness of such a mechanical conception, which robbed the messengers of all individuality and reduced them to the level of mere instruments.

Such was not God's method, and it is very significant that divine providence had so arranged matters that no written words have come down from our Lord. The theory of verbal inspiration seeks 'to do what our Lord was careful not to do . . . to put our Gospels in the position that actual writings of our Lord would have held'.[1] Had such writings been sanctioned and adopted as God's means of revealing Himself they might have prevented all further investigation of the truth, except possibly by allegorical methods. There is a further difficulty which the exponents of the theory seem not to have realized—a verbally inspired book cannot be translated. This is the position of Islam where attempts to translate the Qur'ān are regarded as sacrilege. The Jews had provided for this difficulty by the legend that the seventy translators of the Septuagint each produced an identical rendering, and thus demonstrated that they were just as much under the influence of inspiration as the original authors.

Christian scholars, as we have seen, did not reject the idea of inspiration however radically their views might differ from those which had become traditional. To reject it, indeed, would have involved 'the denial of all spiritual influence of God upon man; and the next step is the denial of any true Personality in God Himself'.[2]

It must never be forgotten that there are two sides to inspiration; there is the God who inspires, and there are the agents whom He chooses to receive and transmit the revelation. It 'is not concerned simply with the production of a record, nor does revelation merely denote the record so produced; but the one represents the Godward, the other the manward side of the creative process in religion'.[3]

The presence of inspiration is not to be sought in the separate writings so much as in the Bible as a whole in which 'everything is presented to us as illustrating God's dealings with man'.[4]

[1] Latham, *Pastor Pastorum*, p. 15.
[2] Sanday in a sermon printed in *Inspiration*, p. 445.
[3] Fairbairn, *The Place of Christ in Modern Theology*, pp. 496f.
[4] Gore, *Lux Mundi*, p. 252.

Furthermore it is to be sought in the writers, rather than in the writings. By this means the freedom of the individual is preserved and his special gifts are allowed expression. 'Inspiration is surely not incompatible with considerate workmanship', A. C. Bradley has written of the poet,[1] and the same is true of the authors of the canonical books. Gwatkin would go further and find it also in the work of the devout scholar, declaring that 'sound criticism is as truly a divine revelation as Scripture itself, and we shall fail in our duty to Him who is the truth if we foreclose the question'.

Inspiration may be much more common than is sometimes imagined, may be, indeed, 'the final term of a power of which each individual possesses the rudiments'.[2] It is noteworthy that Sanday testified that in the course of his work on the subject it had been more and more brought home to him that 'to think truly of Inspiration it should be thought of as acting through the mass—here weakly, there strongly—but yet in different degrees permeating the whole'.[3]

The realization of the true nature and function of inspiration, combined with the results of biblical study and the acceptance of the findings of natural science, made necessary a new conception of the meaning of revelation. Fairbairn considered that to achieve it there was need for 'the restoration of the organic union, in the Holy Spirit, of God, the Reason, the Church, the Scriptures'.[4]

Our conception of revelation must depend ultimately on our conception of God. If we lay emphasis on His transcendence we shall find revelation in outward events or in the delivery through duly accredited messengers of the divine word. If, on the other hand, we emphasize His immanence we shall see in revelation, as did Schleiermacher, the inward answer to human hopes and aspirations.

Those who, in our period, thought of God primarily as

---

[1] *Shakespearean Tragedy*, p. 68.

[2] Evelyn Underhill, *Mysticism*, p. 87.

[3] *Op. cit.*, p. xi. He did not, of course, deny that selected individuals, some of them anonymous, were the recipients of revelation (p. 443).

[4] *Op. cit.*, pp. 511f.

immanent could no longer accept the idea of revelation as coming from a God outside the world who gave it in the form of infallible oracles and imperative decrees which must be received without question.[1] They demanded an idea less static and legalistic, an idea which would deal 'with man, not as a stationary being, but as advancing with a continuous growth'.[2] In other words they were much more concerned with revelation as a present reality than as something which had happened in the past. 'When we are quite sure that God is speaking now . . . we shall not grow wild in discussing how He spoke once.'[3]

One of the first English theologians to proclaim the progressive nature of revelation was T. D. Bernard in his Bampton Lectures for 1864. He affirmed that in view of the work of criticism the Bible must be regarded as the record of a revelation that was still incomplete, and that, as a consequence, revelation could not be confined to the Bible and to a message delivered long ago. The advocates of this view maintained that God was ever disclosing Himself through His acts in history, both that of the Church and of the world at large, and also in the physical universe, for 'Earth's most exquisite disclosure may be Heaven's own God in evidence.'[4] A growing knowledge of other religions also demonstrated that God had not left Himself without witness among non-Jewish and non-Christian peoples; they too had had their inspired teachers and prophets.[5]

We thus find in existence two extreme attitudes towards revelation; one which viewed it as delivered to man through some miraculous superhuman communication, the other seeing revelation in the fact that man possessed a nature (given him by God) which enabled him, by the exercise of his powers of

[1] For some 'an authoritative revelation implies the incompetence of human reason either to discover or to criticize its content'. (Caird, *The Philosophy of Religion*, p. 6.)

[2] Westcott, *The Gospel of Life*, p. 288.

[3] *Life of Westcott*, Vol. II, p. 68.

[4] Browning, *La Saisiaz*, 6.

[5] Cf. the rather grudging admission of Sanday, *op. cit.*, p. 128 (note the small *i*); 'In claiming for the Bible Inspiration we do not exclude the possibility of other lower forms of inspiration in other literatures.'

reflection and imagination, to arrive at the same results. Between these apparently irreconcilable positions there is, however, no complete or necessary contradiction. The message which God reveals to His servants before it can be accepted by others must convince them of its divine sanction and origin, must in effect agree with notions already cherished of what is worthy of such a source. Coleridge long before had insisted that the objective revelation contained in the Bible must be made to correspond with the subjective revelation acquired by the spirit of man. Man is not confronted with mysteries intended to baffle his reason, but with the expression of principles which that reason has already enabled him to work out. Even the most primitive and lowly attempts to explain God, man, and the universe, may be used as a means of revelation.[1]

The conflict between the idea of a revelation given once and for all and a revelation which is continuous and still going on is capable of reconciliation if it is granted that the 'statement' of the revelation is distinct from the revelation itself. The latter is 'Absolute in its essence [but] relative so far as the human apprehension of it at any time is concerned.'[2] No age has yet fathomed the full meaning of the revelation given in Jesus Christ, and fresh experience is ever bringing out new aspects of its significance, as God fulfils Himself in many ways. That revelation was complete in itself and nothing need, or, indeed, can be added to it, 'but all history and all nature are a commentary upon it'.[3]

The idea of the divine disclosure, like the divine creation, as being a continuous process shifted the emphasis from revelation as the act of God, to revelation as the discovery of man. To some thinkers this seemed like a substitution of natural for revealed

[1] Cf. F. H. Chase, *The Lord's Prayer in the Early Church*: 'The method of divine revelation often lies in the absorption of some popular belief which is afterwards purified and spiritualized by a process of co-ordination.'

[2] Westcott, *The Gospel of Life*, p. xxiii.

[3] Westcott, *Religious Thought in the West*, p. 360. Cf. Gore in *Lux Mundi*, p. xxx. 'Progress in Christianity is always reversion to an original and perfect type, not addition to it: it is progress only in the understanding of Christ.'

religion.[1] But this is really a false antithesis and to make too sharp a division between them is to repeat the error of the medieval schoolmen.[2] All religion must have in it an element of revelation, for unless God willed it man could discover nothing concerning Him.[3] Here it may be observed that Clement of Alexandria refused to make any distinction between what man discovers and God reveals;[4] and it is not out of place to compare Westcott's description of inspiration as partly the insight of holiness and partly its divine reward. God is not only the object of man's search, but is Himself present in those who seek. There may be an 'initiative of the eternal', but man's search must precede God's response;[5] for until man sets out to find God he is unable to appreciate that which may meet him by the way. Thus Christianity was 'envisaged as the culmination of a universal process which was at once God's revelation of Himself to man and man's discovery of God; for how could God be discovered except by His own act, or reveal Himself except to a mind prepared for the reception of the revelation?'[6] None the less the idea that man had any significant part in the process was obnoxious to many theologians as liable to undermine the authority of religion. Robertson Smith made an interesting comment on this.

There is a positive element in all religion, an element which we have learned from those who went before us. If what is so learned is true, we must ultimately come back to a point in history when it was new truth, acquired ... by some particular man or circle of men who, as they did not learn it from their predecessors, must have got it by personal revelation from God Himself. To deny that

[1] Cf. Martineau's distinction, 'Natural religion is that in which man finds God; revealed religion is that in which God finds man.' (*The Seat of Authority in Religion*, p. 302.)

[2] Cf. Quick, *Doctrines of the Creed*, pp. 9 ff. and Inge, *Studies of English Mystics*, pp. 1 f.

[3] 'About God it is possible to learn only from God.' (Athenagoras).

[4] See *Protrept.* VI, *Strom.* I, v and xix.

[5] Hort, *The Way, the Truth, the Life*, p. 1.

[6] C. C. J. Webb, *op. cit.*, p. 167. Cf. A. L. Moore in *Lux Mundi*, p. 66: 'A truth revealed by God is never a truth out of relation with previous thought. He leads men to feel their moral and intellectual needs before He satisfies either.'

13

Christianity can ultimately be traced back to such acts of revelation
. . . involves in the last resort a denial that there is any true religion
at all, or that religion is anything more than a mere subjective feeling.[1]

None the less it was the opinion of J. B. Mozley that 'People
will not respect their own creation of religion; and it is mere
folly to think they will let it command or coerce them.'[2]

Dr. Mozley thus objected to the new views on practical
grounds; but for many they were unsatisfactory on intellectual
grounds, as fostering uncertainty and depriving man of knowledge which he thought that he possessed. Such an attitude,
however, was based on a wrong idea of the purpose of revelation.
It was given primarily, not to satisfy the intellect, but to set men
in the way of salvation; for 'the Gospel claims to be "a power of
God unto salvation" and not simply a declaration of the nature
and will of God'.[3] The motive and impulse of the very first
chapter of the Bible was, as Gore pointed out, 'not the satisfaction
of a fantastic curiosity, nor the later interest in scientific discovery,
but to reveal certain fundamental religious principles'.[4]

The attempt to limit any genuine revelation to a single line of
development, that contained in the Bible, was to condemn man,
as Mansel in effect had done, 'to a dark night of agnosticism
concerning God, apart from the light given by revelation'.[5]
None the less to deny this limitation is not necessarily to deny
that God in a special sense disclosed Himself to the Jewish people.
Such would seem to be the divine method. 'The election was
simply a method of procedure adopted by God in His wisdom
by which He designed to fit the few for blessing the many, one
for blessing all.'[6]

The Christian claim to possess a special revelation—and apart
from this claim Christianity has no message for mankind which
mankind could not receive through other channels—depends

---

[1] *The Prophets of Israel*, p. 12.   [2] *Letters*, p. 284.
[3] Westcott, *The Gospel of Life*, p. 297.
[4] In *Lux Mundi*, p. 252.
[5] J. K. Mozley, *Some Tendencies in British Theology*, p. 154.
[6] A. B. Bruce, *The Chief End of Revelation*, p. 116.

ultimately for its justification on the manner in which it is upheld in the history of the world and of the Church; on whether, as H. G. Hamilton has written, 'when the scientific process is over, there are facts and considerations which make such an interpretation appear as part of a moral and intelligible system of progress'.[1] That such a revelation is continuous should present no difficulty to those who believe in the work of the Holy Spirit through the Church; provided always that there is no belittling of the unique revelation in the historic Christ. 'The Gospel', Gwatkin has said, 'is not a growth of this world, but a revelation from the unseen. Men do not set forth in it their passing opinions about God, but God reveals in Christ His own eternal thoughts.'[2]

The new conception of revelation by rejecting the notion that the Bible is a kind of legal code did not deny its value. The Bible is the record of certain happenings in history by which God revealed Himself; happenings, moreover, inspired and controlled by Him for the furtherance of man's salvation. Such a view gives full recognition to the demands of the historian and the philosopher, and above all it recognizes a rational element in man which is one of the proofs that he is made in the image of that God who was revealed in Jesus Christ not only as the Way and the Life, but also as the Truth.

The application of the new methods to the Bible naturally aroused alarm and disquiet in the minds of many Christians, especially among simple folk; but for the educated it brought definite gains, since they were now able to read the Bible in such a way as still to find in it a message from God to the individual and the race which they could receive without mental qualms. The Bible, moreover, seemed to gain a new kind of authority with the mere discovery that religion had not come out of the Bible, but that the Bible had come out of religion.[3] Thus the

---

[1] *The People of God*, Vol. I, p. xxxi. Cf. Westcott, *The Incarnation and Common Life*, p. vi. 'The highest conceivable attestation of a divine revelation lies in its power to meet each new want of man as it arises, and to gain fresh force from the growth of human knowledge.'

[2] *The Sacrifice of Thankfulness*, p. 10.

[3] H. Drummond, *The New Evangelism*, p. 54.

new methods, even if at first sight they seemed to rob men of things which they valued, might on fuller reflection be understood as the means of teaching fresh lessons and of quickening insight into divine truth. As such they were welcomed by many serious and devout believers who came to recognize the hand of God behind what had looked like sheer deprivation. It is thus that God ever trains His children. 'If He takes away any familiar signs of His presence, it is because they are becoming hindrances to the ripening of discipleship.'[1] In 1888 Westcott could assert that 'already we are coming to know the blessing which the withdrawal of old opinions discloses; to know, as we have never known before, that the Bible is a living Book'.[2]

That even a minority of Christians should have come to the realization of the Bible as a living book was all to the good, for it carried with it the recognition that the writers 'though illuminated from on high were yet of like passions with themselves'.[3] This applied, in the Old Testament, especially to the prophets, who were now studied in the context of their own times, and their message interpreted accordingly. A further stage came with the realization that their social teaching had still a meaning, and could be applied to conditions as they were in the late nineteenth century. This could never have taken place had their writings continued to be regarded as merely collections of texts. For apologetics the new standpoint may have involved the abandonment of the old mechanical idea of the detailed fulfilment of prophecy; but that idea had been crude and unworthy, and its loss was really an advantage, for the argument still had force when transformed 'by the increased power to apprehend its breadth and solidity which our historically trained modern minds should have gained'.[4] The same was true of the New Testament, where 'the Apostolic epistles [gained] immeasurably in freshness and felt reality by the

---

[1] Hort, *The Way, the Truth, the Life*, p. 34.

[2] From a sermon in Westminster Abbey on 'The Conditions of Progressive Revelation' printed in *The Incarnation and Common Life*, pp. 375 ff. The quotation occurs on p. 383.

[3] Sanday, *op. cit.*, pp. 430 f.

[4] E. S. Talbot in *Lux Mundi*, p. 119.

growing anxiety to read them in the light of the personal and historic circumstances out of which they sprang'.[1]

If 'a far more vivid and more real apprehension of the Old Testament both as history and religion [had] been obtained',[2] so also the new outlook helped to remove many stumbling-blocks. This applied especially to the moral difficulties of the Old Testament to which believers had been strangely blind, or if they recognized them had explained them away by allegory.[3] Such evasions could no longer be practised when the Bible was treated like any other book. Scholars now saw in them examples of the process by which Christianity had been raised from very lowly beginnings. It may be noticed that some of the early Fathers of the Church, having discerned the shortcomings of the Old Testament, had regarded them as part of the necessary training of the Jewish people.

To have such an explanation available, especially as it fitted in with the prevailing belief in evolution, was pure gain. Henry Drummond in an article in *The Expositor* for February 1885 on 'The Contribution of Science to Christianity' had admitted that there were things in the Old Testament which, cast in the teeth of the apologist, left him without any answer under the traditional views, but that a 'new exegesis, a reconsideration of the historic setting' changed them 'from barriers into bulwarks of the faith'. Thus even the moral deficiencies of parts of the Old Testament and their crude conceptions of the Almighty were capable of being turned to good account. 'To the modern mind the Bible would be incomplete ... if it did not include the traces of childhood's faith as well as the matured experience of the perfect man.'[4]

Thus for scholars and people of education the authority of the

---

[1] Hort, *The Christian Ecclesia*, p. 235. (From the sermon preached at Westcott's consecration in 1890.)

[2] Sanday, *op. cit.*, p. 122.

[3] Mansel had put forward the suggestion that there might be suspensions of the moral law parallel to the suspension of the natural law in the case of miracles. See C. C. J. Webb, *Religious Thought in England*, p. 91.

[4] Allen, *The Continuity of Christian Thought*, p. 393.

Bible had been enhanced as a result of the intense process of criticism to which it had been subjected. If it was no longer accepted as 'infallible', and had lost something of its absoluteness, it was far less vulnerable and had a more rational basis. But even so the Church had a grave problem to face, a problem, indeed, which had been anticipated by Lessing, that of how 'to preserve the spiritual authority of Christianity when criticism was weakening the historical evidence for it'.[1] Much of this historical evidence was to be found in the Bible itself, which an age-long tradition had accepted as inerrant. C. C. J. Webb considered that the abandonment of this attitude was

> a greater theological revolution than any which has taken place in Christendom since those very early days in which it came to be realized that the Lord's return was not to be expected before the generation which has seen Him in the flesh had passed away and the Church was called to face the necessity of finding a *modus vivendi* with a world which showed no signs of coming to an abrupt and catastrophic end. For now the Church must accommodate itself to a situation in which it can no longer take the Bible for granted.[2]

No one, I suppose, would deny that even the simplest reader can obtain spiritual help from reading the Bible; but to appreciate its deeper meaning more than simple faith is necessary, for the Bible is far from self-explanatory. That those who read it may require someone to guide them is shown by the story of Philip and the Ethiopian eunuch (Acts 8:27 ff.). From quite early times various attempts at interpretation were invoked to bring out its meaning.[3] Those who believed that every single word in Scripture was inspired naturally sought for hidden meanings beneath the literary sense, often by the use of allegory. Such a method of interpretation has constantly been applied to writings which are held in particular honour and esteem and are thought to possess

---

[1] Storr, p. 163. [2] In *J.T.S.* (1953), p. 289.

[3] See F. W. Farrar, *The History of Interpretation* (the Bampton Lectures for 1885.) This volume is a vast store of varied learning and should counteract the idea that Farrar was merely a popular expositor with a slightly sentimental outlook.

some special inspiration;[1] but its employment is at bottom a confession that some desired interpretation is not to be discovered on the surface, and, in fact, that it has to be read into the text. The extent to which the method was pressed by many believers in verbal inspiration involved them in ridicule; such as in the cult of 'prophecy', a cult which provided so useful an occupation at one time for retired army officers in our inland watering-places. Its popularity may have been undermined by the not dissimilar crossword puzzle. No one, of course, would deny that new light is ever breaking forth from the Bible, for as George Herbert wrote in 'The Flower': 'Thy word is all if we could spell',[2] but methods of interpretation must be controlled by reason, and it may be added, by a seemly reverence.

The older interpreters had made a great use of isolated texts, and, indeed, treated the Bible as if it had been a legal code or a formal treatise. Modern methods are very different, and study the general development of ideas and institutions; they also endeavour to discover what message the original writers intended to convey to their day and generation.[3] Another popular notion had also to be abandoned, the idea that the best commentary on the Bible is the Bible itself. There is, of course, much truth in this notion; but its utility is strictly limited by the fact that since the authors of the different books came from an immense variety of times and circumstances the views which they put forth are often impossible to reconcile. Even in the New Testament the same terms may be used by different writers in different senses.

The problem of biblical interpretation was no new one, for men had ever come to the Scriptures with preconceived ideas,

---

[1] Cf. Sanday, *op. cit.*, p. 39: 'Only in a book which is regarded as possessing peculiar sacredness and authority is the attempt likely to be made to elicit another sense from the words than the obvious and literal one.'

[2] Cf. John Smith, *Select Discourses*, p. 184; *Nos non habemus aures, sicut Deus habet linguam.*

[3] Cf. A. B. Davidson, *The Called of God*, p. 35. 'There has been too much tendency to dissever revelation from any relation to the human mind in its origin, and to the men of its immediate times in its application. We have been too apt to look at it as coming from heaven like a meteoric stone, amazing to the spectators, but to be analysed and used only by a subsequent era.'

and were only too apt, in consequence, to ignore those elements which did not square with them. The contents of the Bible, indeed, had been constantly made to buttress contradictory doctrines as men read their own thoughts into it; for

> Echo with never a tongue
> Sings back to each bird in answer the song each bird has sung.

The conclusions of those who approach the Bible in this spirit would seem to have little more significance than the cry of the cuckoo who 'shouts all day at nothing'. But that is not all; such an approach, and the reading into the Bible of private meanings, may blind the eyes to fresh revelation. 'The Jews were close students of their Scriptures . . . and they failed to find in them the Christ as He was when He came. They had formed from the Scriptures a wrong conception of what He was to be, and therefore they could not accept Him.'[1]

One great disadvantage for the average Christian which followed on the new attitude to the Bible was that it could no longer be read and understood as in the days when it was regarded merely as a collection of texts; study and effort were demanded such as many of them were incapable of achieving. Hence perhaps the decay of the habit of reading the Bible. It is true that 'Helps' were now provided for those who cared to use them; but such volumes were not of much real value, since they tended to concentrate on small points of detail, such as might be useful for examination purposes, but were of small avail in bringing out the spiritual meaning. The Oxford Press produced *Helps to the Study of the Bible* in 1896, but it was conservative in tone and ignored even the most moderate results of criticism. The *Cambridge Companion to the Bible* published three years earlier was much superior in this respect.

Although a belief in the inerrancy of the Bible had been abandoned by scholars, it still persisted, and like an uneasy ghost unconsciously affected their outlook and methods. Such was the

---

[1] See a sermon on John, 5:39f. by J. F. Bethune-Baker printed in *The Faith of the Apostles' Creed*, pp. 197ff.

opinion of Sanday, who looking back in 1920 said 'I cannot help thinking that our method of theological study in the past has been too predominantly dogmatic. We are still haunted by the old belief in the infallibility of scripture and by the method of authority in teaching.'[1]

If scholars and the better educated were capable of adjusting themselves to the new way of regarding the Bible and at the same time of retaining a recognition of its authority this was not the case with men in general. For them the Bible, taken literally, had been the bedrock of their religion, and since Englishmen are a forth-right and truth-loving race, and disinclined to make fine distinctions, it was a case of all or nothing. If some things in the Bible were untrue, so they argued, could anything be accepted? Who were they to decide on particular statements when scholars were often in antagonism? So there followed a strong reaction from the narrow and even superstitious views of inspiration and infallibility which had once been accepted without question. The consequences of this change of attitude were disastrous; for the Bible fell into neglect, and even its noblest teaching was robbed of authority.[2]

[1] *Divine Overruling*, pp. 96f.
[2] Possibly something of this growing distrust lies behind the story of the small girl who, during the South African War, on being told about Jonah and the whale by her mother asked if it were true. On receiving the reply, 'Of course it's true, it's in the Bible,' she remarked, 'Yes, Mummy—but has it been confirmed by the War Office?'

Chapter Nine

COMPARATIVE RELIGION[1]

SHORTLY before the beginning of our period Jowett had ventured to prophesy that no influence was more likely to have greater effect on theology than an increasing knowledge of the religions of mankind.[2] As with not a few of his forecasts, though by no means all, this was justified in the event and the latter half of the nineteenth century was characterized by an intensive study of the subject. S. A. Cook has claimed that the application of anthropological and comparative methods, the unbiased co-ordination of all comparable data, irrespective of context or age, was amongst the most conspicuous features of modern research.[3]

The study was really a new one, for though the early Fathers, and even scholars in the Middle Ages, had noticed parallels between Christianity and other religions, except in regard to the Greeks and Romans,[4] and later Islam, they had had little available material, and in any case their work and methods had been quite unscientific. Popular interest in the subject had been aroused by Carlyle's lecture on Mohammed in May 1840, delivered as part of the series *On Heroes and Hero Worship*, and F. D. Maurice had

[1] For a useful summary of the subject see S. A. Cook in *E.R.E.*, Vol. x., pp. 664 ff. Studies published in the nineteenth century include E. Caird, *The Evolution of Religion*; F. B. Jevons, *Introduction to the History of Religion*; Max Müller, *The Origin and Growth of Religion*; Grant Allen, *The Evolution of the Idea of God*; Andrew Lang, *Myth, Literature and Religion* and *The Making of Religion*.

[2] *The Epistles of St. Paul*, Vol. II, p. 186.

[3] *Op. cit.*, p. 664. F. S. Marvin held that the tracing out of the development of religion was 'among the greatest conquests of the nineteenth century'. (*The Century of Hope*, p. 220.)

[4] Conyers Middleton in his *Letter from Rome* (1729) had drawn attention to the close similarities between modern Romanism and classical paganism.

taken *The Religions of the World* as the subject of the Boyle Lectures published in 1846.

It is difficult to understand why, save in the case of classical and Semitic religions the study had not attracted attention earlier; probably it was due to prejudice, for it was felt that there was something 'offensive in a theory which seems to include under the common designation of 'religion' the superstitions of heathenism and the spiritual faith of Christianity'.[1] But it was not only the beliefs of primitive peoples which were neglected, there was a similar ignoring by theologians of the great historical religions.[2] There were, of course, scholars who had a wider outlook, and in January 1874 R. W. Church could say: 'It is not surprising that these mysterious utterances, breaking on us . . . from the dawn of time, should have awakened a very deep interest. They seem to require us to revise our judgments and widen our thoughts.'[3]

The impulse to pursue the study was one manifestation of the desire of the age to get down to fundamentals, and it was provoked by the unveiling of vast quantities of new material upon which to work. This revealed, as Frazer has put it, 'the faith and the practice, the hopes and the ideals, not of two highly gifted races only, but of all mankind . . . We of today must recognize a new province of knowledge which will task the energies of students to master.'

The accumulation of new material came from a variety of sources; there were the numerous narratives of travellers, such as Isabella Bird Bishop's *Unbeaten Tracks in Japan* and Mary Kingsley's *Travels in West Africa*; there were the reports of Christian missionaries who were often the first to make any sympathetic contact with simple peoples and to obtain any real knowledge of their beliefs and customs;[4]

---

[1] Caird, *The Philosophy of Religion*, p. 327.

[2] Cf. Hastings Rashdall, *Philosophy and Religion*, p. 149: 'To under-estimate the importance of the great historical Religions and their creators has been the besetting sin of technical religious Philosophy.'

[3] *The Gifts of Civilisation*, p. 382. His primary reference was to the Vedas.

[4] Such efforts were not always appreciated by the societies which employed them. See *Religion in the Victorian Era*, p. 178.

then administrators began to take an interest in the matter; archaeologists also provided material for ancient civilizations, and knowledge of the great religions of the East was facilitated by the publication of translations of their literature; even natural scientists were drawn in, such as the geologist William Boyd Dawkins who published his *Cave Hunting* in 1874 and followed it up six years later by *Early Man in Britain*.

Attempts to co-ordinate the material, especially as it concerned primitive peoples, were made by the new science of social anthropology, which included the study of folk-lore,[1] a study which had already attracted the attention of the brothers Grimm who investigated it, and even fairy-tales, in their search for man's ideas in the past. Much of this study was the work of what may be called amateurs who pursued it from pure pleasure. One of the first of these was E. B. Tylor, a country gentleman of Quaker stock and a great traveller. Among his writings may be mentioned *Researches into the Early History of Mankind* (1865) and *Primitive Culture* (1871).

The great name as a pioneer in the study of Comparative Religion was Robertson Smith. It was he who 'opened out a new field of research or rather he opened it out in a new manner'.[2] Many of those who followed owed much to him, among them Sir James Frazer,[3] F. B. Jevons, and S. A. Cook who edited some of his works. His importance was recognized abroad by scholars such as Reinach[4] in France and Stade in Germany.[5] Robertson Smith's main interest was, of course, Semitic religions and we can now see that he tended to isolate them unduly from other religions; but that was excusable in an age when much

[1] In England no sharp line is drawn between folk-lore and social anthropology. See *Enc. Brit.*, Vol. IX, p. 446.

[2] In *The Religion of the Semites* (third edition), p. xxix.

[3] Frazer himself gladly acknowledged his debt dedicating *The Golden Bough* to him 'in gratitude and admiration'.

[4] Cf. *Cultes, Mythes et Religions*, Vol. IV, p. 23, where he wrote that Roberston Smith 'genuit Frazerum'.

[5] *The Religion of the Semites* was translated by R. Stübe.

material which we now possess was not yet available.[1] Frazer, who is today much more widely known than his master and forerunner, originally approached the subject from the classics as the title of his best-known work, *The Golden Bough*, clearly reveals. The first edition of *The Golden Bough* in two volumes appeared in 1890,[2] to what Gilbert Murray has called 'the combined shock of interest and almost of horror' of his fellow classical scholars. In it he attempted some kind of synthesis of the available evidence, but it was really too soon for such an enterprise. Frazer collected a vast quantity of material, and whatever may be thought of some of his theories, his works will be for long a useful storehouse for the student. But it was not merely, or even primarily, for students that they were written for he hoped to reach a wider public. As he wrote in a clear and attractive style, which rose at times to almost poetic levels, he succeeded in his endeavour; in fact Frazer may be said to have brought anthropology into literature. Furthermore, the popularity and wide circulation of his writings enabled him to exercise a profound influence on the ideas and outlook of contemporary thought, especially as it concerned religion and ritual.

For anthropologists in general, religion was but one interest out of many, and they attached little if any value to the spiritual nature of their discoveries.[3] Religion for E. B. Tylor was 'a belief in spiritual beings', and for Frazer a means of 'propitiation or conciliation of powers superior to man'. To approach religion in a spirit of scientific detachment, however, cannot lead to any fruitful outcome, though it may throw fresh light on ritual customs and other external manifestations. For there is 'no such

---

[1] This applies especially to Sumerian influences. Robertson Smith himself realized that Semitic religion was not very different from other early religions. 'The differences between Semitic and Aryan religion, for example, are not so primitive or fundamental as is often supposed.' (*Religion of the Semites*, p. 32: cf. pp. 54, 214f.)

[2] Later and much enlarged editions appeared in 1907 and 1915.

[3] This attitude naturally aroused the disapproval of Robertson Smith. 'Religion is conceived as a morbid condition, affecting certain stages of human development; and the study of its phenomena forms part of the science of social pathology'. (*Lectures and Essays*, p. 309.)

thing as religion in general,[1] apart from all particular or positive religions; it is only in and through particular and positive religious experience that we have come to know anything about religion'.[2]

The material available for the anthropologist was so vast and so diverse that to reach any completely satisfactory arrangement of it, much less to assess its real value, was out of the question. The new ideas, as happens not infrequently, were speedily welcomed by many as providing a solution of much that had previously been obscure. It was not yet perceived that the comparative method suffered from certain grave weaknesses; one of the gravest of which was the exaggerated emphasis placed on similarities, often of a superficial or doubtful kind, and the passing over in silence of differences which were sometimes fundamental.[3] The fact that similar apparatus and methods, or even similar expressions, are employed is no evidence that the underlying ideas, and these are the important matter, are even approximately the same. Specialists in the various departments of learning, such as classical and theological studies, were highly critical of many suggested explanations; theologians, for example, resented attempts to account for Christian beliefs and rites in the light of primitive notions and practices.[4]

Anthropologists, or those who claimed the title, naturally differed among themselves, and some certainly advanced very curious theories. Such aberrations were admitted by Frazer who deplored the discredit brought on the study by the claims of over-enthusiastic advocates to have found solutions for many of the problems surrounding the early history of mankind.[5] Some of Frazer's own fondly cherished ideas, such as tracing back religion

[1] Cf. C. C. J. Webb, *Group Theories of Religion*, p. 59: 'I do not myself believe that Religion *can* be defined.'

[2] Caird, *The Philosophy of Religion*, p. 305.

[3] Caird asserted that 'superficial resemblances may lead us to connect religions which are essentially different, apparent differences to dissociate those between which there is the closest affinity.' (*Op. cit.*, p. 310.)

[4] If we 'study origins without a reference to the things which they originate our historic method at once degenerates into pedantic antiquarianism.' (Illingworth, *Personality: Human and Divine*, p. 200.)

[5] *The Magic Art*, Vol. I, pp. 333 f.

to magic, and the divine kingship, have of late come under sharp criticism;[1] but nothing can make scholars forget the deep debt which they owe to him as a pioneer and a collector of material.

Contemporary anthropologists are no longer greatly interested in origins, which, in view of the lack of the necessary evidence, they put aside as beyond man's power to discover. This attitude, in part at least, had already been adopted by Caird, who concluded that the 'ultimate origin of religion is not one to which tradition or historical research, however exact and recondite, can penetrate'.[2] Religion to many anthropologists was merely something which men as they became more rational would outgrow and eventually discard. But their researches produced evidence that religion was universally diffused and that even the most primitive peoples had their notions of it. Frazer had supported his theory that magic always went before religion by the example of the Australian aborigines, the most primitive people then known; but unfortunately for his notion it has now been found that they actually possessed religion as well as magic. This is also the case among even more primitive races discovered since his time.

Although there is evidence of the universal diffusion of religion, nothing discovered by anthropologists goes to support the ancient and widespread idea of a primitive world-wide revelation, knowledge of which was subsequently lost.[3] The belief in a revelation to primitive man is certainly widespread; Gladstone claimed to have found traces of it in Homer, where he saw in Athene, the embodiment of the divine wisdom, and Apollo, the organ of the divine utterance, 'disintegrated elements of a primitive tradition'.[4] The older apologists had seen in pagan religions a corruption of the primitive revelation to Adam, and the same opinion was held by Bishop Butler who wrote: 'it is a certain historical fact, so far as we can trace things up, that this whole system of belief, that there is one God, the Creator and moral

[1] Cf. Engnell, *Studies in the Divine Kingship*, p. 1.
[2] *Op. cit.*, p. 297.
[3] Cf. Westermarck, *Moral Ideas*, Vol. II, pp. 670 ff. and S. A. Cook in *The Religion of the Semites* (3rd ed.), pp. 529 ff.
[4] *Homeric Studies*, Vol. II, pp. 139 ff.

Governor of the world, and that mankind is in a state of religion, was received in the first ages'.[1]

The opinion that religion is but a passing phase in the life of mankind might readily suggest itself to those who became aware of the diverse, degrading, and contradictory forms which belief and worship had assumed in the past; for they had 'to become acquainted with so many grovelling and horrible superstitions that a presumption easily arises . . . that any belief which is religious is probably false'.[2] Such a view, however, fails to take account of the ability which religions have shown gradually to purify themselves from unworthy and degrading elements. 'The very development of religion from lowly levels is a guarantee of its power of reinterpreting itself from time to time and of advancing to higher stages.'[3] Religion in its early stages undeniably shows 'a melancholy spectacle of gross superstitions and ferocious forms of worship'; but that stage has been left behind and need not make man ashamed of the lowly origin of his noblest ideas and religious usages.

> The real ground for humiliation is not in the fetishism out of which religion is said to have sprung, or in the childish superstitions and irrational observances that have been the accidents of its history, but rather in the element of fetishism and unreason that often still clings to it, in the admixture of vulgar magic which still deforms its worship, and in the remains of meaningless and irrational dogma which still corrupt its faith.[4]

The idea of God and the desire to hold communion with Him would seem to be so deeply planted in the human soul that to eradicate it is not the easy task which some suppose; a circumstance which totalitarian States may one day discover to their cost and confusion.

So far we have been discussing for the most part the material concerning primitive tribes provided by the anthropologist; but

---

[1] *Analogy of Religion* etc., Pt. I, Ch. VI.
[2] William James, *Varieties of Religious Experience*, p. 490.
[3] S. A. Cook, *The Study of Religions*, p. 4.
[4] Caird, *op. cit.*, p. 330.

far more useful for the student of comparative religion are the great religions of the distant past, and the equally great religions of the present. These provide him with nobler and more elevated ideas and customs than those of savage peoples and may even bear comparison with Christianity itself. Much work was done upon them during our period, but to discuss it would require at least a volume as large as that devoted to our present study, and so we must be content to refer to authoritative treatises on the various faiths, which appeared during the period, both concerning religions of the past[1] and those which still claimed numerous adherents.[2]

Popular demand for knowledge of non-Christian religious systems was met by the very useful series of volumes, written by experts, issued by the Society for Promoting Christian Knowledge; whilst for scholars and those desiring further acquaintance with the literature, there was the famous collection of translations 'The Sacred Books of the East'. This series was financed jointly by Oxford University and the Government of India and originated with Max Müller who devoted the greater part of the last twenty-five years of his life to furthering it.[3] The first volume came from his hand, a translation of the *Upanishads* which appeared in 1879.

There is one great difficulty which confronts the student of comparative religion—that of discovering the real meaning, for those who held them, of the various ideas and ceremonies. This is especially the case where dead religions are concerned, or the

---

[1] See Wiedemann, *The Religion of the Ancient Egyptians*; W. Robertson Smith, *The Religion of the Semites*; A. H. Sayce *The Religion of the Ancient Babylonians* (the Hibbert Lectures for 1887), and Jastrow, *The Religion of Babylon and Assyria.*

[2] See M. Monier Williams, *Hinduism*; A. A. Macdonell, *Vedic Mythology*; T. W. Rhys Davids, *Buddhism*; James Legge, *The Religions of China*; J. W. H. Stobart, *Islam and its Founder*, and William Muir, *The Coran.*

[3] For the aims of the series see *Life of Max Müller*, Vol. II, pp. 9 ff. It was the firm conviction of Max Müller that 'the real history of man is the history of religion: the wonderful ways by which the different families of the human race advanced towards a truer knowledge and a deeper love of God'. (*Chips from a German Workshop*, Vol. I, p. 21.)

14

beliefs of primitive peoples. Archaeology, it is true, provides much material for the religions of the ancient world, but such material is seldom accompanied by explanations as to its meaning or function. This is naturally the case, for everybody was well acquainted with them. So too in regard to primitive peoples in both the past and the present. It is a grave mistake to imagine that their religious notions were necessarily simple; apparent simplicity may be due to the absence of the ability to express them in ways which can be understood by the modern mind, and by the abundant recourse to symbol and metaphor. Perhaps one of the best representations of the mind of the primitive savage is to be found in Browning's *Caliban on Setebos*,[1] where we have a recognition of vague ancestral or tribal traditions being handed down (in this case from his mother Sycorax), coupled with an attitude of indifference, and even of defiance, when things go well, but one of grovelling terror when they seem to threaten danger.

Another important aspect of non-Christian religions which cannot be ignored is, that like Christianity itself, they have a long history behind them during which they have changed considerably; the differences between the religion of the Vedas and later Hinduism is a case in point. There is a very definite risk in speaking of the 'evolution' of religion and religious ideas, since the development followed no straight or single path, and a later stage may actually be a decline from an earlier, a comparatively lofty period being followed by one which is ruder and less organized.[2] It has also to be remembered that different conceptions often persist side by side. It may be that religion originated in a sense of awe inspired by the phenomena of nature,[3] and that later it advanced as man pondered over their meaning and faced the mysteries of existence and the powers which lay behind nature. But the more worthy conception did not always drive

---

[1] In *The Tempest* Shakespeare had used Caliban to point a contrast between the noble savage and the degenerate representatives of civilization personified by Trinculo and Stephano.

[2] See S. A. Cook, in *E.R.E.*, Vol. x, p. 665.

[3] Cf. Petronius: *Primus in orbe Deos fecit timor.*

out the humbler, the latter often survived alongside the other. Moreover it is necessary to bear in mind that the state of religion among a people cannot be judged in the light of its surviving literature alone. No one, for instance, would take the lofty utterances of the Hebrew prophets as an index of the religious condition of the nation at large. Religion, after all, is primarily a practical matter and must be studied in the lives of its votaries rather than in the ideals set forth by their spiritual guides.

The traditional attitude of Christianity towards its rivals, an attitude which goes back to the early days of the Church, was that they were at best ineffective, at worst positively evil. There were, of course, some who held more worthy views; Justin Martyr had recognized that even before Christ there had been those who had a genuine knowledge of God,[1] whilst Clement of Alexandria could declare his belief that 'the same God to whom we owe the Old and New Testaments gave also to the Greeks their Greek philosophy by which the Almighty is glorified among the Greeks',[2] and that it came not from 'the mythology of Dionysius, but from the theology of the Eternal Word'.[3] Such a liberal outlook, however, was exceptional and the prevailing view was very different; even the undeniable resemblances to certain Christian rites and beliefs were condemned as the work of the devil designed to confuse and perplex the believer. Christian writers were not slow to point out the glaring defects in paganism and to deride the moral lapses of the gods to whom the heathen paid their worship. This line of attack, abundantly illustrated in St. Augustine's *De Civitate Dei*, was not unknown in our period, as can be seen in *Popular Hinduism* (1890), the work of Paul Savarimuttoo, an Indian Christian. Hinduism, of course, is very vulnerable to such onslaughts and the writers of the Puranas seem to take a delight in showing that the gods are not amenable to moral restrictions. As in the case of similar stories among the ancient Greeks and in the Old Testament a free use of allegory

[1] *First Apology*, xlvi. Among the Greeks he specified Heraclitus and Socrates as living 'according to reason', and so to be reckoned as Christians before Christ.

[2] *Stromateis*, VI, v, 42.   [3] *Op. cit.*, I, 13.

can overcome such blemishes and even find in them illustrations of lofty spiritual truths.

Such an intolerant and unsympathetic attitude is unworthy of the Gospel of love, and, moreover, is bad 'tactics'. 'There can be no greater mistake—from an apologetic point of view than to depreciate the ethnic religions in the supposed interest of an exclusive revelation.'[1] To exclude the evidence contained in the non-Christian religions means depriving the student of comparative religion of much valuable material, an intolerable position; hence 'the wisest among theologians recognize that the supreme object of theology must be the exhibition of the organic unity of all the doctrines and truths of religion'.[2]

Long before our period an attitude of greater tolerance had been growing up. This can be seen in Lessing's *Nathan der Weise*. Lessing found value in every stage of religious development and looked upon even the most primitive expressions as a means for interpreting the process as a whole. Like Herder he had come to recognize that national religions were the natural expressions of the minds and characters of the various peoples. It must not be forgotten that the Old Testament 'before it passed into Christian hands was exclusively a national book'.[3] Schleiermacher, it may be noticed, found in different religions expressions of special types of feeling.

The student of comparative religion must approach his subject with an entirely open mind, assuming only that 'religion is a thing which has developed from the first, as law has, or as art has';[4] certainly he has no right to regard one religion as true, and the rest as false; he seems, indeed, to be faced by two alternatives, either to look upon all religions as human inventions and therefore equally false, or to regard them as all equally inspired and therefore equally true. This raises the pertinent question as to whether the Gospel is but one among many other faiths, and whether a day may not come when it will be superseded by a

---

[1] Illingworth, *Personality, Human and Divine*, p. 167.
[2] Storr, p. 15.   [3] Illingworth, *op. cit.*, p. 188.
[4] Menzies, *The History of Religion*, p. 6.

higher synthesis in which all that is best in Christianity will be combined with all that is best in other religions.

It must not be forgotten that Christianity, when compared with other religions, was by no means immune to criticism, for like its rivals it had preserved a number of myths and fables. One cause of Darwin's religious doubts had been the realization that the Old Testament was 'no more to be trusted than the sacred books of the Hindoos'.[1] Moreover scholars had found that the study of other religions had, here and there, helped to a fuller understanding of Christianity itself. Thus for the candid theologian a new outlook was necessary, since it had to be admitted that religion had not been confined to a single line of development, that going back to the Old Testament and the Jewish people.

The intense and sympathetic study of the non-Christian religions, coupled perhaps with the realization of past injustice towards them, led in some unbalanced minds to too great a reaction; the good in them was exaggerated and their serious deficiencies passed by. If it tended to promote tolerance it also weakened dogma, and might lead to a virtual abandonment of the belief in the absolute and unique character of Christianity as a final revelation, even if not fully worked out, from God. One manifestation of the new spirit of tolerance was the holding of what were called Parliaments of Religions, in which representatives of different creeds expounded their several points of view. Christians who attended such gatherings may have been careful to explain that their presence did not in any way imply an acceptance of the equality of all religions; but, in spite of disclaimers in which not all Christians joined, this was the impression made on their colleagues, some of whom eagerly welcomed it as a confession of the inadequacy of Christianity. At the first of these assemblies held at Chicago in 1893 a Japanese did not scruple to assert that the holding of a Parliament of Religions was a sign that the Western nations had come to recognize the weakness and insufficiency of their own faith, and, in their

[1] *The Life of Charles Darwin*, Vol. I, p. 308.

perplexity, were turning to the East for guidance. But Christian students of comparative religion, though they might acquire greater tolerance, were by no means disposed to respond to appeals to share in 'the common search after fuller truth and the higher life on equal terms'. Even if they admitted that knowledge of God might come through other channels, those who believed that the supreme revelation was in Jesus could not but regard their faith as unique, and also final. For them it was final because 'inseparable from the final victory which Christ accomplished'.[1]

Such a position seemed to many who did not share it utterly illogical. They could understand the attitude of those who rejected non-Christian religions out of hand, but not that of those who, while admitting that they contained elements of truth and even recognized in them a measure of inspiration, refused to place them on an equality with the Gospel. Why could they not combine with other religions to form the best possible faith for mankind?

In response to this plea it was argued that in the Gospel every aspiration of mankind could find its fulfilment and that there was no need for it to borrow from other faiths. This was the line taken by John Wordsworth in the Bampton Lectures for 1881, *The One Religion: Truth, Holiness, and Peace desired by the Nations, and revealed by Jesus Christ.* The lectures were the fruit of wide reading, but Wordsworth had no real mastery of the subject, which was then only in a pioneer stage, although Max Müller was already rousing interest in it, especially in Oxford. Nor did he realize that the argument tells both ways; for if Christianity realizes an ideal which other religions have failed to reach may it not be that Christianity itself is merely the crown of a process of evolution, the result of a natural development? In which case there is no need to bring in the idea of a revelation. Those who knew the history of the Church were well aware of the extent to which it had adopted both ideas and practices from other religions during the course of its long development. This might confirm the argument. Others, however, saw in its capacity to

[1] Quick, *Doctrines of the Creed*, p. 143.

absorb elements from outside strong evidence for thinking that Christianity was the final religion. The most powerful argument in favour of the hypothesis, however, was the fact that though Christianity might have taken over elements from other faiths and philosophies and had much in it that was shared with other religions, it had also its own peculiar characteristics. Above all there was its claim to a supernatural basis.

> Supernaturalism is of the essence of Christianity, which claims to be from above, both in its origin and in the power which it wields for the redemption of human life. . . . On the other hand, thought cannot rest content with any crude antithesis of natural and supernatural. What is needed is some reconciliation between the two, some definition of Christianity which, while it preserves its uniqueness, shall set it forth in its universal relation to all other faiths. It is in this direction that the deepest theological thought of the time is moving.[1]

But this is not all. Christianity is the only religion which really faces the problem of sin and offers to provide a remedy; it is the one faith which gives an adequate place to personality, both human and divine; whilst its great ideals of service, purity, humility, holiness, the recognition of the equal rights of all men, are not to be found elsewhere, save when there has been definite borrowing from it. It is, beyond all its rivals, a religion capable of progress, and so alone is fitted to survive in an age of constant change and transition.[2]

The arguments in support of the claim of Christianity to be the final religion so far adduced have been based on general grounds and are such as will appeal to believers and non-believers alike. For the Christian, however, there is another argument, and that of overwhelming force, which separates his faith by a vast chasm from all others, however lofty and admirable may be their teaching. Christianity for him is unique because its founder was divine. Jesus for the Christian is accepted, not as merely one

---

[1] Storr, p. 158.
[2] Cf. *Letters of J. R. Green*, p. 118: 'In former times, at each great advance of human thought, a religion fell dead and vanished away; Christianity survives because it is capable of adjusting itself to new conditions.'

among a number of inspired teachers competing for man's discipleship, but as Lord and Saviour. 'Calvary', as R. E. Speer has finely said, 'closes the issue of comparative religion.'[1]

The Christian faith is that God has finally revealed Himself in His Son, though, as has been seen, the working out of all the implications of that revelation and the disclosure of the immensity of the treasures contained in it may still go on through the operations of the Holy Spirit. The doctrine of the Incarnation is the all-sufficient justification for the claim that Christianity is unique, and if the Incarnation is but a man-made doctrine, then Christianity has no universal and eternal validity and may well in the course of time be superseded; for if, as L. S. Thornton has written, 'we regard Christ as a human individual in the organic series, in whom there is a unique manifestation of the eternal order, then we have no ground for supposing that Christianity has the final character which Christians have ever found in it'.[2]

Although the study of comparative religion may fail to furnish any assured proof of the uniqueness of Christianity, on the whole it can be said to reinforce the theistic position, and so to strengthen the Christian outlook even if it does not go so far as to establish religion as 'a biological necessity implanted in mankind by the author of life'.[3] In the opinion of some scholars it also supports the idea that Providence is benevolent. 'The unbiased student of religions can hardly escape the conviction that the Supreme Power, whom we call God, while enabling man to work out within limits, his own career, desires the furtherance of those aims and ideals which are for the advance of mankind.'[4] Comparative religion also helps to support the belief that man is religious by nature and, in addition, provides illustrations of the many paths by which he has sought to find out God. These different approaches to the divine can be perceived in the different manner in which man has expressed his desires and longings. Even the variety of names by which men have called Him, and the strangely

---

[1] *Missionary Principles and Practice*, p. 110.
[2] *The Incarnate Lord*, p. 259.   [3] Gowen, *A History of Religion*, p. 1.
[4] S. A. Cook, *The Study of Religions*, p. 427.

divergent conceptions of His being and nature which they have formed, are but so many milestones in the long road which man-kind has travelled in its search. If some of the ideas seem strange and repulsive to the modern mind they help to show 'what man is and what he strives to gain'.[1] Closer and more sympathetic study has revealed that much in primitive religion, not excluding that of the Hebrews, was not sheer superstition. Primitive man did not worship stones and trees as such, but because he believed that they were the abode of the deity. We can no longer accept the idea that pagans

> still in heathen darkness dwell
> Without one thought of heaven or hell,

for we know that such thoughts were often in their minds and that they prompted many of their actions.

Furthermore, comparative religion shows us that God did not leave Himself without witness in any people; though they might worship Him in ignorance (Acts 14:17, 17:23 ff.), it was His Spirit that was at work among them.

> All souls that struggle and aspire,
> All hearts of prayer by Thee are lit,
> And dim or clear Thy tongues of fire
> On dusky tribes and centuries sit.
>
> Nor bounds nor clime nor creed Thou know'st,
> Wide as our need Thy favours fall.
> The white wings of the Holy Ghost
> Stoop unseen o'er the heads of all.
>
> WHITTIER

Such a conception, and the fact that experiences thought to be the sole privilege of Christians were also enjoyed by the adherents of other faiths, were a great difficulty to old-fashioned believers; though the prologue of the fourth gospel affirms that Christ is

---

[1] Westcott, *The Gospel of Life*, p. 99.

the light which lighteth every man (John 1:9). Had some ultra-orthodox souls been better acquainted with the Logos theology they might have been saved much needless heart-burning.

Rumours of the conclusions reached by students of comparative religion had a very disquieting effect on the average Christian, for they seemed to show that not only had Judaism much in common with other Semitic religions, but also that pagan elements had entered into the practice of the Church and even that pagan philosophies had had a part in shaping its doctrines. This disclosure of the genesis of much in which he believed and which he practised seemed to rob them of their sacred character. Others, more wisely, held that origin does not affect validity; though such a conclusion is not without its drawbacks, for as Farnell has said: 'We can imagine how difficult it might be to maintain a fervid Mariolatry among sincere Christians, if the worshipper were vividly conscious that he was worshipping, not the historical personage, but another form of the great Pagan goddess of the Mediterranean.'[1]

In view of these doubts and disquiets it was not surprising that many conservative Christians came to look upon the advocates of what to them was an excessive tolerance as little better than traitors to the Master. Such believers held that there must ever be a clear distinction between the religion which He came to reveal and all other faiths, whatever there might be in them which was noble and uplifting. Any attempt at reconciliation was an impossible and even a reprehensible task, since it involved, or so it seemed, the abandonment of the unique position of Jesus and the admission that His was *not* the only name whereby men must be saved.

Efforts to bring home to the general public the real meaning and value of comparative religion were few; a matter for regret, since the subject was so disquieting for those who knew of it only from vague rumours and exaggerated claims. The first considerable exposition, from a Christian point of view, did not come until 1887 when Boyd Carpenter delivered the Bampton Lecture

[1] *The Attributes of God*, p. 8.

on *The Permanent Elements in Religion*. It was a bold undertaking, and in some minds at least the suspicion was aroused that the lecturer himself was infected by a kind of lurking infidelity.

Interest in the subject was undoubtedly spreading among educated people, though it is to be feared that in the majority of instances intellectual curiosity rather than moral earnestness was the outstanding motive. There were even some who took to dabbling in Oriental cults; a practice more common in America than in England. They certainly provided exciting alternatives for those who felt that they had exhausted the possibilities of Christianity, and were anxious to sample some new thing. Illingworth told of a couple of ladies who, having been persuaded to attend a missionary study circle, came to the conclusion that Brahminism was much more interesting than Christianity.[1]

Before leaving the subject it may be noted that in Germany the Ritschlians, in view of their belief that only in Christ was there any revelation of God, gave no encouragement to its study. When it was proposed to establish a chair of comparative religion in the theological faculty at Berlin, Harnack opposed the suggestion on the ground that other religions, though they might be studied with profit in connexion with philosophy and history, could make no useful contribution to theology.

[1] *Life of J. R. Illingworth*, pp. 191 f.

Chapter Ten

DOGMATIC THEOLOGY[1]

THERE was in our period probably less progress made in this department, Christology apart, than in any other. Writing in 1888 Dale considered that for many years Systematic Theology had been neglected in both the theological colleges and in ministerial studies. Its value had been deprecated and it had even been regarded 'as unfriendly to a free and generous development of the Christian life'. To this neglect he attributed 'very much of the poverty and confusion of theological thought, very much of the religious uncertainty, and some of the more serious defects in the practical religious life'.[2] Four years later, in the preface to the translation of his *Grundriss der Dogmengeschichte*, Harnack considered that whilst English and American theological literature possessed excellent works they were 'not rich in products within the realm of the History of Dogma'. Westcott, as has been seen,[3] had hoped to produce a treatise on Doctrine, but only partially achieved his purpose in *The Gospel of Life*, a volume rightly so named, for to him the Gospel was 'the message of a Life ... made known to us through life and ... apprehended throughout the ages and still apprehended in life'.[4]

The subject was indeed being taught in theological colleges, but too much on traditional lines. Pearson *On the Creeds* was still a text-book, with Harold Browne's *Exposition of the Thirty-nine Articles*, first published in 1850, and frequently reprinted but never revised, as a supplement. A much needed step forward

[1] I have called this chapter 'dogmatic' theology in accordance with the conventional usage, but I prefer the term 'doctrinal' theology as being more fluid. Dogmas are often the hardening of doctrines.

[2] *Life of Dale*, p. 573.   [3] See above, p. 123.   [4] *Op. cit.*, p. 284.

was made when in 1896 E. C. S. Gibson produced *The Thirty-nine Articles of the Church of England*. His volume, however, was not intended to provide a complete system of theology, but to explain the various Articles and especially the first eight. Evangelicals had E. A. Litton's *Introduction to Dogmatic Theology* and Handley Moule's *Outlines of Christian Doctrine* (1889), of a mildly Calvinistic tinge. Interest in doctrine, however, as containing 'at once the most certain and the most important truths of man's history, nature and destiny, in this world and for ever',[1] was fostered by the publication of *Lux Mundi*.

The desire to penetrate into the meaning of things is part of the endowment of normal man and more than anything else distinguishes him from the rest of the animal creation.[2] Man finds himself in a seemingly ordered world over which he can exercise little if any control and he is excusably curious as to the character and nature of the powers behind it.[3] 'Who can help being a philosopher and asking "Why?" when he sees a man die or the sun set?'[4] But though the desire to know, and to come face to face with reality, may be part of man's natural endowment, in most men it is generally dormant, and in all it may vary from time to time, being only too liable to be overcome by the pervasive influence of their earthly environment, as the 'shades of the prison house' become ever more opaque.

It was the common man's failure to use this faculty, or even to realize that he possessed it, that led in the ancient world to the divorce between philosophy and religion. The philosopher might feel that the unexamined life was not to be endured and might be consumed by an intellectual passion, but in this he was exceptional, and his search after reality had, moreover, no connexion with religion; religion was the concern of the State or the community, and was confined to the performance of certain ritual acts. So long as men took their part in such acts they were

[1] R. C. Moberly in *Lux Mundi*, p. 158.
[2] Cf. Aquinas, *Summa contra Gentiles*, Bk. III, ch. xxxvii.
[3] Cf. Westcott, *Lessons from Work*, p. 89: 'Our mind has a characteristic desire of knowing the truth of God and the causes of things.'
[4] *Life of Max Müller*, Vol. II, p. 315.

free to interpret them as they thought fit. Such a condition of affairs could not satisfy the Christian Church, and from early days attempts were made to formulate its fundamental beliefs, and 'to meet the craving for intellectual satisfaction by constructing theological definitions and dogmas, and weaving them into systems freed from anything that wars with logical self-consistency'.[1]

As there is in mankind a desire to penetrate into the meaning of things, so there is also what may be termed an instinct for totality, and when once man begins to ask questions he can never be satisfied this side of omniscience. So the mind is driven on to ever wider apprehensions. In the same way the Christian dogmatic system, by which theology attempts to meet this need, is continually striving to be all-inclusive, to extend the area of its application. Hence the tendency to multiply doctrines.

Such a process can never be entirely successful, for it seeks to express in human language and human forms eternal truths which ever elude them. Nature has no outlines, and those who gaze on the sun miss the form through being dazzled by the light; similarly no verbal statement can adequately convey a spiritual reality. Dogma is nothing more than 'the partial and progressive approximation towards the complete intellectual expression of the Truth manifested to men once and for all in the Incarnation'.[2]

None the less, in spite of such a limitation, some definite pattern of belief was necessary; for dogma not only crystallizes experience, it should also promote it; though in the process it may require restatement in different ages and climes. Dogma is not an end in itself, but must lead 'to something higher—to the sacramental participation in the atoning sacrifice of Christ'.[3] In other words, beliefs which are accepted merely on 'authority' may be completely barren of results; men must work out their implications if they are to become a motive power in their lives. It has to be realized that the bare intellectual acceptance of a

[1] Caird, *The Philosophy of Religion*, p. 199.
[2] Westcott, *Lessons from Work*, p. 63.
[3] W. Shirley, *The Church in the Apostolic Age*, p. 103.

creed has no spiritual value, and is, as Dr. Lock has said, 'like the answer to a sum which a school boy takes from a key'.[1] The Christian creed is not 'a mere systematized collection of technical definitions which may be learnt and used with dangerous facility'.[2] There is a further danger which may follow such an attitude—faith in a doctrinal system may become a substitute for faith in a Person.

It was the conviction of Schleiermacher that 'Dogmatics must start . . . from the basis of Christian experience, must not travel beyond it, and must make that experience the standard by which it tests its intellectual constructions.'[3] But if dogma is based on experience the process of defining it can never be complete;[4] and, as a consequence, no age, however venerable, has the right to seal up the 'deposit'. This does not mean that what has grown old is to be entirely repudiated; rather by fresh application it may be quickened into new life. Since wider experience may involve a transformation and adjustment of dogma any statement which is apparently clear and harmonious must, in view of man's defective knowledge, arouse the suspicion that its seeming finality and consistency is the result of the ignoring of factors which are really vital. Dogmas are working hypotheses to be tested by practical religious experiment, and every age must conduct its own tests and be prepared if necessary to make the consequent adjustments, for a too rigid doctrinal system may erect barriers to the fuller knowledge of things divine and preclude further progress. The Christian faith is not a kind of Maginot Line behind which the Church takes shelter against the intrusion of new and unwelcome ideas.

August Sabatier laid it down that 'The history of dogma is its inevitable criticism.' This is undoubtedly true, for every dogma

---

[1] *The Bible and Christian Life*, p. 244.

[2] Westcott, *op. cit.*, p. 64. Cf. *The Gospel of Life*, p. 58: 'Right doctrine is an inexhaustible spring of strength if it be translated into deed: it is a paralysis if it be held as an intellectual notion.'

[3] Storr, p. 239.

[4] Cf. Westcott, *Lessons from Work*, p. 13: 'as long as experience is incomplete there can be no finality in the definition of doctrine'.

achieved formulation under known historical conditions, and these must be understood if the dogma itself is rightly to be comprehended. Fresh investigation has revealed more fully than ever before the background against which the Christian system received its shape, as also the various influences to which the Church was exposed when the process was going on. Many of the notions adopted came in from outside, and some of them were but imperfectly Christianized; as a consequence 'later theology [was] largely occupied with providing a basis in Scripture and philosophy for opinions which have no real connexion with either the one or the other'.[1]

The development of doctrine is no unbroken advance; it involves readjustment, and the substitution of new forms of expression for those which are outmoded. But in the process care has to be taken that the substance of the original doctrine is not lost or impaired. 'Progress in theology', Hort has declared, 'does not consist in mutilation, but in purification. It is not the great facts or ideas that are false, but the way in which they are conceived.'[2]

The early Fathers of the Church had not been at pains to define the faith too narrowly or too exactly. Not only did they appreciate the impracticability of discovering adequate language, but they were also conscious that full knowledge was unattainable. Athanasius himself has said, 'God has His being beyond human discovery',[3] and in the less speculative West, Hilary of Poitiers was equally outspoken. He pointed out that it was the erroneous teaching of heretics which compelled the Church to dare 'to embody in human terms truths which ought to be hidden in the silent veneration of the heart', and even ventured to admit that the Church in so doing had dealt with 'unlawful matters and trespassed on forbidden ground', and that attempts to describe the divine nature were 'helpful to man rather than descriptive of God'.[4] Such admissions of man's limited knowledge and the

---

[1] C. Bigg, *Wayside Sketches*, pp. 50 ff.

[2] *The Way, the Truth, the Life*, p. 186.　　　　[3] *Contra Gentes*, Bk. II.

[4] See *De Trin.*, Bk. I, ch. 19, Bk. II, ch. 2, etc. and, on the reluctance to define, Illingworth, *The Doctrine of the Trinity*, Ch. VI.

early reluctance to add to the number of definitions need to be borne in mind in considering the doctrinal theology of the nineteenth century.

Attempts to express divine truths in human language are of necessity imperfect, and it follows that they may even misrepresent or distort them. 'We must not claim for phrases of earthly coinage a more than earthly and relative completeness.'[1] Plato had realized this fact ages before, and knowing that truth cannot be stated in abstract terms made use of myths. Dogmas, be it remembered, are only symbols of something which can never find expression in words;[2] Newman had recognized that, as the product of man's reason, they were untrustworthy, and only to be accepted when guaranteed by an authority of sufficient competence. But in speaking of dogmas as symbols we are not using the word as it is used in art and literature, where symbols may be nothing more than the product of aesthetic or fanciful inventiveness; the test of any symbol is its effectiveness, the extent to which it is able to convey the truth which it strives to present and preserve.

It is a matter for regret that subsequent Christian thought did not sufficiently imitate the reticence of the early Church, nor recognize the limitations which attend upon all human definitions. In its desire to leave nothing unexplained it added dogma to dogma with an ever increasing elaboration. After all the claim to have answers to all questions is not a characteristic of the ablest minds which are usually more quick to discern problems than to solve them. There are many questions on which an open mind is the only proper attitude, questions where too ready answers may be a bar to genuine progress, and arouse the opposition of more candid seekers after truth. This was the case with Scholasticism which 'knew so much about the deepest mysteries of God, that it almost provoked an agnostic reaction, in the interests of reverence and intellectual modesty'.[3] Dean Colet

---

[1] R. C. Moberly in *Lux Mundi*, p. 187.

[2] Archbishop Lang always regarded 'any attempts, however authoritative, to formulate beliefs in God as necessarily only "symbols" '. (J. G. Lockhart, *Cosmo Gordon Lang*, p. 13.)   [3] A. L. Moore in *Lux Mundi*, p. 73.

condemned this excessive desire as due to 'temerity and pride', and Erasmus made merry over those who seriously discussed such questions as whether God could have taken the form of a cucumber, and, if so, how He could have preached, performed miracles, and been crucified, and over those who claimed to be able to give an exact explanation of the mystery of transubstantiation 'on a blackboard'. In a more serious vein he pleaded that statements concerning the faith should be as few and as simple as possible. But his warning passed unheeded.

In the Church of Rome the itch to multiply dogmas has persisted; perhaps in order to make a 'hedge about the Law', and so to protect vital beliefs; perhaps also to demonstrate that it still possesses the necessary inspiration. Such fencing of the truth by additional barriers seems very far from the methods of Jesus, and the elaboration of doctrines may strain the allegiance of the thoughtful and those who desire to preserve their intellectual integrity. It may also be an obstacle to some from outside who would otherwise enter in; Florence Nightingale once told Cardinal Manning that though her heart was urging her to find a long-desired refuge in the Church of Rome, her head refused to assent to Roman doctrines.

The Christian faith as it came down to the later nineteenth century was full of discords and apparent contradictions. Such apparent contradictions may, of course, arise from an imperfect analysis, a failure to recognize subtle distinctions; but this was not the explanation of the discords in Christian thought. These represented definite and opposing points of view, the result of attempts to combine diverse strands of tradition. Some of the differences were of long standing and went back to the struggle between the Hebraic and Hellenistic elements in the primitive Church. Now the influx of new knowledge had increased the discords and difficulties. Hostile critics went even further and declared that the whole Christian dogmatic system was as dead as the geocentric astronomy which was the presupposition of many of its formularies. Liberal Christians, whilst admitting that there was much in the faith which ought to be discarded or restated, were convinced that the rest was capable of being defended, so long as there was no obstinate clinging to partial or misleading statements which could only result in errors and misapprehensions.

The sixth of the Thirty-nine Articles of the Church of England affirms that all doctrines derive their authority from the Scriptures. If this claim is admitted, and it was not everyone who was prepared to accept it, then it follows that the results of biblical criticism made it imperative that doctrines should be re-examined, and that adequate methods of interpretation should be applied in the process, for as F. H. Chase has said: 'The History of Doctrine cannot rightly be understood apart from the History of Interpretation.'[1]

Difficulties over dogmatic statements brought about by the changing climate of thought seldom arouse anxiety in the mind of the average churchgoer. By long usage and habit he takes so much for granted without inquiring into its exact meaning or implications. He has, for example, been told that the *seventh* day is to be hallowed, when everybody knows that it is the *first* that is meant. To the outsider, however, even if his attitude to Christianity is sympathetic, the persistence of such anomalies is a cause of amazement and gives him the impression that there are different standards of truth in the Church and in the world of scholarship.[2] This view was to some extent shared by the better educated and more thoughtful churchmen, and there was a demand, which grew in intensity during the last quarter of the century, for a clarification of the situation and for some attempt to adapt the traditional doctrines to contemporary thought and ideas, and for the elimination of expressions of belief which had become obsolete. Such demands received the sympathetic consideration of so conservative a scholar as Dr. Swete, for, as he wrote, 'The disciples of the Word dare not turn away from any

---

[1] *Chrysostom: A Study in the History of Biblical Interpretation*, p. viii.

[2] It may be pointed out that the retention of terms which have lost their meaning is not confined to religion; we still speak of the sunrise, and of electric currents, and even of splitting the atom, which is sheer nonsense, for an 'atom' is that which cannot be divided.

of the teachings of God in Nature and History because they may be thought to involve reconstruction of some of their cherished beliefs.'[1]

The so-called Athanasian Creed was an especial stumbling-block. A writer of wide influence wrote to Archbishop Tait: 'I believe that this Creed has done more to alienate the minds of intellectual men from the Church of England than all other causes.'[2] Hort also disapproved of the creed and felt that in England any real faith in the Trinity had been killed 'by that hapless *Quicunque vult*, and its substitution of geometry for life'.[3] Even if the statements contained in it were exactly true it was quite unfitted for public use in an age when the Christological controversies which had called it forth were no longer remembered, save by scholars, and its language was certainly liable to misunderstanding by worshippers who were untrained in such niceties.[4]

But it was not only on intellectual grounds that there was criticism of Christian dogmas; some of them revolted the increasingly sensitive moral perceptibility of the age. This attitude, however, was not without precedent, for Coleridge had pointed out that moral difficulties, as distinct from speculative, might be a barrier to belief.[5] There were two doctrines in particular which caused offence, the Atonement as generally interpreted, and the belief in eternal punishment. Both had been attacked by Bishop Colenso in his commentary on *Romans*

---

[1] In *Cambridge Theological Essays*, p. ix.

[2] Davidson, *Life of A. C. Tait*, Vol. II, p. 129.

[3] *Life*, II, p. 140. A distinguished Cambridge scholar of the next generation took a very different line: 'I much prefer to state my own beliefs, "theological" and "Christological", in the terms of the Athanasian Creed. It is the only Creed that precludes the tritheistic ideas always latent in the faith of Christians. . . . To the trained theologian its assertions. . . . ring as true to-day, as ever. But only he can make its terms his own. They are merely *hocus-pocus* to anyone else.' (Bethune-Baker, *The Faith of the Apostles' Creed*, p. 67, note.)

[4] For an account of the controversy over the use of the creed, see Warre Cornish, *A History of the English Church in the Nineteenth Century*, Vol. II, pp. 160 ff.

[5] *Aids to Reflection*, XCVI (2).

published in 1861, but his onslaught was soon forgotten in the still greater excitement over his criticisms of the Pentateuch.

In spite of demands for restatement from many quarters there was much reluctance to undertake the task, or even to countenance it. For those who rejected biblical criticism and stood firmly in the old paths it was, of course, unnecessary; and even some who were prepared to accept the more moderate results of criticism retained a veneration for traditional definitions of doctrine, and were unprepared to allow the legitimacy of amending them. Such an attempt seemed to question the guidance of the Holy Spirit in the past. Ecclesiastical pronouncements, it may be observed, like other authoritative utterances, especially if they claim a supernatural sanction, often acquire undue weight, for it is easy to imagine that

> our puny boundaries are things
> That we perceive and not that we have made.

The more timid were afraid of the consequences of making the slightest concessions even in non-essentials; for they failed to distinguish between the central truths and the mass of explanatory teaching which had grown up around them, and that the 'current mode of explaining a doctrine in one age, and bringing it home by illustrations to the imagination of men, may be discredited and superseded in another'.[1] It is an old difficulty; for the work of adjustment is always troublesome and liable to arouse suspicion and resentment. Were not the works of St. Thomas Aquinas condemned in both Paris and Oxford and denounced by Archbishop Peckam?[2]

One reason why the narrowly orthodox regarded any tampering with even a single doctrine as perilous, was the traditional idea that all doctrines were closely interlocked, and that, in consequence, to abandon or even to restate one of them might jeopardize the entire structure. 'You must accept the whole or reject the whole; attenuation does but enfeeble, and amputation

---

[1] R. C. Moberly in *Lux Mundi*, p. 183.
[2] Cf. my *Decline and Fall of the Medieval Papacy*, pp. 83 f.

mutilates.'[1] In this statement Newman regarded the faith, not as a machine, but as an organism which might receive permanent and even fatal damage by the removal of a single part. This is, however, a deceptive analogy, though more enlightening and more in accord with contemporary thought than the figure of a machine, for there are cases where amputation may be necessary for the preservation of the life of the organism. Even the enlightened A. L. Moore acquiesced in this view and could write: 'It seems to me impossible to defend Christianity on anything less than the whole of the Church's Creed.'[2] But though this was the traditional view, if it precluded any restatement, it was patently contradicted by the facts of history; for, as J. R. Illingworth wrote in 1876: 'The theology of the past gains a fictitious unity for us, chiefly from our ignorance of it. The more we look into it, the more we find that it has changed its language again and again.'[3] A more worthy attitude was that of F. H. Chase who declared that: 'The thoughtful Christian . . . will be content to admit that round his central beliefs there lies a margin of admittedly open questions. The cry "all or nothing" is the confession of despair.'[4]

There is, of course, a sense in which the faith is a whole, the parts of which supplement and throw light on each other. All doctrines are descriptive of the relations of God and man, and none taken in isolation is more than a partial application of that relationship. It is when the notion is pressed too far and too narrowly that it becomes burdensome. Moreover there lies behind it the false assumption that all the facts have been included and accounted for, so that nothing fresh may be allowed to intrude. A balanced system of doctrine in which all the parts are nicely distributed may be convenient for the theologian, and he may resent any interference with it; but such interference cannot be rejected if it is demanded by new knowledge, and, let it not be forgotten, by fresh experience. Theology is not religion, but the

---

[1] Newman, *The Development of Christian Doctrine*, p. 94.
[2] *Science and the Faith*, p. xii. [3] *Life*, p. 46.
[4] In *Cambridge Theological Essays*, p. 417.

science of religion, and like every other science worthy of the name, it must be prepared to adjust itself to meet new conditions. Christianity for Bishop Butler was 'a scheme or system imperfectly comprehended', but have not additional discoveries and a wider range of living helped to lessen its incomprehensibility?

The current insistence on the faith as a single whole had some justification, for many quite genuine and candid attempts at restatement were vitiated by the lack of a sense of proportion. This again was no new thing; for Christianity has repeatedly been misunderstood, not to say, misrepresented, by certain aspects of it being isolated and even regarded as the sum total of the Gospel. The temptation to over-emphasize a few cherished doctrines is a potent one, and where it has been allowed to have its way there has followed a shifting of balance, consequent upon confusing the part with the whole. The position is made worse when, as has sometimes been the case, the part is worked up into an apparently complete scheme of salvation.[1] The Christian faith, it would seem, is so great that no age and no individual teacher can grasp it in its entirety and with a due heed to proportion.

In regard to the need for restatement, as in other matters, there was a notable difference of opinion between the older and the younger adherents of the Oxford Movement. This can be seen by a comparison of two utterances. Liddon had affirmed that 'A particular intellectual presentation of Truth may be modified, but nothing of the kind is possible with any article of the Christian Faith';[2] but Illingworth could write: 'Christian truth, in virtue of its very vitality . . . must be for ever outgrowing the clothes with which successive ages invest it.'[3]

Before proceeding to consider the various doctrines in detail mention must be made of a feature of the period which affected many of them—a fresh turning to Greek theology. A knowledge of Greek theology had been characteristic of the Caroline divines;

---

[1] Sanday poured out his scorn upon those who demanded the 'all' of some little system which fitted together like a piece of mechanism. *Inspiration*, p. 428.
[2] *Life*, p. 366.   [3] *Life*, p. 45.

hence, in the judgment of Hort, their largeness of mind.[1] But after their day the study of Greek theology had been neglected; the Tractarians, in particular, had been attracted to the more rigid theology of the Latins.[2] A reaction was undoubtedly overdue. This was recognized by Liddon who wrote to Max Müller, 'You have the Alexandrians behind you, and the modern Church has too hastily forgotten them';[3] whilst in the preface to *Logic and Life* (1882) Scott Holland in emphatic terms lamented the loss which English theology had sustained in consequence of this neglect. Four years earlier Westcott in an essay on 'Origen and the Beginnings of Christian Philosophy' in *The Contemporary Review*,[4] had found hope for the triumph of Christianity in the conflicts of his day from its achievements in the third century. He considered that a turning to Greek theology would lighten the Church from 'the heavy burden of the materialistic conceptions' imposed upon it by Latin theology[5] from its first beginnings with Tertullian and its development by Augustine. In 1883 in an essay on 'Dionysius the Areopagite'[6] he could declare that 'it is not too much to say that a work remains for Greek divinity in the nineteenth century hardly less pregnant with results than that wrought by the Greek classics in the fifteenth'.[7] One feature of the Greek Church had been its fearless encouragement of free inquiry and the belief that the results of such inquiry must be ultimately to establish the truth of Christianity.

[1] *Life*, Vol. II, p. 38.

[2] The leaders read some of the Greek Fathers, Newman especially delighted in them (see R. D. Middleton, *Newman at Oxford*, pp. 73 f., 106 f., but their influence on the movement was inconsiderable. *I nar barn our by the Tra*

[3] *Life of Max Müller*, Vol. II, p. 47.

[4] Reprinted in *Religious Thought in the West*, pp. 194 ff.

[5] But Greek theology was not entirely free from this defect. William Temple in *Foundations*, p. 231 said that Greek theology 'noble as it is, suffers from a latent materialism; its doctrine of substance is in essence materialistic'.

[6] Reprinted from *The Contemporary Review* in *Religious Thought in the West*, pp. 142 ff. In this essay Westcott mentions a mild revival of interest in Scholasticism, a revival which has since attained great proportions.

[7] Westcott, like his contemporaries, entertained an exaggerated notion of the part which Greek played in the Renaissance: see my *Erasmus the Reformer*, pp. 4 f. and F. X. Kraus in *Cambridge Modern History*, Vol. II, p. 3.

The revival of interest in Greek theology was due in part to F. D. Maurice. Essentially a theologian, all his religious teaching was based on theology; but on a theology which was the fruit not of thought and meditation alone but of practical experience in real life. His influence would undoubtedly have been much more extensive had it not been hampered by obscurities of style, and even of thought. Men suspected him, as he himself confessed in April 1862, of hiding some esoteric meaning behind utterances which were intended to be taken quite literally. In 1873, after the death of Maurice, Matthew Arnold wrote: 'The truth must at last be said, that in theology he passed his life beating the bush . . . and never starting the hare.'[1] But in spite of these handicaps, real or imaginary, Maurice exercised a profound influence on some of his younger contemporaries, such as Hort, though strangely enough, in view of the similarity of many of their views, not on Westcott. Westcott although he valued *Social Morality*, 'one of my very few favourite books',[2] deliberately abstained from reading Maurice from fear of being unduly influenced by him. On reading *The Life of Maurice* in 1884 he wrote: 'I never knew before how deep my sympathy is with most of his characteristic thoughts.'[3] He did, however, quote from the *Moral and Metaphysical Philosophy* in an essay written in 1866.[4]

For many devout Churchmen religion without dogma seemed meaningless,[5] and even some who might not fully merit the term saw its importance. Did not Disraeli once say to Dean Stanley, 'Mr. Dean, no dogmas, no deans'?[6] The necessity of

[1] *Literature and Dogma*, p. 345.
[2] *Life*, Vol. II, p. 160.   [3] *Op. cit.*, Vol. II, p. 37.
[4] See *Religious Thought in the West*, p. 48, note 1. For a fuller discussion of the relations between Maurice and Westcott see *Religion in the Victorian Era*, pp. 296f.
[5] Cf. Newman, *Apologia*, p. 54: 'I cannot enter into the idea of any other sort of religion; religion as a mere sentiment, is to me a dream and a mockery.' Lord Salisbury believed that 'Religion can no more be separated from dogma than light from the sun.' Cf. also Robertson Smith, *Lectures and Essays*, p. 310: 'A religion without theology means, for the most part, a religion without God.'
[6] *Memoir of Alfred, Lord Tennyson*, Vol. II, p. 232.

dogma was also recognized by some who were generally regarded as advanced Liberals; Hastings Rashdall, for example, affirmed that 'Religion can only be handed down, diffused, propagated by an organized society: and a religious society must have some means of handing on its religious ideas.'[1] But the tendency of the age was moving in an opposite direction, and moving so strongly that the future of dogmatic religion seemed to be hazardous. Newman had written from the Oratory at Birmingham that he despaired 'about the cause of dogmatic truth in England'.[2]

In the opinion of T. H. Green dogmatic theology was already a thing of the past, and he looked upon it as 'a phase of the human mind in which, having lost its hold on the original religious experiences of the founders of Christianity, it substitutes for them chains of reasoning the same in kind as those by which it would explain or establish any physical or historical phenomenon'.[3] A similar conclusion had been reached, rather plaintively, by Matthew Arnold in 'Dover Beach' and 'Obermann Once More':

> Alone, self-poised, henceforward man
> Must labour; must resign
> His all too human creeds, and scan
> Simply the way divine.

The reasons which may be invoked to account for the move away from dogmatic religion were many and various. One contributory cause was probably the feeling among some quite orthodox believers that the process of definition had gone too far, that the piling up of dogmas had obscured the simple Gospel.[4] There was also a suspicion that theologians were too much inclined to devote themselves to the solution of minute points

---

[1] *Philosophy and Religion*, p. 174.

[2] *Autobiography of Isaac Williams*, p. 131.

[3] Nettleship, *Memoir of T. H. Green*, p. 147. Cf. William James, *Varieties of Religious Experience*, p. 448: 'We must bid a definite good-bye to dogmatic theology. In all sincerity our faith must do without this warrant.'

[4] Hampden in his Bampton Lectures for 1832 had urged the need for greater simplicity in doctrinal statements.

which did not really matter, and that they professed to have knowledge of things which were beyond man's power to comprehend. It cannot be denied that there was some justification for this suspicion, or that some attempts to explain such mysteries as the doctrine of the Atonement and the nature of the sacramental presence were far from convincing. They depended, moreover, on the large use of outworn philosophical notions; for the terms in which some dogmas were stated had become mere words from which the reality they had once enshrined had long ago departed. The efforts of theologians to preserve the old forms, whilst giving them new meaning, may have been sincere and indeed praiseworthy, but were not calculated to increase their credit with the masses. Another factor which cannot be ignored was the influence of the poets, whose religious and theological notions carried so much weight. Many of them were very vague in their beliefs. Browning is here typical, for after he had thrown off the narrow Nonconformity of his youth he held views that were far from orthodox. 'His early Christian faith had expanded and taken the non-historical form of a Humanitarian Theism courageously accepted, not as a complete account of the Unknowable, but as the best provisional conception which we are competent to form.'[1]

There was also a growing dislike of metaphysics, for which the influence of Ritschl and his followers may in part have been responsible, though the limited extent to which their views were current in England during our period makes this unlikely. To this was allied what was perhaps the most potent cause of the flight from dogmatic religion, the dislike of anything which smacked of the supernatural or the miraculous. It could not be denied that not only the Bible, but also the Creeds, countenance a belief in such events. Many of the exponents of undogmatic Christianity believed that if once the faith could be freed from this element it would gain in strength and be capable of a much wider appeal. Pfleiderer ended his survey of *The Development of Theology in the Nineteenth Century* by affirming that it was certain

[1] Dowden, *Life of Robert Browning*, p. 364.

that the labours of the best and wisest of all the theologians of this century . . . however various the courses they followed may have been in detail, have still all pointed towards the one end, the deliverance of Christianity from its dogmatic impedimenta, that it may evince its world-subduing virtue in the ethical idealism of a love bound to God and binding mankind in one bond of brotherhood. (p. 454.)

This statement is a patent exaggeration, so far as England is concerned, but it is not without some truth.

In their efforts to arrive at what would now be called a 'basic' Christianity, extreme liberal thinkers were not only moved by the desire to purge from Christianity 'the falsifications of dogmatic theology and popular superstition', they also wished, in view of the prevailing unsettlement, to establish 'an intellectual position for the Christian faith which should not be called in question by every advance in historical evidence and in physical science'.[1] This seems a cowardly attitude to adopt, and so open-minded a theologian as Hort denounced it as 'a baseless contrivance for generating results of conduct such as would please God and make men happy'.[2]

The attempt to separate what were regarded as the permanent values of Christianity from what was obsolete or secondary might make an appeal to intellectuals, especially to those who had had an emotional experience of the comfort and power of religion, but even so, efforts to promote communities of 'believers' to foster religion apart from the organized churches were almost uniformly unsuccessful. In 1868 Henry Sidgwick and others founded what they called a 'Free Christian Union'; but it had a brief existence only. This is hardly surprising, for what they attempted to provide was there already, and not finding much favour, in the Unitarian congregations.

Some optimistic souls cherished the idea that a non-miraculous and simplified form of Christianity would make an appeal to the labouring classes who were growing in influence and in mental

---

[1] Arnold Toynbee's preface to T. H. Green, *Two Sermons*.
[2] *The Way, the Truth, the Life*, p. 45.

ability. J. R. Green, who had worked among them in Bethnal Green, was persuaded that the faith of the future would be found in the union of mysticism with freedom of thought and inquiry.[1] But the masses found nothing attractive in the new religion; in fact it made no appeal to them whatsoever. If religion was such an uncertain thing why bother about it at all?

For many earnest seekers after truth dogmas were a positive burden fettering the free movement of thought;[2] truth, so they opined, could only be attained by the healthy conflict of ideas, and in such an endeavour those whose minds were already bound by ecclesiastical formulas could take no useful part. But such was not the universal opinion of those who could no longer accept the Christian faith; there was something fixed about doctrines, even if only for the purpose of rejecting them. 'The absence of definite dogmas', wrote John Addington Symonds in 1882, 'accentuates our present differences and makes isolation of souls more painful.'[3]

In the decay of dogmatic religion many consoled themselves with the thought, so well suited to a humanitarian and philanthropic age, that what really mattered was to live a Christian life, to follow the teaching and example of Jesus, not to hold any special doctrines about His person;[4] conduct was the vital test, not the acceptance of credal statements. Those who had reached this conclusion appealed to the attitude of Jesus Himself, as portrayed in the Synoptic gospels, and one of the contributors to *Essays and Reviews* had contrasted His severity towards the practical failings of the Pharisees with His apparent unconcern over the doctrinal defects of their rivals. Others quite openly rejoiced at what they regarded as the collapse of dogmatic religion.

---

[1] *Letters of J. R. Green*, p. 80.
[2] Before our period F. W. Newman had appealed for the free movement of personal intuition, unfettered by creed or definition: see Storr, p. 375.
[3] *Letters*, p. 141.
[4] Though they rejected existing forms of worship they were 'definitely religious and sympathized with all religious activities that did not involve affirmations which might prove inconsistent with complete freedom of scientific and historical inquiry'. Webb, *op. cit.*, p. 115.

'The worship of deities has passed into the service of man', wrote Cotter Morison.

In so far as they emphasized the practical nature of religion, demands for an undogmatic Christianity served a useful purpose and helped to counterbalance the tendency of theologians to look upon the faith from too intellectual a point of view, to the neglect of its direct application to life. Pusey had written to Stanley in 1864 on this matter: 'I think that one of the great dangers of the present day is to conceive matters of faith as if they were matters of opinion.'[1] This was not the attitude, it need scarcely be said, of all, or even the majority, of theologians. In the very year after Pusey's letter to Stanley, Westcott had written in the preface to *The Gospel of the Resurrection*; 'The subject *is not a vain thing for us: it is our life.*'

That religious dogma should have been underrated by many was a little anomalous in an age which was not averse to dogmatism in other spheres; some scientists, for instance, were exceedingly dogmatic, and it seemed as though the theologian alone was to be deprived of the privilege.

The disparagement of Christian dogma was followed by a consequence which few had foreseen and most would have deplored; its effects on conduct. It is an indisputable fact that creed and conduct are closely connected and that conduct depends largely on creed. On this, as so many other matters, the credit of having contributed the last word belongs to Lightfoot: 'Christianity, it is said, is a life, not a creed. It could more truly be called a life in a creed.'[2] The men of the nineteenth century were unduly optimistic when they imagined that the Christian way of life and Christian ethical standards could be preserved apart from dogmatic beliefs. The tree soon decays when cut off from its roots. That is all very obvious to us now; but even then its truth was beginning to be realized. When *Ecce Homo* was published in 1866 Westcott commented: 'It is this so-called Christian morality as the "sum of the Gospel" which makes

[1] *Life of Stanley*, Vol. II, p. 165.
[2] *Notes on Epistles of St. Paul*, p. 186.

Christianity so powerless now.'[1] That surely is true; for the attempt to reduce Christianity to a bare morality leaves man very much to his own resources and is in reality only another form of naturalism.

Such a reduced Christianity, even if men could be persuaded to accept it—which they have never shown signs of doing—has no message of hope for those who are tied and bound by the weight of their sins and bewildered by the darkness which surrounds them. It is certainly far removed from the historic faith which found expression in the lives of the saints, and inspired countless thousands to witness to it by their deaths.

[1] *Life*, Vol. I, p. 289.

Chapter Eleven

THE IDEA OF GOD:
CHRISTOLOGY: THE FUTURE LIFE

TURNING to the different articles of belief we begin naturally with the idea of God, for this is fundamental to all theological thought; fundamental, moreover, for conduct as well, since our conception of the moral law must vary with our idea of God. Ethics for the Christian cannot be divorced from metaphysics.

The idea of God is one which demands constant rethinking in the light of fuller knowledge and richer experience, even the struggles and confusions of an era may be the means of gaining fresh revelations. The attempt to obtain new insight is itself salutary, for as William Temple has said: 'Nowhere is the danger of resting in abstract universals more serious than in Theology. We are liable to argue in support of the Being of God, without troubling ourselves as to what sort of God we are establishing.'[1]

The predominant feature of our period, following on the revived interest in Greek theology, was a new emphasis on the divine immanence. The deity was thought of more and more, not as standing outside the world, but as continually active in human affairs. There were even some, such as William James, who believed in a kind of 'progressive' God whose own life was enriched by new experiences and by His participation in the struggles of life. This new emphasis was also in agreement with the discoveries of natural science, for so long as heaven was regarded as a definite place, situated above the earth, it was natural to think of it as the dwelling-place of God. The abandonment of such a notion clearly demanded a fresh attitude. Furthermore

[1] *Mens Creatrix*, p. 20.

the conception of creation, not as an event in the distant past, but as continuous, fitted in with the thought of an immanent deity. 'The doctrine ... of God's immanence means that the laws of Nature are the thoughts of God.'[1]

The thought of God as almost purely transcendent was an inheritance from Deism, and it was high time that it should be modified, for as Tennyson wrote in 1869, 'The general English idea of God is as an immeasurable clergyman: and some mistake the devil for God.'[2] But too great an emphasis on the divine immanence was not without its dangers. A transcendent deity may be far off, but He is definite and distinct from the world; an immanent God may become a mere abstraction. Furthermore undue emphasis on the divine immanence may take away from the uniqueness of the Incarnation, and suggest that some kind of incarnation is possible for all men.[3] Immanence, in any case, may verge on Pantheism, a belief which proved very attractive in our period,[4] especially in the form of what was known as the Higher Pantheism, a kind of cosmic emotion, which made a strong appeal to romantic and poetic minds.

A really adequate and balanced idea of the deity demands that both His immanence and His transcendence shall receive equal weight. Such a conception seems to meet the apparent paradox, first formulated by Plato (*Timaeus* 27), which philosophers find so baffling, of Being and Becoming.

One problem concerning the nature of God provoked considerable discussion—how to reconcile the Christian idea that

---

[1] Gwatkin, *The Sacrifice of Thankfulness*, p. 53. He saw in immanence but a new name for the old attribute of omnipresence, but an omnipresence viewed in the light of science and history (*op. cit.*, p. 54).

[2] *Memoir*, Vol. II, p. 90.

[3] This danger seems to attach itself to T. H. Green's description of God. 'He is a Being in whom we exist, with whom we are in principle one: with whom the human spirit is identical, in the sense that He *is* all which the human spirit is capable of becoming.' (*Prolegomena to Ethics*, §187.)

[4] Cf. Caird, *Philosophy of Religion*, p. 221. 'The attraction of Pantheism and of pantheistic systems of philosophy lies in this, that they meet the craving of the religious mind for absolute union with God, and of the speculative mind for intellectual unity.'

He is Love with the existence of evil in the world. The latter
fact was difficult to account for and led many to deny the truth of
Christianity altogether.[1] The age was peculiarly sensitive to
suffering of any kind, a feature of a high state of civilization,
and much of it was unselfish—sympathy for the sufferings of
others. There was a tendency, indeed, to limit evil to suffering,
and to forget that, for the Christian at least, the worst evil is sin.

This reminds us that one of the great difficulties about the
problem of evil is that it assumes so many different forms.
There is physical evil—such as suffering and disease, and grave
disasters like earthquakes and floods. There is moral evil which
is the outcome of man's own acts, though not necessarily nor
invariably the fault of the victim; much of it is due to cruelty,
greed, and injustice. In the Old Testament this distinction is
clearly recognized; moral evil is due to man's wilfulness, physical
evil is God's punishment for sin, usually of the nation rather than
the individual. Another form of evil, the denial or distortion
of the truth, has become much more familiar to us than it was to
men in the nineteenth century.

The problem of evil, in spite of endless discussions, has never
found a satisfactory solution; probably it is beyond man with
his restricted knowledge to arrive at any solution. It is a difficulty
not only for religion, but perhaps even more for naturalism; for
pain 'is one of those facts of universal experience which are
peculiarly intractable from the point of view of a merely materialistic philosophy'.[2] Spinoza might dismiss evil as a human concept
and not an absolute, declaring that nothing is either good or bad
in itself; and optimists, like Browning, could proclaim that 'evil
is null, is nought, is silence implying sound';[3] but these attempted
solutions were really a refusal to face the facts, even if it
be admitted that much which seems to be physical evil comes

---

[1] 'Popular unbelief—and sometimes the unbelief of more cultivated persons—
rests mainly upon the existence of evil.' Hastings Rashdall, *Philosophy and
Religion*, p. 85.

[2] Underhill, *Mysticism*, p. 23. A materialist, of course, could not suggest the
possibility of compensation in a future life.

[3] *Abt Vogler*, ix. 6.

from an over-emphasis on 'the disparity between the course of nature and the values of man'.[1] It is, however, not physical but moral evil which raises the problem in its most acute form; since 'moral evil, independently of any theory of its nature or its origin, is a plain palpable fact, a fact of such stupendous magnitude as to constitute by far the most serious problem of our life'.[2]

If it seems impossible to reconcile the belief that God is Love with the existence of evil the question remains, and it is a question which raises issues of profound importance, as to how it is that men ever came to entertain such a conception. Since nature is 'red in tooth and claw' no contemplation of it could have suggested to man the thought that the Creator was merciful and loving.[3] Yet there were pious souls, even in the Old Testament, who had risen to the height of this conception (cf. Exodus 34:6f.). The only explanation would seem to be that they had arrived at it, not by contemplating nature, but human relationships in their noblest and most unselfish forms. It must not be forgotten that Jesus, who brought the supreme revelation of God as Love, had a deeper consciousness of the presence of evil than any other religious teacher.

The existence of evil and sorrow in the world can only be reconciled with the idea of God as Love (and without such a hypothesis the universe seems inexplicable) along two lines: by showing that 'evil overcome of good contributes to a greater good than was otherwise attainable', and that God 'through His love' has taken upon Himself the burden of the evil of the world.[4] As to the first, it cannot be denied that the presence of moral evil is bound up with the grant of 'freewill' to man; for

[1] Cf. Inge, *Outspoken Essays*, Vol. II, p. 22.

[2] J. R. Illingworth in *Lux Mundi*, p. 153.

[3] Cf. Sanday, *Inspiration*, p. 152: 'The presence of evil in the world, of pain and sorrow and sin, prevents us from arguing directly from the character of Creation to the character of the Creator.'

[4] Cf. William Temple, *Mens Creatrix*, p. 351 and Gore, *The Incarnation*, p. 120 who wrote that Christ 'made it, in His bitter passion and death upon the cross, the very occasion for expressing the depth of the divine self-sacrifice'.

had there been no possibility of vice, there could have been no possibility of virtue. Pain also may be a form of punishment warning the offender of the consequences of his conduct; it may also be purgatorial and corrective. One of the complications over moral evil is that it can never be found in a 'pure' form, for good and evil are ever intermingled. Pain, however, may help to distinguish them and bring about different reactions. It thus serves as a form of discipline, for it is, as Illingworth has said, 'the men of sorrows who are the men of influence. . . . Even more than knowledge pain is power.' Pain, too, has a unifying effect and draws out compassion in others. In connexion with the relation of the evil of the world and Christianity it may be noticed that the latter was often charged with being a religion 'which has increased the sum of actual and the expectation of prospective pain'.[1] Pain for the religious man may, indeed, be regarded as something to be offered to God, for there is 'an instinctive tendency in all religions, from the savage upwards, to view pain, whether in the form of asceticism or sacrifice, as inseparably connected with an acceptable service of the gods or God'.[2] As to the second point: if Christianity provides no solution of the problem of moral evil it sets forth a remedy for sin in the Crucifixion; and the Cross gave a divine significance to pain; 'the sight of perfect sinlessness, combined with perfect suffering has cleared our view for ever'.[3] The Atonement demonstrated, once and for all, that 'there is no sinning upon cheap and easy terms'.

It has to be confessed that theologians and philosophers, though they might make use of the old arguments, some of them weighty, brought little fresh light to illuminate the problem of pain and evil; Illingworth, however, wrote wisely and under-standingly upon it, and James Hinton in *The Mystery of Pain* produced an important study.

If little fresh light was thrown during our period on the problem of pain and evil, the same was true of the doctrine of the Trinity. This is not surprising, for discussions on the subject go

---

[1] Illingworth in *Lux Mundi*, p. 82.   [2] *Op. cit.*, p. 88.   [3] *Op. cit.*, p. 90.

back to the age of the Fathers, and their arguments in support of the doctrine seem to exhaust the matter. There was, moreover, a tendency to treat the doctrine as of only secondary importance; it was incomprehensible and therefore best left alone. For some it seemed an unnecessary addition to the faith and even an embarrassment. Yet the Trinity, rightly understood, is almost a philosophical necessity to the Faith, and, as Barth nowadays affirms, the very corner-stone of theology.

Although the doctrine is not 'discoverable by reason', it is 'agreeable to reason',[1] and enriches our conception of the nature of the Godhead. A lonely and isolated Creator, dwelling aloof, might arouse awe and reverence, but is too remote to evoke the affections of men. Much more satisfying is the idea of a living 'society', a diversity in unity, at the heart of the universe. The doctrine of the Trinity 'preserves the divine transcendence which gives fixity to all relative existence without sacrificing the divine immanence which makes life and progress possible'.[2]

Christian idealists found in the doctrine of 'persons' in the unity of the divine essence the suggestion that 'rightly conceived, the mutual differences of persons would be found to involve the unity of these different persons in a fellowship, to the constitution of which these differences were at the same time permanently necessary'.[3]

Personality is the highest thing of which we have knowledge; personality therefore is the least inadequate symbol by means of which we can represent God, and 'the doctrine of the Trinity as dogmatically elaborated, is ... the most philosophical attempt to conceive of God as Personal'.[4]

Person, as a theological term, preserves its primary meaning of status, condition, or character of existence, but its use to describe the Father, Son, and Holy Spirit was apt to be misunderstood by simple souls, and the belief of many Christians

---

[1] Gore, *The Incarnation*, p. 134. Cf. Aquinas *Summa Theol.* I, XXXIII, 2.
[2] *Life of J. R. Illingworth*, p. 275.
[3] C. C. J. Webb, *Religious Thought*, etc., p. 118.
[4] Illingworth, *Personality: Human and Divine*, p. 67.

was, in fact, a kind of Tritheism, a belief in three Gods. They did not comprehend that 'in the Christian conception of God, Father, Son, and Spirit are alike equally essential to His Being. There never was One of the Three alone: the Three together are GOD.'[1] Hastings Rashdall, at the price of being suspected of unorthodoxy, tried to correct the popular error by pointing out that in the teaching of the older theologians the three persons were not regarded as 'distinct centres of consciousness', but as 'eternally distinct activities of One Divine Mind'.

The common notion that the doctrine of the Trinity was a kind of metaphysical puzzle which had no relation to practical life was far removed from the truth, and any attempt to vindicate it from a purely speculative angle 'must always be incomplete, and must fail to do justice to the fullness of moral truth which the doctrine enshrines'.[2] The influence of Greek theology, with its emphasis on the conception of the Second Person in the Trinity as the Word, did something to counteract the popular tendency, at least for theologians. As a consequence the philosophical truth became 'an integral part of that Christian doctrine of God, which, while it safeguarded religion and satisfied reason, had won its first and greatest victories in the field of morals'.[3]

Teaching about the work of the Holy Spirit became very prominent during our period, but in the practical life of religion, mainly owing to the activity of what was known as the Keswick School. For theologians it was beset by difficulties, for it was not easy to distinguish the operations of the Holy Spirit from those of the Word. Bishop Thirlwall, shortly before his death in 1875, declared that the great intellectual and religious struggle of our day turned mainly on the question whether there was a Holy Ghost.

If our period was not characterized by much progress in the elucidation of Christian doctrines in general this could not be said of the work done on Christology. Problems in connexion with

---

[1] Bethune-Baker, *The Faith of the Apostles' Creed*, p. 157.
[2] Storr, p. 336.　　　[3] See A. L. Moore in *Lux Mundi*, pp. 70f.

it had already been forced into prominence by Hegel's failure to present a satisfactory account of the Person of Christ, and these fell into three divisions—the recovery of the historical Jesus, the definition of the Christ of theology, and the determination of the relationship between them.[1]

Theologians of all schools recognized the importance of the doctrine of the Incarnation and the need to explore its possible applications. 'Faith in the Incarnation, with all that it involved, has been the sole and exclusive source of our historic Christianity', wrote Illingworth;[2] while Westcott considered that it alone was 'able to give reality to human knowledge',[3] and that the Incarnation as the 'central fact of history . . . illuminates the problems which meet us alike in our daily work and in our boldest speculations'.[4] Westcott wrote much on the subject, but dealt mainly with the practical applications of the doctrine; Illingworth, in addition to many incidental references, contributed an essay to *Lux Mundi* in which he endeavoured to remove popular misconceptions of the doctrine, to draw attention to some more or less forgotten aspects, and to suggest fresh ways of viewing it;[5] R. C. Moberly also had an essay in the same volume on 'The Incarnation as the Basis of Dogma'.

Turning to larger works we notice first Liddon's famous Bampton Lectures for 1866 on *The Divinity of our Lord and Saviour Jesus Christ*, which, though a powerful and persuasive restatement of the traditional position, cannot be said to have made any fresh contribution to theology. Liddon laid great stress on the claims which Jesus made for Himself, and poses the dilemma *aut Deus aut homo non bonus*. In digressions he affirmed that the Mosaic authorship of the Pentateuch must be accepted as recognized by Jesus, and he also connected the Incarnation with the efficacy of the sacraments. Equally famous, and much more apposite to

[1] Cf. Storr, p. 218.   [2] *Personality: Human and Divine*, p. 199.
[3] *Life*, Vol. II, p. 88.   [4] *Lessons from Work*, pref.
[5] R. W. Church, *The Gifts of Civilisation*, p. 109, had drawn attention to the extent to which different ideas of the Incarnation arise in different ages and with different observers: 'We behold Him through the medium of our own minds and hearts.'

the times, were Gore's Bampton Lectures delivered in 1891 with the title of *The Incarnation of the Son of God*. The lectures were designed for the general public rather than for professional scholars, though they contain evidence of wide reading and deep thought. Gore himself claimed that he had made 'a profound and sympathetic study of the facts', and especially of the evidence of the gospels, including that of St. John, the apostolic authorship of which he accepted. The whole work is typical of his general position, for whilst it appeals to reason, the binding nature of the creeds is affirmed. He exposes the weakness of the medieval method of laying down dogma, and then arguing from it that certain consequences must follow; indeed, he reviews nature and history before going on to examine definitions and dogmatic statements. Christ as the crown of creation is both natural and supernatural, and Christianity is faith in His person. The humanity of Jesus is emphasized in view of the danger of its being obscured and forgotten, and there is a statement of the Kenotic theory in the form in which Gore held it. The most considerable study surveying the history of the doctrine was that of R. L. Ottley, *The Doctrine of the Incarnation* (1896). In it he laid stress on the dogmatic element in Scripture in opposition to the theories of Hatch and Harnack, who looked upon the theology of the Church as 'merely a product of Greek metaphysics'. He concludes that 'a far more considerable element in the development of dogma than "Hellenism" has been the influence of the Scriptures'.[1]

Hastings Rashdall, at the risk of being accused of unorthodoxy, laid stress on the perfect manhood of our Lord. This was very necessary; for in popular belief Jesus was regarded as 'not really man at all, but simply God walking about with a human body';[2] and there were even theologians who attempted 'to modify or refine away to a mere docetic phantom the human side of Christ's person so as to make it capable of union with the Divine'.[3]

[1] *Op. cit.*, Vol. I, p. vi, with a reference to C. Bigg, *Neoplatonism*, Ch. VIII.
[2] *Principles and Precepts*, p. 41.
[3] Caird, *Philosophy of Religion*, p. 202.

One interesting development was the abandonment by some theologians of unquestioned orthodoxy of the supposed distinction between our Lord as 'Man' and as 'a man'. 'Let us frankly recognize in Him 'a man', as He calls Himself.'[1]

One outcome of the popular notion of our Lord led to what might be called 'Jesus-worship'; for it is not the historic Jesus who is worshipped by Christians, but the eternal and omnipresent Word. In 1865 Hort wrote to Westcott:

> I have been persuaded for many years that Mary-worship[2] and 'Jesus' worship have very much in common in their causes and results. In Protestant countries (there is) the fearful notion 'Christ the believer's God', (whilst in) Romish countries the Virgin is a nearer and more attractive object, and not rejected by the dominant creed.[3]

John Wordsworth also saw the dangers inherent in the popular view, and 'emphasized the importance of a Trinitarian religious worship as against a one-sided adoration of the Second Person of the Holy Trinity in His human nature'.[4]

The neglect of the humanity of Christ must ultimately make Him an unreal figure. Such had been the experience of Henry Drummond, who confessed that, after hearing hundreds of sermons and addresses on His Person and Work, 'the ruling idea left in my mind was that Christ was a mere convenience . . . the creation of theology, and His function was purely utilitarian'.[5]

For Westcott the essence of the doctrine of the Incarnation lay 'not in the recognition of a distinct divine person, but in the

---

[1] A. J. Mason, *The Chalcedonian Doctrine of the Incarnation*, p. 60.

[2] Newman defended 'Mariolatry' on the ground that 'we want the idea of an ascended humanity as well as a descended Godhead': see *Life of F. D. Maurice*, Vol. II, p. 517. Such a notion reveals an imperfect appreciation of the humanity of our Lord.

[3] *Life*, Vol. II, p. 50.

[4] E. W. Watson, *Life of Bishop John Wordsworth*, p. 391.

[5] *The New Evangelism*, p. 15. Cf. Illingworth, *Divine Immanence*, p. 151 'all attempts to present religious doctrine in a philosophical connexion run a certain risk of conveying the impression that it is only philosophy.'

personal and final union of the Godhead and humanity'.[1] This
recalls the opinion current in some Russian Orthodox circles,
especially in the teaching of Solovyev and Berdyaev, that Christ
was 'the revelation of the universal principle of God-manhood'
and a symbol of the relation between God and man. These
theologians, however, recognized the unique character of the
Incarnation.

The revived emphasis on the human nature of Christ was in
some quarters, and above all in Germany, carried to such lengths
as to reduce Him to the level of the great teachers and prophets
of the past, though it was admitted that He far exceeded them.
Those who held such a view professed to find in the gospels,
when critically examined, a justification for their position. But
such a conception of Jesus could only be maintained by stripping
Him of His most characteristic features, and it is no wonder that
some eccentric scholars went so far as to deny that He had ever
existed. The Christ of the extreme Liberal theologians was
indeed an impossible figure.

Ritschl and his followers tried to find a middle way between
orthodox belief and a merely humanitarian conception of Christ,
and their views met with considerable favour. They came to
'a generation prepared by long discussion of the history of early
Christianity to welcome a system which made it seem possible
to worship Jesus Christ while saturated with scepticism as to the
supernatural . . . and despair as to the historical'. They believed
that Christ revealed God and also that He founded a community
in which the meaning of the revelation was first realized. He
made known the Father and so 'completely did He absorb the
divine will . . . that in Him, His faith, His obedience, His love,
we see the love, the grace, of God towards us. Thus Christ, in
the famous phrase, has for us "the value of God".'[2] One of the
most striking expositions of this position was contained in
Harnack's well-known lectures, delivered at Berlin in the winter
of 1899–1900, under the title *Das Wesen des Christentums*, and
translated into English soon afterwards as *What is Christianity?*

[1] *The Gospel of Life*, p. 252.   [2] *E.R.E.*, Vol. VII, p. 542.

Harnack professed to believe in the divinity of Christ, but was impatient of orthodox attempts to explain it.

The traditional theology of the Church had treated the relation of the divine and the human in our Lord as primarily a question of metaphysics. For medieval theologians, as for the popular notion of the Incarnation in the nineteenth century, the divinity was all important, the manhood little more than a mask. But now the problem was being approached from a different angle, in consequence of the new interest in history and in psychology.

For philosophy the doctrine of the Incarnation raises many difficult problems which largely remain unsolved, for they concern the relation of a concrete human life to a divine universal, and who can say where the human ends and the divine begins? Theologians, too, were engrossed in our period over the relation of the Jesus of history and the Christ of dogma, a problem that had become more acute with the increasing emphasis on the humanity of our Lord.

Jesus could be called the Jesus of history in the sense that He was born into the world at a particular time and in a particular place. But since His coming belongs to history it was open to critics to explain Him as a mere product of development, and to reject the claims made for Him by the Church as implying a breach of the natural order. Schleiermacher had asserted that His coming was to be regarded as normal and non-miraculous in its mode, even if a special act of God lay behind it. For believers the coming in history did not blind them to the fact that He who came into history was also its Lord, standing over and apart from it and directing its course; though He appeared on earth in abasement and poverty He was still the ruler and governor of all things.

This dual circumstance seemed almost a paradox, and some tried to avoid it by suggesting that while He was incarnate He ceased to exercise His divine powers in the universe. These, so it was suggested by the Swiss theologian Godet, He abandoned for the time as part of His self-emptying. In Germany Gess went so far as to declare that the eternal generation of the Son and the procession of the Holy Spirit through the Son, were suspended during His earthly life, and that 'the Word took the place of the human soul in Jesus as actually having become a human soul'.[1] Gore, on the other hand, believed that we are to suppose that 'the humiliation and the self-limitation of the incarnate state was compatible with the continued exercise of divine and cosmic functions'.[2]

This idea was an extreme form of what was known as the Kenotic theory, a term derived from our Lord's 'self-emptying' (Phil. 2:5ff.), but by no means dependent upon it, as is often inferred, for it derives support from other New Testament passages.[3] The Kenotic theory sought to account for the limitations, real or assumed, in our Lord's knowledge. These are recognized in the Synoptic gospels, which not only speak of His growth in knowledge, but also of His ignorance in certain matters (Mark 13:32; Luke 2:52; cf. John 11:34). The orthodox position was that the human mind of Christ possessed all knowledge, and in the West His admissions of ignorance had been explained as 'economic', being put forth for purposes of edification.[4] The idea had occurred in the writings of Thomasius (d. 1875), and was made familiar to English scholars by the translation of Godet's *Biblical Studies* in 1875; it also received notice in J. B. Heard's *Old and New Theology* (1884). What, however, brought it into prominence was its acceptance by Fairbairn in *The Place of Christ in Modern Theology* (1893). Fairbairn took up a middle position similar to that of Thomasius, but not so extreme as that of Gess, for he distinguished between the physical and the ethical attributes of the divine nature; the

---

[1] See Gore, *Dissertations*, p. 188.

[2] *Op. cit.*, p. 93.

[3] Cf. Bethune-Baker, *The Faith of the Apostles' Creed*, p. 12: 'The term itself, though derived, I believe, from a mistaken interpretation of a phrase of St. Paul's, expresses a doctrine necessary to the scientific theologian.'

[4] Cf. Bethune-Baker, *op. cit.*, p. 10: 'The master-builders and sculptors of Greece knew and practised the *entasis* of the column, that it might produce the effect of straightness at the distance they desired: and the Master Teacher of spiritual things may well have practised a kind of intellectual and spiritual *entasis*.'

latter were still exercised during the Incarnation, it was the former alone which were laid aside. A still more moderate position was that of Gore, who brought the theory into general notice in *Lux Mundi*, and afterwards elaborated it in the sixth of his Bampton Lectures, as well as in a long essay on 'The Consciousness of our Lord in His Mortal Life' in his *Dissertations*.

Gore entered upon the inquiry into the theory with reluctance, having the traditional Anglican dislike of prying too deeply into the mysteries of the faith; for Anglican theologians, in the words of Jeremy Taylor, do not 'love to serve God in hard questions'. The following were his provisional conclusions:

1. The Son of God, without ceasing to be God ... and without ceasing to be conscious of His divine relations as Son to the Father, yet, in assuming human nature, so truly entered into it as really to grow and live as Son of Man under properly human conditions ... [But] He did ... —doubtless by the voluntary action of His own self-limiting and self-restraining love—cease from the exercise of those divine functions and powers, including divine omniscience, which would have been incompatible with a truly human experience.
2. Jesus Christ, the Son of God incarnate, was ... at every moment and in every act, both God and man, personally God made man ... The Son of God really became and lived as Son of Man.[1]

Although the Kenotic theory was not widely adopted, it served to draw attention to the fact that, as depicted in the Synoptic gospels, Jesus possessed only the historical and scientific knowledge of His day.[2] This might have been expected, for unless Jesus lived under such limitations His mind can hardly be said to have been truly human.

The sub-title of *Lux Mundi* had been 'A Series of Studies in the Religion of the Incarnation',[3] and in it was reflected a change of

---

[1] *Op. cit.*, pp. 94f.

[2] Gore pointed out that 'Christ never enlarges our stock of natural knowledge, physical or historical, out of the divine omniscience.' (*The Incarnation*, p. 150.)

[3] Fairbairn, perhaps a little perversely, commented: 'Curiously the Incarnation is the very thing the book does not, in any more than the most nominal sense, either discuss or construe.' (*The Place of Christ in Modern Theology*, p. 451, note 1.)

emphasis in English doctrinal theology. The prevailing Protestantism had made much of the Atonement as the central dogma of Christianity, a circumstance readily understood, since the consciousness of the work of Christ in the individual soul was to many so vivid that it was for them the most certain proof of Christianity itself. The Cross was the divine remedy for the fall of man and the sole hope of the race.

The renewed study of the Greek Fathers, however, and in particular of the Alexandrians, showed that there were other ways of viewing the matter. They believed that the Incarnation was no mere afterthought, made necessary by man's failure, but that it had been part of the divine plan from the beginning, and was, indeed, the natural sequel to the creation of man. Man had been made in the divine image, and the Logos, or Word of God, had been continually active in the world, preparing the way for the supreme revelation of Himself in a historical person. Thus the Incarnation, as the crown of a long process and not as the remedy for a catastrophe, could itself be regarded as the Atonement, the bringing together of God and man.[1] The death of Jesus was not to be isolated from the life of Jesus, for that life, whatever else it did, had taught men 'that in the conditions of the highest human life we have access as nowhere else, to the inmost nature of the Divine'.[2]

By suggesting that the Incarnation, as the culmination of a long process, was in some sense itself the Atonement, the writers of *Lux Mundi* introduced the notions of evolution and divine immanence 'into the very heart of the traditional scheme of doctrine'; but this conception seemed to reduce the Cross almost to an accidental, though inseparable, accompaniment of the Incarnation, and showed an imperfect appreciation of the place which the Atonement had always held in Western theology, and even of the balance of the New Testament itself. The Cross, after

---

[1] 'In soteriology the Greek notion was metaphysical and personal, and so found its centre and symbol in the Incarnation; but the Latin was legal and forensic, and so emphasized justification and atonement.' (Fairbairn, *op. cit.*, p. 74.)

[2] Pringle-Pattison, *The Idea of God in Recent Theology*, p. 157.

all, had been in every age the symbol of Christianity.[1] None the less it served to correct that over-emphasis on the Atonement at the expense of the Incarnation which had become prevalent in popular representations of the Gospel teaching. In its crudest form this representation might seem to suppose that had Jesus given no teaching, but had been content only to offer His life, the Gospel could have been preached in all its fullness, and that the object of the Incarnation was to provide a divine victim without which Atonement would have been impossible. Dale was especially insistent on redressing the balance between the two doctrines in this relationship, considering that to regard the Incarnation merely as a remedy for sin was to misconceive its whole nature.[2]

The renewed insistence on the importance of the Incarnation, even if it involved some depreciation of the Atonement, did at least unite the death to the life work of Jesus, and also brought out more adequately the moral and spiritual elements in the doctrine. It also served as a reminder that the Cross had a man-ward as well as a Godward aspect.[3]

If the new emphasis on the Incarnation tended to lessen the importance of the Atonement in Christian thought and life other factors were also at work in the same direction; there was, indeed, almost a revolt, not so much against the doctrine itself as against the crude theories which had been put forward to explain it; for the Atonement accepted joyfully in the simple language of the New Testament may become repellent when couched in terms of scientific theology, and 'circumscribed by the presuppositions of self-interest'.[4]

[1] Cf. J. M. Creed in *Mysterium Christi*, p. 129: 'Unless the doctrine of the Incarnation is nailed to the Cross it tends to lose definition and to evaporate into a cosmic principle.' Recent Anglo-Catholics recognize the inadequacy of the *Lux Mundi* treatment of the Atonement: see J. K. Mozley, *Some Tendencies*, p. 79.

[2] *Life of R. W. Dale*, p. 604.

[3] Cf. Westcott, *Christus Consummator*, p. 24. 'The currents of theological speculation have led us to consider the sufferings of Christ in relation to God as a propitiation for sin, rather than in relation to man as a discipline, a consummation of humanity.'

[4] Cf. Oman, *Vision and Authority*, p. 240.

No doctrine has suffered more than that of the Atonement from human attempts to define and elaborate it. In many of them a division seemed to be made between the Father and the Son, who were regarded, when legal analogies were employed, as though they were opposing parties in a lawsuit. In their crudity they suggested that the Father was akin to the Zeus of Aeschylus rather than to the God revealed by Jesus, and the lonely figure on Calvary might well have said with Prometheus:

> Mercy I had for Man: and therefore I
> Must meet no mercy, but hang crucified
> In witness of God's cruelty and pride.[1]

Thus there was a greater need to restate the doctrine of the Atonement in terms which would commend it to modern educated thought than in the case of any other doctrine. There was, however, in view of the immense difficulties of the task, reluctance to enter upon fresh attempts at explanation or definition. But such an attitude cannot be maintained indefinitely; the Atonement

> must be related to the world of thought in which modern men are living, and shown to be as capable of explanation and defence in the moral and spiritual terms which have become controlling for our modern thought of God as in the legal and judicial categories so familiar to the older theology.[2]

It must be remembered that, as in the case of Inspiration, the Church has never adopted or sanctioned any 'official' theory of the Atonement, and Gregory of Nazianzus could say that the death of Christ is an article of faith about which it was not dangerous to be mistaken. None the less certain views had become traditional. These may be divided into three groups.[3]

The first to be considered is the theory held by St. Anselm,

---

[1] *Prometheus Vinctus*, 241–3 (Gilbert Murray's translation).

[2] *E.R.E.*, Vol. v, p. 647.

[3] See further J. K. Mozley, *The Doctrine of the Atonement*, pp. 173 ff., and the collected volume of essays *The Atonement in Modern Religion* (1900).

the Reformers, and prominently in Evangelical teaching, by which Christ suffered in the place of sinners, and so made expiation to the Father. This view found classic expression in *The Atonement* by R. W. Dale, published in 1875. The volume originated in a series of ten lectures which aroused much attention; the first eight, however, are given up to establishing the fact of the Atonement, and it is only in the last two that any theory is elaborated. In them Dale endeavours to retain the juridical significance of the Atonement, but at the same time to avoid the artificiality and legalism of previous statements. He looks upon the death of Christ as justly inflicted upon Him as the voluntary representative and head of the race, in order to satisfy the eternal law of righteousness which is one in essence with the will of God. The recognition that Christ was not merely a substitute, but also the head and representative of humanity, links his theory with that to be considered later.[1] Although Dale insisted on the 'legal' and 'objective' theory he thought it not inconsistent with the 'moral' theory; though the latter by itself represented only part of the truth. The death of Christ was a manifestation of the Love of God by which a change 'is wrought in us, a change by which we are reconciled to God'.[2] Similar views were put forward by J. Scott Lidgett in *The Spiritual Principle of the Atonement* (1897), but he differed from Dale in finding the necessity for penal satisfaction in the nature of fatherhood itself.

Next in order is what is known as the Representative theory, a theory which went back to the Greek Fathers and looked upon Christ as performing an act of vicarious penance on behalf of the race as a whole. It had been set forth by McLeod Campbell in *The Nature of the Atonement* (1856),[3] who believed that 'while Christ suffered for our sins as an atoning sacrifice, what He

---

[1] Hort went even further, holding that 'the absolute union of man with Christ was the spiritual truth of which the popular doctrine of substitution was an immoral and material counterfeit'. *Life*, Vol. 1, p. 430.

[2] R. C. Moberly considered that Dale's exposition was onesided and did not give sufficient importance to the redemptive aspect. Its gravest defect was the absence of any reference to the Holy Spirit.

[3] Summarized by Storr, pp. 424 ff.

suffered was not . . . a punishment'.[1] Campbell denied that there was anything redemptive in suffering itself, 'the essence of Christ's atoning work was in its moral quality as obedience'. But in substituting vicarious repentance for vicarious punishment he merely exchanged one difficulty for another.[2] Campbell's real interest, however, was not so much in the transference of the benefits of Christ's repentance, as in the conditions under which man may be forgiven. The whole idea of substitution in religion is only possible 'in the sphere of the moral and spiritual relationships of which the family rather than the law-court or the civil government gives us the most helpful example'.[3]

Finally, there is the theory, associated with the name of Abailard,[4] by which the effect of the Atonement is regarded as entirely subjective, an appeal to man to respond to God's love as exhibited in Christ's sacrifice on the Cross. This aspect had, of course, been present in other theories, but not as a complete explanation of the work of Christ, and has compelling power.

> Wouldest thou love one who never died
> For thee, or ever die for one who had not died for thee?[5]

Reviewing the work done on the Atonement during our period two tendencies may be noted: (*a*) a desire to moralize the doctrine, and to free it from the crudities which had disfigured older attempts at explanation, crudities which still persisted in much popular teaching; (*b*) a gradual abandonment of a merely individual application of the Atonement in favour of something wider.

[1] *Op. cit.*, p. 101. Cf. J. M. Wilson, *The Gospel of the Atonement*, p. 94: 'It is not only permissible but obligatory for us to eliminate from our thought of the reconciling work of Christ every trace of expiation or penalty as illustrations such as might be given in parables or metaphors.'

[2] *E.R.E.*, Vol. v, p. 648.   [3] *Idem.*

[4] The word is one of four syllables; the common form Abelard, derived from the French, is therefore incorrect.

[5] Blake, 'Jerusalem', xcv, 23 f. This view was later set out with great skill and power by Hastings Rashdall in the Bampton Lectures for 1915 on *The Idea of the Atonement in Christian Theology*.

(a) The theory that Christ gave His life as a 'ransom' had caused much embarrassment to the older theologians who could not decide whether it had been paid to God or to the devil. It had been rejected by St. Anselm in *Cur Deus Homo*, and was no longer taken in its literal sense by serious thinkers. The whole theory, of course, was based on a misunderstanding of Hebrew mentality. It is obvious, for example, that when God is said to have redeemed Israel out of Egypt there was no question of His having paid any price to Pharaoh; so too when in Judges we are repeatedly told that He sold Israel into the hands of various oppressors we are not intended to suppose that He received any payment.

(b) Although interpretations of the Atonement had mainly concentrated on its effects on the relations of God and the individual soul, there had not been lacking from early days a recognition that it had also a wider application, the redemption of the race as a whole and the establishment of the Kingdom of God on earth. This aspect was brought out strongly by Westcott in *Social Aspects of Christianity*. He declared that in 'every part of the New Testament the object of Redemption is set before us, not simply as the deliverance of individual souls, but as the establishment of a Divine Society'; the early Christians looked for a 'transformation of human society, to correspond to the Resurrection of the individual'.[1] Ritschl held a very similar view which he had expressed in *Die christliche Lehre von der Rechtfertigung und Versöhnung*.[2] Such a conception of salvation and atonement is more ethical than that commonly preached, for it 'takes its departure from the social nature of personality and finds the primary object of Christ's death in the creation of a community in which the bond of union is the acceptance of his principle of self-sacrificing love'.[3]

Other Anglican writers of an outlook different from that of

[1] *Op. cit.*, pp. 86 and 89.
[2] Published between 1870 and 1874 but not translated, under the title of *Justification and Reconciliation*, until 1900.
[3] *E.R.E.*, Vol. v, p. 649.

Westcott, though not uninfluenced by his teaching, were also reviving this conception of the Atonement, largely in connexion with the notion of the Church as a continuation of the Incarnation,[1] and also with the object of linking the Atonement and the sacraments. One very important study from this school lies just outside our period, R. C. Moberly's *Atonement and Personality*, which J. K. Mozley regarded as 'one of the most impressive theological works of its age'.[2]

The wider aspects of the Atonement received further attention after our period in the writings of P. T. Forsyth, especially in *The Work of Christ* (1910), in which he gave them still further extension, for he insisted that the reconciliation made by the Cross was 'a reconciliation of the world as a cosmic whole'. (p. 77.)

Some extreme critics, especially in Germany, belittled the whole doctrine of the Atonement and refused to give it any dogmatic importance, attributing the stress laid upon the death of Christ to the influence of St. Paul. From non-Christian sources also there came objections to the doctrine. Any idea of the possibility of atonement for sin was rejected, for the law of consequences must work itself out. This was a central point in the teaching of George Eliot who 'thought that the world would be infinitely better and happier if men could be made to feel that there is no escape from the inexorable law that we reap what we have sown'.[3]

One further reason why the doctrine of the Atonement began to fall into the background was that men were no longer worrying about their sins;[4] and many, accepting views based on evolution, regarded evil as something from which man would gradually free himself, thus treating a moral as though it were a physical

---

[1] The Incarnation 'opened heaven, for it was the revelation of the Word; but it also reconsecrated earth, for the Word was made Flesh and dwelt among us'. (Illingworth in *Lux Mundi*, p. 155.)

[2] *Some Tendencies in British Theology*, p. 25.

[3] Lord Acton, *Historical Essays and Studies*, p. 284.

[4] W. H. Moberly has remarked that 'the sense of sin is apt to be in inverse ratio to its actual presence' (in *Foundations*, p. 276).

defect. According to these thinkers, who emphasized man's dignity and denied his depravity, the worst evil was the inability of man to realize his true nature. The thought of 'sin', that is disobedience to a divine law, was completely ignored. Furthermore, belief in the doctrine of 'original sin' had been weakened by the recognition that the story in Genesis 3 was symbol and not history.[1] But there is much evidence to support the notion that there is in human nature some such bias, even if the idea of the Fall as accounting for it is rejected.[2] Kant, it may be noted, after a candid survey of the whole history of the race, had accepted the theory, and scientists might see in it the theological equivalent of heredity.

Criticisms of current theories of the Atonement, especially of those which involved substitution or representation, naturally caused considerable alarm, above all in Evangelical circles. They had, however, a beneficial side, since the traditional views had tended to foster too narrow a conception of religion by making it too individual, not to say too self-regarding, and by erecting a barrier between the secular and the religious had excluded whole areas of human activity from its sphere. It was one of the merits of the *Lux Mundi* group that they reminded men that the great theologians of the past had regarded redemption as a means to an end greater than the salvation of the individual, namely 'the reconsecration of the whole universe to God'.[3]

We come now to the doctrine of a Future Life.[4] Any religion worthy of the name accepts the existence of a world out of sight and claims to be able to provide a link between it and that of which we are immediately conscious. But not all religions affirm that man's connexion with the unseen world extends beyond the life of the body; though the belief that the soul survives death is

[1] It is a noteworthy fact that in the Old Testament there is 'no reference of human peccability to the event described in Gen. iii'. (Toy, *Proverbs*, p. 386.)

[2] Cf. *Life and Letters of Dean Church*, p. 248. 'The fact of what is meant by original sin is as mysterious and inexplicable as the origin of evil, but it is obviously as much a fact.'

[3] *Lux Mundi*, p. 134.

[4] See R. H. Charles, *A Critical History of the Doctrine of a Future Life* (1899).

widespread among primitive peoples.[1] But even when the possibilities of such a survival were recognized the future existence was dim and shadowy; Achilles would rather be a slave on earth than 'reign the sceptred monarch of the dead', and the Jewish psalmists held that only in this life could man have relations with God.[2]

During our period the doctrine did not attract much attention in either theology or religion. Men's thoughts were occupied so keenly with the affairs of this life that even where they retained some kind of belief in the hereafter they seldom paused to consider it. Some, indeed, had no desire for any kind of immortality, and felt that, as Anatole France once wrote, they ought to have the right to cut the entail. Popular neglect and even popular unbelief were largely the result of the unattractive and even repellent forms in which the future life had been represented, especially where biblical imagery was taken literally.

Idealist philosophers, although they might regard this life as designed for 'the training and development of immortal spirits',[3] were 'above all things concerned to find within *this* world . . . those religious values which had so often been thought of as belonging to another world'.[4]

Man seemed to be entrapped in a vicious circle; for absorption in the things of this life tells against any belief in a life hereafter, and it is by a belief in the immortality of the soul that a materialistic outlook can most effectively be corrected.[5] Moreover, life on this earth itself is robbed of much of its worth and interest if it is thought to end at death. 'When earth is an ante-room to heaven . . . earth itself is full of beauty and goodness.'[6]

[1] See Tylor, *Primitive Culture*, Vol. II, p. 1.

[2] See 6:5, 30:9, 88:5, 11f., 115:17; cf. Isaiah 38:18f.; Job 7:9.

[3] Edward Caird, *Lay Sermons*, p. 381.

[4] C. C. J. Webb, *op. cit.*, pp. 107f.

[5] Cf. Hastings Rashdall, *Philosophy and Religion*, p. 79: 'Disbelief in Immortality would, I believe, in the long run and for the vast majority of men, carry with it an enormous enhancement of the value of the carnal and the sensual over the spiritual and intellectual elements in life.'

[6] *Letters of Christina Rossetti*, p. 39.

Belief in immortality[1] and of man's survival of the death of the body were for many made difficult by the growth of scientific knowledge, and especially by the demonstration of the close dependence of the mind on the brain. If the death of the body involved that of the soul the whole question of any future life was ruled out and speculations concerning it were futile.

Whatever thoughts concerning the future life may have been cherished by the Victorians they certainly took death very solemnly, and seemed to take a delight in surrounding it with the most distasteful and gloomy circumstances. Even those who professed to hold the Christian hope laid emphasis on its melancholy aspects. By the end of the century 'the era of professional mourners and nodding plumes, and streaming hat-bands, had scarcely closed'.[2] Respect for the dead may also be seen in the heavy ornamental railings by which cemeteries were usually surrounded. The use of black-edged note-paper was universal; Disraeli, after the death of his wife, always wrote on paper with a wide black edging although he survived her for eight years.

Various arguments on behalf of a future life were advanced. Kant had admitted that man's survival could never be proved by reason, since reason can be applied only to things of space and time, but he regarded a future life as a necessary postulate of our moral nature, since it could provide a compensation for the inequalities of earthly existence. This was not a very compelling argument, and T. H. Green supported the belief on other grounds. He pointed out that 'there are capacities of the human spirit not realizable in persons under the conditions of any society that we know, or can positively conceive, or that may be capable of existing on earth';[3] and, furthermore, that the whole process of

[1] Immortality may include pre-existence as well as survival. This aspect does not seem to have aroused much speculation or interest, though Browning may have believed in some kind of pre-existence: cf. *Cristina*, v.
> Ages past the soul existed,
> Here an age 'tis merely resting.

[2] Crewe, *Life of Lord Rosebery*, p. 413.

[3] *Prolegomena to Ethics*, §185. Cf. Illingworth, *The Doctrine of the Trinity*, p. 23: 'If man's life were limited to this world, he is immeasurably over-endowed for the petty part he has to play.'

human development lost all meaning 'if we suppose the end of development to be one in the attainment of which persons—agents who are ends in themselves—are extinguished'.[1] If this earth will one day come to an end, as science suggests, and spiritual beings have no future existence apart from it, then the whole story of the human race becomes a mockery; for the course of evolution would seem to find its highest point in the production of such beings, who form what Henry Drummond called a 'third kingdom' above the merely animal and merely human. This line of argument by no means demands the survival of all men; in fact it might be maintained that only those who had fitted themselves during their earthly life for a new spiritual environment would do so, and the rest be 'cast as rubbish to the void'. Hence there arose the idea of 'conditional immortality'. This idea was accepted by some Christian thinkers in the form that immortality was not part of man's nature, but could be attained by union with Christ. 'He that hath the Son hath the life and he that hath not the Son hath not the life' (1 John 5:12). To many, however, the thought that the individuals who make up humanity had no permanent significance, but were only elements out of which would develop something more worthy, was utterly abhorrent.

> Oh dreadful thought if all our sires and we
> Are but foundations of a race to be—
> Stones which one thrusts in earth and builds thereon
> A white delight, a Parian Parthenon.

Those who rejected the idea of man's immortality tried to find compensations for the loss. The Positivists by combining what was noble and good in the lives of the great men and women of the past into an object of worship claimed to give them a kind of immortality. Comte himself had said that 'the dead do not cease to live and even to think in us and by us', and George Eliot had expressed a not dissimilar opinion:

[1] *Op. cit.*, §189.

> Oh may I join the choir invisible
> Of those immortal dead who live again
> In minds made better by their presence.

This, however, was a very defective substitute, and is mainly significant as a testimony to the interest still taken in those who were gone.

The question as to whether anything lay beyond 'the last dark river's shore' caused much perplexity among thoughtful people, and some of them endeavoured to find positive proof of man's survival by what came to be known as psychic research, a science which cannot always be distinguished from the more vulgar line of inquiry through spiritism or spiritualism.

The Society for Psychical Research was founded in 1882, with Henry Sidgwick, who had long been interested in the subject, as its first president. Before this the inquiry had achieved a respectable position through the participation of a number of scientists;[1] Mr. (later Sir) William Crookes as early as 1871 had contributed articles on the subject to various reviews, and Alfred Russell Wallace had written an impressive essay which appeared in *The Fortnightly Review* in 1874. Others who took a leading part in the investigations were F. W. H. Myers, whose *Human Personality and Its Survival of Bodily Death* was published posthumously in 1903; F. Podmore, who had collaborated with Myers in *Phantasms of the Living* (1886) and published *Studies in Psychical Research* in 1897; and Edmund Gurney (after overcoming an early reluctance to pursue the study.)[2]

But even if psychic research had succeeded in obtaining incontestable proofs of the genuineness of psychical phenomena its success would have been of a limited nature, and its very claims

---

[1] An earlier attempt to investigate the subject had been undertaken by the 'Ghostly Guild' founded in Cambridge in 1851. Among its members were Westcott, Hort, and Benson. They abandoned their investigations as unlikely to produce worthwhile results. See further, *Religion in the Victorian Era*, pp. 296 ff.

[2] Both Podmore and Gurney had tragic deaths. The latter died in 1888 from an overdose of a narcotic drug and the former was found drowned near Malvern in 1910.

aroused disquieting problems. The establishment of the genuineness of the phenomena was very difficult, for many mediums
who had been accepted as entirely trustworthy proved in the end
to be fraudulent, as Henry Sidgwick found to his continued disgust. The so-called revelations carried no guarantee as to the
source from which they emanated; some quite frankly regarded
them as due to demonic influence. Even if they could be accepted,
they amounted to very little; the dead with whom contact was
supposed to be established were living a life very like that on
earth, and their communications were exceedingly trifling and
seemed hardly worth making, save as possible evidence that those
who made them still survived.

Among the less learned and less thoughtful, spiritualism had a
considerable vogue, and came even to be regarded as a substitute
for religion. There were, indeed, those who asserted that it was
a religion, and even that it underlay all the faiths of mankind.
Of these its votaries were, in general, abundantly tolerant; though
some became definitely antagonistic towards Christianity; among
them was F. W. H. Myers, a strange ending for the poet who
wrote 'St. Paul'. But Myers, as he once confessed to Wilfrid
Ward, had undergone such a variety of religious experiences,
and even ecstacies, that he could no longer attach much importance
to them.[1]

Although spiritualism seemed to seek by means of 'material'
proofs to establish the reality of man's survival, it claimed to offer
a spiritual explanation of the universe and a refuge from the
material outlook on life which was so common. It was this
aspect which first attracted Conan Doyle who began to take an
interest in it as early as 1887,[2] though it was not until after our
period that he finally became convinced of its truth, and, as a
result, to devote the last years of his life to ardent propaganda
on its behalf.

To speculate as to what life will be like in that other world is
obviously useless, and may be mischievous. The Bible itself

[1] *The Wilfrid Wards and the Transition*, p. 366.
[2] See J. Dickson Carr, *Life of Sir Arthur Conan Doyle*, p. 69.

describes it by symbols drawn from a variety of sources (the 'four-fold city' of Revelation 21 : 16 seems to be an anticipation of the 'cubists'), and many current ideas of heaven and hell were definitely pagan. The discoveries of natural science, moreover, had demonstrated that heaven could no longer be regarded as a 'place', and that, as a consequence, the descriptive imagery of the Bible could not be taken literally, as men somewhat surprisingly had been accustomed to take it.[1] In view of the reticence of the Scriptures curiosity had in it something of the nature of presumption.

Among theologians there was speculation as to the nature and meaning of 'the resurrection body'.[2] The popular idea was, and probably still is, that the very material of our bodies will be reassembled—a task of extraordinary difficulty when it is considered what this would involve! A more worthy doctrine postulates only the preservation of personality. This was no novel refinement, forced on the defenders of Christianity by the necessities of the situation, but a revival of the teaching of Origen (based on that of St. Paul) that the body is the same, not by material continuity, but by virtue of being the organ of the same spirit. Some philosophers and theologians regarded the resurrection body as purely spiritual and as existing apart from all contact with or relation to matter. In this case the use of the term is merely symbolical.

In the early Church there was some excuse for the prevalence of crude and materialistic views, for thinkers then made no clear distinction between mind and matter; but this can hardly be said of the framers of the Thirty-nine Articles, the fourth of which is distinctly materialistic. The insistence on the resurrection of the 'body', moreover, was doubtless intended to show that the Christian doctrine was not, as with the Greeks, mere immortality.

[1] Gore, *The Incarnation*, p. 179 wrote of our Lord's teaching: 'The old metaphors . . . are filled with new moral meaning, but supplemented by hardly any disclosure to satisfy the imagination or curiosity.'

[2] Tennyson's 'Tithonius', first contributed to *The Cornhill Magazine* in 1860, deals with the case of an immortal linked to a decaying body, and may be evidence of interest in the subject.

In this connexion Lightfoot enunciated two valuable principles: (1) So far as we know the union of the soul of man with an external framework is essential; and (2) We must not suppose that the resurrection body is like our present body.[1]

Questions about the future life in general, although they aroused some popular interest, did not provoke any violent controversy. This cannot be said of one aspect of the matter, the punishment of the wicked. This had become a subject for dispute before 1860, for F. D. Maurice had affirmed in 1853 that 'eternal'[2] punishment did not mean something which went on for ever, with no hope of repentance on the part of the sinner. The controversy broke out afresh in 1878 when Canon Farrar, as he then was, proclaimed the notion of what he called 'Eternal Hope'; a notion which met with the approval of Westcott, it was 'just what he had himself been teaching for the last ten years'.[3] Severely orthodox theologians, however, refused to countenance it. Liddon, although he confessed that the idea of men being tortured for endless ages was 'unspeakably awful', held that as a revealed doctrine it could not be challenged.[4] More liberal theologians rejected this argument on two grounds; not only was the idea of endless punishment repugnant to their moral sense,[5] but, in view of passages which suggest a very different conception, they could not agree that it was the clear teaching of the Bible.[6]

Criticism of the doctrine of endless punishment, needful

---

[1] *Notes on the Epistles of St. Paul*, p. 215.

[2] Maurice made a distinction between 'eternal' and 'ever-lasting'. The problem of the exact meaning of 'everlasting' is also found in Zoroastrianism: see J. H. Moulton, *Early Zoroastrianism*, p. 312.

[3] Quoted Rashdall, *Principles and Precepts*, p. 169.

[4] *Life*, p. 225.

[5] Conan Doyle's Roman Catholic mother gave him two pieces of advice: 'Wear flannel next your skin . . . and *never* believe in eternal punishment.' In spite of Roman Catholicism being her ancestral faith she evidently found it too narrow and restrictive, and after the death of her husband she joined the Church of England. See J. Dickson Carr, *The Life of Sir Arthur Conan Doyle*, pp. 28 and 80.

[6] New ideas on the subject, its terms and presuppositions, became current through the recovery of Jewish Apocryphal writings: see C. W. Emmet in *Immortality*, pp. 176ff.

though it was, undoubtedly robbed the preacher of a potent weapon, and may have contributed to lax views about sin. Like so many reactions it was often carried too far, and men, in spite of Christ's warnings as to future retribution, came to look upon God as too good-natured to inflict punishment at all.

Chapter Twelve

THE CHURCH AND MINISTRY:
THE SACRAMENTS

THE subject of the Church[1] had become prominent owing to the rise of the Oxford Movement, and all through our period it continued to arouse much interest and discussion and to call forth very diverse and conflicting views. If the expositions of the Tractarians and their successors contained few novelties, they served to revive aspects of the doctrine which were in danger of being neglected. 'Historic Christianity is fundamentally ecclesiastical . . . and if the Oxford Movement had done nothing else besides reviving and restoring this crucial idea of the Church, it would still have laid English-speaking Christendom under a profound obligation.'[2]

Dr. Lock in his essay in *Lux Mundi* specified three functions of the Church: it was a school of virtue, the guardian of truth, and the home of worship. It is interesting to notice that first in order he placed the idea of the Church as a school of virtue; this was a conception which also appealed strongly to a thinker of a very different school, Hastings Rashdall, who declared that 'The Church is not a close oligarchy of perfected or mature Christian men, but a great educational institution in which men are gradually brought ever more completely and directly within the circle of Christ's influence.'[3]

One question which aroused much controversy was whether it

[1] See, *Essays on the Early History of the Church and Ministry* (ed. H. B. Swete) which, though not published until 1918, throws light on the views held in the latter part of the nineteenth century, and A. J. Carlyle, 'The Church' in *Contentio Veritatis*, pp. 243 ff.

[2] N. P. Williams in *Northern Catholicism*, p. 198.

[3] *Doctrine and Development*, p. 158.

had been the intention of Jesus to establish such a body as the Church. That He did so is definitely stated in Matthew 16:18; but this passage is rejected by many New Testament scholars, though not by Hort. It must not, however, be forgotten that even if Jesus never uttered the words they represent a very early tradition.

Typical of those scholars who denied that Jesus intended to establish a community of believers was Hatch, who expounded his ideas in *The Organization of the Early Christian Churches*, the Bampton Lectures for 1880. By him the various statements in the gospels, and particularly in St. John, were explained away as due to the natural tendency of the early Church to bolster up its authority, and he held that the establishment of an organized society was really the work of St. Paul. This negative opinion found fresh support with the rise of the eschatological school towards the close of the century, for if Jesus was convinced that His return would be almost immediate there was no object in forming such a society.

The traditional view, however, received support from quarters which were not regarded as strictly orthodox. Seeley, for example, saw in Christ above all else the founder of a society, and his avowed aim in *Ecce Homo* was not only to set forth His earthly life as an example to His followers, but also 'to furnish an answer to the question, "What was Christ's object in founding the Society which is called by his name, and how is it adapted to attain [its] object?"'

Hort, in a series of lectures in 1888–9 (published in 1897 under the title of *The Christian Ecclesia*), examined the meaning of 'ecclesia',[1] chiefly as used in the New Testament. The first Christian ecclesia was formed by the apostles after the confession of St. Peter. Although the word is applied to various local communities in the epistles, behind this use is the idea of the One Ecclesia, which is made up, not of communities, but of individual men. 'The One Ecclesia includes all members of all

---

[1] He rejected the usual derivation as a body of men 'called out' from a larger whole (p. 5).

partial Ecclesiae; but its relations to them all are direct, not mediate.' (p. 168.) The One Ecclesia was not to be identified with the Kingdom of God. (p. 19.)

For the orthodox the Church was, in St. Paul's words, the Body of Christ; and, following a suggestion by the Roman Catholic scholar Moehler, they saw in the term no mere metaphor but actual fact, the Church was in very truth an extension of the Incarnation, taking the place of the human frame which Christ had borne on earth, and through it He still worked His age-long task of redemption. This theory, it may be remarked, was in accord with the prevailing idea of development; for it set forth a conception of the Church as organic and living, and so capable of limitless growth. It was thus a suggestion of outstanding significance, though not without its dangers if pressed unduly. It was certainly an aspect of the Church which required emphasis.

Traditional theories of the Church, especially as revived by the Oxford Movement, were severely criticized by A. M. Fairbairn in *Catholicism: Roman and Anglican*. He distinguished two types of Churches: those in which 'the political' and those in which 'the theological' idea was supreme. In the former any action of God outside its boundaries was regarded as 'irregular, illicit, or uncovenanted'; in the latter the Church was, as it were, the visible image of Christ. Christ 'is too large to be confined within the institutions of men, they too hard and narrow to be equal to His penetrative and expansive grace'.[1] He held that in the New Testament as regards material character the Church is 'the people, the society of the Sons of God', and as regards formal character it is 'described in theocratic, ethical, and social terms, but not in sacerdotal or ceremonial'.[2]

The renewed emphasis on the idea of the Church was on the whole beneficial, for it helped to counteract the excessive regard for the individual which was characteristic of Evangelical teaching in the Church of England and among Nonconformists. The leaders of the Oxford Movement, however, in laying stress on the collective idea of Christianity did not ignore its individual

[1] *The Place of Christ in Modern Theology*, pp. 154f.   [2] *Op. cit.*, p. 535.

side. Newman in his Anglican days had recognized 'two only supreme and luminously self-evident beings', the soul and its Maker;[1] and no finer exposition of the relation of the individual soul to God could be desired than that contained in R. W. Church's sermons on *The Discipline of the Christian Character*.[2] Hort, also, drew attention to the careful balancing of the community and the individual in St. Paul's epistles; the individual 'is not to be lost in the community, as in so many societies of the ancient world'.[3]

Thus the idea that the Church was a living and organic body, with a life of its own apart from that of its members, and not a mere collection of believers, was being strongly urged and it slowly made its way.[4] Since our period it has been welcomed in what would then have been regarded as most unlikely quarters. One reason for this was undoubtedly the growing stress on community life in general which was a characteristic of contemporary thought. At the same time it brought Christianity face to face with the very difficult problem of the exact relation between the community and the individuals who make it up, and of their respective values. This is, of course, a problem which is by no means confined to religion, as an American observer has pointed out; 'Stating it in as broad a form as I can, this is the philosophical problem that faces the community at the present time: How are we to get the universality involved, the general

---

[1] *Parochial and Plain Sermons*, Vol. I, p. 23; cf. *Apologia*, p. 5.

[2] Cf. *The Gifts of Civilisation*, p. 338: 'Christianity addresses itself primarily and directly to individuals. In its proper action, its purpose and its business is to make men saints; what it has to do with souls is far other, both in its discipline and its scope, from what it has to do with nations and societies.'

[3] See the sermon attached to *The Christian Ecclesia*, pp. 239 ff.

[4] Mention may here be made of the theories of Rudolf Sohm, although they did not exercise much influence in England until the following century. The publication of his *Kirchenrecht* in 1892 may be said to have marked an epoch in the study of the doctrine of the Church. Denying that Catholicism was part of primitive Christianity Sohm sought to shew where within it lay the germ from which Catholicism later developed. He made no distinction between the Church as a religious conception and the corporate society. See the fair, though critical, account in Harnack, *The Constitution and Law of the Church*, pp. 175–258, and also *Essays* (ed. Swete), pp. 9 f., 20–22, 32.

18

statement which must go with any interpretation of the world, and still make use of the differences which belong to the individual as an individual?'[1]

It had been a fixed principle with Coleridge that 'A Christianity without a Church exercising authority is vanity and dissolution';[2] yet rather oddly the increasing emphasis on the importance of the Church coincided with a serious decline in its authority and influence during the closing years of the nineteenth century, and especially within the Anglican communion. For this decline a number of reasons may be adduced. The emphasis which the Tractarians and their successors had laid on the Catholic aspect of the Church had served to weaken its national character, and the extreme form in which it was stated by some Anglo-Catholic theologians (in conjunction with the striking growth of ritual) had provoked a reaction in the popular mind. It savoured too much of Popery. (Englishmen have ever been anti-clerical and averse to ecclesiastical domination.) What, however, did more than anything else to undermine the prestige of the Church of England was the refusal of individual members to submit to its rulings. This was especially true in the controversy over ritual, which attracted wide attention and even violent public outbreaks. There was much talk of 'clerical lawbreakers', and the defiant attitude towards the bishops, the constitutional instrument by which the Church expressed its mind and administered its affairs, aroused very unfavourable comment. If the Church could not impose its authority upon its own clergy, it was obviously in no position to retain influence with those outside its boundaries, or even their respect.

Christianity in general had lost influence and prestige owing to its failure to restate its message in terms which could be understood and appreciated by contemporary thought, and because of its apparent unawareness of the wider implications of its Gospel. It was considered that the Church was too tolerant of ancient and exploded ideas, and too tender in its dealings with

---

[1] Mead, *Movements of Thought in the Nineteenth Century*, p. 417.
[2] *Aids to Reflection*, Aph. CXII note.

superstitious survivals in both thought and practice. A suspicion was widespread that there was one standard of truth for the scientist and another for the ecclesiastic; a suspicion which was strengthened by the refusal of many traditionalists to make the least concession to modern ideas, and to condemn those who were willing to do so. Liddon felt that in *Lux Mundi* there had been an abandonment of ground won by the Oxford Movement, and a willingness to substitute private judgment and literary criticism for the authority of the Church.[1]

Turning to work done on the Ministry we have first to notice Lightfoot's famous essay attached to his commentary on the *Philippians* which was published in 1868. His conclusion was that the lists of functions exercised by various members of the congregation contained in the Pauline epistles were intended to be exhaustive, and that the threefold ministry of bishops, priests, and deacons, gradually emerged 'as the Church assumed a more settled form, and the higher but temporary offices, such as the apostolate fell away'. He thought that the diaconate (which he equated with the Seven of Acts 6:5—a doubtful identification, in spite of Irenaeus) was the first order to be established; then came the presbyters, on the model of the Jewish elders, who were also called bishops in Gentile churches, 'in the apostolic writings the two are only different designations of one and the same office'.[2] The later exaltation of the bishops arose from practical needs, the usefulness of having a single 'president', as St. James had been at Jerusalem, to act as ruler over the Church and to be its representative.

Lightfoot's conclusions were taken, much to his surprise, by Nonconformists as supporting their idea of the ministry (Nonconformists for their part were often bewildered by the strong Churchmanship of Lightfoot and Westcott) and when the

[1] *Life*, p. 371.
[2] It is worth pointing out, as this is seldom realized, that the Church of Rome does not recognize a separate order of bishops, they are a 'grade' within the priesthood. Later scholarship accepts the interchangeability of the terms, but considers that while 'all bishops were presbyters, not all presbyters were termed bishops'. (Armitage Robinson in *Essays*, p. 84.)

essay was republished in 1901 his comments, from *Dissertations on the Apostolic Age*, pp. 241 ff., were added as a protest against perversions which had arisen because he had been 'scrupulously anxious not to overstate the evidence'. Criticisms naturally came from those who held a more Catholic position, and R. C. Moberly in *Ministerial Priesthood* (1897) condemned some of Lightfoot's conclusions as based on a number of unproved assertions.[1]

The discovery of *The Teaching of the Twelve Apostles* (*The Didache*) in 1875 suggested that the Church had not been so highly organized as had been supposed, and Harnack in his edition of the book in *Texte und Untersuchungen* (1884) advanced the theory of a 'charismatic' ministry of apostles, prophets, and teachers, as having existed alongside the 'official' ministry which eventually displaced it. The suggestion received sympathetic consideration from a number of scholars; but later judgment has tended to be more critical.[2]

Hatch, in his Bampton Lectures, drew a comparison between the churches and the religious associations which were a feature of the period. He laid great emphasis on the philanthropic element as a factor in the development of the ministry; just as the presidents of associations gained importance by their responsibilities for the administration of charitable funds so did the bishops. In this work they were assisted by the deacons. The presbyters originated from imitation of the Jewish elders and the similar respect paid to older and more experienced men among the Gentiles. Hatch also investigated the relation of the clergy and the laity, and, carrying on his inquiries down to the fall of the Western Empire, he maintained that until Christianity became a recognized religion there was no separate class of clergy.

In *The Christian Ecclesia* Hort expressed views which came in for some criticism. He considered that originally there was no question of 'offices', but only of 'functions', and that much

---

[1] For a careful re-examination of Lightfoot's arguments in the light of later discussions see Armitage Robinson in *Essays*, pp. 79 ff.

[2] See *Essays*, pp. 60 ff. and my *Beginnings of Western Christendom*, pp. 314 ff.

'profitless labour had been spent on trying to force the various terms used into meaning so many definite ecclesiastical offices'.[1] Furthermore, he professed to find no evidence that Jesus ever gave the Apostles any formal commission to govern the Church; they were sent to 'witness'. 'Discipleship, not apostleship, was the primary active function . . . of the Twelve till the Ascension, and . . . remained always their fundamental function.'[2] The high place occupied by the Apostles in the primitive Church was due to the spontaneous homage of their fellow believers. He saw in the directions issued after the Council of Jerusalem (Acts 15) 'a claim to deference rather than a right to be obeyed', though he did not deny that this 'moral' authority was very real and effective.[3]

The position of the Anglo-Catholics was marked by a rigid clinging to the traditional views of the ministry.[4] Some of them advocated a conception of the apostolical succession which was decidedly materialistic, relying as it did on 'a transmission of grace from consecrator to consecrated'. The 'succession' in the New Testament is not concerned with 'grace', but with the authoritative handing on of 'office'. This was pointed out by Headlam,[5] and accepted by C. H. Turner.[6] Fairbairn, with his habitual hostility to 'High Church' views, indulged in the sarcastic remark that 'the rise of the sacerdotal orders marks a long descent from the Apostolic age, but is certainly no thing of Apostolic descent'.[7]

Turning to the Sacraments[8] we find little that was novel;

---

[1] *Op. cit.*, pp. 157 f.   [2] *Op. cit.*, p. 29.   [3] *Op. cit.*, pp. 81 ff.

[4] See Gore, *The Church and the Ministry* (1888: revised edition by C. H. Turner, 1900).

[5] *The Doctrine of the Church and Reunion*, p. 131.

[6] *Catholic and Apostolic*, pp. 280 f. He also quoted, in *Essays*, p. 193, St. Augustine's view that 'the apostolic succession of the Church of Rome is, as with St. Irenaeus, from holder to holder not from consecrator to consecrated'.

[7] *The Place of Christ in Modern Theology*, p. 534.

[8] For different views see Dimock, *The Doctrine of the Sacraments*; W. R. Inge, in *Contentio Veritatis*; Illingworth, *Divine Immanence*, pp. 125 ff., and F. Paget in *Lux Mundi*. Liddon (*Life*, p. 367) regarded the last as a real contribution to Christian theology.

controversies of ancient origin were fought out afresh with each side occupying much the same ground and repeating the old arguments. The fact that there were no conciliar definitions of the sacraments which commanded universal acceptance, and that in early days 'the only test of Church-fellowship was willingness to use the sacraments rather than any specific belief about them',[1] made the situation very flexible.

The Oxford Movement attached immense value to the sacraments, and above all to the eucharist, opportunities for attending which were multiplied and its ritual accompaniments elaborated. But such a feeling was by no means confined to one party. Bishop Creighton, who was no advanced sacerdotalist, gave it as his opinion that 'the sacramental system is the only means of holding the nearness of Christ to the believer . . . it is a matter of fact that all bodies which reject or explain away the Sacraments drift into Unitarianism. They push our Lord farther and farther away, till He is lost to their eyes.'[2] The observance of the sacraments certainly helped to provide something stable and reliable in a religious world which was inclined to give too high a place to the feelings.

As regards Baptism it must be confessed that, though a good deal was written about it, agreement over the age-long problems which beset it was not brought any nearer. Such problems included the question as to how far it was right to admit infants to membership of the Church since they had no conscious faith and were incapable of expressing it; the relation of Baptism to Confirmation; the proper person to administer the ceremony;[3] and, finally, the meaning of the rite and what exactly was accomplished by it. On this last point there was much difference of opinion. Maurice had declared that Baptism was 'a declaration of the actual relation in which men stood to God. They were His children; baptism did not make them so.'[4] The Evangelicals had no very clear or agreed views on the matter, and Dean Church

[1] N. P. Williams in *Northern Catholicism*, p. 197.   [2] *Life*, Vol. I, p. 415.
[3] This was not a very vital issue: but see Elwin, *The Minister in Baptism* (1889).
[4] See Storr, p. 343.

considered that their 'negations and vagueness' had gravely endangered the place of Baptism in the living system of the English Church.[1]

The closing years of the previous period had witnessed the very acrimonious dispute over Baptismal Regeneration which centred round Mr. Gorham.[2] There was a sequel to it in J. B. Mozley's *Review of the Baptismal Controversy* (published in 1862) in which he admitted that his own former views had been mistaken, and that it was necessary to make a clear distinction between the grace received and those who received it.[3] As Mozley was an honoured leader of the Tractarian party his retraction caused some misgivings among High Churchmen.

The question of Baptismal Regeneration had divided Evangelicals from the first. It had been strenuously upheld by John Wesley, who declared that 'it is certain that our Church supposes that all who are baptized in their infancy are at the same time born again'; but most of the early leaders had other views.[4] In our period Dimock argued that there was a distinction between sacramental and actual regeneration,[5] and Goode quoted St. Jerome: 'They that receive not Baptism with perfect faith, receive the water, but the Holy Ghost they receive not.'[6] Some compared the grace in Baptism to a seed which might or might not bear fruit. Many Evangelicals preferred not to investigate too deeply the meaning of regeneration. Chavasse wrote to one who was troubled over the matter: 'Be content to accept the simple and, I think, commonsense view that regeneration means admission into the outward family of God, and the sealing to the individual of the promises made to the Church at large. It may mean more, but surely it means this much.'[7]

One point among those previously mentioned came under discussion—the relation of Baptism and Confirmation. It was

---

[1] *The Oxford Movement*, p. 263.　　　　[2] See Storr, pp. 407f.
[3] It is a striking fact that the Church never uses the term 'regeneration' except in connexion with the grace given in Baptism.
[4] See my *The Early Evangelicals*, pp. 393 f.
[5] *The Doctrine of the Sacraments*, pp. 11 ff.
[6] *Infant Baptism*, p. 253.　　　　[7] Lancelot, *Francis James Chavasse*, p. 97.

argued that if Baptism admits to full membership of the Church and carries with it the gift of the Holy Spirit there is no need for any subsequent rite. This criticism was met by A. J. Mason in *The Relation of Confirmation to Baptism*, who drew a distinction between the gifts of the Spirit received in the two ceremonies.

After the close of the seventeenth century eucharistic theology had been rather neglected in England, but the rise of the Oxford Movement aroused renewed interest in it.[1] There were also other reasons for attention being again drawn to the subject. These were a consequence of the study of Comparative Religion and of Historical Criticism.

The researches of anthropologists had brought to light many examples of acts of communion, and Robertson Smith advanced the view that all sacrifices had this origin. These additions to knowledge and the novel theories which they evoked, were in reality of little help, for the suggested parallels were far from congruous. It was, however, a very different matter with the questions raised by New Testament critics. These questions were mainly concerned with the origin of the rite.[2] Many critics were doubtful whether Jesus Himself intended that the Last Supper should be repeated. The evidence is by no means clear, and the matter far more complicated than is sometimes realized.[3] Most scholars, at least among the orthodox, in view of the practice of the early Church, accepted the assumption that a repetition had been intended. But even here there were critics who questioned whether the early eucharists could legitimately be regarded as in any sense a continuation of the Last Supper; they might merely have gone back to the Jewish custom by which the head of the house offered thanksgiving at every meal.

Turning to a more strictly theological consideration of the doctrine, attention may be drawn to a tendency, in accord with the general outlook of the era, to regard the eucharist from a less

[1] For the eucharist in general see Gore, *The Body of Christ* (1901) and Darwell Stone, *The History of the Doctrine of the Holy Eucharist* (1909).

[2] One minor point was whether the Supper was a passover meal or not.

[3] See Sanday in *H.D.B.*, Vol. II, p. 638.

individual point of view. Men were reminded that it had a Godward as well as a manward aspect; it was not only a means of providing spiritual food for the soul of the believer, but also an offering to God by the whole Church.[1]

This brings up the much debated question as to how far and in what sense the eucharist could be regarded as a sacrifice. In Catholic doctrine it was often associated, not with the Last Supper, but with Calvary; some scholars even saw in it a repetition of the sacrifice there offered, though they were careful to guard against the notion that the priest actually 'slays' Christ afresh in the Mass. Anglicans, however, favoured the idea that there was only a pleading of the sacrifice, not a repetition; Gore, for example, though affirming that the eucharist had from the first been regarded as a sacrifice, would not hear of any thought of repetition,[2] and earlier still William Bright had written: 'There is no one, we may trust, in the Church of England, who would admit, even in thought, the notion of a repetition of the one atoning sacrifice; who would not repudiate it absolutely, *ex animo*, in all senses and without reserve.'[3]

Another matter which had long been debated aroused fierce controversy, that is the nature of the eucharistic presence, and its connexion, if any, with the elements of bread and wine.[4] All Churchmen were agreed that these were no bare signs; Bishop Moule, the Evangelical leader, regarded them, as also the water in Baptism, as divine seals, 'covenating rites in which God in Christ, through ordered human ministration, is present to meet spiritual faith with material token'. A similar view was held by some Nonconformists; P. T. Forsyth considered that there was no greater error in regard to the sacrament of the Lord's Supper than to regard it as a mere memorial service, whilst Dale's views involved him in a bitter dispute with his fellow Congregationalists who denounced ideas which he had expounded in *A Manual of*

[1] See F. Paget in *Lux Mundi*, p. 308.
[2] See *The Body of Christ*, pp. 156, 174 ff.
[3] In a letter to *The Guardian* written in 1871 and reprinted in *Letters of William Bright*, pp. 100f.
[4] See Dimock, *op. cit.*, pp. 8 ff., and 23 ff., and Gore, *op. cit.*, pp. 71 ff.

Congregational Principles (1884) as sacerdotal and 'rank Romanism'. Dale defended himself by asserting that, though he accepted a 'real presence' in the sacrament, he rejected any connexion with the elements. He also claimed that his view was that of the older Congregationalists and akin to that of Calvin.[1]

Westcott rejected any connexion between the 'presence' and the elements.

> One grave point I am utterly unable to understand—how 'the Body broken' and 'the Blood shed' can be identified with the Person of the Lord. I find no warrant in our Prayer Book or ancient authorities for such an identification ... The Lord Himself offers His Body given and His Blood shed. But these gifts are not either separately (as the Council of Trent) or in combination Himself.[2]

The whole conception of the presence is beset by difficulties, for Christians believe that Christ is everywhere present and to speak of a 'special presence' is misleading. 'A person is either present or not present. He cannot be 'specially present' though He can be present with a special purpose or intention.'[3]

The increasing emphasis on the 'real presence' tended to force other aspects of the Holy Communion into the background and had other dubious consequences, for it 'made an immense change in the whole balance of Eucharistic devotion when there emerged that concentration on the moment and the object'.[4] It also led to the practice of non-communicating attendance, a practice which had been condemned by Keble, and was also denounced by Gore who wrote: 'It cannot be said too strongly that any practice which divorces eucharistic worship and sacrifice from communion, or which rests content at the "high service" with the communion of the priest alone, really represents a seriously defective theology.'[5]

Some High Churchmen in their desire to exalt the eucharistic

---

[1] See *Life*, pp. 351 f.   [2] *Life*, Vol. II, p. 351.
[3] Storr, *Spiritual Liberty*, p. 116.   [4] Gore, *Reservation*, p. 41.
[5] *The Body of Christ*, p. 276. Elsewhere Gore pointed out that in the Church of Rome only those who actually communicate participate in the sacrifice. (*The Holy Spirit and the Church*, p. 221.)

presence not only exhibited 'defective' theology, but actually fell into doctrinal errors. This was the case with W. J. E. Bennett who was prosecuted in 1870. He had spoken of the visible presence of the Lord and of adoration of the consecrated elements. It is strange that Bennett should have fallen into this error, which is guarded against in Pusey's *The Presence of Christ in the Holy Eucharist* (1853), a work which one may suppose he ought to have known. Newman also had said: 'Our Lord neither descends from heaven upon our altars, nor moves when carried in procession. The visible species change their position, but He does not move.'[1]

The Roman doctrine of transubstantiation (in formulating which St. Thomas Aquinas, by affirming that the accidents of bread and wine persisted without their substance, departed from the teaching of Aristotle) was discussed at some length by Gore in his *Dissertations*, pp. ix and 229–84. He felt that it was a necessary task in view of 'the lack of exact histories of eucharistic doctrine'.

Attempts to bring Anglicans of different views more closely together were made from time to time. In 1898 Lord Halifax proposed to Handley Moule a meeting for this purpose. Then in October 1900 Bishop Creighton, shortly before his death, called a Round Table[2] Conference at Fulham Palace. It was attended by fifteen representatives of different types of thought, and included Moule, N. Dimock, Lord Halifax, A. Robertson (later Bishop of Exeter), Sanday, Armitage Robinson, and Gore, with Dr. Wace as chairman. The actual results of the gathering were disappointing, as it was found that the differences went too deep for any agreement to be possible. It had, however, the effect of drawing the exponents of the various views nearer to one another in sympathy and understanding; if they could not agree, at least they knew more clearly where they stood.

[1] *Via Media* (the revised edition of 1877), Vol. II, p. 220. Cf. Bishop Forbes of Brechin, *Explanation of the Thirty-nine Articles* (1881), p. 556 'what is heavenly cannot be liable to the laws of physics'.

[2] The 'round table' was once the symbol of romantic and ideal endeavours, as now of more prosaic, if not less fruitful, enterprises.

Chapter Thirteen

THE POLITICAL, ECONOMIC AND SOCIAL BACKGROUND: CHRISTIAN ETHICS: CHURCH AND STATE

IT is not my object in the early part of this chapter to give a sketch, even in outline, of the general background of the period or to show in detail how it influenced theology and religion.[1] All I wish to do is to draw attention to its importance as a factor in shaping the forms which they assumed.

Man's outward circumstances, though, in general, matters over which he has but little control, play an enormous part in his life; his whole character, indeed, may be largely the result of the mutable shapes of the society into which he is born and in which he must perforce spend his earthly existence. 'Even the greatest and most original minds, though they may be the foremost exponents of the spirit of their time, can never isolate themselves.'[2] Not least is man's religious outlook affected by his environment, and we cannot afford to ignore what F. L. Lucas has called 'the power of material adjuncts over the soul'.[3] If the effects of environment are mainly in the realm of conduct, they are by no means confined to it, but may influence the expression of beliefs. Even the prevailing political notions—and the most domestic and secluded barometer will record changes in the political atmosphere—may affect the form that religion assumes in any period. So it had been in the eighteenth century,[4] and,

[1] A fuller treatment of the subject will be found in my *Religion in the Victorian Era*; see also John Bowles, *Politics and Opinion in the Nineteenth Century*.

[2] Caird, *The Philosophy of Religion*, p. 295.

[3] *The Decline and Fall of the Romantic Ideal*, p. 14.

[4] See *The Early Evangelicals*, p. 11.

in our period, Matthew Arnold was convinced that there was an intimate connexion 'between the religious doctrine of the middle classes and its social and political philosophy'.[1]

The expression of religious beliefs is the task of theologians, and their outlook, although it may be controlled by other factors, cannot fail to be affected by changes in manners and morals, and, in the period under review, by the slow but inevitable displacement of 'a highly finished civilization with elaborate and fixed standards'[2] by an age which repudiated many previously accepted conventions and traditions and questioned matters upon which that civilization was based. In our own day that repudiation has assumed gigantic forms; but changes were already at work, even if their ultimate effects were not yet fully manifest. John Buchan, looking back, described society as he knew it at the close of the Victorian era as 'friendly and well-bred ... without the vulgarity and the worship of wealth which appeared with the new century'.[3]

Men were becoming accustomed to think in terms of commerce and to apply to all things the foot-rule of the counting-house; it was therefore but natural that writers, desiring to adopt notions and phraseology common among those to whom they hoped to appeal, should be influenced by this tendency, to which even poets were not immune, for Mrs. Browning could aver that 'The soul's Rialto hath its merchandise'.[4] Theology, too, was succumbing to like influences, and F. D. Maurice wrote in 1863: 'Our English theology, popular as well as systematic, has been gradually reconstructing itself on commercial or material bases; I find it the hardest thing possible not to adopt phrases ... which assume its habits and motives.'[5]

Such influences are very subtle, and spread slowly by a kind of infiltration. It is not easy to realize how one department of activity, or even of research, may hand on its presuppositions, and

[1] Trilling, *Matthew Arnold*, p. 224.
[2] Maisie Ward, *The Wilfrid Wards and the Transition*, p. vi.
[3] *Memory Hold-the-Door*, p. 94.
[4] *Sonnets from the Portuguese*, xix.
[5] *Life*, Vol. II, p. 460.

even its methods, to another. Mead, in analysing the social movements of the age found 'an analogy between the procedure in those fields and in what we regard as the sciences properly so-called'.[1] Even the theories of the political economists, with their attempts at simplification, may have had an influence on thought in general. Toynbee goes further and suggests that scientific and historical studies were affected by the methods of the industrial world.[2]

Interest in social questions during our period spread but slowly, for economic theories, such as the place of competition and of *laissez-faire*, were taken for granted, and, as there was still a profound belief in the power of Parliament to remedy abuses, politics seemed to be of primary importance. At the same time there was a suspicion of any kind of State interference. If, however, the forces generated by the Industrial Revolution were not to be injurious to the community the State had to intervene. It became easier to acquiesce in this as new ideas of what was meant by the community and by the State gradually made their way. Westcott wrote in 1886: 'Fifty years ago the term "solidarity" and the idea which it conveys were alike strange or unknown. . . . It was then fashionable to regard a state as an aggregation of individuals bound together by considerations of interest or pleasure.'[3]

Before leaving the subject of political influences it is worth noting the number of prime ministers during the period who were sincere Christians. This was, I think, true even of Disraeli.[4] Gladstone was, of course, here outstanding, and his interest in theological questions never ceased; in fact when Disraeli went to the House of Lords, leaving the Tory party in the Commons without anyone capable of meeting Gladstone on equal terms, he did so under the impression that the latter was about to abandon politics and devote himself to theology.[5] Lord Salisbury

[1] *Movements of Thought in the Nineteenth Century*, p. xi.
[2] *The Study of History*, Vol. I, pp. 2 ff.
[3] *Christus Consummator*, p. 120.   [4] See below, p. 301.
[5] Conversation with Drummond Wolff in W. S. Churchill, *Life of Lord Randolph Churchill*, Vol. I, p. 157.

was a devout Anglo-Catholic and when there seemed to be a possibility that his sons would be unable to make a weekly communion at Eton he made up his mind to remove them if necessary.[1] Rosebery was a regular churchgoer and before kissing hands when he became prime minister in 1894 he made his communion at Christ Church, Piccadilly, 'the church in which I was married'.[2] He was also in the habit of reading sermons to his motherless boys, and on their first going to school he sent them to Mr. Gladstone to receive his blessing.[3]

During the last thirty years of the nineteenth century industry and commerce made immense strides; the population increased, as did wealth and trade; and joint-stock companies innumerable were launched. This rapid development of the industrial system brought into prominence the economic notions on which it was based and aroused drastic criticism in many quarters.

The spirit of competition which prevailed in industry seemed to find justification in the current theories of evolution, with their emphasis on the survival of the fittest and the idea of natural selection. Competition was quite evidently the law of the universe. But as the whole notion was rooted in selfishness, it was scarcely in line with the teaching of the Gospel. As a consequence, Christian ethics had to be considerably diluted before they could be applied to the business world, where the governing factor was economic expediency and not Christian principle, though many of those engaged in commerce were devout Christians and did what they could to mitigate the harshness of the system; but, in common with others, they took it for granted without troubling to examine its underlying presuppositions.

The most notable attack on the system came from John Ruskin, who suddenly emerged as a social and economic reformer. This seemed a very unaccountable development in one who held a foremost position as an art critic; but Ruskin himself found a near

[1] See Gwendolen Cecil, *Life of Robert, Marquis of Salisbury*, Vol. I, pp. 24, 100 f., 120.
[2] Crewe, *Lord Rosebery*, p. 443.
[3] *Op. cit.*, p. 431.

relationship between art and economic theory.[1] He opened his campaign in a series of articles in *The Cornhill Magazine* for 1860, which were later collected into a volume and published in 1862 under the title *Unto This Last*.[2] The choice of a title taken from the New Testament (Matthew 20:14) was significant. A further exposition of his views was contained in articles in *Fraser's Magazine* for 1863, which after a delay of nine years appeared in book form as *Munera Pulveris*.

Many of the theories which Ruskin put forward are now almost commonplaces; but in 1860 they went dead against the accepted political economy. It is not surprising, therefore, that they were received with hostility, and in some quarters with derision. Especially unwelcome was his recognition of the need for State interference.

Ruskin's onslaught on the prevailing notions was based on four considerations: (*a*) They cut off man from the social affections by making relations depend on economic necessity. (*b*) They isolated the individual from society, setting up the motive for effort in the enrichment of the few (at the cost of the impoverishment of the many), and ignoring the good of the community as a whole. (*c*) The terms used had never been precisely or correctly defined—this applied above all to the meaning of wealth, which was not 'money', or 'money's worth', but 'the possession of useful articles which we can use'. 'THERE IS NO WEALTH BUT LIFE. Life, including all its powers of love, of joy, and of admiration.' (*d*) The law of supply and demand was entirely unjust and was ultimately bad economics.[3]

The development of industry on an ever increasing scale carried with it the depression of the individuals employed in its service; a process which has continued into our own day with ever

[1] Inge, *Platonic Tradition in English Theology*, p. 91, said of Ruskin that his great discovery was the close connexion 'of the decay of art with false values in personal and social life'.

[2] Speaking in 1877 Ruskin said that *Unto This Last* was the central work of his life and contained all that he had since had to say. (E. T. Cook, *Life of Ruskin*. Vol. II, p. 2.)

[3] See E. T. Cook, *op. cit.*, Vol. II, pp. 130 ff.

mounting speed. Its results arouse alarm and apprehension. But the nineteenth century also saw the rise of forms of industrial enterprise whose effects were very different. This was especially true of the co-operative movement, which had enormous social repercussions; for it trained the common folk in management and organization, fostered the spirit of self-help and independence, and did much to stimulate intellectual progress among the working classes.

Although the social evils of the times can hardly be said to have had much effect on theology, they were a definite handicap to religious progress; for many of the victims, not without justice, regarded the Church as bolstering up an order of things which for them was based on inequitable and corrupt principles. The same attitude had been adopted by the older Utilitarians, who blamed the prevailing theology for most of the social evils which they strove to remedy.

In both the Old and New Testaments there are constant warnings that the possession and abuse of riches may raise a barrier between the soul and God. It was a hard matter for a rich man to enter into the Kingdom of Heaven. It should be noted that no such warnings are uttered against the spiritual dangers of extreme poverty; in fact the poor and needy seem to have been driven to God by their state of hardship. But here we must remember that poverty in Palestine, with its hot climate and mainly agricultural economy, was not the grinding hardship that it is in Northern lands, and under the conditions of an industrial economy. Here poverty and want are more likely to lead to neglect of God than even riches and luxury; for the continual pressure of material needs and anxieties may easily crush the soul. Lord Shaftesbury once said of the working classes that 'until their housing conditions are Christianized, all hope of moral or social improvement is utterly vain'. The worst evil of slums is that they create the slum mind.[1]

That the Church was so slow in realizing the evils of social

---

[1] On the spiritual effect of bad conditions see further *Religion in the Victorian Era*, pp. 246 f.

conditions and in attempting to provide remedies for them is at first sight difficult to explain or to excuse.[1] We must, however, recall that the outlook of our fathers was very different from that of today, and this difference of approach supplies reasons for the Church's avoidance of meddling in social reform. In the first place, it regarded economic and social matters as the business of experts, and merely acquiesced in their conclusions. Moreover, criticisms of the accepted system savoured of 'socialism', a term which in those days was as damning as 'communism' is now. Secondly, there was a strong aversion on the Church's part to interfere in politics, and this could hardly be avoided if social reforms were to be carried out. Then again, the Church's primary task was to deal with individuals; and if all men were genuine Christians there would be no social problems, the regeneration of society would be brought about by the conversion and renewal of its members.

It was only gradually that it came to be recognized that the Church had in reality a double task; the elevation of the individual, and the elevation of society. Both aspects must be taken into account and neither can be neglected for the sake of the other. This conception of the Church's function, and the growing realization of the evils of the situation, caused many Christians to look upon the prevailing state of things as a definite challenge; for the Church to continue to ignore the hardships and injustices of the social and economic conditions of the times was tantamount to abandoning the moral leadership of the nation.

The Church's opportunities for dealing with individuals had been gravely restricted by the Industrial Revolution, and the consequent growth of huge new centres of population, which had thrown its machinery out of gear. At the same time, as has been seen, Christianity had come to be excluded from the industrial and economic world, or, worse still, perverted to support practices with which it was really inconsistent. Relying on the Old Testament notion that prosperity was a sign of the

---

[1] On the Church's part in coping with social problems see further *op. cit.*, pp. 267 f.

divine favour, the new manufacturers were eagerly pushing ahead, with little regard for the deeper teaching of the New Testament. It was urgently necessary that there should be an application of Christian ethics, not only to individuals, but to society as a whole, a demonstration that the Gospel had a wider scope than was generally supposed. R. W. Church thought that in the first days of Christianity the Church's true attitude in such matters was not at once apprehended, 'as soon as the first great shock was over, which accompanied a Gospel of which the centre was the Cross and Resurrection, it became plain that the mission of the Church was not to remain outside of and apart from society, but to absorb it and act on it in endless ways'.[1] So, too, Hort had declared that 'God in Christ has claimed for His kingdom all things human except the evil that corrupts them.'[2]

The attempt to find practical remedies for definite social evils was no new endeavour; it went back to Wilberforce and Buxton and others who had fought the evil of slavery, to Lord Shaftesbury and his efforts to deal with factory conditions, and to the so-called Christian Socialists. But now the attempt was being undertaken on a far more comprehensive scale. It is, of course, outside the scope of the present study to deal with these practical measures;[3] our concern is with their theological implications, and the working out of a scheme of Christian ethics which would justify and extend them. Before proceeding to consider this aspect it may be pointed out that some of those who gave themselves up to social work did so as a way of escape from the difficulties which they felt in regard to Christianity as a doctrinal system; they, of course, had no contribution to make to theology. The great majority, however, especially among the clergy, were inspired by definite Christian teaching; there were even those who hoped to commend the Gospel by demonstrating its social usefulness, a short-sighted, not to say suicidal, policy.

Much of the credit for awakening the Church to a sense of its

---

[1] *The Gifts of Civilisation*, p. 56.
[2] Sermon appended to *The Christian Ecclesia*, p. 246.
[3] See *Religion in the Victorian Era*, pp. 198, 241 ff.

wider responsibilities must be given to the Oxford Movement. In 1868 Church had lamented that 'the relations between Christianity and the ideas and facts of modern civilised society' had 'not yet been worked out', and averred that 'a great service will be done to our generation by any one who can grasp its leading truths, and do justice to its difficult problems'.[1] The advocates of the movement extended the idea of the Church as a society so as to include the whole of humanity, which came to be viewed 'as an organism in which the various members and parts are so related as to form an organized whole'. Emphasis on the doctrine of the Incarnation told in the same direction, for it suggested that all aspects of human affairs were relevant to Christianity. One of the objects of *Lux Mundi* had been to put the faith in 'its right relation . . . to the modern problems of politics and ethics',[2] and its contributors saw in the new social needs and the development of civilization a challenge as urgent as that presented by the new knowledge and the outlook engendered by scientific studies.[3] They had doubtless been influenced by T. H. Green's interest in social questions, and also owed much to F. D. Maurice, and, even more, to Westcott.[4]

At the end of our period the new attitude towards social questions received official sanction when the Lambeth Conference of 1897 'asserted the right of the Church to speak on all social questions, and rejected the favourite belief of the nineteenth century *laissez-faire* "that economic conditions are to be left to the action of material causes and mechanical laws, uncontrolled by moral responsibility"'.[5] The efforts of the Church and its changed attitude were also recognized by social reformers in general;

[1] Preface to *The Gifts of Civilisation*.

[2] *Op. cit.*, p. x.

[3] Westcott found a close parallel between the new teaching on social questions and biblical criticism, in so far as they were both attempts to bring the faith into the closest connexion with life. (*Lessons from Work*, pp. 177 ff.)

[4] In preaching at Westcott's consecration to the bishopric of Durham Hort described him as one 'who hears in every social distress of our times a cry for the help which only a social interpretation of the Gospel can give'. (*The Christian Ecclesia*, p. 249.) Gore had been Westcott's pupil at Harrow.

[5] Spinks, *Religion in Britain since 1900*, p. 93.

H. J. Laski, for example, wrote that 'whereas a hundred years ago it [society] did not have to square its accounts with the Churches ... today the Churches increasingly insist that the economic system must be judged in terms of their religious message'.[1]

Thus the challenge of the situation called for a fresh statement of Christian ethics and for the fuller development of moral theology; Christianity as a system had to be shown as applicable to 'the diplomacy of daily life' under the new conditions. But there were some thinkers who professed to regard the Gospel message as no longer necessary. Comte, long before, had banished theology and metaphysics from his system, and had tried to demonstrate that man's social life demanded nothing more than a purely scientific treatment for its amelioration. Others, while admitting that Christianity in the past had done good service, now asserted that it had no further benefits to confer, and that appeals to Christian ideals and motives were out of date. Morals, after all, had 'evolved' from very low beginnings, and the ethics of the Bible had shared in the process, and even at their highest might still be capable of further improvement. One remarkable position was that of Benjamin Kidd who, whilst regarding Christianity as incompatible with reason, could still assert that it was 'the active principle of development and progress in the history of society'.[2]

If the common notion that civilization was advancing steadily on an upward grade were admitted, its ideals were, from a Christian point of view, sadly defective, and there were still valuable contributions which the Church alone could make. Civilization, for one thing, was limited to this present life, and gave no place for what was to the Christian the supreme element, the spiritual nature of man. Furthermore, there was need, and the need had grown in intensity with the passing years, for insisting on the Christian standard in sexual morals. This was all the more urgent as current legislation, in its fear of trespassing too far on the rights of individuals, took no account of certain grave evils

[1] *Communism*, p. 249.
[2] *Social Evolution* (1894) quoted by C. C. J. Webb, *op. cit.*, p. 156.

so long as they did not openly affect society. It might condemn bigamy, but was silent on the subject of adultery.

There was thus a pressing need for the proclamation and exposition of Christian ethics. Philosophers had thrown fresh light on the sources and nature of moral obligation,[1] and many of them openly viewed morality not 'as the eternal embodiment of eternal principles of right, but rather as a prudential matter', rejecting the hypothesis of a divinely implanted moral instinct. Religion could no longer, so it was held, offer any secure basis for morals. So far as such views spread among people in general they meant that, deprived of the direction of religion, each man was now compelled to shoulder his own burden of moral responsibility. Is it to be wondered that many found such a burden beyond their strength and fell into a state of uncertainty in moral questions? The spread of Agnosticism in the intellectual sphere was thus accompanied by a refusal to undertake ethical judgments in the moral; for everything had become relative, and with no accepted standards by which to assess it. There were even some who denounced the accepted morality as an obstacle to the production of a higher type of humanity. Men in such a state of moral scepticism are obviously at the mercy of their impulses. It was therefore necessary for the Church once again to affirm that moral obligations have a divine origin and sanction, that the good is not merely an abstract and impersonal conception, but the expression of the will and character of God.[2] Unless such a conception is present, respect for the moral law will scarcely exist, at least among the multitude, and obedience to it will seldom be found if it clashes with deep-seated desires and passions. 'Law will never be welcomed, never be reverenced, unless it is felt that "its seat is the bosom of God, and its voice the harmony of the world".'[3] It follows from this principle that Christian

[1] See, in addition to Green's *Prolegomena*, Sidgwick, *Methods of Ethics* (1874) and Bradley, *Ethical Studies* (1876).

[2] Cf. Ottley in *Lux Mundi*, p. 342: 'The idea of ethical Good is not . . . due to a natural process by which the accumulated social traditions of our race are invested with the name and sanction of moral law.'

[3] Creighton, *The Church and the Nation*, p. 47.

ethics must have a dogmatic foundation; for conduct 'is inseparably related to truth and character to creed'.[1] Above all they
must be based on the doctrine of the Incarnation; Christ's person,
work, and character 'form the central point of ethical inquiry
and contemplation'.[2]

Most schemes for human betterment ignore the fact, fundamental from the Christian point of view, that man is a sinner,
and that, in consequence, he is incapable of working out his own
salvation, even in material things; a change of heart and will is
the only true starting-point of moral improvement.[3] Christian
ethics not only sought to answer the question '*Why* should I do
right?' but the even more difficult '*How* can I be enabled to do
right?' Penetrating more deeply than secular philosophers into
the causes of moral evil, they also offered a remedy, and claimed
'to have at command practical means of solving a problem which
is admittedly abandoned as hopeless by the ethics of naturalism'.[4]
By anti-religious thinkers and reformers this claim was regarded
as tending to weaken the moral ideal, and to lessen the severity
of its demands. 'Theology', wrote Cotter Morison, 'has always
been celebrating the power of Grace to the depreciation of
Ethics.'[5]

Christianity sets up the life of Christ as the perfect example for
all men. But since it also asserts that He was divine and sinless,
critics could reply that, if the claim were admitted, the only
standard that Christ could provide was so far above the reach of
man in his weakness as to be practically valueless. The Church
none the less, whilst recognizing that the example of Christ was
unapproachable, yet declared it 'to be universally binding, and
ever to be attempted, for those who would fulfil the law of their
nature'.[6] It was further alleged that if Christ were not only
sinless, but also divine, He was so unlike other men that He could
not be an example to them. Here again the Church could show

---

[1] Ottley, *op. cit.*, p. 341.   [2] *Op. cit.*, p. 347.
[3] Since man is a fallen creature 'the path of ethical progress is a way of
recovery'. (Ottley, *op. cit.*, p. 346.)
[4] *Op. cit.*, p. 340.   [5] *The Service of Man*, p. 85.
[6] R. W. Church, *The Gifts of Civilisation*, p. 80.

that according to its doctrine He was perfect *man* as well as perfect God.

But if Christian conduct consists, not in the observance of a number of rules and in obedience to legal ordinances, but in imitation of a Person whose life was passed in surroundings so very different from those of subsequent ages, from time to time guidance will be necessary, by which the principles revealed in the life of Christ, eternal and binding as they are, may be restated in terms of current ethical demands and ideas, and in the face of new difficulties and temptations. This task had frequently been undertaken in the past; amongst others by the Schoolmen, the Reformers, and the Caroline divines; but now once again the need had arisen for a statement as clear and precise as possible of Christian ethics.

We have noticed already the pioneer attempt of R. W. Church in *The Gifts of Civilisation* to supply in outline what was required, and also his plea that others better qualified should carry on the undertaking. In 1874–5 Henry Wace, in his Boyle Lectures on *Christianity and Morality*, continued the inquiry; but more important was Westcott's *Social Aspects of Christianity*. This volume contained sermons delivered by him in Westminster Abbey in 1886, and in it he took the opportunity of summarizing various ideas which, in a fragmentary form, he had been proclaiming over a number of years.[1] But the medium he chose for the purpose prevented any comprehensive exposition; such would have been out of place in sermons intended for a popular audience, and the title itself suggests that all he endeavoured to do was to survey various problems which called for solution. Thus the book, valuable as it undoubtedly was, could not be regarded as a systematic treatise on Christian ethics.

A more comprehensive treatment was attempted in two essays in *Lux Mundi*, those on 'Christianity and Politics' by W. J. H. Campion and on 'Christian Ethics' by R. L. Ottley. The latter essay, which with one exception, was the longest in the volume,

---

[1] Westcott acknowledged his indebtedness to Comte's *Politique Positive* which he had read in 1867, and to Maurice's *Social Morality*.

attempted to produce, though only in outline, a definite system. Ottley based his scheme firmly on doctrinal postulates, the Person of God and the nature of man; but he also examined the authority and sanctions of the moral law. Christ is set forth as the perfect example and also the means of man's re-creation. The object for which society exists is to lead up to the consummation of the Kingdom of God. This includes the perfection of human personality, its inner harmony, glory and blessedness, and, in addition, provides for fellowship in a moral community.

Further efforts to enlighten Christian opinion and to direct attention to the need for Christian Ethics and for their application to all departments of life can be found in Creighton's paper read at the Folkstone Church Congress in 1892,[1] and in the Bampton Lectures of T. B. Strong in 1895 on *Christian Ethics*.[2]

Storr deliberately omitted more than a bare consideration of the relation of Church and State (p. 10); and it is, indeed, perhaps more a problem of what may be called ecclesiastical politics than theology in the strict sense of the term, being concerned with practical adjustments between the two bodies which changing conditions make necessary. At the same time the principles underlying the relation may be said to come under Christian Ethics, and so call for at least a brief notice.

At the outset it may be laid down that the Church is not pledged to any special form of government in the State, and in practice accepts that current in the various nations and at the various ages wherein it operates. Such at least is the principle; but there may be difficulties in applying it, e.g. in a totalitarian State. In England, although the Church has often been regarded as more closely bound to the Tory party than to any other, it cannot attach itself to a party without endangering its national character. This, as we have seen, had tended to be obscured by the emphasis laid by the Tractarians on the Church as Catholic.

Hooker, Selden, Burke, Coleridge, Thomas Arnold, and others,

[1] Printed in *The Church and the Nation*, pp. 1 ff.

[2] In America F. G. Peabody published *Jesus Christ and the Social Question* (1900) which aroused much interest in this country.

had identified the Christian commonwealth with the Christian State, the Church was simply the nation on its spiritual side. But such a conception could no longer be held in view of the existence of large numbers of Nonconformist bodies and the decay of religion among masses of the people; even in Hooker's day it had been a Utopian dream, for many Englishmen still clung to the 'old religion'. An attempt to revive it was made by W. H. Fremantle in the Bampton Lectures for 1883, the avowed object of which was 'to restore the idea of the Christian Church as a moral and a social power . . . capable of transforming the whole life of mankind and destined to accomplish the transformation'. Fremantle took the term Church as including all Christians, and he saw in the Christian nation its fullest expression.[1]

Both Church and State have much the same end in view, for both are concerned with the wellbeing of mankind and the orderly conduct of society; but the Church takes notice of matters which lie beyond the cognizance of the State, and appeals to higher motives. Creighton defined the State as 'the community which is concerned with the arrangements of the common life', and the Church as 'the community concerned with setting forth the principles on which all life rests'.[2] The State, indeed, can seldom afford to appeal to the highest motives, and politicians, not necessarily by any deliberate aim, frequently encourage the spirit of self-interest. Moreover, the State is often merely a restraining power, for its laws are in general intended to check or stamp out what is harmful to the community, and by appointing penalties to control the acts of the vicious and self-willed. The Church, where it is established, must also guard against putting its interests before those of the community as a whole, for the ordinary citizen 'will not endure an ecclesiastical system which pursues small objects of its own apart from their connexion with the great stream of national life'.[3] Already in our period the process was beginning by which the Church was deprived of

---

[1] William Temple in his younger days had been fascinated by Arnold's view: see Iremonger, *William Temple, Archbishop of Canterbury*, p. 93.

[2] *Life*, Vol. II, p. 98.   [3] Creighton, *The Church and the Nation*, p. 268.

many of its opportunities of serving the nation; for the State, by broadening its activities, was taking over certain departments of life, such as education, in which the Church had previously had almost a monopoly.

In the Middle Ages both Church and State were regarded as equally religious; so the phrase 'going into the Church' was an equivalent for taking Holy Orders, and a 'churchman' was a cleric, a definition which survived as late as Shakespeare's day. In the same way the theories of Hooker and others had recognized the spiritual nature of the State. But this conception was largely ignored, and in practice the State was looked upon as a purely secular organization; a view which is contradicted by the inauguration of its head with religious rites. The non-religious view was reinforced by the popular cry, during the Disestablishment controversy, that the Church ought to be freed from bondage to the State; on which Creighton commented: 'This representation of the State as something inherently unholy, something stifling to spiritual aspirations, something from which the high minded man longs to be delivered, is very dangerous teaching.'[1]

It is interesting in this connexion to notice the teaching of Hegel, who maintained that 'States and Laws are nothing else than Religion manifesting itself in the relations of the actual world', and recognized 'the Secular as capable of being an embodiment of Truth'.[2]

In the Middle Ages Dante had turned to the Empire, 'as God's predestined minister of truth and righteousness, where the Church had failed';[3] so likewise in the later nineteenth century there were Christian social reformers who were 'inclined to see in the nation or State rather than in the Church the organized expression of the spiritual life which [they were] intent on promoting'.[4] But it is

[1] *Op. cit.*, p. 34.

[2] *The Philosophy of History*, pp. 434, 440. Croce held that the real office of the State was to provide 'the necessary condition of stability for the developing of the highest spiritual functions' (*History as the Story of Liberty*, p. 167).

[3] Church, *The Gifts of Civilisation*, p. 176.

[4] C. C. J. Webb, *op. cit.*, p. 116.

an error to regard religion too exclusively from the standpoint of the reformer or the statesman, that is as something which makes for social and economic justice, and assists in maintaining good order and stability. Christian principles must indeed be applied to remedy the evils of society; but to see in the process the supreme task of the Church is to reduce religion to a mere department of 'civilization', and to ignore its deeper aspects; for it makes no provision for man's spiritual needs, such as the expression of his relations to the Deity in communion and worship.

Before proceeding further, mention may be made of the theories of Gierke concerning the rights of separate communities within the State. He stated them in his *Deutsches Genossenschaftsrecht*, and Sidgwick, when he read it in 1886, commented: 'It is certainly an able work, but I think he carries legal subtleties a little too far back into the naïve beginnings of Germany history.'[1] Part of the treatise was translated into English by F. W. Maitland in 1900 under the title *Political Theories of the Middle Ages* which introduced Gierke's ideas to a wider English public. Their importance for our inquiry lies in their being taken up later by J. N. Figgis and applied to the Church.[2]

In England the relation between Church and State was founded on the basis of an establishment of religion. But political changes had greatly modified the original conception. During the course of the years the actual government of the nation had been taken over from the monarchy by Parliament, and Parliament, from being a lay assembly of the Church of England, had become a body open to all, without any religious qualification. Parliament, moreover, had passed laws, such as that legalizing divorce, which were in conflict with those of the Church, and in 1869 had disestablished the Church of Ireland. This last event had aroused among Nonconformists the hope that the same fate would also befall the Church in England.

Nonconformists were almost to a man Liberals in politics;

---

[1] *Henry Sidgwick*, p. 437.
[2] See his *Churches in the Modern State*, a course of lectures delivered in June 1911 and published in 1913.

and just as they resented control by the State in secular matters,[1] so they sought for freedom from the Church and the abolition of its position of privilege. To work towards this end they had, as early as 1844, founded the Society for the Liberation of Religion from State Control, a somewhat ambiguous title from their point of view. Thus the conflict over Disestablishment had a political as well as a religious aspect. It was, however, not only Nonconformists, in the usually accepted meaning of the term, who wished to sever the link between Church and State; there were also those who denied the truth of Christianity itself and wished to abolish any recognition of religion such as was contained in the establishment. In addition to these two groups there was a third, and it alone could be said to desire the removal of State Control in any literal sense. The Gorham Judgment of 1850 and prosecutions for ritual offences had aroused in the hearts and minds of a number of High Churchmen the conviction that the establishment hampered the Church's freedom, and that it was intolerable for the Church to have to obtain the consent of the State for changes in doctrine or ritual. In addition there were those who argued that, as no one religious organization could possibly express the desires of all citizens, there should be no established Church—an argument which Creighton pointed out would also be fatal to any form of the State itself.[2] Thus the attack on the connexion of Church and State was inspired by very different motives.

Those who supported and defended the establishment were also inspired by very different motives. Tory politicians, such as Disraeli, regarded it as part of the Constitution and attacks upon it, especially as they had the support of what he called 'revolutionary philosophers', as politically dangerous. But he had also a sincere admiration for the system itself: 'to have secured a national profession of faith with an unlimited enjoyment of private judgment in matters spiritual is the solution of the most difficult problem, and one of the triumphs of civilization'.[3] The

[1] See H. Spencer, *Man versus the State* (1884).
[2] *The Church and the Nation*, p. 31.   [3] *Life*, Vol II, p. 529.

maintaining of a national profession of faith was probably the strongest motive inspiring those who valued the establishment, for as Westcott said: 'A national Church alone can consecrate the whole life of a people',[1] and many Churchmen who were liberals in politics opposed any severance of the link between Church and State.[2] Creighton, in his primary charge as Bishop of Peterborough, expressed his conviction that 'Disestablishment would work a more abrupt change in the principles on which national cohesion rests than any other alteration in our political system.'[3]

The outcry against the establishment seems for the most part to have been based on a sense of grievance, rather than on any definite principles; the Nonconformist objection to State Control of Religion was obviously nothing more than a convenient formula, and many who indulged in it had not thought out its wider implications. The controversy was really very unfortunate, for it prevented co-operation between Christians of various denominations in the real work to which they were dedicated. It is a happy circumstance that it is no longer a source of active disagreement.

[1] *Social Aspects of Christianity*, p. 76.
[2] In November 1885 a number of Cambridge resident teachers who were liberals in politics, including Westcott, Hort and Creighton, published a declaration to this effect. See *Life of Hort*, Vol. II, pp. 260 ff.
[3] *The Church and the Nation*, p. 31.

Chapter Fourteen

THE INFLUENCE OF LITERATURE

SOME apology may appear to be needed for devoting a whole chapter to the subject of general literature[1] in a treatise dealing with theology. But I feel that it is justified; for not only did literature reflect the grievous turmoil of opinion and action during our period, but it had, especially in the case of some of the poets, a definite and discernible effect on the religious ideas of the people, and even on the course of theological thought.

During the nineteenth century a great change took place in the general attitude towards Christianity,[2] and this change is to be seen in literature. At the beginning of the century, religion, although it might be criticized or patronized, had been accepted as part of the normal background of life; towards the close it was virtually ignored, as no longer of value as a source of expansion or enlightenment. Religion, in other words, was relegated to a sphere of its own and isolated from literature in general;[3] in spite of the popularity of a few religious writings, orthodox Christianity came to count for as little in the literary world as it did in the political. 'When I was young', wrote W. B. Yeats, who was born in 1865, 'there were as many religious poets as love poets.'[4] There were, indeed, still some poets who took Christianity

---

[1] I have not dealt with the influence of art; for art no longer indulged in what Ruskin has called 'pictorial theology', as it had done in the Middle Ages. It was neither revealing nor didactic, though a few artists still chose religious subjects.

[2] Cf. C. C. J. Webb, *op. cit.*, pp. 171 ff.

[3] Hugh Walpole seems to have thought that the ignoring of Christianity came somewhat later; for he once expressed the wish that his own literary activity had been between 1890 and 1910 'when romanticism was all the *wear*'. See Hart-Davis, *Hugh Walpole: a Biography*, p. 419.

[4] *Oxford Book of Modern Verse*, p. xli.

seriously; but mainly as an influence which stood in the way of progress and enlightenment, an influence which ought to be obliterated. John Davidson, incidentally a son of the manse, could proclaim that

> To purge the world of Christianity,
> The sacrifice of every human life
> That now enjoys or nauseates the sun
> Would not be too exorbitant a price![1]

Attacks of this kind, however, were exceptional; the majority simply ignored Christianity as lacking both interest and importance. There were a few, such as William Watson, who contemplated it with a wistful, but perhaps even more disintegrating, agnosticism, seeming to find a morbid delight in laying wreathes on the unquiet tomb of a long dead faith.[2]

The last decade of the century saw the emergence of a school of writers, of whom Oscar Wilde may be taken as typical, whose attitude to life was one of profound pessimism, a pessimism from which they sought to escape by plunging into a carnival of pleasure seeking. They found a Gospel in the writings of Omar Khayyám, which had become widely popular through the translation, or it would be better to call it the paraphrase, of Edward Fitzgerald. It is, however, difficult to get at the real thoughts of this school of writers owing to their extreme superficiality, for they merely ploughed up the surface of things and never attempted to mine their depths; with the heroine of Browning's poem they might well have exclaimed, 'Who knows but the world may end tonight'—so why bother about it? Their influence was probably confined to a small circle of intellectuals,

---

[1] *Mammon and His Message*, p. 103.
[2] Cf. also Thomas Hardy's poem 'The Oxen'
> I feel
> If someone said on Christmas Eve
> Come, let us see the oxen kneel
> . . . I should go with him in the gloom
> Hoping it might be so.

for though crowds might flock to the plays of Oscar Wilde and be amused by his pungent wit, they regarded him merely as a superior kind of buffoon. None the less such an atmosphere had its dangers for religious belief and practice.

The effects of the earlier Romantic movement in literature,[1] even if they did not persist as long as Hugh Walpole imagined,[2] lingered on, and the beauty of the natural world was still recognized as having a spiritual significance; nor had the interest in things medieval entirely disappeared (the Oxford Movement helped to keep it alive), though people were apt, as G. K. Chesterton has somewhere said, to see them by moonlight, and their attempts to reconstruct the Middle Ages hardly fitted the facts as known to scholars.

The Romantic movement was undoubtedly of service to religion, and did something to counteract the too prosaic outlook of the mass of mankind, for it recognized the importance of the imagination, alongside the reason, in their joint creative task. Romance need not be fantastic, and in its saner and healthier expressions scarcely deserves Professor Abercrombie's definition as 'a withdrawal from outer experience to concentrate on inner experience'; such a withdrawal, indeed, if not carried too far, may enhance the true value of life. For the Christian, at any rate, the cultivation of the imagination means 'the vivifying of truth, not the spectral embodiment of a lie'.[3]

Writers and movements such as these affected theology and religion only indirectly; but their influence, although elusive and difficult to assess, was none the less important and significant. We turn now to those men of letters who wrote definitely on theological subjects. Their influence was largely due to the fact that they dealt with the mysteries of life from an emotional rather than an intellectual standpoint (Browning, indeed, was anti-intellectual); and as the great majority of mankind, and

[1] On these see Storr, pp. 126 ff.
[2] F. L. Lucas, *The Decline and Fall of the Romantic Ideal*, p. 100 thinks that in England it 'could still inspire true poetry, in Pre-Raphaelite hands, as late as the 'seventies'.
[3] R. C. Moberly in *Lux Mundi*, p. 172.

20

Englishmen not least, are left cold by the demands of logic, this line of approach made an especial appeal.

Inge once declared that: 'The poets have been our most influential prophets and preachers in the nineteenth century.'[1] This influence is difficult for us to understand; for poets, perhaps because they lack the great names of the Victorian era, no longer arouse the same wide interest, and we do not now look upon the appearance of a new work by one of them as an exciting or significant event. But there can be no doubt of the truth of Inge's judgment, which is supported by other testimony; it was the opinion of Hastings Rashdall, for example, that 'Tennyson and Browning were the greatest theological teachers of their generation';[2] and, going further back, we have the confession of Robertson Smith that the impression made upon him by *Ecce Homo* was nothing like so deep as that made by *Christmas Eve and Easter Day*.[3] The explanation of the place held by the poets was, I would suggest, provided by T. H. Green when, in the introduction to *Prolegomena to Ethics* (1868), he put forth the view that in works such as *In Memoriam* and *Rabbi Ben Ezra* 'many thoughtful men find the expression of their deepest convictions'. There was a turning away from professed theologians, with their reserve and restraint, to guides who were unshackled and free to proclaim what they had felt and experienced. It may be, indeed, that poetry is a more adequate medium for expressing the true essence of Christianity than dogmatic theology.[4] This, however, does not mean that we are to agree with Santayana when from his monastery in Rome he wrote: 'As in poetry, so in religion, the question whether the events described actually occurred is trivial and irrelevant.'[5]

It is rather an odd circumstance that the decay of poetic influence has coincided with the spread of what Matthew Arnold

---

[1] *Studies of English Mystics*, p. 35.

[2] Matheson, *Life of Hastings Rashdall*, p. 177.

[3] Black and Chrystal, *William Robertson Smith*, p. 535.

[4] Aristotle (*Poetics*, ix) held that poetry was more philosophical, and also more elevated, than history. For Bentham all poetry was misrepresentation.

[5] *The Idea of Christ in the Gospels*, p. 10.

would have called 'culture'—the term has now fallen somewhat out of favour. In his eyes culture possessed a religious element, and he adopted from Bishop Wilson the maxim that its function was 'to make reason and the will of God prevail'. Contrary to the popular notion, he had no wish to confine its possession to the privileged few, but desired as many as possible to be partakers of its 'sweetness and light'. But culture is not something that can be handed over, as it were, in a parcel; it needs an atmosphere in which it can flourish, and antecedent traditions; otherwise it degenerates into a superficial veneer. It may also be that the supply of culture is limited, that there is not enough to go round, and a system of rationing may mean more equal shares, but no increase in the amount available. Certainly, since life in its higher reaches of grace and charm has been opened up to the many it seems to have lost some of its essence.

As the primary object of the poet is not truth or edification, but beauty—though we must not forget that Keats held that 'Beauty is truth, truth beauty'—any contribution that he may make to thought or morals is in some sense only incidental. Yet this incidental contribution may have the highest value. Matthew Arnold, in his essay on 'The Study of Poetry', foretold that eventually it would displace both religion and philosophy, that we should more and more 'have to turn to poetry to interpret life for us, to console us, to sustain us. Without poetry our science will appear incomplete; and most of what now passes for religion and philosophy will be replaced by poetry.' Earlier still, in 'The Youth of Nature', he had spoken of the poet as becoming

> a priest to us all
> Of the wonder and bloom of the world,
> Which we see with his eyes and are glad.

This same idea, though with a wider application, long persisted, and W. B. Yeats, before the turn of the century, could also venture on prophecy, and affirm that the arts were 'about to take upon their shoulders the burdens that have fallen from the shoulders of the priests'.

Some preachers pandered to, or were even led astray by, their desire to conform to the prevailing taste. R. W. Dale referred to 'one conspicuous man', whom he did not further specify, as openly confessing that he got his sermons from novels rather than from the Bible.[1] The result might be more attractive preaching, but only at the cost of depth and genuine instruction in the faith. The fashion of turning to secular literature as a basis for Christian teaching had been made popular by Stopford Brooke, who in 1872, while still an Anglican, delivered a course of sermons from his pulpit in St. James Chapel, York Street, on 'Theology in the English Poets'. Twenty-seven years later he would make a more comprehensive survey in *Religion in Life and Literature*.

Tennyson, after a period of disparagement, is now being hailed by some critics as likely to be the most enduring poet of the century, and certainly in his own day his writings, with their freedom from dogmatism and width of application, gave him a position of predominance, at least after the shock of some of his earlier utterances had been absorbed. When *In Memoriam* first appeared it caused bewilderment among older people, so Hort has told us, but for Hort's own generation it spoke with a force which few other writings could rival.[2] It is, however, probable, that great as was the influence of Tennyson, that of Browning was even greater. At the beginning of our period Oxford was already taking him very seriously, and the abler undergraduates analysed his poems, corresponded about their different interpretations, and discussed his writings in essay clubs.[3] Browning, it need hardly be said, was no trained theologian; but he had a wide and comprehensive knowledge of the Bible and had penetrated into some by-ways of religion and theology which were little known to the theologians of his day. He had also a remarkable insight into the minds of the writers of the Scriptures and of those whom they portray. This can be seen with regard to the Old Testament in 'Saul', and in regard to the

---

[1] *Life*, p. 680.   [2] *Life of Hort*, Vol. II, pp. 61 f.
[3] See E. W. Watson, *Bishop John Wordsworth*, p. 27.

New in 'A Death in the Desert', which William Temple described as the best commentary on the fourth gospel.[1] One of his great merits was an insistence on the inadequacy and relativity of natural science,[2] and the need to take further account of the affections and their intuitions. He had also a faculty for applying the teaching of Christianity to the conditions of the time.[3]

It is a little remarkable that Matthew Arnold—in spite of his forecast of the place that poetry was to take as displacing religion and philosophy and his belief that the function of the poet was 'to interpret human life afresh and to supply a new spiritual basis to it'—when he became seriously interested in theological and religious questions, like Coleridge before him, abandoned poetry for prose. His standing as a literary critic had been firmly established with the publication of *Essays in Criticism* (1865), now he would exercise his critical powers in another field. Between 1870 and 1877 (after which his thoughts were switched over to politics) he produced four works, *St. Paul and Protestantism, Literature and Dogma, God and the Bible*, and *Last Essays on Church and Religion*.[4]

Westcott thought that in his theological and critical writings Matthew Arnold exhibited a vanity from which his poetry was free.[5] In them he undoubtedly made a far wider use of irony and satire, especially at the expense of all forms of conventional religion and his special bugbear, Nonconformity. But this was no mere pose. In spite of occasional lapses into flippancy, there can be little doubt that Matthew Arnold was in deadly earnest

[1] In *Foundations*, p. 216, note 1.

[2] His interest in scientific discoveries and their effects was, however, far less than that of Tennyson.

[3] In a vacation lecture to clergy at Oxford in 1893 E. L. Hicks gave Browning as an example of one who knew how 'to enunciate the Gospel in the phrases and ideas of modern life'. See also Westcott 'On Some Points in Browning's View of Life' in *Religious Thought in the West*, pp. 253 ff, and Henry Jones, *Browning as a Religious and Philosophical Teacher*.

[4] Meredith considered that if his prose and poetry are both taken into account Matthew Arnold was the most considerable writer of his age. See Trevelyan, *A Layman's Love of Letters*, p. 22.

[5] *Life of Westcott*, Vol. II, p. 58.

over religion. His religious teaching, however, was based on a somewhat eccentric type of theology, and since he rejected the idea of a personal God its appeal was very limited. Arnold's object was not to disturb the faith of believers, but to convince the unorthodox and sceptical that they need not relinquish a spiritual view of life. It must, however, be said that his influence, even if his intentions were good, was on the whole subversive rather than constructive. Though he had a considerable knowledge of theological literature his ideas were almost entirely derived from others and contained little that was original; it is as a disseminator of the views of more profound thinkers that he was mainly valuable, and, also, as reflecting the ideas of the times. Arnold was too versatile and too much the child of his day to make any valuable contribution to theology; though Percy Gardner considered that *St. Paul and Protestantism* contained the best account of the Pauline Theology that he knew.[1] Arnold was too fond of deceiving himself and his readers by the use of phrases, in the coining of which he was an adept; outwardly they have a very convincing air, but in reality mean nothing. F. H. Bradley, who made a violent exposure of his methods called them 'clap-trap'.[2]

In spite of these defects, the importance of Matthew Arnold for theology, even if it did not extend to the making of any original contribution and was weakened by a lack of clear thinking, must not be underestimated. In an age when men who desired to be thought cultivated were prone to scoff at religion and those who still clung to it, he came forward, in the name of culture itself, to affirm that religion was necessary for man, and that in Christianity (as interpreted by himself) its most adequate manifestation was to be found.

Turning to novelists, we may notice the influence of Disraeli, for though his writings belong to an earlier period they continued

---

[1] *The Religious Experience of St. Paul*, p. vii.

[2] See *Ethical Studies*, p. 283. Bradley was quite merciless in his comments, and said of Arnold's notion of God as 'the Eternal not ourselves which makes for righteousness' that 'the habit of washing . . . might be termed "the Eternal not ourselves that makes for cleanliness".'

to be read. Most of them are concerned mainly with politics, but some have a strong religious and even theological interest. This is true above all of *Tancred*, in which he advocated a recognition of the authority of the creeds as a means of curing the many and various diseases of contemporary society. In his general outlook he was ever at pains to emphasize the spiritual view of life and to counteract the growing materialism.[1]

In the famous debate on Darwinism at the Oxford Conference in 1864 Disraeli had declared that he was on the side of the angels, and his religious outlook was definitely anti-critical. This was part of his general conservative attitude to life, but here reinforced by his dislike and fear of anything which might weaken 'Semitic' influence.[2] Disraeli was an omniverous reader (though his claim to have read 'all the writings of the critics'[3] must be dismissed as a rhetorical exaggeration) and made it his business to keep in touch with the currents of thought. He had, moreover, a remarkable understanding of the views of those from whom he differed, such as Roman Catholics and Broad Churchmen.[4] That Disraeli was a sincere Christian seems beyond question; for as a Jew by race he regarded Christianity as the finest and necessary development of Old Testament religion, and in his *Life of Lord George Bentinck* expressed his regret 'that several million Jews still persist in believing only part of their religion'.

If Disraeli showed an understanding of the views of Roman Catholics the same could hardly be said of Charles Kingsley (1819–75) who exercised a vigorous and Protestant influence. Distrusting all forms of religion which seemed to him to be unmanly and based on a false asceticism, he was the sworn enemy of fads and affectations. It is easy to dismiss him as the advocate of 'muscular Christianity' (a term which he himself disliked and repudiated), but he performed a real service by bringing religion into the open air and in sweeping out some of its close and dusty corners. Kingsley was a man of wide if not very profound culture, and had a respectable knowledge of natural science. Men might

---

[1] Monypenny and Buckle, *Life of Disraeli*, Vol. II, pp. 605 f.
[2] *Op. cit.*, p. 84.   [3] *Op. cit.*, p. 106.   [4] *Op. cit.*, p. 495.

scoff at his appointment as Regius Professor of Modern History at Cambridge; but his acquaintance with the subject was probably as great, if not greater, than that of many of his predecessors. He might be only a 'popular novelist', but his historical novels were based on deep and painstaking research. 'I wish I knew any one generation as you know that of Hypatia', wrote Stanley in 1858.[1] His best known work is, of course, *Westward Ho* (1855), but others, such as *Yeast* and *Alton Locke* (both published in 1849), had great influence in their day. Many of them continued to be read after his death, and are still reprinted.

One result of Kingsley's dislike of what he regarded as affectations and subtleties was the unfortunate controversy with Newman. In a review of Froude's *History of England* in *Macmillan's Magazine* for 1864, Kingsley remarked that 'Father Newman informs us that truth for its own sake need not be, and on the whole ought not to be, a virtue of the Roman clergy.' Newman responded by writing his famous *Apologia pro Vita Sua* —perhaps the one happy outcome of the affair.

The contest was most unequal, for Newman as a controversialist was far superior to his opponent; and it was made more bitter by the inability of both combatants to understand the point of view of the other. The two men were, indeed, totally removed in ideas and methods. Newman had been trained in the Oxford school and delighted in subtle distinctions and arguments (even in his Oxford days many of his contemporaries looked upon him as disingenuous); Kingsley had no patience with such approaches, and his methods suggested a bull charging at a gate.[2] The result was that Newman seemed to gain an easy victory, for he fought on ground chosen by himself; none the less doubts still remained,

---

[1] Prothero, *Life of Dean Stanley*, Vol. II, p. 1.

[2] F. D. Maurice, who understood Newman's mentality, wrote: 'I would have given much that Kingsley had not got into this dispute with Newman. In spite of all apparent evidence, I do believe that Newman loves truth in his heart of hearts, and more now than when he was an Anglican.' (*Life*, Vol. II, pp. 478 f.) Hort considered that Kingsley was much to blame 'for his recklessly exaggerated epigram, though it had but too sad a foundation of truth. Newman's reply, however, was sickening to read, for the cruelty and insolence with which he trampled on his assailant.' (*Life*, Vol. II, p. 424: cf. pp. 30 and 35.)

and some who sympathized with his point of view were not very happy over his triumph.[1]

Newman died in 1890, and Lord Rosebery, as he gazed down on his death-bed, commented: 'And this was the end of the young Calvinist, the Oxford don, the austere vicar of St. Mary's. It seemed as if a whole cycle of human thought and life were concentrated in that august repose.'[2]

George Eliot was born in the same year as Kingsley and died in 1880. Her *Scenes from Clerical Life* (1853) aroused the admiration of Leslie Stephen for 'their unforced power, their pathos, and the sympathetic appreciation of the old-fashioned times'. George Eliot was notorious for her unorthodox views,[3] though these appear in her novels merely by the way. The somewhat austere conception of life and its duties which they set forth rendered her writings a little heavy for the general reader, and her characters tended to become mere personifications of ideas rather than living beings; there was also a touch of sentimentalism about them, which led Walter Raleigh to scoff at her 'twopenny meliorism'.[4]

A wholly different writer was George Eliot's slightly junior contemporary (who long survived her), Charlotte Yonge (1823–1901). Charlotte Yonge had been greatly influenced by John Keble, and her earlier novels exhibit a mild form of Tractarian piety. They became very popular, and found admirers in some most unexpected quarters—William Morris and Burne Jones were immensely impressed by her best known work *The Heir of Redcliffe* (1850)—whilst *The Daisy Chain* (1856) became a household favourite; on one occasion Frederick Temple and Lord Rosebery were found discussing the careers of the May family as if they had been real people.[5] Among her other devotees were Tennyson, and Henry Sidgwick; the latter, as a young man, admired her ability to make one feel 'how full of interest the narrowest sphere of life is'.[6] Her later writings, though

---

[1] Von Hügel never really liked 'Newman's pulverization of Kingsley in the personal parts of the *Apologia*'. (De la Bedoyère, *The Life of Baron von Hügel*, p. 32.)   [2] Crewe, *Life of Lord Rosebery*, p. 357.
[3] See *Religion in the Victorian Era*, p. 151.   [4] *Letters*, p. 45.
[5] *Memoir of Frederick Temple*, Vol. II, p. 21.   [6] *Henry Sidgwick*, p. 109.

of inferior quality, had large circulations; and the earlier ones have been continually reprinted.

The influence of Charlotte Yonge's works was largely practical, for they portrayed, in attractive colours, the lives of ordinary people as they developed under a strong sense of duty and discipline; but as everything was based on definite doctrinal beliefs they had a significance for theology also, and helped to arouse interest in theological and doctrinal ideas.

In view of his pleasant sketches of clerical life, especially in the famous Barchester series (1855–67), some attention might seem to be called for in the case of Anthony Trollope. But though he has handed down a valuable record of a bygone state of affairs (and even here one is tempted to doubt whether the representation had any very close relation to the reality) his novels can hardly have exerted any great influence on theology. More worthy of consideration is a novel which appeared in 1881, just before Trollope's death, J. H. Shorthouse's *John Inglesant*. The author called it a philosophical romance, a new term; for though Sterne had used *Tristram Shandy* as a means of popularizing the ideas of Locke,[1] he had not so openly revealed his intentions. Shorthouse (1834–1903) had been brought up as a Quaker, but joined the Church of England in 1861. The first and the most famous of his novels was not written until he was forty, being probably born of his own religious questings. Much of its attraction lies in the grave and delicate style in which it was written, and also in the vivid pictures of English life in the seventeenth century (much in them simply transcribed from contemporary sources). In addition the theme of the volume, which was in effect the superiority of culture over fanaticism in life, and, not least, in religion, went straight to the hearts of that growing public which, like Shorthouse himself, was vaguely feeling after a more refined outlook.[2] The immediate success of the work owed much to the patronage of Mr. Gladstone, who not only invited the author

---

[1] See *The Early Evangelicals*, p. 56.

[2] No less attractive to some was the large place given to the ceremonial side of religion.

to breakfast, but even allowed a photograph of himself with the book on his knees to be circulated.

John Inglesant was indebted for its publication to the influence of Mrs. Humphry Ward; a somewhat surprising fact in view of her very different views. Mrs. Ward was a niece of Matthew Arnold, and many of his theological and religious notions gained currency through her novels.[1] But this did not mean that she had merely adopted them; the similarity was largely due to the fact that their minds worked in the same direction, and in the case of Mrs. Ward they had an independent origin, for when little more than a girl she had come under the influence of Mark Pattison, by whose advice she undertook an intensive study of early Spanish history and literature, a subject then little known in England, and became a recognized authority on it.[2] Her views were first proclaimed in *Robert Elsmere*, which when it appeared in 1888 created a storm in the theological world. Her other novels during our period were not so deliberately outspoken, the point of view set forth in *Robert Elsmere* being taken for granted,[3] though just at its close *Helbeck of Bannisdale* had a definitely theological subject, and it may be said that it was treated with a maturity and grip of her material far superior to that exhibited in its predecessor.

Mrs. Ward's novels may well be called 'period pieces'; of great interest and value as setting forth the ideas and background of her times, and as such they may well survive. As works of art, however, they have certain fundamental weaknesses. For one thing the various characters, especially on the religious side, are often merely reflections of the mind and ideas of their creator, and exhibit, to adapt a phrase of Matthew Arnold, rationalism touched by emotion. This was the consequence of another weakness—the subordination of art to propaganda. It was a

[1] See further C. C. J. Webb, *A Study of Religious Thought in England from 1850*, pp. 115 f.

[2] Later she was invited to contribute the lives of the early Spanish Kings and Churchmen to the *Dictionary of Christian Biography*.

[3] Trilling, *Matthew Arnold*, p. 303 has written: 'Robert Elsmere was far more than the hero of an enormously successful novel; he was the protagonist in a great social and intellectual crisis that in one way or another involved all thinking people.'

shrewd warning which Bishop Creighton gave her quite early in her career, that '*Tendency* is a foe to art.'[1] In choosing the novel as a medium for the propagation of religious ideas Mrs. Ward was not, of course, a pioneer, but was reverting to earlier models. The method had been utilised by Plato and by Cicero in discussing the great questions which press upon mankind, and, in more recent times and with a closer parallel, Voltaire had employed it in *Candide*. But to present such serious matters in the form of fiction was then a little unusual, and, in the opinion of old-fashioned people, even blameworthy.

Before leaving the consideration of the effect upon religion and theology of English novelists, we must notice two who probably enjoyed, at least among the more intellectual portion of the public, a greater reputation than any of their fellows— George Meredith (1828–1909) and Thomas Hardy (1840–1928). Neither of them had much sympathy with orthodox religion; they may, indeed, be regarded as advocates of a kind of revived paganism, though a paganism very different from that of Swinburne with its seductive and alluring appeal. Meredith's religious philosophy was severe and bracing, and underpinned by a regard for strict honesty in both thought and aim; though at times it has a trace of mysticism it was far removed from anything metaphysical or doctrinal. Hardy was a determinist, and, indeed, obsessed by the thought of man's weakness in the hands of fate; life as described in his novels, the last of which *Jude the Obscure* appeared in 1895, was a vast and almost unendurable tragedy.

Our survey of the men of letters who exerted influence has of necessity been restricted, and had space allowed other names might well have been included; for many had a hand in forming that general atmosphere of thought in which religion had to breathe and with which theology had to make its account. So far, we have noticed only those influences which arose from the native soil; but there were others, only little less important, which came from across the seas. Emerson, for example, exercised

[1] *Life*, Vol. II, p. 101.

a very stimulating influence, and his writings, according to Martineau, 'recalled natural faiths which had been explained away, and boldly appealed to feelings which had been struck down; they touched the springs of sleeping enthusiasm, and carried us forward from the outer temple of devout science to the inner shrine of self-denying duty'.[1] But Emerson had no real contribution to make to theology as such; his own views were too vague,[2] and his teaching lacked consistency and any firm underlying foundation upon which others could build, and, so far as dogmatic theology was concerned, they were apt to be disintegrating.[3]

Another influence from America was Walt Whitman. His *Leaves of Grass* first appeared in 1855, though it later received numerous additions, especially poems dealing with the Civil War. Whitman owed some of his ideas to Hegel, but much was original, and expressed in rough-hewn verse. Refusing to be daunted by the evils and problems of his day he faced life with an optimism which seemed to have little to justify it; he could even in 'Song of Sunrise' proclaim that he did 'not see one imperfection in the universe'. His optimism was based on a profound belief in democracy and in the power of fellowship. Such notions naturally made a strong appeal to the young, and in England he numbered among his admirers the youthful Gerard Manley Hopkins.

Turning to European writers, we notice first of all the influence of Ibsen. Ibsen was a great opponent of conventional ideas and among them conventional Christianity, and for this reason many regarded him as opposed to Christianity in any form. But this was to misunderstand him, for his attacks on a spineless Christianity were themselves inspired by a belief, though of a somewhat eccentric and mystical character, in the Gospel. Ibsen's most cherished convictions were the right of the individual to freedom,

[1] J. Estlin Carpenter, *James Martineau*, p. 174.

[2] York Powell dismissed them as 'sandy inconsequence and vague culture'. (*F. York Powell*, Vol. 1, p. 152.)

[3] Emerson belongs to religion rather than theology: see further *Religion in the Victorian Era*, pp. 140f.

and the ultimate evil as a denial of love. It was P. H. Wicksteed's *Four Lectures on Ibsen* (1888) which brought him to the knowledge of English people; but his teaching and ideas had at first no favourable reception, and even liberal minds such as Martineau and Mrs. Humphry Ward denounced and condemned them.

Although both Tolstoy (1828–1910) and Dostoyevsky (1821–81) wrote their chief works well within our period, and although they were to exercise great influence in the following century, they cannot be considered of any great account for our study, as their writings remained untranslated. Tolstoy, it is true, aroused curiosity owing to the romantic stories that were in circulation about him, but that was all. The Russian Pole, Sienkiewicz (1846–1916), however, by his famous novel *Quo Vadis?*, which appeared in 1895 and was translated in the following year, aroused much interest in religious questions, even if he did not contribute to our knowledge concerning them. A later Russian novelist and thinker, Merezhkovsky (born 1865), received attention in certain select circles by his mystical attempt to combine paganism and Christianity, the flesh and the spirit; but it was not until the new century that his ideas began to spread in England. *Smert Bogov*, the first of his famous trilogy, was written only in 1895, and was not translated into English, as *The Death of the Gods*, until 1901.

To trace the influence of other European literatures[1] would be a vast undertaking demanding space which we cannot afford; but what has been attempted at the conclusion of this chapter should be enough to remind us that there were outside influences, of a literary character, entering into the minds and having their effects upon the thoughts of men and women in this country. They may not have been of any great volume when compared with those which flowed from our own writers, but entirely to ignore them, as is often done, would be a mistake, even though we cannot exactly assess their significance.

[1] Mention may be made of Fogazzaro whose *Piccolo Mondo Antico* was published in 1896 and aroused something of a sensation in Italy. It was not, however, until the translation of *Il Santo*, the third of the famous trilogy, in 1906, that he began to exercise much influence in England.

Chapter Fifteen

THE SPREAD OF LIBERAL VIEWS

THE spread of liberal views in theology was as inevitable as their spread in politics. In the latter, when once the tide had set in that direction, though attempts might be made to check or control it, each party as it came into power was perforce borne on by it. Change and revolution in the religious and intellectual spheres are the result of much the same causes as in the political and social, a growing feeling of discontent and dissatisfaction; and their course is not invariably directed by wisdom, nor is it necessarily beneficial in its operation. Even the most ardent reformers are often aware of the mistakes and shortcomings of their predecessors, but this does not deter them, for they are convinced that in the long run the good will outweigh the evil. So the pioneer in religious thought must ever 'venture on a sea where many have been drowned and where many derelicts and phantom ships endanger and beguile the voyager'.[1]

Everywhere the new spirit was at work and even the Church of Rome, in spite of official disapproval, was not unaffected.[2] There the advocates of liberal views found an excuse for their critical activities by claiming that the decrees of the Council of Trent applied only to the theological sense of the Scriptures, and that modern methods of research might be used in historical and critical matters. As early as 1885 Baron von Hügel had begun to work on biblical criticism, learning Hebrew for the purpose. He also contributed articles to *The Dublin Review* in October 1894 and April and October 1895. On the Continent articles of a

[1] A. C. Turner in *Concerning Prayer*, p. 372.
[2] See A. R. Vidler, *The Modernist Movement in the Roman Church* and Rivière, *Modernisme dans l'Église*.

liberal character had appeared in Duchesne's *Bulletin Critique*, whilst Lagrange had made contributions to *Revue Biblique* which exhibited the same tendency. These were but the small beginnings of a movement which would attain great proportions in the twentieth century. The outstanding name in connexion with it would be that of Abbé Loisy. Although Loisy in *Histoire du Canon de l'Ancien Testament* (1890) had accepted the theories of Kuenen and Wellhausen no notice was taken by the authorities; the book indeed, attracted little attention, and it was not until his reply to Harnack's *Das Wesen des Christentums* appeared in 1902 under the title of *L'Évangile et l'Église* that he became notorious.

In England the most significant and perhaps the most surprising example of the spread of liberal views was their emergence amongst the followers of the Oxford Movement. One of the great objects of that movement had been to protest against liberalism as then understood, though it was a liberalism of a very mild brand when compared with that current in the 'eighties,[1] and their whole conception of theology was narrow and restricted. It was

> not the science of a living God who was fulfilling Himself in many ways, but rather the formal study of the defined beliefs of the Christian Church at a certain period of its existence; a period which they assumed was to be the norm and pattern for all time . . . They could not view Christianity as a life and a spirit. They could view it only as a life expressed in one particular type of ecclesiastical organization.[2]

For a time the movement appeared to be stemming the tide of liberalism, especially in Oxford; but a strong reaction took place led by Jowett and Stanley, with the sinister figure of Mark Pattison in the background. Mark Pattison had at last become Rector of Lincoln in 1861 and lived on until 1884, but his chief interest was in literary studies. A man of a cynical and bitter disposition his influence was mainly negative, and a warning

---

[1] In 1874 Church wrote 'what had been called Liberalism in the days of Whately was mere blind and stagnant Conservatism'. (*Occasional Papers*, Vol. II, p. 347.)   [2] Storr, pp. 257f.

against the dangers of disillusionment.[1] Liberalism at Oxford, once it got under way, advanced swiftly, and its advocates were apt to be a little scornful of those who in earlier days had borne the burden and heat of the day. It left Pusey in lonely isolation at Christ Church, and even Liddon became disheartened. The foundation of Keble College in 1870 had done something to check extreme liberalism, but soon in a milder form it would seep into the movement itself. The extent to which this had taken place first became widely known with the publication of *Lux Mundi* in 1889. Most of the contributors had been members of the graduate class (it would now be called a seminar) which J. B. Mozley had started in 1874, and, being resident in Oxford, had for a considerable time been in the habit of discussing theological questions among themselves. Thus the volume was 'the expression of a common mind and a common hope'. Its appearance proclaimed the rise of a new school in English theology, that of Liberal Catholicism; a fact of the highest moment, for, as J. K. Mozley has said: 'Few books in modern times have so clearly marked the presence of a new era and so deeply influenced its character.'[2]

The writers welcomed the discoveries of natural science and the results of moderate biblical criticism, looking upon them as helps and not hindrances to the Christian faith. In striking contrast with the pessimism which had fallen on Liddon and many of the older generation, they were eager to take the offensive, to meet the opponents of Christianity on their own ground and with their own weapons. It was their assured conviction that the thought of the age, instead of being resisted and condemned, should be incorporated into the faith, and that it was capable of throwing new light on Christianity and of disburdening it of obsolete notions. Looking back in later years Scott Holland recalled the spirit which moved them: 'We did not desire to die

[1] Henry Sidgwick (*Memoir*, p. 404) wrote: 'I cannot but admit that his life is a moral fiasco, which the orthodox have a right to point to as a warning against infidelity.' Robertson Smith on meeting him was not very favourably impressed: see Black and Chrystal, *W. Robertson Smith*, p. 170.

[2] *Some Tendencies in British Theology*, p. 17.

in the last ditch, but to throw defences and ramparts behind us, and to charge with flags flying, and see what we could do with a clear field and no favour.'[1]

Lux Mundi was attacked in Convocation by Archdeacon Denison, who denounced the principle of making the Bible conform to the supposed results of criticism, and suggested that the methods of the writers would place anthropology above theology. Convocation, however, and the English Church Union, both refused to condemn the volume, and it received more favourable notice from some of the older High Churchmen, such as Dean Church, the close friend of Liddon and his ally on many fronts.

Though the centre of controversy was Gore's treatment of Inspiration, it was the volume as a whole which was important, both because of its emphasis on the Incarnation, and, still more, as an attempt to reconcile the new knowledge with the traditional faith of the Church.

If liberal views were being welcomed by at least one section of the Anglo-Catholic party in the Church of England the same could not be said of the Evangelical wing. To them all such views were abhorrent, and, above all, any attempt to criticize the Bible, on which their rather narrow and rigid creed was so dependent. In contrast with the *Lux Mundi* group they were unwilling, and indeed lacking in the necessary attainments, to meet the upholders of the new knowledge on their own ground. In any case the limitations of their outlook led them to regard with suspicion the effects of any movement that was not definitely 'religious'. In consequence such subjects as art, literature, and philosophy, though they might furnish pleasant means of relaxation, were regarded by them as of small importance. There was an immense gap between the wisdom of the world and the wisdom of the Gospel.[2]

[1] *A Bundle of Memories*, p. 58.
[2] V. F. Storr had been brought up in a narrowly Evangelical home, but had imbibed more liberal views under J. M. Wilson at Clifton and from R. L. Nettleship at Oxford. In consequence of the clash between the old and the new he delayed his ordination until 1900 when he was thirty-one.

Evangelicals had never been conspicuous for depth or originality of thought, being prone to attach greater value to the instinctive and emotional than to the products of the reason. Their considerable and praiseworthy energies found their chief outlet in practical work and were devoted to the spread of the Gospel at home and abroad. Zeal and a spotless orthodoxy were prized above intellectual ability or theological research; the latter, indeed, might often arouse their suspicions. It must not, however, be supposed that the Evangelicals entirely lacked able and learned theologians; they had Henry Wace (1836–1924) the future Dean of Canterbury, who was widely read in the Reformation writings and proved a doughty opponent of Huxley. His width of knowledge was recognized by his being chosen as the editor of the *Dictionary of Christian Biography*. Dimock had vast liturgical knowledge, and Gwatkin was a highly competent historian. But, like Pusey, they were men of learning rather than discoverers, and their thinking, save for Gwatkin, was hampered by a too obstinate regard for tradition and a refusal to examine the foundations on which it was laid. Standing too solidly in the old paths, they could contribute little that was new. Few of them showed much interest in philosophical developments and they rejected, except in a very mild form, any criticism of the Bible. It is surprising, when one remembers the immense devotion to the study of the Bible exhibited by Evangelicals, that they did not build up a more impressive body of theology. But they came to the Bible with a presupposed 'scheme' of doctrine and read it in the light of that 'scheme'; such texts as proved intractable they carefully ignored, or explained away.

Apart from Charles Simeon, Daniel Wilson, and a few others, the Evangelical Movement produced no great clerics; but by way of compensation it enrolled under its banner an impressive array of outstanding laymen, one need but mention William Wilberforce and his fellows of the Clapham Sect, T. F. Buxton, and Lord Shaftesbury. These laymen formed the backbone of the party, and did much to keep it on conservative lines. Some of them were not at all averse to meddling in theological questions;

a proceeding which called forth the criticism of Westcott, who, in spite of his admiration for their services in other fields, regretted that they would stray into domains where 'we want an unusual endowment of modesty'.[1]

In the early days of the movement no Evangelical could hope for promotion in the Church, and for much of our period there was a reluctance to raise them to high office. In September 1868 Queen Victoria wrote to Disraeli: 'It will *not* do merely to encourage the ultra-Evangelical party, than which there is none so narrow-minded, and thereby destructive to the well-being and permanence of the Church of England.'[2]

In doctrine the Evangelicals still clung for the most part to that mild form of Calvinism which had characterized the party from its inception. They laid immense emphasis on the Atonement as 'a penal substitutionary sacrifice', and had no sympathy with attempts to shift the emphasis to the Incarnation. So far as their doctrine had a metaphysical basis they looked upon the Deity as transcendent rather than immanent; the Gospel was in their eyes a sudden incursion into the world of the supernatural (though not without its preparation in the Old Testament). Apart from the Old Testament, they refused to recognize the spiritual value of other religions; nor did they see in the new scientific theories any contribution towards the understanding of the world which God had made. Creation for them was an event which had taken place once and for all in the remote past, and it included the creation of the separate species. It is true that more than any other party in the Church they recognized the work of the Holy Spirit; but His divine activities were largely confined to influencing the individual believer. The fate of the individual was decided by his earthly life, and all wider aspects of the Atonement were ignored or given but a secondary place.

To counteract the growth of rationalism and ritualism and to provide a better instructed ministry, the Evangelicals founded

[1] *Life*, Vol. ii, p. 45.

[2] *Life of Disraeli*, Vol. ii, p. 402. There had, however, been appointments of Evangelicals under Lord Palmerston who sought the advice of Lord Shaftesbury to whom he was related.

two famous theological colleges; Wycliffe Hall at Oxford in 1877 with R. B. Girdlestone as its principal, and Ridley Hall at Cambridge four years later under Handley Moule. Moule[1] was a fine classical scholar and had been a Fellow of Trinity, and a pupil of Lightfoot. He was also a man of literary taste and no mean poet. In 1899 he succeeded Armitage Robinson as Norrisian Professor of Divinity, but held the post for a brief period only, as in 1901 he was called to follow Westcott at Durham. In spite of his undoubted scholarship, Moule held the traditional beliefs, and by his teaching and example did much to check the growth of liberal views among Evangelicals. 'Intensely conservative in mind and outlook, he shrank from and never mastered the new learning; and some of his pupils remember their wonder at his reluctance to make definite mental decisions on many of the important issues which were occupying thoughtful minds in the University.'[2] Moule published a number of theological and devotional works, including several volumes in the Cambridge Bible for Schools; but these, though valuable for their spiritual teaching, hardly gave that attention to scholarship which the series required.

The counter-part of Moule at Oxford was F. J. Chavasse[3] who became principal of Wycliffe Hall in 1889. Though he came of Roman Catholic stock, Chavasse was a sincere and humble-minded Evangelical. If he could not compare with Moule as a scholar, his outlook was more open, and he courageously faced the new views and their implications, advising his pupils to come to no hasty decision in regard to the higher criticism, though he himself went so far as to admit that it was 'likely enough that some of the Psalms which have been attributed to David were not written by him'.[4] When Bishop of Liverpool, he preached to the British Association at Southport, and in his sermon showed that he was alive to the gains which theology could derive from the reverent study of nature. 'Once . . . they

[1] See Harford and Macdonald, *Bishop Handley Moule.*
[2] E. S. Woods, *Theodore, Bishop of Winchester,* pp. 30f.
[3] See Lancelot, *Francis James Chavasse.*
[4] *Op. cit.,* p. 124.

thought of creation as an act: now they knew that it was a process.'[1]

Although the Evangelicals, as a whole, reacted unfavourably towards the new views, there were already signs that they were at work among them. Evangelical ordinands, who went up to the universities, attended lectures in which they were set forth; some might in consequence feel that the outlook of the party was unduly narrow and cramping and part company with it, others would remain, but not without sympathy for a wider point of view. In the coming century liberal views would at last prevail among the thoughtful, and prove as unwelcome to the older minds, as had *Lux Mundi* to Liddon and his friends a generation earlier. But even in the closing years of the century such views were already apparent. Dr. Thorold, Bishop of Winchester, in a letter to R. W. Dale on 7 December 1894, 'thought Evangelical teaching ... among thoughtful men, not cankered by party spirit, [was] filling out and completing itself everywhere'.[2]

If liberal views were making but slow progress among Evangelicals, and were still regarded with suspicion by many Anglo-Catholics, in other quarters they were spreading rapidly, and were even becoming accepted in works of reference such as the *Encyclopaedia Britannica*, of which Robertson Smith became editor in 1881. An impetus to their further diffusion among educated people who took an interest in theological matters, came through the foundation of the Hibbert Lectures, an enterprise in which James Martineau took a prominent part. The series was inaugurated by Max Müller, who delivered the first lecture 'On the Origin and Growth of Religion' in the chapterhouse at Westminster in 1878.

The defenders of the old views seem, however, to have been blind to the progress which was being made by liberalism in the Church, for in 1884 it was declared that 'the Broad Church party had been extinguished by popular clamour'. This brought forth a reply from a young Oxford don, Hastings Rashdall by name,

---

[1] *Op. cit.*, p. 159.　　　　[2] *Life of R. W. Dale*, p. 684.

in *The Oxford Magazine* that on the contrary it had succeeded in 'leavening the tone of theological thought and theological temper among the clergy and religious world at large'.[1]

The designation 'Broad Church' as a party label, was apparently recognized by 1853, when it was so used by Conybeare in an article in *The Edinburgh Review*, and was loosely applied to those Churchmen who held liberal views in one form or another; though they were not really a 'party' as were the Evangelicals and the Anglo-Catholics. F. D. Maurice, who resented being called a Broad Churchman in the popular sense, had used the term of the Church of England as comprehending different views, and not as implying any tendency towards Latitudinarianism.[2]

Those who were roughly classed as Broad Churchmen, naturally welcomed the new views; they were also being unconsciously imbibed by others, including some who had once condemned them. In 1888 Jowett could write: 'Our problems are not so serious as those of thirty or forty years ago. Then men thought they had to receive a revelation from God which conflicted with their sense of justice, and puzzled themselves with trying to reconcile God's goodness with the doctrine of eternal punishment.'[3] The whole atmosphere had been changed by a gradual process; so gradual indeed that it had scarcely been noticed. This can be seen by the reception of *Lux Mundi*; for though it caused much commotion among the older Anglo-Catholics, it was as nothing when compared with the outcry against earlier works of a liberal trend. The veteran Archdeacon Denison, who in his younger days had taken a strong line against *Essays and Reviews*, admitted that he would no longer be willing to sign the denunciation of that work.[4] Another token of the different atmosphere was the pacific acceptance of R. L. Ottley's Bampton Lectures *On the Incarnation* in 1897; upon which

---

[1] *Life*, p. 45.

[2] *Life*, Vol. II, p. 607. Daniel Wilson, Bishop of Calcutta, also spoke of 'The broad, tangible, undoubted doctrine of the New Testament, as held by the Church of England.' See Carus, *Memoirs of the Life of Charles Simeon*, p. 834.

[3] *Life*, Vol. II, p. 305.   [4] Bell, *Randall Davidson*, p. 109.

Hastings Rashdall remarked: 'In 1860 the saintly Ottley would have been a persecuted heretic.'[1]

But although liberal views were spreading, the position of such of the clergy as held them was still difficult; they might, indeed, find themselves denounced by those who had advanced some distance in a liberal direction; an article by Fremantle in *The Fortnightly Review* in 1887, for example, met with criticism from Gore. One burning question was continually cropping up; the conduct of those of the clergy who recited the public offices of the Church whilst not accepting some of the statements contained in them in their literal and obvious sense. (Liturgical reform it may be pointed out, had not kept pace with doctrinal restatement, nor taken any account of even those milder results of biblical criticism which were accepted by most scholars.) E. A. Abbott in *The Kernel and the Husk* (published anonymously in 1886) argued that they were justified, since in such recitations, including the saying of the creed, they were acting, not in any personal capacity, but as mouthpieces of the Church. This was a position held by not a few of the clergy; but it laid them open to severe criticism in some quarters. An article by Henry Sidgwick in *The International Journal of Ethics* in 1896 brought matters to a head. Though he was willing to allow some latitude to the laity, he utterly condemned any of the clergy who made declarations of assent to statements which they did not really accept. Such conduct was a breach of veracity and good faith, and blameworthy on moral grounds. Hastings Rashdall replied by an article in the same periodical in the following January, and by so doing caused a dispute with Gore who agreed with Sidgwick. The controversy was summed up by the editor, Bernard Bosanquet, in 1898. He considered that if a man conscientiously believed that he could find his best life work as a clergyman, the fact that he had to make use of formularies which to him were obsolete, ought not to debar him from the ministry. In such a case 'the question of veracity would be so greatly modified as to present little difficulty'.

[1] *Life*, p. 86.

The spread of liberal views raised in an acute form the problem of authority. Scholars had established the right to pursue their investigations unhampered by outworn conceptions of the authority of the Bible or the Church; but they did not repudiate the authority of either the Bible or of the Church when rightly understood. But for ordinary folk the matter was far from simple. They were aware that both the Church and the Bible were being criticized, and that their authority was no longer accepted unconditionally; how were they to decide the extent to which it could still be applied? It is little wonder that many came to the conclusion that such authority need no longer be recognized at all.

The problem of authority is one of the most urgent, as also one of the most baffling, of all those which confront religious systems, Christianity not excepted. Consciously or not, authority governs to some extent every region of life and thought; but for religion and theology it is a prime necessity.[1] The debatable point is how and where to apply it. For Newman 'the essence of all religion is authority and obedience';[2] but this was not the view of Hort, who held that authority is 'salutary only in so far as it is propaedeutic, placing men in the best attitude for forming a judgment and helping them in the process, but never demanding to be listened to against judgment'.[3]

In a paper on 'Authority, Scientific and Theological' Sidgwick pointed out that authority in theological and religious matters may be accepted on one of two grounds; (a) because those exercising it possess better knowledge, or (b) because disobedience may be followed by penalties.[4] Authority may thus be recognized on account of its ability to impart knowledge of things divine which man could not discover by his own unaided efforts; or because it possesses powers of compulsion. But what may be termed dictatorial authority had lost its prestige owing

---

[1] Cf. Streeter, *Restatement and Reunion*, p. 39. 'Authority must necessarily occupy a far more important place in religion than in any other department of thought or life.'

[2] *Development of Christian Doctrine*, p. 87.

[3] *Life*, Vol. II, p. 435.   [4] Printed in *Henry Sidgwick*, pp. 608 ff.

to the advance of historical and biblical studies, and the whole intellectual climate was averse to any insistence on blind obedience, especially where the authority refused to submit its supposed claims to the examination of reason. The idea of accepting beliefs arbitrarily imposed was utterly repugnant to the outlook of the age, which found the so-called Religion of the Spirit much more attractive.

R. W. Dale saw the highest authority, not in the Bible, but in a combination of the witness of the individual and that of the Church, affirming in *The Living Christ and the Four Gospels* (1890) that faith was trust in a Person, not belief in a Book, and 'that the ultimate foundation of faith is personal knowledge of Christ, and its originating cause the personal testimony of those who in our own time and before it have trusted in Christ and found their faith verified in spiritual experience'.[1]

The above quotation brings up the further question as to the seat of authority. Is it to be sought in an organization, a book, or in some more or less vague 'inner light'? For pure Protestantism the sole authority was the Bible; for others the sole authority was the Church; a much more flexible and progressive guide, it may be remarked, in theory if not always in practice. But the two authorities are closely linked; so much so, indeed, that as represented by orthodox apologists from Aquinas onward they seem to involve an argument in a circle; the Bible is to be accepted on the authority of the Church, and that of the Church because it can be demonstrated from the Bible.[2] This was an argument urged against the *Lux Mundi* position by that doughty champion of popular Protestantism, Sir Robert Anderson.

The Bible is not infallible, but the Church is infallible, and upon the authority of the Church our faith can find a sure foundation. But

---

[1] Quoted *Life*, p. 593.

[2] This was not held by all Roman Catholics. Bishop Manet wrote to Baron von Hügel in 1894: 'If the Church depends only on the Scriptures I would tremble, but happily the Church proves herself.' See *Life of Von Hügel*, p. 77. Newman had declared in Tract LXXXV that all persons, with very few exceptions, who try to go by Scripture only fall away from the Church and her doctrines.

how do we know the Church is to be trusted? The ready answer is, We know it upon the authority of the Bible. . . . It is a bad case of 'the confidence trick'.[1]

Many who were perplexed and bewildered by the weakening of external authority turned to the witness of the lives of Christians as the most powerful argument for the truth of Christianity.[2] Such an appeal is, indeed, more persuasive than any formal apologetic, and could affect a much wider constituency, since it is capable of appealing to the multitude who have no opportunity for studying theological questions, and are seldom interested in them.[3] The lives of the saints can undoubtedly serve as lamps, providing some illumination for feet which are stumbling in the gloom of uncertainty.[4]

Others sought for proof in intuition and internal assurance. Martineau, in *The Seat of Authority in Religion* (1890), declared that there was a faculty in man which enabled him to recognize the working of God in nature, in history, and in humanity. But the appeal to any kind of intuition or internal assurance, although not without value, cannot stand alone. 'Immediate knowledge, as being merely empirical and subjective, cannot be accepted as its own guarantee.'[5]

There was also a revived interest in mysticism, as furnishing the believer with direct experience of the God whom he worships. This was, of course, no new means of approach; Coleridge, for example, had found help from the writings of the German mystics, and George Fox and William Law had been to him 'a pillar of fire by night in the wilderness of doubt' through

[1] *The Silence of God*, p. 92.

[2] This argument was elaborated by Francis Paget in *Studies in the Christian Character* (1895); cf. also Inge, *Studies of English Mystics*, p. 5.

[3] Cf. Streeter's essay on 'The Simplicity of Christianity' in *Restatement and Reunion*, pp. 1 ff.

[4] This is the line taken by C. C. J. Webb in his valuable little book *Religious Experience*. He admits that such an appeal may not provide an infallible guide, but it does assure us of a belief in 'the living God present with us, speaking to the conscience, enlightening the mind, impelling to charity, but always, as St. Paul says, imparting to us this heavenly treasure in earthen vessels.'

[5] Caird, *Philosophy of Religion*, p. 53.

which he travelled before finding intellectual satisfaction in the
teaching of Kant. But now it was being worked out in a more
scientific and systematic manner.[1] Max Müller in the last series
of his Gifford Lectures, *Theosophy or Psychological Religion*, had
turned back to the Alexandrian Fathers and their teaching on the
Logos, and also found much that was congenial in the German
mystics, Eckhard and Tauler. About the same time Inge, who
had just migrated to Oxford from Cambridge, began the study
of Christian Mysticism in 'order to find a sound intellectual basis'
for his religious beliefs.[2] One result of his studies was the Bampton
Lectures for 1899 which attracted much attention, and placed
mysticism on a new footing, redeeming it from the reproach of
haziness and even unorthodoxy, which, for many thoughtful
people, had long enveloped it. Interest in mysticism was, indeed,
not confined to religion; for it was being fostered in literary
circles by the Celtic school and by the writings of Theodore
Watts-Dunton, whose essay on 'The Renascence of Wonder' in
Chamber's *Cyclopaedia of English Literature* was widely read, as
was his novel *Aylwin*, first published in 1898.

But though there was a revived interest in mysticism, and
curiosity as to the teaching and experiences of the mystics in all
ages, it failed to obtain an unreserved welcome from scholars as a
whole, and even from some religious leaders. Mysticism is hard
to 'fit in', dealing as it does with certain great departments of
human experience, such as the aesthetic and devotional (including
'love' of every kind) which do not admit of any logical or
philosophical treatment.[3] Mysticism, moreover, has a number
of undeniable dangers and defects. A faith based on mystical
experiences may become entirely subjective and divorced from

---

[1] See further *Religion in the Victorian Era*, pp. 289 ff., Von Hügel, *The Mystical Element in Religion* (1908) and Evelyn Underhill's careful and comprehensive study, *Mysticism* (1911).

[2] *Vale*, p. 32. Cf. *Outspoken Essays*, Vol. II, pp. 14 f. 'Formless and vague and fleeting as it is, the mystical experience is the bedrock of religious faith. In it the soul, acting as a unity with all its faculties, rises above itself and becomes spirit.'

[3] See further A. J. Balfour, *Questionings on Criticism and Beauty*.

the institutional and intellectual aspects of religion. The mystics certainly made but little contribution to pure theology, though they might witness to the depth and reality of spiritual life. (Mystics rarely attempt to formulate their experiences, and when they do so, almost invariably interpret them in terms of the creeds which they had previously held.) Many were content to stand aside from the ecclesiastical systems of their day, or even to criticize them; for those who are convinced that they are under internal guidance are apt to resent doctrinal or other restraints, and to exalt their individual experiences unduly.[1] There was a further danger—such experiences might become a means of escape from the harsh realities of life, and so foster a gloomy and pessimistic attitude to existence, though such a procedure was not found in the great mystics.

Mysticism and a reliance on spiritual intuition, though they might help to bolster up the faith of those who were religious by temperament or upbringing, were of little avail to common men and women for whom the traditional religion, received on authority, had had no personal verification. It was all too vague and subjective and alien to their own experience of life. So long as they were able to accept them the old biblical myths, such as Creation in six days, had satisfied their curiosity as to the meaning of existence, or at least as to its origins and supposed purpose. But when authority could no longer be accepted, everything seemed to be the sport of chance, and their own lives to lose significance. Confused and disquieted, many abandoned religion, as a matter beyond their comprehension, and sought, by ceaseless occupation, to shut out anxiety over the inevitable mysteries which surrounded them. There was, in consequence, a steady drift towards indifference and agnosticism.

Confusion was aggravated by the freedom with which religious questions were discussed in the public Press; generally by those

---

[1] F. D. Maurice had already condemned 'the tendency to invest certain feelings, consciousnesses, temperaments, of individual men with the sacredness which belongs only to such truths as are of an universal character, and may be brought to an universal test'. (*The Kingdom of Christ*, Vol. I, p. 53.)

who possessed but slender qualifications for dealing with them. The very fact that fundamental beliefs were being so discussed was itself disquieting for the uneducated, and had the effect of enveloping them in a haze of uncertainty. Towards the close of our period the sudden increase of literacy had stimulated the habit of reading newspapers by a new class of the public, and this had been exploited by Alfred Harmsworth and others who followed in his wake. In opening their columns to the discussion of religious matters the proprietors of such organs had no sincere wish to promote investigation of the question involved—otherwise they would have been more careful in the choice of their contributors—all that concerned them was to encourage circulation by pandering to public demand. Thus the opinions of some popular figure were canvassed, and it was but seldom that an expert was invited to take part in what might extend to a long series of articles. The assurance of some of these scratch collections of writers was only equalled by their ignorance. They might claim to represent the 'lay' point of view; but if so they justified Sir James Baillie's definition in *Reflections on Life and Religion*: 'A layman is a man who is prepared to lay down the law on matters which he does not profess to understand.' No newspaper proprietor or editor would for a moment have entrusted articles on scientific subjects to any but experts; theology, however, was apparently a subject upon which no special knowledge was required, and anyone was qualified to give his or her opinion upon it.

Agnosticism, which may be regarded as an extreme form of liberalism, was a term invented by Huxley in 1869.[1] He disliked Atheism as being too negative, and failing to find any other '-ism' which satisfied him, he started one of his own. The word was suggested to him by 'the unknown god' of Acts 27:23; but he used it in the sense of 'unknowable',[2] for at the time he held that man's powers were incapable of discovering ultimate reality.

[1] *Collected Essays*, Vol. v, pp. 239f.
[2] Agnosticism is a very unsatisfactory term for, as Lucretius had long ago pointed out, if nothing can be known we cannot know that we know nothing.

In this he was going beyond the teaching of Kant, and apparently endeavouring to combine it with that of Hume,[1] which, incidentally, Kant had tried to answer. Huxley was certainly no atheist, and in later life he was impressed by the evidence in the universe for a god who might even be kindly. 'One thing', he wrote, 'which weighs with me against pessimism and tells for a benevolent author of the universe is my enjoyment of scenery and music. I do not see how they can have helped in the struggle for existence. They are gratuitous gifts.'[2]

Agnosticism was much more a widely diffused attitude of mind than an explicit doctrine; though with some it stood for the definite denial of the possibility of any positive beliefs, and is really a phase of scepticism,[3] applied, indeed, in a narrow sphere, for it does not deny the possibility of all knowledge, but only the knowledge of things ultimate.

Agnosticism was developed with great energy and persistence by Herbert Spencer; so much so, in fact, that Bradley once remarked that he had told us more about the Unknowable than the rashest of theologians had ever ventured to tell us about God. His *First Principles* had as its avowed object the reconciliation of science and religion. This was to be brought about by a division of territory; science was to have what was 'knowable', religion what was 'unknowable'. Spencer's position, in its general outline, is not unlike that taken up by Hamilton and Mansel, for they accepted the agnostic conclusions of Kant, but got round them by making Christian doctrine depend entirely on revelation; a step which Spencer himself would not have taken.

The great weakness of agnosticism is that, as I have already pointed out, it tends to confuse the unknown with the unknowable, and 'rejects probabilities because we cannot have certainties, and insists on knowing nothing because we cannot

[1] Hume, it may be remarked, looked upon dogmatic atheism as 'multiplied indiscretion and imprudence'.

[2] *The Wilfrid Wards and the Transition*, p. 347.

[3] Cf. Fairbairn, *The Place of Christ in Modern Theology*, p. 204: 'Agnosticism is just scepticism become too proud or too perverse to confess its real nature.'

know everything'.[1] No one can deny that, in view of man's limited powers and endowments, a measure of agnosticism is inseparable from human thought, even when reinforced by revelation; the danger lies in acquiescing in narrow boundaries, for 'it is not the limitation of our knowledge which is perilous, but our tendency to regard the limited as absolute and to treat the part as the whole'.[2] There is a devout and praiseworthy agnosticism which patiently accepts man's burden of ignorance and is content to walk by faith where sight is as yet unavailable; but this is an outlook far removed from the point of view of those who aver that the only certainty is that nothing is certain, and whose only hope is a stern despair.

Some of those who, in spite of intellectual difficulties, were determined at all costs to preserve their religious beliefs, sought for an infallible authority which would give them the necessary assurance in return for a blind surrender, for as Sohm once said: 'The natural man is a born Catholic.' But though infallibility meets this natural craving, it 'meets it in the most fatal form',[3] involving not only a repudiation of personal responsibility, but also, what is in effect an act of intellectual suicide, the abandonment of all search for the truth. In the eyes of more robust thinkers such timid souls provoked a comparison to inexperienced travellers who hand themselves over, bag and baggage, to a tourist agency. They might achieve earthly content, but only at the price of missing a celestial crown, that tried but serene knowledge which comes to those alone who have dared to confront and wrestle with doubt and uncertainty. Difficulties may be stumbling-blocks, but they can also be stepping-stones.

The attraction of a Church which claimed to have answers to all doubts and uncertainties, and whose agents were inflexible in their conviction that they were the instruments of an infallible authority, was naturally strong for souls plunged in despair. The fact that its supposed authority had to be taken for granted

---

[1] Hastings Rashdall, *Philosophy and Religion*, p. 48.
[2] Westcott, *The Incarnation and Common Life*, p. 280.
[3] H. Drummond, *The New Evangelism*, p. 22.

seemed to make little difference. Hort wrote in 1862: 'There is so strong a craving for . . . an oracular voice that the mere claim to possess it is eagerly accepted without question.'[1]

Others there were, and they perhaps reflected more nearly the prevailing spirit of the times, who, convinced that Christianity in any of its orthodox forms had finally been discredited, turned to what may be described as 'fancy religions'. Most of these were either derived from Oriental sources, or were mere rehashings of forgotten heresies, and, though their advocates might recommend them as 'up-to-date' Christianity, they were in reality nothing more than reversions to discarded types.

The rejection of the accepted religion had left a vacuum and men were making for themselves false gods whom they could worship. For 'the religious emotions, if they no longer find their object in a God of Righteousness . . . will avenge themselves, as they have done again and again, in superstition'.[2] Those who adopted such substitutes for the living God frequently met with disappointment and disillusionment; but this did not deter them from fresh adventures, nor deprive them of their sanguine outlook; when one 'religion' failed them they turned eagerly to the next. In exactly the same way men in the days of the Roman Empire had been initiated into one mystery religion after another, hoping to find a compass to guide them over the dark and unknown seas of life and bring them at last to a safe haven.[3]

Some of these new faiths offered the consolations of religion on very easy terms, especially in America, where they aroused the scathing satire of Stephen Leacock in his *Arcadian Adventures with the Idle Rich*. But this was by no means true of all of them; in some cases, indeed, their new-found votaries took them exceedingly seriously and exhibited an intensity of devotion which put the conventional Christian to shame. This is, of course, a frequent characteristic of small, despised coteries, and what is

---

[1] *Life*, Vol. I, p. 466.
[2] A. L. Moore in *Lux Mundi*, p. 59. Cf. William Blake: 'Man must and will have some religion; if he has not the religion of Jesus he will have the religion of Satan.'
[3] See Elliott-Binns, *The Beginnings of Western Christendom*, p. 61.

22

novel will often call forth unforeseen energies in those who had grown lax in their following of the old.

Much in these various 'religions' was merely fanciful or even absurd, such as the eccentric notions of Jehovah's Witnesses and the British Israelites; but their success clearly demonstrated that they made an appeal to certain temperaments. In addition, they provided channels for self-expression and activity for many who, for one cause or another, had failed to find them in the orthodox denominations; that women should have been so prominent in many of them (as Mrs. Eddy in Christian Science and Mrs. Annie Besant in Theosophy) was surely no accidental circumstance. Furthermore, it can hardly be denied that some of these faiths took up aspects of religion which Christianity, in its orthodox form, appeared to have forgotten. They also undertook to provide answers to questions which had long baffled the minds of men. Christian Science, for example, offered an explanation of pain and evil—by the simple device of denying their existence. Theosophy met the same problem, and the apparent injustice of the universe, by the doctrines of Karma and Reincarnation; its avowal that all religions were in essence the same, although revealed through the mouth of different teachers, was in line with the new ideas which had come in by way of the study of Comparative Religion. In general Theosophy made a strong appeal to those who were attracted by the vague cosmic emotion then becoming popular, and it seemed fitting that light and guidance should come to the bemused Western world from the quarter of light. Those who had lived for a time in the East were often open to such notions, which were reinforced by the growing knowledge of the historic Oriental religions. Esoteric Bhuddism had its adherents, and some even became Moslems.

Spiritualism attracted many, especially in times of bereavement; and here again a 'fancy' religion stepped in to meet a human need, for the Church of the day was opposed to prayers for the dead, and in the Burial Service seemed to place all the emphasis on the sorrow of parting, and to neglect the note of Christian joy. It had also apparently forgotten the meaning of the communion of saints. It is not surprising therefore that the claim of Spiritualism to give information as to the state of the departed, and to provide means by which intercourse with them might be maintained, proved so attractive.

Any contemplation of the period as a whole from this aspect recalls the oft-quoted saying of Plato that 'The maker and father of the Universe it is difficult to discover; nor, if he were discovered, could he be declared to all men',[1] but it hardly justifies the opinion which Arnold Bennett (that rather quaint person whose influence and popularity, although only transient, seem so inexplicable today) expressed in a letter to H. G. Wells in 1905: 'I hope you aren't going to defend the worn-out platitude to the effect that religion is a necessity to man's nature. Because it isn't. Religion is done for—any sort of religion.' Such a sweeping judgment could only arise in an arrogant and ignorant mind; for unless the future is to be very different from the past man needs 'religion', and if he cannot acquire it from traditional sources will find for himself something to take its place, an object of 'worship' outside himself. This new 'idol' may be disguised and take on incongruous forms, such as Natural Science or the totalitarian State, but it witnesses to the existence of a vacuum in the soul which must somehow be filled.

Although liberal views were slowly penetrating almost all sections of the Church, and in some cases overflowing into definite unorthodoxy, the movement as a whole, and especially in its more extreme forms, suffered from a variety of weaknesses which in the end were bound to provoke a reaction. Many of them were, indeed, recognized by the wisest of its leaders.

In the first place, its aims were too negative. Many liberals, in their determination to rely on their own understandings and to bring the faith into line with contemporary notions, showed a contempt for all authority, whether it were the traditions of the Church or of learning. It is true that before a new building can be erected on an old site there must be considerable demolition,

---

[1] *Timaeus*, 28 C.

but it is sometimes unwise to carry this process too far, especially if comprehensive plans are lacking for what is to come. But in all ages of transition there are never lacking those who are more concerned with being in advance of their fellows than in giving consideration to what has stood the test of time. Minds of this type, like Flecker's pilgrims, must go 'always a little further'. In their obsession with what is novel they are disdainful of the past, and might even seem ready to sacrifice the abiding elements in the Gospel for the sake of adjustments which in their very nature could only be temporary. R. W. Church complained that liberals in their efforts to place Christian history in a new light were impatient and at times careless of Christianity itself,[1] and one who was himself an ardent advocate of liberal views could write: 'The sudden withdrawal of all reverence for the past has generated a type of intellect which is not only offensive to taste, but is unsound in training.'[2]

It is not enough calmly to dismiss much in traditional theology as obsolete and conventional; before doing so it is advisable to inquire into 'the rational ground or basis in human nature on which the convention proceeds'.[3] Many liberals forgot this principle, and in their eagerness and over-optimism were apt to isolate the Spirit from the forms by which it was mediated.[4] Novel ideas may be exciting and attractive when compared with the old, but there is need to exercise some restraint before adopting them, and a wise and manly attitude will not embrace them without careful examination, and will be on its guard against the tendency to over-rate them. 'One who forgets the discoveries of all the years of yesterday will never see but a broken fragment of the truth.'[5] A. C. Turner aptly compared the objects of the Modernists in theology with those of the Futurists in art: 'Both try to escape from the traditionalism and materialism with which the modern world is beset, into a psychological heaven of their

---

[1] *Occasional Papers*, Vol. II, p. 141.
[2] Mark Pattison, *Memoirs*, p. 240.
[3] Jowett, *Cratylus*, Vol. I, p. 256.
[4] A. E. J. Rawlinson in *Foundations*, p. 390.
[5] B. H. Streeter in *Foundations*, p. 78.

own contrivance; one would throw overboard the nuisance of history and the other the boredom of natural form.'[1]

The liberal approach suffered from another fundamental weakness, it was too exclusively intellectual, and adopted with too great a facility the presuppositions of current ideas. One consequence of this was that it exposed Christianity, as liberals understood it, to attacks on ground chosen by its opponents. Liberalism might provide fresh illumination, but in doing so it sacrificed heat and, as G. K. Chesterton has said, 'light without heat is moonshine'.[2] Its advocates might think that they possessed the Truth, and even that they had discovered the Way, but they had small experience of the Life. The enthusiasm which had marked the early stages of the movement had waned, and it had lost some of its soaring aspirations, leaving behind 'the wreckage of unfulfilled dreams'. Liberals had to learn anew the lesson taught by the eighteenth century 'that a faith which never gets beyond preaching up reason and morality is powerless to reform society or to meet the spiritual longings of the individual'.[3] Liberalism had been too optimistic in its conceptions of man's rationality and innate virtue; it had, moreover, forgotten his need of redemption.

This liberal weakness was the outcome of a defective psychology. Truth is not to be discovered by logic alone, and other factors must be brought into account—those dispositions and moral habits of the mind which are indispensable for the search. There are, as Newman in *The Grammar of Assent* rightly maintained, sub-conscious grounds of belief, and in practical life convictions are generally based on a kind of intuition, rather than on logic; intuition, indeed, may often give the death-blow to a mistaken application of logic. 'The facts of religion address themselves to the whole nature of man; and it is only by the whole nature of

[1] In *op. cit.*, p. 382, note 1.
[2] *Orthodoxy*, p. 49. Cf. Jowett's confession, above, p. 126. Liberalism alone is not sufficient. 'A devout Christian may be a Liberal Protestant or a Liberal Catholic; he can hardly be a Liberal without any qualification.' (Inge, *Vale*, p. 74.)
[3] *The Early Evangelicals*, p. 95.

man that they can ever be fully apprehended.'[1] Any genuine presentation of the truth must be capable of bringing satisfaction to the conscience and the heart as well as to the mind. To ignore them in the search for truth is therefore hazardous.

In its concentration on the intellectual expression of religion liberalism tended to ignore or belittle its other aspects. It had no really adequate sense of the wonder and mystery of life; and, in spite of all man's amazing discoveries, mystery still covers much of existence, and will, one imagines, continue to do so till time shall be no more. The sense of wonder and mystery raises life above the earthly and material, and by the sanctities of reverence and awe hallows and enriches it. But all this was to many liberals a closed book; hence their habitual disregard of the ceremonial and sacramental expressions of religion.[2] Their outlook was too 'spiritual', using the term in a narrow sense, and therefore wanting in breadth and comprehensiveness.

> The religion which attempts to be rid of the bodily side of things spiritual, sooner or later loses hold on all reality. Pure spiritualism, however noble the aspiration, however living the energy with which it starts, always has ended at last, and will always end, in evanescence.[3]

In England there was the beginnings of an organized Liberal Catholicism in the *Lux Mundi* school, but Liberal Protestantism remained vague and inchoate. There were some Broad Churchmen who might be included in its ranks, but the failure of liberal views to spread, for the present, among Evangelicals stood in the way of its advancement in the Church of England, though it was better represented in the Nonconformist bodies. This failure of Liberal Protestantism to attain any kind of organized system in England meant that theologians of this type turned largely to Germany for direction and stimulus. Liberal Protestantism in Germany had most of the defects of liberalism in general, and

[1] R. C. Moberly in *Lux Mundi*, p. 167.

[2] This statement does not apply, of course, to all those who shewed sympathy with liberal views, the *Lux Mundi* group, is an obvious exception.

[3] R. C. Moberly in *op. cit.*, p. 200.

often in an exaggerated form. It conformed too readily to current modes of thought, and though there was a deep and searching study of the New Testament and of the history of the Primitive Church, it was prone to concentrate on certain aspects only and to neglect the rest. The Kingdom of God, upon which the Ritschlians laid such stress, was to come by a gradual process of permeation and was concerned with this world only. Christ Himself, for Liberal Protestants, was valued mainly as a teacher of ethics, and the ideals which He set before His followers were presented in a form which made them approximate to those desired by cultivated thinkers of the nineteenth century; in fact they made 'the Christ of the Gospels . . . a prophet of modern civilisation'.[1] Such a representation of the Christ failed entirely to account for the effect which He had had upon His first followers, and for the progress of the Church; it needed only the suggestion of a few eccentric minds that He had never existed at all to show that this line of criticism had reached a dead end.

The picture of Jesus which Liberal Protestants had sketched was the outcome of a process of selection and ignored elements in the Gospel which cannot be made to square with the notion that He was nothing more than the greatest of ethical teachers—those elements which are usually spoken of by theologians as eschatological. In many passages Jesus is represented, not simply as a teacher of morals who hoped that men would respond to His message by repenting and that so the Kingdom would slowly spread, but as one who looked for a sudden and supernatural intervention, in which He Himself would be the central figure. The Kingdom would arrive, not as the result of a gradual and pervasive process, but through a catastrophic event. Attention to this neglected aspect of the Gospel picture of Jesus was aroused first in Germany, being a natural reaction to the prevailing and inadequate conception, and was the work mainly of Johannes Weiss and of Albert Schweitzer, that strange genius who is not only a theologian but also a great musician and a medical missionary. It was the translation of the latter's volume *The Quest*

[1] C. C. J. Webb, *Religious Thought in England*, etc., p. 55.

of the Historical Jesus (*Von Reimarus zu Wrede*) which made such views popular in England and marked an epoch in theological thought in this country, as it had marked an epoch in Germany. But this did not take place until 1910.

In considering the defects of liberalism we have so far confined our attention to its content; but in addition there was a tactical weakness which stood in the way of its progress—a lack of unity when compared with its traditionalist opponents. These latter were inspired by a single idea and had a single object on which they were all agreed—to resist to the uttermost any teaching which seemed to them to be in conflict with their conception of the Gospel. But liberals were of all shades of opinion, and were far from agreeing among themselves; their ideas, moreover, were in a constant state of flux, as new knowledge came flowing in. Here the liberal ideal, as dynamic and ready to welcome truth from whatever quarter it might come, was infinitely higher than the static attitude of the obscurantists, but it laid them open to the charge of inconsistency and vacillation. Really deep and sincere thinkers can never be wholly consistent; for the truth has many facets, and now one and now another will seem more important, as fresh facts emerge which demand consideration; conclusions can therefore be only tentative. It is the rigid exponents of a narrow system who alone can maintain absolute consistency; for they are inflexibly opposed to anything which cannot be fitted into their scheme of things and are blind to truth if it comes in a novel form. Consistency is no necessary virtue in either an individual or a movement, but there can be no question as to its utility as a factor making for union and solidarity.

Newman in his *Apologia* defined liberalism as 'the anti-dogmatic principle and its developments', and the fact that liberals were suspicious of dogmas was another source of disunion; for the ideal of an undogmatic religion, though it may attract the individual, can never provide a firm basis for a community. The corporate side of religion, indeed, made little appeal to liberals, and many of them were only too conscious of the deep cleavage between the Church as it existed in primitive times and its later developments. All this led to their remaining a collection of more or less isolated units with no very effective bond to draw them together. An attempt, not without important consequences, was made in 1898 to consolidate Liberal Churchmen by the formation of The Churchmen's Union, later to be known as The Modern Churchmen's Union.[1] It professed to have five objects, of which the fifth deserves special notice, the support of 'those who are honestly and loyally endeavouring to vindicate the truths of Christianity by the light of scholarship and research'.

But if there were fundamental weaknesses in the liberal position, and if there was a lack of cohesion and unity amongst those who maintained it, they themselves at the close of the century were confident, and even self-complacent. They felt that 'the flowing tide was with them', and would inevitably sweep away all opposition. But, even then, voices were raised to question the value and permanency of their achievements. Men had struggled to obtain freedom in religious questions and the right to believe as they chose; but for many the result was to rob them of all settled convictions. One thing seemed as good as another, and nothing had abiding significance; all had become relative, but with no reliable standard to which it could be related.[2] Observers, moreover, were asking for more positive and constructive results; and it was not long after our period that G. K. Chesterton put this criticism into a pregnant phrase: 'It is time we gave up looking for questions and began to look for answers.'[3] As is the case with so many revolutionary movements, the destruction of an ancient tyranny might be followed, all unconsciously, by the setting up of one equally burdensome, in the exchange of 'old prejudices for new, which then, as much as the old ones, serve as leading-strings to the unthinking crowd'.[4]

---

[1] See further *Religion in the Victorian Era*, pp. 496f.

[2] Cf. *Henry Sidgwick*, p. 539 (written in 1895). 'What does freedom bring us to? It brings us face to face with atheistic science: the faith in God and Immortality, which we had been struggling to clear from superstition, suddenly seems to be *in the air*.'

[3] *Orthodoxy*, p. 64.   [4] Pfleiderer, *Development of Theology*, p. 4.

To criticize a movement and its advocates is an easy task, as it is easy to ignore the tremendous difficulties which they had to face. The task of the liberals was certainly beset by enormous difficulties, and unless these are taken into consideration we shall do them an injustice. As Matthew Arnold has said, referring to the work of Dean Stanley:

> It is one of the hardest tasks in the world to make new intellectual ideas harmonize truly with the religious life, to place them in the right light for that life. The moments in which such a change is accomplished are epochs in religious history; the men through whose instrumentality it is accomplished are the great religious reformers.

After confessing that no such reformer had yet arisen in his day, he went on:

> Till he appears, the true religious teacher is he who, not yet reconciling all things, at least esteems things still in their due order . . . who shutting his mind against no ideas brought by the spirit of the time, sets these ideas, in the sphere of the religious life, in their right prominence, and still puts that first which is first; who, under the pressure of new thoughts, keeps the centre of the religious life where it should be.

In addition to those who criticized the achievements of liberalism there were some who thought that they could already discern a movement against its predominence in theology. In two unsigned articles in *The Quarterly Review* for January and April 1899 Wilfrid Ward expressed the view that

> We are now witnessing a religious reaction. . . . There is a strong tendency to fall back upon the old religious beliefs . . . not indeed with the clear definite faith of early days, yet with a vague and undefined sense of their worth. . . . We have lived to see the disenchantments which Liberalism has undergone.

This was perhaps a little premature; but the coming years would undoubtedly teach liberal theologians many bitter lessons. But the reaction, as is the habit of reactions, has surely gone too far, and even the services which liberalism has rendered, and they cannot be denied, have tended to be forgotten. Liberal views might have been applied too drastically, but they had 'awakened men to believe that there was a freshness and reality in things they had by use become dulled to'.[1]

An uncontrolled liberalism can be dangerous to religious faith, but a sober liberalism is a necessary element in the life of the Church. The spirit in which the best thought of nineteenth-century liberalism pursued its task was the spirit of John 8:32: 'Ye shall know the truth and the truth shall make you free', and if some of its findings have to be abandoned, that would not have surprised those who advanced them, for they were aware of the complexity of the problems with which they had to deal, and knew only too well that the tide of knowledge ebbs and flows. But they know also that even the errors of sincere and selfless scholars may in the end be found of service. A recent writer has said that

> liberalism is not to be identified with the particular manifestation of it which was dominant in Western Protestantism at the beginning of the century. It is the spirit which holds all expressions of the truth, its own included, in subjection to the truth itself. As such it cannot die. But it needs to learn ... that freedom requires the support of tradition, though it may never surrender to tradition.[2]

In *The International Review of Missions* 1938, pp. 589 ff., Oliver Quick, after pointing out that the reaction against liberalism was a return to a Hebraic outlook, pleaded for a more balanced judgment.

> The Church is now, or soon will be, the only remaining trustee of all the treasures of Hellenism—its belief in reason, persuasion, beauty, justice, freedom and the moral consciousness of man. Before we repudiate this heritage as a legacy of original sin, let us be sure that we are really doing the will of Him who in Jesus Christ revealed His love for the men whom He created. (*Op. cit.*, p. 580.)

[1] Church, *Occasional Papers*, Vol. II, p. 269.
[2] E. L. Allen in *Religion in Britain Since 1900*, p. 197.

Chapter Sixteen

THE POSITION AT THE CLOSE
OF THE CENTURY

AFTER making due allowance for the developments already considered, it may be said that the position at the close of the century did not differ very materially from that in 1860. Yet changes there had been, for the endeavours of the passing years had not gone unrewarded. If many of the same problems still awaited solution, there had been a shift of emphasis; theologians were now in a better position to comprehend their scope and dimensions and to distinguish between those which were fundamental and those which were merely secondary. Some problems, moreover, had been solved, whilst others could be stated more accurately. Unsolved problems are like the hidden rocks which may bring shipwreck and disaster; to chart them is an outstanding service to future voyagers over the same seas. In all branches of knowledge progress is achieved mainly by discovering what are the right questions to ask, and even if the immediate answers are mistaken or incomplete, so long as they do not become barriers to further advance, this is not of supreme importance, for 'the better thought could not have come if the weaker thought had not come first, and died in sustaining the better. If we think honestly our thoughts will not only live usefully, but even perish usefully.'[1] The passage of two generations had, indeed, altered the shape of many problems, and some inchoate tendencies had now achieved definite form. 'The problem of life is not changed by the lapse of centuries, but the conditions are changed.'[2] Scholars had richer and more abundant materials upon which

[1] Ruskin, *Proserpina*, Vol. I, Ch. I.
[2] Westcott, *Religious Thought in the West*, p. 49.

to work, and had learned new methods of handling them; moreover, they had now greater freedom and a complete liberty of investigation.

One feature of the end of the period deserves notice—the immense prestige that had been acquired by German theology.[1] The old aloofness had entirely disappeared, and Harnack in the preface to *Outlines of the History of Dogma* (1892) could affirm that 'there no longer exists any distinction between German and English theological science. The exchange is now so brisk that scientific theologians of all evangelical lands form already one Concilium.' The findings of German theologians, in some quarters at least, were looked upon as being above criticism, and the docile spirit in which they were accepted now arouses our wonder. It was not until the war of 1914 that this attitude was disturbed.

If, however, the problems were much the same they had acquired a new urgency. The spread of education and public controversy had made them more widely known and realized. In addition, room had to be found for the many new facts and notions which had come pressing in. If a renewed study of the Greek Fathers and a better understanding with science had in some respects eased the situation, it cannot be said that theologians had at all adequately met the demands made upon them. This, however, was not so obvious then as it is now. There were many who thought that all necessary adjustments had been made, and that there was nothing more to be feared from the advance of knowledge. The orthodox were certainly very confident, and a writer in *The Quarterly Review* commenting on *Robert Elsmere* in 1888, actually dismissed the critical process as 'a phase of thought long ago lived through and practically dead'. Even Bishop Creighton seems to have shared this view, for as late as 1896 he could write: 'For my part I believe the attack on Christianity is intellectually repulsed.'[2]

[1] This was, of course, not true of all scholars; Ramsay, for example, has left an interesting account of his reaction from a too submissive attitude: see the preface to *The Church in the Roman Empire* (cf. also pp. 5 f.).

[2] *Life*, Vol. II, p. 191.

One factor which made for optimism was the realization that the older rationalism had fallen from favour; even in France Alfred de Musset, writing before our period, had made one of his characters complain that he had been nurtured on 'the sterile milk of impiety', and now the realization that impiety was, indeed, sterile was becoming widespread. Herbert Spencer himself admitted it when he wrote: 'Religious creeds, which in one way or another occupy the sphere that material interpretation seeks to occupy and fails the more it seeks, I have come to regard with a sympathy based on community of need.'[1] Science, too, was moving away from a purely deterministic idea of the universe and adopting a dynamic rather than a static outlook; even before the rise of Einstein there was a move in the direction of greater freedom. One result of this was the gradual dying down of the conflict between science and religion. This was all to the good, but the advocates of Christianity were a little premature in their optimism, for they failed to discern that the prevalence of materialistic and mechanical views had been due, not only to the spread of scientific knowledge, but perhaps even more to the weakening of faith and the decay of the spirit of adventure in the Church itself. Moreover, there was danger in accepting too eagerly the retreat from determinism.[2] The most disquieting feature of the situation, however, was that the full implication of scientific discoveries had not been realized nor the proportions that they would one day assume. Space and time might be terrifying spectres, but they were not yet credited with the vastness we know today, when men can speak of millions of years as casually as they would of a few weeks; though even then it required a robust faith to 'refuse to accept space as a measure of being . . . time as a measure of the soul'.[3]

Science had given to both thought and life a new framework and promised to provide mankind with a unity such as it had

[1] *Autobiography*, Vol. II, p. 471.

[2] Cf. Webb, *A Study of Religious Thought in England from 1850*, p. 155, 'it would be prudent in the defenders of religion not to welcome too warmly the admission of indeterminacy in nature by certain men of science'.

[3] Westcott, *Christus Consummator*, p. 22.

not known since the Reformation, and in this, perhaps half unconsciously, lay its attraction. Men found once more by its aid a common speech. But to this unification there was one striking exception, Christianity still expressed itself in terms of biblical mythology, a mythology which was no longer characteristic of the age nor understood by common folk. Theology was confronted by the task of finding new forms in which the Gospel could be preached to an age which thought in entirely different terms.[1]

Furthermore, even if a mechanical explanation of the universe was no longer accepted as a satisfactory solution by the majority of philosophers, in practical life the machine was becoming more and more a predominant factor. Man seemed to be at the mercy of instruments of his own devising,[2] and was little short of obsessed by his mechanical surroundings; so much so that for many there was a feeling of insecurity unless they were linked up to a machine. Man, as someone has said, is now 'a displaced person in a mechanical environment of his own creation'.

Carlyle has told us that it is hazardous to foretell the coming of a new age, for it is often heralded by false warnings. Yet for many believers the coming of a new century brought the hope of an era of affirmation and faith far different from the spirit of doubt and hesitancy which had marked the Victorian Age on its intellectual and spiritual side. Each century seems, by a curious kind of law, to react to its predecessor, and some were probably not averse to casting fresh earth on the grave of a passing era. Men felt that they had gone through Purgatory, and could now rest awhile in the Earthly Paradise which they had won. Little did they anticipate that no Paradise lay ahead, but the Inferno of two world wars. But even if there had been no major conflicts, it is

[1] The writings of H. G. Wells did much in the 'nineties to make the scientific outlook familiar to the average man and woman, and encouraged them to revolt against all restrictive influences; at the same time they suggested positive, if somewhat impractical, ideals for the conduct of their lives.

[2] Cf. John Galsworthy in the preface to *The Forsyte Saga*: 'Men are . . . quite unable to control their own inventions; they at best develop adaptability to the new conditions those inventions create.'

doubtful whether such an attitude could long have been maintained. Humanity is constantly endeavouring to create for itself
a quiet garden secluded from the chaos which surrounds it, but
inevitably its peace is disturbed by that latent spirit of curiosity
which cannot remain at rest, 'the Serpent, that never allows man
to abide long in any Eden'.[1]

The lull could not last, for its maintenance depended on
ignorance and the shutting out of unpleasant facts. Much would
come to disturb it; from a more drastic biblical criticism, from
the study of comparative religion, perhaps above all from the
inroads of the new psychology.

In regard to biblical criticism it was now recognized that the
Old Testament was not so important as had once been supposed.
As Gore commented: 'The battle of historic truth cannot be
fought on the field of the Old Testament, as it can on that of the
New, because it is so vast and indecisive, and because ... very
little of the early record can be securely traced to a period near
the events.'[2] Liberal views were, as a consequence, no longer
looked upon as highly dangerous. In 1894 Huxley wrote: 'Thirty
years ago, criticism of "Moses" was held by most respectable
people to be a deadly sin; now it has sunk to the rank of a mere
peccadillo.'[3] As to the New Testament there was a comfortable
feeling that the attack had been thrown back by the Cambridge
school. 'What Bishop Lightfoot has tested and approved, we
believe we may accept as proven', wrote J. B. Mayor in 1897,
though he was careful to add, 'so far as present lights go.'[4] But
the Cambridge contribution, valuable as it undoubtedly was,
was merely a transitional attempt to deal with the problems, and
in Cambridge itself many would move far beyond its conclusions.
At Oxford, Sanday had already pointed the way they would
follow by his greater readiness to sit at the feet of German
scholars. There were few who then recognized that principles
which had been accepted for the Old Testament would be applied

[1] Berenson, *The Italian Painters of the Renaissance*, p. 174.
[2] In *Lux Mundi*, p. 258.
[3] *Science and the Christian Tradition*, p. xi.
[4] *The Epistle of St. James*, p. cxlix.

as ruthlessly to the New; whilst the storm which would rage round eschatology had hardly broken. Eschatology would, indeed, bring much distress of mind to simple souls, for the figure of Jesus presented by its advocates, so far as it was at all intelligible, seemed repellent rather than attractive.

The deeper implications of comparative religion were also hidden. It was, indeed, admitted that Christianity had no monopoly of spiritual teaching and achievement; but other faiths, apart from Judaism and Islam, because they had little concern for morals, might be held to rank as metaphysical systems rather than as religions. The threat contained in efforts to account for both Judaism and Christianity as having developed along purely natural lines was scarcely understood save by scholars. None the less, there was among the educated considerable unsettlement owing to the popularization of the results of anthropology. 'Men asked themselves whether rules regarded in England or in Christendom at large as sacred may after all be no better than *taboos*.'[1] S. A. Cook considered that such knowledge was, more than any other study, the cause of loss of faith on the part of the well-informed.[2]

Another threat, perhaps even more dangerous, because more insidious, and one to which the believer was even more open than the public in general, came from developments in the study of psychology.[3] Such a study was, of course, no new departure, it went back at least to Aristotle's *De Anima*, and there is perhaps no more searching treatment of the subject than *The Confessions* of St. Augustine; but now it was making ambitious claims for itself, although looked down upon and even derided by scientists. A new era in the study may be dated from the opening of Wundt's psychological laboratory at Leipzig in 1875.

Whatever view may be taken of psychology, or of its claims

---

[1] Webb, *op. cit.*, p. 52.   [2] *The Study of Religions*, pp. 7 f.

[3] 'The older psychology was structural. That is, it took experience as we find it to pieces and found certain relations between the various elements of it. These it explained by association. The later psychology is functional rather than structural. It recognizes certain functions of conduct.' (Mead, *Movements of Thought in the Nineteenth Century*, p. 386.)

23

to be a science, there can be no doubt that the researches of psychologists concerning both normal and abnormal subjects revealed vast unexplored possibilities in the mental life of man, and raised, in an acute form, the relation of the thinking mind and the brain which is its instrument. They also brought about an increasing awareness of the mutual effects of mind upon matter and of matter upon mind. Hort, for example, was ready to grant that no mental or spiritual movement took place without 'a concomitant physical movement'.[1]

What made the threat from psychology most disquieting was that its operations were so subtle and so elusive, and the fact that they were concerned, not with external events, but with mental processes; in particular they offered an explanation of religious experience, and in so doing seemed to undermine that trust in spiritual intuition which for many Christians, and above all for Evangelicals, was the securest foundation of their faith. Especially alarming was the idea that the mind of man was capable of working below the level of consciousness, from which it dispatched 'messages' having an air of independent authority.[2] The notion of the subliminal self, as it was termed, like all fresh discoveries tended to be overworked, until it became what Evelyn Underhill has called 'the Mesopotamia of Liberal Christianity'.[3] Religion, it might seem, could be discounted as merely subjective, 'an uprush from the sub-conscious', with the desire for salvation as nothing more than an expression of the instinct for self-preservation, and prayer as but a form of auto-suggestion. There were, indeed, some extreme advocates of the new psychology who dismissed all spiritual phenomena as pathological, an attitude of mind which William James derided as 'Medical Materialism'.[4] Such notions were at times accompanied by the patronizing admission that religion was not without its uses, even if its truth were a matter of indifference.

[1] *The Way, the Truth, the Life*, p. 188.
[2] The idea was not entirely new. Descartes had hinted at such a possibility, and Leibniz had openly suggested that there was a mental life going on below the threshold of consciousness.
[3] *Mysticism*, p. 62.　　　　[4] *Varieties of Religious Experience*, p. 13.

This new challenge to orthodox Christianity found definite, if moderate, expression in William James's Gifford Lectures for 1901-2 *The Varieties of Religious Experience*.[1] James was himself a Christian, though not of an exactly orthodox kind, and this made his work more alarming; for earlier attempts to account for religious experiences by the application of psychology had come from open enemies, such as Bain in *The Senses and the Intellect* published in 1855, and Herbert Spencer in *Principles of Psychology* which appeared in 1870-2.

Although theologians might recognize much in the new ideas which was helpful and even admit the truth of some of the claims made on their behalf, they were not blind to serious defects in them. One weakness in the psychological approach was, that though it might account for the origin and growth of certain notions or beliefs, it provided no standard by which to test their value. (No doubt the psychologist would have said that this was not a matter with which he was concerned.) The whole outlook was unsatisfactory because it was too materialistic. The physical causes and effects of the emotions may be recorded, as the varying temperatures are recorded on a hospital chart; but this does not throw much light on them. There is no microscope by which we can examine a soul. Christians, therefore, although agreeing that spiritual experiences might be conditioned by bodily or mental states, and even recognizing that they followed definite laws, had no patience with those who would dismiss them as dependent for their origin and constitution upon such states. The fact was that some psychologists were apparently unaware that they were dealing solely with means, and not with ends, and that the material upon which they worked was entirely supplied by human consciousness. To explain the origin and development of a process does not account for it, nor assess its real significance.[2]

[1] Hastings Rashdall referred to it as 'that rather painful work'. (*Philosophy and Religion*, p. 109.)

[2] Cf. Hastings Rashdall, *Philosophy and Religion*, p. 111: 'The business of Psychology is to tell us what actually goes on in the human mind. It cannot possibly tell us whether the beliefs which are found there are true or false.'

In the case of prayer, for example, to dismiss it as mere self-suggestion leaves unexplained the self that makes the suggestion.

Thus, educated and thoughtful Christians, whilst recognizing the value of psychology within strict limits, were not greatly troubled by some of the exaggerated and even fantastic claims that were made on its behalf. But the position was far different with the uninstructed public, and as vague notions of what was afoot drifted down to them they aroused much consternation.

The importance of the subject for religion had been realized before our period by Schleiermacher, and his work must not be forgotten, for from him 'is largely derived our modern interest in the psychology of religion and our insistence that in our final interpretation of reality religious experience . . . has a right to be heard'.[1] That psychology would increasingly be applied to religion had long been anticipated, as well as the unsettlement to which it might lead. Frederick Temple had written to Scott in 1857: 'Our theology has been cast in a scholastic mould, *i.e.* all based on logic. We are in need of and we are being gradually forced into a theology based on psychology. The transition, I fear, will not be without much pain; but nothing can prevent it.'[2] About the same time Jowett was endeavouring to reassure those who might be alarmed at the forthcoming developments: 'Why should it be thought incredible that God should give law and order to the spiritual no less than to the natural creation?'[3] It was not, however, until Boyd Carpenter delivered the Hulsean Lectures in 1878, that the usefulness of psychology for religion was publicly proclaimed.

Viewed in its totality the atmosphere of the age was over-critical and the defects of all systems were apt to loom larger than their merits. This was true above all of its attitude to the various systems of belief, especially if they were traditional. In the past men might have been credulous in accepting beliefs because they found them congenial and helpful, now the process had gone

---

[1] Storr, p. 243.
[2] *Memoirs of Frederick Temple*, Vol. II, p. 517.
[3] *The Epistles of St. Paul*, Vol. II, p. 235.

into reverse, and denial and negation were commended. New knowledge and new ideas were pouring in, but there was no centre around which they might be grouped, nothing to give them coherence, meaning, or consistency. The exponents of criticism had no agreed standard of values upon which to base their findings and so confusion was increased, as when 'ignorant armies clash by night' in a turmoil of meaningless strife. The age was one of intellectual chaos without promise of any clarity in the foreseeable future. This spirit of negation was by no means confined to religion, it was found too in literature where criticism had become an end in itself, for critics had forgotten that their primary task was one of interpretation. Criticism for its own sake had become almost a mania, or at least a disease, and F. L. Lucas, speaking of a later period, could term it 'that influenza of modern intellectuals'.[1]

A critical spirit is often a manifestation of the daring and captiousness of youth, as when men in the dawn of time sought to defy the elements; now it seemed to be the product of senility and evidence of the loss of hope and of creative power. The spirit of pessimism was indeed abroad, a spirit which would soon arouse the derisive scorn of G. K. Chesterton—*The Defendant* was published in 1901—and some observers who were far from orthodox Christians deplored what George Moore once called 'the vulgar details of a vulgar age'.

A purely critical phase, whether in thought or literature, is incapable of producing fruit, and sooner or later provokes a reaction, not always of a healthy kind. Negations are not attractive in themselves, though they may tempt some to adopt them as a pose; but even so they are apt to arouse resentment in stronger intellects, as when Goethe in a somewhat petulant outburst, wrote to one of them: 'If you must tell me your opinions, tell me what you believe in. I have plenty of doubts of my own.' The spirit of denial leads nowhere, and can offer no solution for the pains and difficulties and contradictions of life;[2]

---

[1] *The Decline and Fall of the Romantic Ideal*, p. 143.
[2] Cf. Westcott, *Christus Consummator*, p. 153.

any kind of criticism 'which does not either end in construction or make it more possible, is . . . without any scientific character or function'.[1] If not unduly prolonged, and in themselves, 'critical and sceptical phases . . . can never . . . be other than temporary',[2] such periods have their usefulness in clearing the way for new forms of affirmation.

Regular churchgoers were probably not greatly influenced by the uncertainties of the times, of which they were often ignorant or deliberately unregarding. Religion, as is generally the case, mainly flourished among the middle classes; and the middle classes, here at one with the sovereign whom they so ardently revered, were little affected by the changes in the intellectual climate. J. B. Mozley once opined that George Eliot's antipathy towards them had been aroused by their fixity of belief and apparent immunity to the disturbing force of new ideas in beliefs and morals.[3] Attendance at divine worship was for them a token of respectability rather than an open confession of faith in Christ, and the habit had not yet been threatened by changes in social outlook nor the opportunities which the cheap motor-car and the attractions of week-ends away from home would bring about.

But beneath much of the criticism of the Church and of Christianity there lay a cause which was much more fundamental and damaging. It was voiced by Bishop Westcott when he said: 'The startling contrast between the Christian faith and the life of Christians has created a widespread distrust in the claims of the Gospel.'[4] Long before, R. W. Church had found in the same contrast an example of 'the incredible facility of self-deception' which characterized the times. The life of the average church-goer might be innocent and without offence, and he might contemplate 'the New Testament with perhaps longing or respectful or wondering awe', but he remained 'at an infinite

---

[1] Fairbairn, *The Place of Christ in Modern Theology*, p. vii.

[2] Illingworth, *Divine Immanence*, p. v, and cf. *Personality: Human and Divine*, p. 84.

[3] *Letters of J. B. Mozley*, p. 333.

[4] *Lessons from Work*, p. 287.

distance from its spirit and temper'.[1] Great duties go not well with little souls, and the failure of Christianity was to be attributed, not to defects in the Gospel, but to the all too patent limitations of those who professed it. Conventional religion can be very deadening, and Lightfoot thought it well to warn his ordination candidates that, 'If vice is the death of the irreligious many, formalism is the death of the religious few.'[2]

Englishmen as a whole are notoriously suspicious of speculation, and for the most part are averse to hard and prolonged thinking; they prefer action to thought, and have so often shown themselves capable of 'muddling through' that to indulge in it seems scarcely profitable.[3] There were naturally but few who had the necessary equipment or opportunity to face up to the difficulties of the times, or patience to accept the discomfort of suspended judgment on things fundamental; the great majority either took such matters for granted or put them aside as incapable of solution. Some, in accord with the prevailing spirit of the age, did this deliberately, for inquiry might only lead to additional perplexity and mental stress. There can be no doubt that the most serious enemy of genuine religion was the cowardice or levity which dissuaded men from thinking things out.[4] Fred Bason, the Bermondsey bookseller, belongs to a later period, but his comment on the poor demand for theological literature can be applied to conditions at the end of the nineteenth century. 'Why', he asks, 'don't religion sell? Do people know all about God?'[5]

---

[1] *The Gifts of Civilisation*, pp. 40f.   [2] *Ordination Addresses*, p. 171.

[3] Cf. *Letters of J. Addington Symonds*, p. 49: 'We are . . . now too interested in phenomena, too bent on actual discovery to embark on speculation. Yet this is one-sided . . . we are contented with the examination of matter and neglect the problems of mind.'

[4] Cf. Quick, *Doctrines of the Creed*, p. 6: 'The real faithlessness of the modern world is seen in its half-despairing, half-complacent agreement to give up ultimate questions.'

[5] *Fred Bason's Diary* (edited by Nicholas Bentley), p. 26. In 1870 religious books headed the list of new titles, but by 1886 fiction had gained the first place, religion being second. By the end of the century it had dropped still further down the list.

One possible sign of the diminution of interest in religion may perhaps be found in the falling off in the number of ordinands. In 1885 the figure had been round about 870, but by the end of the century it had dropped to about 700. This decline was not entirely due to a loss of religious fervour; account must also be taken of changes in social habits, such as the emergence of other openings for the sons of the professional classes and of the smaller landed gentry who at one time would have avoided any occupation which savoured of 'trade'.

The loss of interest in religion may be accounted for in various ways, apart from the prevailing unsettlement. People, as always, were intently absorbed in their own affairs and problems, and had little energy for dwelling upon things more fundamental. There seemed no longer any direct relation between them and faith in God. Then there were the many competing interests which had arisen as distractions from religion. Not the least of these was the growth of literacy and the multiplication of reading matter. The time when the Bible was almost the only book to be read had passed away before such rivals as the daily paper, the monthly magazine, and cheap editions of literature of all kinds, from the classics to modern fiction. And so the Bible was neglected a loss not only to the religious life of men and women, but to their intellectual life as well. One evidence of this loss was the disappearance of the antique idiom of the Scriptures which had given a quaint savour to the common speech of an older generation.

We have thus the beginnings of that spirit of indifference, which in our own day has reached such distressing proportions, when sport and the cinema, not to mention wireless and television, have come to play so important a part in the mind of the average man and woman, that more serious matters are crowded out, including religion itself. How different had it been in the Middle Ages when, as in Chaucer's time, the lengthening days of spring and summer had urged men to go on pilgrimage to Canterbury or other shrines; now they were wending their way to Brighton or Southend, to Blackpool or the Isle of Man. Those who still professed to be interested in religion were not taken very seriously by their neighbours; if they found it an attractive hobby that was their affair, and quite harmless, so long as it did not lead them to become censorious of other people. There was undoubtedly a danger that Christians themselves would aquiesce in such a condition, and the Church become merely 'a school of culture in the religious art for persons of leisure and education'.[1]

The Church, indeed, seemed curiously indifferent to the crisis which faced it, and its leaders not unduly alarmed by its loss of influence. The guardians of the established order are apt to be more disturbed by religious vagaries than by religious torpor, and so the 'Crisis in the Church', which provided headlines in the religious weeklies and even in the popular Press, was concerned, not with the things that really mattered, but with the interpretation of the Ornaments' Rubric.[2] This dispute was to rob the Church of England of one of the greatest and wisest of her bishops, for there can be little doubt that efforts to deal with it shortened the life of Mandell Creighton.

To suggest that interest in religion and the life of the spirit was confined to the organized denominations would, of course, be ridiculous; but such outside interest tended to move away from religion in its organized forms and to concentrate on its practical application and to ignore its dogmatic aspects. Philanthropy, not doctrine, seemed all important, and to strive to help others a sufficient expression of religious faith. There were also many sincere men and women who, finding themselves no longer able to make use of the ministrations of the Church in which they had been brought up, gradually drifted away.[3] Some form of Unitarianism might have satisfied them, but they were repelled by its ugliness and provincialism, and, ceasing to maintain contact with religion, they sought to fill their lives with other manifestations

[1] J. H. Skrine, *Pastor Futurus*, p. 10.

[2] The extent to which such disputes obscured the danger of attacks on the faith aroused the amazement of Randall Davidson, the future archbishop. See Bell, *Randall Davidson*, p. 153.

[3] In this they differed from many of an older generation: see above, pp. 11 ff.

of the spirit, such as art and music, and allied forms of non-material enterprise. Even the influence of Browning was declining, and literary critics of the younger generation, though they retained their admiration for his less intellectual poems with their emotional insight and glowing splendour of colour, could sneer at what they regarded as his morbid interest in religion.[1]

Yet there persisted with many of them a wistful looking back and a sense of something lacking. It can be seen in some of the poets,[2] and with a deeper sounding tone in Romanes's utterance:

> I am far from being able to agree with those who affirm that the twilight doctrine of the 'new faith' is a desirable substitute for the waning splendour of 'the old', I am not ashamed to confess that with this virtual negation of God, the universe to me has lost its soul of loveliness.[3]

Romanes, it may be noted, later recovered his faith, a not unexpected sequel to his earnest search. With some this 'nostalgic' feeling was probably little more than a pose; they found a morbid pleasure in hunting shadow-land for the lost ideals of their youth, or at best desired a 'religion' which would give them pleasurable sensations and at the same time make small demands on their conduct. *Sehnsucht* is one of the most parasitical of the emotions.

Of definite opposition to Christianity there was but little, and that of not much account. The real threat to the future of religion was contained, not in opposition, but in indifference. There was no widely organized movement to draw men away from the faith, but a collapse of belief in the hearts of individuals which penetrated into the very roots of society as a whole. People were not atheists in the technical sense, they did not deny the existence of God, but they ignored Him, save perhaps in some sudden emergency, and were content to live in a world in which He had no place. There were, of course, political extremists who saw in all religion an enemy of the people, one of the many devices of the

---

[1] It must not, however, be forgotten that Henry Jones's *Browning as a Religious and Philosophical Teacher* appeared in 1891.

[2] See above, p. 294.   [3] *A Candid Examination of Theism*, p. 114.

possessing classes to keep them under, or it might be a token ot middle-class respectability. But the great majority outside the Church bore it no enmity; they simply could not understand its meaning or what useful function it could play. Religion, in their eyes, was no longer a vital question and had become one of life's luxuries, not one of its necessities.

An impassioned opponent of natural selection had once exclaimed: 'Leave me my ancestors in Paradise, and I will grant you yours in the Zoological Gardens'; but the real danger came, not from ancestors in the Zoo, but from the growth of a feeling that man was merely a superior species of animal, bereft of any spiritual endowments. Where such a view is accepted it inevitably follows that man's endeavours will be confined to providing the race with what are in effect nothing more than the most convenient and hygenic cages. There lay the most destructive threat. Man was limiting his aspirations to the things of this life, and forgetting his eternal destiny; the steady growth of comfort and a feeling of security had weakened his moral and spiritual sinews. It is comfort, the object of the many, rather than luxury, which can be but the possession of the few, that is most insidious in hampering the pursuit of the ideal.[1]

This lethargic and complacent spirit had even invaded the religious world, and many of those who still conformed demanded a cheap and easy faith, a faith that would make little call upon them for self-denial or sacrifice. They expected to be provided, at little cost to themselves, with opportunities for the appropriate religious exercises, at suitable times, and in comfortable buildings. Their attitude recalls that summed up in the old Ionian proverb— they were content 'to worship God with other people's incense'.[2]

The relegation, by the great mass of the people, of religion to a region apart, the decay of the study of the Bible, and, in general, the weakening of the authority of the Church, had a grave and almost unforeseen consequence—the progressive

---

[1] Plato had foreseen the possibility that a time would come when mankind, content with material luxury and comfort, would miss the highest. (*Politicus*, 270 C.) [2] Cf. Pausanias, Bk. IX, Ch. xxx, § 1.

decline in the moral state of society. Those who, in the earlier days of our period had attacked Christian dogmas, had taken it for granted that Christian moral standards would still be observed, even after the removal of their supernatural sanctions. They failed to realize the extent to which moral ideals are dependent on fixed beliefs, or that a time would come when governments, alarmed by the moral state of society, might by their actions almost suggest that if God did not exist, it would be necessary to invent Him. In the case of the individual, lax morals often follow on the decay of belief, for the character 'having been integrated by the religious sentiment, collapses through the destruction of the belief in God'.[1] The same is also true of the community, for to take a merely pragmatic ideal as the basis of public morals is a hazardous device, since such an ideal is largely conditioned by the moral quality of the very society it is desired to elevate.[2]

The older generation, having repudiated Christianity as a dogmatic system, still clung to its ethical teaching; but by the close of the century that system was itself being called in question, and the religious basis of morality criticized in the name of scientific humanism. Such criticisms were welcomed, as also the prevailing uncertainty about the truths of Christianity, by not a few, who found in them a ready excuse for throwing off moral restraints which they had resented, although in the absence of this new teaching, had not dared overtly to defy. The last decade of the century saw a growth of 'levity, if not of laxity', which made the term 'the naughty nineties' no misnomer.[3]

Morality is a delicately balanced structure, the slow work of countless generations, and its foundations, like those of an actual building, lie well below the surface. The conventions which control it are ultimately the outcome of a rational process; but this process is so complex and so involved that it is never quite apparent, for it is the work of both society itself and of the

---

[1] McDougall, *Character and the Conduct of Life*, p. 114.

[2] Cf. Hastings Rashdall, *Philosophy and Religion*, p. 75: 'The tendency of all naturalistic Ethics is to make a God of public opinion.'

[3] G. M. Trevelyan, *English Social History*, p. 568.

individuals of which it is composed. So long as conventions are generally accepted they are powerful; but their basis is exceedingly precarious, and anything which seems to weaken the grounds upon which they rest, even when such grounds have never been consciously recognized by the bulk of mankind, may have serious consequences. The common folk, although they may not always conform to such conventions, accept them as part of the received notions of their day; being seldom capable of themselves formulating moral judgments they depend on what is customary and generally received.

Religious beliefs had aroused a sense of responsibility and of obligation in men, and given some kind of meaning to their lives. But the prevailing materialism was robbing religion of this power. Man was part of nature, but nature was apparently unaware of his separate existence and took no interest in him. Is it strange that those who embraced such views lost all sense of meaning or purpose in life, or that their wills became unstrung? At the same time the extension of the theory of physical evolution from the race to the individual undermined the sense of sin.[1] Sin, so-called, might be ignored as due to nothing more than the survival of animal instincts which would gradually be eliminated or overcome; in the meantime men could hardly be blamed for giving way to them.

It was, of course, but slowly that the effects of the change in outlook became manifest. For in these matters, as Oman has said, 'Habit and custom often confuse the issue. Men cannot rid themselves at once of old associations, old views, old habits.'[2] But such habits would in any event have been threatened by the growing complexity of existence. When a man's relations with his fellows are concerned with persons known to one another, as they are in small communities, they have binding force; but such force is often lost when vague and massive entities are in question. Hence, probably, the growing disrespect for law; which came to be regarded as something, whose objects and

---

[1] Nature, moreover, seemed indifferent to moral values.
[2] *Vision and Authority*, pp. 180f.

meaning they did not comprehend, imposed upon them from above.[1]

There is a further difficulty. Many offences against the moral ideal do not count as 'crimes', that is as acts which the law is prepared to punish; adultery, is a case in point, as is sexual immorality unless indulged in a manner calculated to attract public notice.

Another difficulty which hampers those who desire to maintain or elevate ethical standards is the odd fact that popular notions of what constitutes morality are so largely sentimental and emotional, and so seldom depend on principles. 'Generosity ranks far before justice, sympathy before truth, love before chastity, a pliant and obliging disposition before a rigidly honest one. In brief, the less admixture of intellect required for the practice of any virtue, the higher it stands in popular estimation.'[2]

As late as 1908 Dr. Figgis could maintain that a new spirit was at work, counteracting the doubts and hesitations of the Victorian era. But this was too optimistic a judgment, for it was true of a few finer spirits only, such as J. M. Keynes and his set,[3] who put before them 'the assertion of truth, the unveiling of illusion, the dissipation of hate, the enlargement of men's minds and hearts', as the things for which they were striving. Under the surface, and in the popular mind, there was in reality an alarming decay of the cultivation of ideals; and, in spite of outward peace and the prevalence of a spirit of self-complacency, the seeds of the coming tragic years were slowly maturing.

Notwithstanding their doubts and uncertainties over ultimate things the Victorians had been supremely confident in regard to worldly issues. Their material achievements had been such as no previous age had rivalled, and this had given them an optimism which, until the close of the era, seemed unassailable. Civilization

---

[1] Cf. Westcott, *The Incarnation and Common Life*, p. 33. 'Premature legislation is not only ineffective: it is demoralizing. It brings the majesty of law into disregard.'

[2] C. F. G. Masterman, *The Condition of England*, p. 115.

[3] Keynes went up to Cambridge in 1903, and was deeply influenced by G. E. Moore. See his memoir, *My Early Beliefs*.

was not yet at the cross-roads, and any notion that its survival might be threatened was remote from their minds. But by the end of our period this boundless confidence was beginning to show signs of wear, as if the weariness of a dying epoch had come upon it. In the early years of the century the French Revolution had caused a flood of optimism to flow over all Europe, but it had long ago lost its momentum. One of its effects had been to undermine the unity, far from complete it is true, which was based on religion. Even in Matthew Arnold's poetic period this had become obvious:

> The glow of central fire is done
> Which with its fusing flame
> Knit all your parts, and kept you one.

Pessimism was slowly invading the scene, and Sanday, preaching before Oxford University on 21 October 1894, declared that, 'Even among the leaders in literature and thought, there is plenty of pessimism.'[1]

Then came the shock of the sudden outbreak of the South African War, with its early reverses. War had seemed so remote, but now it had raised its head amidst a world which seemed so secure and so comfortable; and for many it brought disillusionment, and began that disintegration of the settled state of things which two world wars have hastened so drastically. Its effects told most severely upon the few disinterested and noble spirits whose ideals seemed to be challenged and threatened, and they led to a loss of faith and hope. For those who have lived through one or both of the great world wars these have become landmarks, and we commonly speak of 'before the war' as of a different epoch in our lives. Though, so far as I can recall, this expression was never used of the Boer War, its significance must not be underrated, coming as it did without previous warning. It gave Bishop Gore the opportunity, preaching on the last day of the century, to deliver, what his biographer has called, 'a most despondent sermon on the hollowness of modern progress'.[2]

[1] Printed in *Inspiration*, p. 437.　　[2] G. L. Prestige, *Life of Charles Gore*, p. 225.

But the bishop was right in his judgment, for the popular belief in inevitable progress was a mere superstition, without justification in either history or science. Science itself, in the person of Huxley, had indeed already dealt the notion a shrewd blow when, in the Romanes Lecture for 1893, he affirmed that there was nothing in natural science to support it. The mind of the populace, and some more informed who might have known better, confused progress with movement and change; they did not ask whither they were 'progressing', being content to follow a devious path towards an unknown goal. This attitude is seen in the teaching of Walt Whitman, which someone has paraphrased: 'I have urged you forward, and still urge you, without the slightest idea of our destination.'

The dangers and deceptiveness of such an outlook had been exposed already by Westcott. 'Change, even if it is popular, is not necessarily progress, nor movement however rapid, . . . the test of progress is character.'[1] This judgment recalls the distinction drawn by Theodore Watts-Dunton—a shrewd critic of humanity as well as of literature—between a genuine and a bastard civilization. The former results in a widening and enriching of human life; the latter is little more than the invention of fictitious wants and the means of supplying them, it adds nothing to man's stature and leaves him discontented and poorer than ever, with new desires and longings for which there can be no permanent satisfaction.[2]

The Boer War had indeed given a shock to the self-conceit of Englishmen, and 'it was a somewhat sobered John Bull who picked himself up off the pavement the morning after the Mafeking debauch'.[3] But the effects wore off, and a renewed spirit of confidence, though in a modified form, soon returned. It seemed to be justified by the uninterrupted flood of new inventions and new means of adding to the comforts of living, and, most impressive of all, trade and commerce were booming.

---

[1] *Lessons from Work*, pp. 387, 396.
[2] James Douglas, *Theodore Watts-Dunton*, p. 71.
[3] G. M. Trevelyan, *British History in the Nineteenth Century 1782–1901*, p. 426.

The material prosperity upon which so many vaunted themselves, like Tyre of old, was, however, a structure full of flaws, and these at any time might bring about its collapse; those social injustices which a somewhat tardy legislation had done little to mitigate, the spirit of competition, and the scramble for international markets. Looking back we can clearly discern the gulf between the situation as it actually was, and the way in which men, apart from a few thinkers and social reformers, continued to regard it.

But it was not only in the commercial and economic world that there were gaps between the real situation and what men imagined it to be; similar gaps in theology and religion were also to be found. It might, indeed, be said with some truth that theology and religion were moving apart. On the one hand there was little comprehension on the part of the average clergyman or minister of what was being done by theologians; and, on the other, many of the clergy and ministers held views which they were chary of proclaiming in their naked truth to their congregations. Most of them were too solidly immersed in practical work to have much time for reading after they had left the university or theological college, and such reading as they fitted in was often confined to the occasional perusal of small handbooks or of some favourite religious journal. Even those who wished to continue their studies were handicapped by the inability to acquire the necessary books and by the absence of appropriate direction. Help was, indeed, forthcoming for some, from Clerical Reading Societies, Dr. Bray's Library, and, after 1899, the Central Society for Sacred Study.

Those who, in spite of all difficulties and discouragements, were successful in keeping up their reading, often felt themselves out of touch with the learned world. Scholars were so fond of using technical terms and of writing in a heavy and unattractive style, possibly reminiscent of the days when it was thought that all serious subjects could only be worthily discussed in Latin. They seemed to fear that any lightness of touch might suggest a flippant approach, and did not realize that to be profound one

24

need not always be ponderous. The literary artist often strives in vain for 'the grace of a perfect utterance'; writers on learned subjects, and theologians among them, might seem to suppose that such an attempt was beneath the dignity of their theme. Theology, after all, was the queen of the sciences, and she ought to be presented in a becoming garb, and not left, like some poor Cinderella, in her working clothes.

Another difficulty was that the outlook of theologians seemed to have so little relation to life, and failed to deal with the problems that confronted those engaged in ministerial work. Men of scholarly mind, as they brood beside 'their studious lamps', may be tempted to regard theology as an abstract science which raises interesting problems for the mind and to forget their practical issues; some theologians, indeed, arouse the suspicion that they prefer complex to simple explanations, and invent difficulties in order to demonstrate their skill in meeting them.[1]

Such an attitude of mind ignores the fact that for the majority of believers uncertainty in matters of faith may be a grievous hardship; for them, at least, there is urgent need of 'some sure song in the dark, some story against fear'. But religion must have its foundations in truth; and if the truths enunciated by scholars seem to deal mainly with matters remote from practical and pastoral concerns, in reality they are concerned with fundamentals, and can only be ignored to the ultimate hurt of religion as a whole; 'little profit brings speed in the van and blindness in the rear'.

If the gap between theology and religion was harmful to the faith—for beliefs, in the absence of intellectual scrutiny, may easily degenerate into superstitions—it was not without drawbacks for theology, since 'theology, however much it may be a matter for revelation in the sources of its knowledge, must be a science of experience in putting its truth to the test'.[2] The same is true, also, of the theologian. A scholar may have a comprehensive and profound knowledge of theology, but if his religious life is

---

[1] Coleridge, *Aids to Reflection* Aphorism LX, had asserted that theological studies are 'alike defective when pursued *without* increase of knowledge, and when pursued chiefly *for* increase of knowledge'.

[2] Oman, *Vision and Authority*, p. 190.

defective his work as a scholar may be handicapped, and his personal faith become dimmed. 'I am not a theologian', wrote Duchesne to Von Hügel, 'that is why I can praise God with joy', and, he wickedly added, *Non mortui laudabunt te, Domine, sed nos qui vivimus*.[1] One reason why theologians are often out of touch with the life of the Church in general is that most of those engaged in the study are attached to universities, and it is easy for them to get into the habit of regarding themselves as members of an academic society rather than as teachers responsible to a Church.

Thus the danger is twofold. On the one hand, theology may develop into a mere abstract science, devoid of life, and incomprehensible to the simple and unthinking who form the great bulk of believers; and, on the other hand, for these latter religion may sink down into nothing more than a ritual exercise, the participating in rites and ceremonies whose exact significance and utility they understand but dimly.

If there was a gap between the study and the pulpit there was an equally dangerous gulf between the pulpit and the pew.[2] This arose from two not unrelated causes. Preachers who could no longer accept certain doctrines in their traditional form nor make use of the traditional language, were prone to confine their sermons to such matters as they still held in common with their people, and, it might be, limit themselves to instruction on practical life. By others, reserve was deliberately exercised; so as not to upset the faith of simple souls who had no idea of the difficulties raised by the progress of science and of biblical criticism and were incapable of understanding discussions concerning them. But whilst it may be true that the majority of churchgoers are simple folk, conservative in their outlook and uninterested in the nicer points of theology, there are others of the better educated who are attracted by them. Many of the latter were vaguely aware that the Church's teaching, especially as based on

---

[1] Cf. the remark of John Smith, the Cambridge Platonist, 'To seek our divinity merely in books and writings, is to seek the living among the dead.' (*Select Discourses*, p. 5.)

[2] See some interesting comments on this in Hamilton, *The People of God*, Vol. I, pp. xx ff.

the Bible, was being questioned, but they were ignorant of the meaning of such attacks and of their extent and scope. They therefore felt that they had a right to look to the pulpit for guidance and information on such matters, and for suggestions as to the reinterpretations of the faith which seemed to be involved in the discovery of fresh truths.

For the Church to be silent over its fundamental doctrines and to restrict its preaching to ethics, would be a dereliction of duty, which could not fail to lower still further its prestige. It may be true that the main object of preaching, apart from special courses, is to promote a worthy Christian life; but to live such a life the enabling grace of the Holy Spirit is necessary, and the whole endeavour must be firmly rooted in truth. Strictly speaking the simplest practical instruction, for the Christian minister must involve ultimate ideas. Henry Drummond, in addressing a theological society in Glasgow, put forward the view that the reason why the Gospel had lost much of its old appeal was because its preaching was unsuited to the age, a new 'Evangelism' was needed, an Evangelism based on the new outlook in theology.[1] Bishop Creighton, though fully aware of the position, did not consider that such questions were suitable for discussion in the pulpit during the ordinary services of the Church;[2] whilst Frederick Temple thought that the proper course was 'to preach sermons in which the true conception is presupposed, but not definitely stated, then people who think will find it out and be benefited, and those who do not think will not be unduly disturbed'.[3]

A preacher may, of course, take the line that his congregation is not yet fitted to absorb the new ideas, or he may, if he himself holds conservative views, consider that in desiring to know more about them they are committing a sin. Such an attitude, however, seems not in accord with the relation of preacher and congregation in modern times; though it was the view of St. Anselm, who saw

---

[1] *The New Evangelism*, pp. 3 ff.
[2] *The Church and the Nation*, p. 91.
[3] Sandford, *Frederick Temple, an Appreciation*, p. 305.

in the Fall of Adam and Eve a punishment for attempting to acquire knowledge prematurely, and by unlawful means.

Any kind of economy in handling the truth may have unfortunate consequences; for it may foster the idea either that the clergy preach things which they no longer believe, or that they are unable to meet the difficulties occasioned by the advance of knowledge. Congregations have often a much greater awareness of such difficulties than those who minister to them suppose, for they become acquainted with them through reading the newspapers and in other ways. In 1890 Archbishop Benson was amazed to discover that a group of highly educated Churchwomen whom he was instructing were dubious about the authorship of the fourth gospel, uncertain as to whether we know much about the life of our Lord, and not at all willing to accept the personality of the Holy Ghost.[1] So, too, C. F. G. Masterman, writing a little later than 1900, could affirm that 'definite statements of the average belief, set out in black and white by the average congregation, would astonish the average preacher'.[2]

The matter is certainly beset with problems. No one, of course, has any right to teach doctrines which he himself cannot accept as true; but, on the other hand, as the representative of a Church, he may feel justified in handing on its official teaching on matters about which he is uncertain.[3] In the latter case, however, his message will lack the energy and conviction which alone can bring it home to his hearers. Divided in himself he will remain divided from his people, unless, indeed, he assumes an air of assurance which he does not fully feel; as a medical man has often to give the impression, in order not to arouse misgivings in a patient, that he understands a case about which he may be completely puzzled. There is a further difficulty. The preacher, in his desire not to hurt the feelings of the older and simpler people, may impart to his younger hearers views which they will

---

[1] *Life of E. W. Benson*, Vol. II, p. 299.   [2] *The Condition of England*, p. 18.
[3] Morley, in *Compromise*, attacked the intellectual honesty of men who, when ordained at twenty-three, committed themselves more or less blindly to the acceptance of certain positions, not knowing what the future may bring in the way of new knowledge and experience.

inevitably be compelled to abandon in the light of fuller knowledge. If so, he will be the cause of unnecessary doubt and
unsettlement, and even alienate the rising generation.

Considerations such as these, although they may involve
problems for the preacher, do not affect the theologian, who is
bound to proclaim the truth as he sees it, whatever may be the
consequences. Temporary doubt and unsettlement are inevitably
the lot of those who demand a faith of their own, and are not
content merely to accept what they have been told. Creighton,
in his younger days, held that 'unintelligent acquiescence in
opinions, though these might be true, was immoral and
dangerous'.[1]

In the closing years of the century there was still much
obscurantism, due in part to the mental cowardice which seeks
refuge in conventions and in part to the intellectual stagnation
which is unwilling to think things out afresh. Those who clung
to outworn interpretations were in danger of turning the Church
into a museum of antiquities, and of robbing doctrines, which
once had engendered life, of all meaning and potency. Growth
involves the full exercise and use of powers already possessed,
and not their careful preservation in a napkin. The spirit of
conservatism was indeed rife, and that not only among the
clergy. Many of the laity were well represented by Oscar Wilde's
Lord Murchison who was 'the stoutest of Tories, and believed in
the Pentateuch as firmly as he believed in the House of Peers'.

The whole situation naturally aroused the deep concern of all
who were anxious to adjust the faith to the new conditions and
saw in them a fresh opportunity for advance.

> It is impossible when we look at the subjects and methods of current
> controversy not to ask ourselves sadly whether we ourselves are
> busy in building the tomb of Christ (cf. Matthew 23 : 29 f.), or really
> ready to recognize Him if He comes to us in the form of new
> life. . . . Men cling almost desperately to traditional phrases and
> customs [and] forget the call of Christ to occupy new regions of
> thought and labour in His name.[2]

[1] *Life*, Vol. I, p. 36.   [2] Westcott, *The Revelation of the Risen Lord*, pp. 27 f.

The position of the obscurantists had as its basis a general distrust of reason, 'a sentiment of jealousy towards intelligence as something not wholly good in its nature'.[1] For some of them it involved the deliberate attempt to suppress or conceal knowledge, and, whether through ignorance or malice, even the misrepresentation of the views of those whose conclusions were in conflict with traditional notions. They clung obstinately to their old ideas in the face of an encroaching world, a world which they did not attempt to understand, but which they felt to be a threat to all that they held dear.

To condemn all the defenders of strict orthodoxy as blind opponents of what was new, merely because it was new, would be unjust. There were sound reasons for their state of alarm; for ideas were being put forth by some adventurous theologians, which they or their less well-informed followers were pleased to call 'assured results' (a better description would have been 'probable hypotheses'), which could not fail to arouse suspicion and disquiet. They were shocked and antagonized by being called upon to abandon teaching which had proved so effective in the past, and even in the present was still producing results. This was, of course, especially true of the Evangelicals and their scheme of salvation. After all what the ordinary man so sorely needed was not up-to-date knowledge, but forgiveness and power. Hence Canon Ainger's protest:

> With eager knife that oft has sliced
> At Gentile gloss or Jewish fable,
> Before the crowd you lay the Christ
> Upon the Lecture table.

> From bondage to the old beliefs
> You say our rescue must begin—
> But *I*—want refuge from my griefs,
> And saving from my sin.[2]

[1] Mark Pattison. For a vigorous attack on the obscurantist position see his *Sermons* (1885) especially pp. 138f.
[2] 'On reading a Volume of Modern Sermons.'

There was certainly much to be said for them on this score, for theologically trained clergymen and ministers seemed unable to reach the lowest and most degraded elements of the population, whereas the 'hot gospel' of the Salvation Army with its stern and unbending orthodoxy was certainly doing so, converting drunkards and criminals and sending them forth to save their late associates. A tacit recognition of the failure of the new ideas to advance spiritual life was contained in Fairbairn's comment: 'It is neither said nor meant that our age is distinguished by a deeper reverence or purer love for the Redeemer, or even a stronger faith in Him. In these respects we might claim pre-eminence for other ages than our own.'[1]

If the majority of those who still clung to old-fashioned views did so because they found that they still worked, and if few of them had any competent knowledge of the position of those whom they condemned, they were not entirely without more learned support. In 1888 Bishop John Wordsworth, a really able scholar it need hardly be said, had declared that if the accepted date and authorship of the Pentateuch were given up there would be a decay of faith in the Gospel among the public. Later he came to modify his views of the Old Testament, though he never accepted modern views of the New.[2] Wordsworth himself was quite unaffected by the intellectual difficulties of the times, and he could never understand why they should affect others. Another learned prelate, C. J. Ellicott, Bishop of Gloucester, in his charge of 1891 declared that 'any attempt to utilize the critical view of the Old Testament for the sake of helping the distressed faith of a few, may end, we had almost said, must end, in endangering the faith, and it may be, the salvation of thousands'.[3]

But obscurantism was not the monopoly of orthodox Christians. In Lord Keynes' memoirs there is a description of an atmosphere in which the non-existence of God and the falsity of Christianity were so much taken for granted that any thought

---

[1] *The Place of Christ in Modern Theology*, p. 19.
[2] See E. W. Watson, *Life of Bishop John Wordsworth*, p. 189.
[3] *Christus Comprobator*, p. 190.

even of discussing them would have seemed ridiculous. This summary dismissal of Christianity and much of its teaching was due in large measure to the persistent notion that believers still accepted in their literal sense myths and legends which had been exploded by the advance of knowledge. Even today it is commonly imagined that the Church believes in verbal inspiration, hell fire, and a material heaven 'with streets of shining gold',[1] as well as the miracles of the Old Testament.

People no longer thought in biblical terms and images, but in those derived from natural science;[2] and though Christian theology might be, in the words of Lily Dougall, 'the greatest of all the structural growths of human thought about God and man',[3] it was in danger of being misunderstood and neglected because written in a dead language. 'What is an interpretation for one age, becomes "a tongue not understood" in the next. Hence when a revival of religious life comes, it frequently shows itself in an attack on the received theology.'[4]

There was thus a twofold work for Christian Apologetics. On the one hand its representatives had to defend the faith against the extreme ideas of heterodox scholars, and in so doing to enter into regions far beyond the comprehension of those untrained in any theological discipline; on the other they had to consider the simple folk who cherished mistaken ideas of the Gospel and were easily misled by superficial and inaccurate criticisms of Christianity. The need for this type of defence seems to have been especially pressing in Scotland, where Robertson Smith, writing in the 'seventies, declared that

> our whole theological literature, even when not apologetical in subject, is impregnated with an apologetical flavour; that the most popular commentaries, the most current works of doctrine, do little

---

[1] Many popular ideas of what Christianity stands for are derived from hymns, which, it need hardly be said, no longer represent its outlook, though still retained in its worship.

[2] See above, pp. 48 f.

[3] In *Immortality*, p. 357.

[4] A. L. Moore in *Lux Mundi*, p. 64.

or nothing to carry theology forward to new results, and direct all
their energy to the refutation of attacks from without.[1]

But this was a wasteful method, and not a very effective one,
for as Hort had said 'in order to preserve and restore it is necessary
to advance'.[2] Apologists accordingly sought new methods, and
in place of seeking to meet criticisms in detail, as the evidence of
witnesses in a law court is weighed and assessed, endeavoured to
defend it on the widest grounds. Here their task was made harder
by the prevailing scepticism or uncertainty over certain fundamental beliefs which Christians shared with others who had a
religious outlook.[3]

Perhaps the most helpful line of approach was to show that
Christianity was able to offer an explanation of the scheme of
things, and to meet the religious needs of mankind. In 1891
Westcott collected a number of essays, written in earlier years,
and published them under the title of *Religious Thought in the
West*. The object of the volume was to show how the hopes and
desires, and even the errors of early Western teachers, pointed
forward to the Gospel as satisfying man's natural aspirations, and
as illuminating the dark places of his life. 'The Faith welcomes
all truth, while it supplements external lessons by its own peculiar
witness, and places partial and limited expressions of truth in their
right relations to one another and to the whole.' (*Op. cit.*, p. vi).
The object of this attempt was to combine the traditional teaching
of the Church with what had become known through the
advances in secular knowledge, and at the same time to preserve
the peculiar essence of the Gospel message.[4] This was the only
effective policy; for any religion which is to retain its vitality
must be perpetually renewed and reinvigorated by the new truths

---

[1] *Lectures and Essays*, p. 315.   [2] *The Way, the Truth, the Life*, p. 24.
[3] 'It is, I believe, more and more coming to be true that men's attitude
towards Christianity is determined mainly by their attitude towards Theism.'
(Hastings Rashdall in *Contentio Veritatis*, p. 3.)
[4] Cf. Bosanquet, *The Principle of Individuality and Value*, 'all logical activity is
a world of content reshaping itself by its own spirit and laws in the presence of
new suggestions'. (p. 333.)

which God Himself is ever disclosing. To reject them is to suffer intellectual, and even spiritual, impoverishment.

The most important qualification for apologists is an intimate acquaintance with the contemporary situation in all its relevant aspects; otherwise their efforts will be as futile as those of an anti-aircraft battery which continues firing at objects which have passed outside its range. It is important, too, that apologists, so far as is possible, should avoid the appearance of being mere advocates of a cause; though the fact that they have belief in what they affirm should be no bar to a sympathetic hearing; a witness, after all, is not disqualified by an honest conviction that he is bearing testimony to the truth. It is, however, easy for an apologist to take on the guise of a special pleader; in which case he will throw himself open to the suspicion of selecting from the new knowledge only such material as will serve his purpose, instead of unconditionally applying it as a whole. Absolute honesty in the restatement of the faith was essential, and, where necessary, the confession of ignorance.

There was thus an urgent need for theological leadership, and for the presentation of Christian beliefs and the Christian way of life, in such a manner that they would be understood and appreciated, not only by the highly educated, but also by ordinary folk, for they too have their intellectual difficulties. Many of them, moreover, had become vaguely aware that much in Christianity as popularly understood was being criticized by the learned, and in the absence of skilful guidance were in danger of confusing its permanent elements with the transient forms in which they had been embodied. Some form of restatement was demanded which would bring not only intellectual satisfaction to the educated, but also enlightenment and reassurance to the simple, and, avoiding exact and minute definitions of the lesser mysteries of the faith, would concentrate on essentials.

It has, however, to be admitted that theologians did not rise fully to meet the needs of the situation, though a great deal more was being done than is commonly supposed. Dr. Lock ended his inaugural lecture at Oxford in 1896 with these words: 'There is at the present moment no sphere of study, unless it be that of natural science, in which there is so much of movement, of progress, of fresh light, and so certain assurance that toil will meet with its due reward.'[1] Henry Drummond, writing five years earlier, had stated his conviction that even the bewilderment of doubt was a price worth paying for 'the stimulus of working in an age when theology is no longer stagnant, but the most living of all the sciences'.[2]

But though many new books were produced by theologians, their efforts were largely unco-ordinated and dispersed, and much of their writing was in the nature of supplying mere palliatives intended to meet temporary needs. There was in theology a lack of proper organization, and an absence of any long-term or comprehensive policy. In this matter the theologian differs from the artist and is nearer allied to the scientist. The artist may derive benefit from working alone and in secret until his masterpiece is completed; the scientist gains by sharing even the most slender of his hypotheses with fellow scientists. Theology, like science, is best advanced by the pooling of resources. The nearest approach to such a combined enterprise was in the group of scholars who produced *Lux Mundi*, and that was only made possible through the presence, in and near Oxford, of a number of remarkable men.

When placed alongside the growing richness of religious experience theology was comparatively barren. In other words the intellectual presentation of the Christian faith was not keeping pace with its practical and emotional expressions. Theology is 'the history of the Church's soul. The work of the theologian . . . is to keep the record up to date.'[3] But to keep the record up to date is no easy task; thought is ever in arrear of life, and as Hegel has put it, 'the owl of Minerva does not start upon its flight until the evening twilight has begun to fall'.

Theologians were undoubtedly overcautious. It may be that

[1] *The Bible and Christian Life*, p. 96.
[2] *The New Evangelism*, p. 47.
[3] J. H. Skrine, *Pastor Futurus*, p. 141.

they feared, if they were members of the Church, the condemnation of the ecclesiastical authorities, or even popular outcry,
if they were too venturesome. There were, however, other
causes at work to account for their caution. There is real danger
in an age when all things are in a state of fluidity, and when the
hidden watersprings of feeling and emotion are breaking through
the crust of conventional life, that changes may be made in
religion and theology which, though seemingly wise and progressive, will in the end lead only to loss and the painful return
to older paths. Then again, in that age of specialization theologians were conscious of the inadequacy of their knowledge.
Theology was no longer the queen of the sciences as once she
had been, for her subjects had proved unruly, and she herself was
apt to stand aloof from other studies. But 'an isolated theology
is no living theology, and . . . without frank interchange of
thought between the theologian and investigators in all other
fields of knowledge theology ceases to be of interest'.[1] This was
the opinion of Hort, who wished that all studies should be
permeated by theology, and that theology should permeate all
other studies. For this reason he opposed the setting up of a
Theological Tripos.[2]

In England, however, an interest in theology was much more
widespread among students of other subjects than on the
Continent, as Sanday pointed out in the introduction to his
Bampton Lectures:

> We may count it as one of the happiest of English traditions, and
> in fact the main compensation for the backwardness of much of our
> theology proper, that a [class of highly trained and intelligent laity]
> has never ceased to take an active interest in all matters connected
> with religion.[3]

There was one man who might have undertaken the task of
restatement with some prospect of success, and that was Hort
himself; for his knowledge covered a very wide field, or number
of fields. But he was strangely tongue-tied, in spite of many

---

[1] Storr, p. 12.　　　[2] *Life*, Vol. I, p. 63.　　　[3] *Inspiration*, p. xiii.

appeals,[1] and his only major contribution, the Hulsean Lectures for 1871, was not published until after his death. After their delivery he made many additions and alterations, but no finally satisfactory form had, in his eyes, been achieved. Even so *The Way, the Truth, the Life*, is one of the most valuable and suggestive theological works produced in England during our period. Although it passes by in silence what was being done or had been done by others, it is obvious that there was little of which Hort had not taken full account, little which he had not assimilated and made his own. The volume is so packed with wisdom and learning, so compressed, that only those who read it with intense concentration can hope to gain a full appreciation of its merits. There is in it little that on the surface deals directly with contemporary problems, for Hort chose to raise the discussion of such difficulties to a higher plane, to appeal to great and abiding principles, and so to suggest the lines along which they would find their ultimate solution. The outstanding value of *The Way, the Truth, the Life* lies not in the provision of facile answers to current criticisms of the faith, but in the setting forth of a point of view or method by which truth as a whole is to be apprehended. It was perhaps the strongest conviction in Hort's mind that truth was an organic whole, and that all truth must at last meet in Christ.[2] The approaches to truth are so varied and so numberless, and none can be neglected without loss, that caution and restraint are inevitable; and so Hort felt unable to give complete expression to the measure of truth to which he thought he had attained. He regarded himself as still a learner, but a learner who had his steps on the right way, even if his progress along it had been but slight and tentative. Many therefore found

---

[1] Cf. *Life*, Vol. II, pp. 370f. 'Hort suffered much distress from the growing feeling that on the highest debated question of the time he had much to say, but could not say it.' Sanday in *The Contemporary Review* for July 1889 had appealed to him to break silence, but he was unable to respond.

[2] Storr has said of him: 'No one understood more clearly . . . that truth enters the mind of man by many avenues, and that the ripest thought and the clearest illumination come only to those who seek to see truth in its many-sidedness, and to grow into its fulness.' (*Development and Divine Purpose*, p. 2.)

his method unsatisfactory, for it seemed to raise problems and to leave them unsolved. But Hort was himself aware of this limitation, and, indeed, rejoiced over it, declaring that if the lectures did not suggest more questions than they answered their intention was not fulfilled (p. xxxv).

The close of the period, and the first years of the twentieth century, was characterized by a decline of interest in pure theology. In biblical studies there was too great a concentration on the text of documents and their linguistic and historical aspects, a necessary stage, no doubt, if firm foundations were to be laid, but one which robbed theology of much of its vitality. In acknowledging the gift of Moule's inaugural lecture as Norrisian Professor of Divinity in 1899, Gwatkin wrote: 'I think that our Cambridge school is getting too much absorbed in prolegomena and literary details and needs a call to higher and wider things.'[1] In the same year Pringle-Pattison, a sympathetic observer, had written to Hastings Rashdall: 'The surprising thing is that in the great Church of England there is so little of the leaven of thinking Christianity. And it has so good an historical title to exist in the Anglican Church with its Cambridge School of Christian Platonists.'[2]

One cause of the decay of Anglican learning was the steep decline in the number of clerical 'dons' in the universities. So long as fellowships had been largely confined to the clergy learning was necessarily cultivated by them, and in it not a few saw a definite means of fulfilling their ministry. Another cause was the growing tendency to use residentiary canonries in cathedrals, not for the promotion of scholars, but as a means of subsidizing diocesan officials. The process began earlier than is sometimes realized, for in 1869 there was a proposal that one canonry out of four in every cathedral should be abolished in order to endow suffragan bishoprics. Behind these lesser causes, however, lay one that was more fundamental, the fact that not many of the clergy were deeply interested in theology as a science. The period

[1] Harford and Macdonald, *Bishop Handley Moule*, p. 153.
[2] Quoted Matheson, *The Life of Hastings Rashdall*, pp. 92 f.

had seen much admirable activity in the parishes, and a great extension of social work and of missionary endeavour, and these had absorbed the whole energies of a number of able men who might have made a real contribution to learning. Among Anglo-Catholics the intellectual expression of the faith had for many ardent souls been subordinated to its expression in ceremonial.

There is another circumstance which militated against any truly comprehensive restatement of the faith—theology had no underlying, agreed philosophy. English theologians had always maintained an aloof and even suspicious attitude towards philosophy; though this had been a little modified during the later years of our period, as the advantages of reconciliation between them had been realized. 'Philosophy and religion have both been enriched by wider knowledge, and as their knowledge has become deeper and fuller, the adjustment of their claims has become more imperatively necessary.'[1] None the less the gulf remained largely unbridged.

This, however, was not so serious a deprivation as it might have been, since philosophy itself was going through a state of considerable confusion. In France there had been a strong reaction from the dogmatic assumptions of Positivism, and by the close of the century philosophers everywhere were striving to liberate themselves from its tyranny. Philosophy, moreover, had, like theology, failed to assimilate much of the new knowledge; whilst the warfare between its antagonistic schools had lowered its prestige. For philosophers, in the words of Professor Caldecott, the century was 'closing in a mood of depression through our failure to secure a commanding and dominant result . . . after so much mental activity'.[2]

For theology, too, the century was closing with its tasks unfulfilled, though the extent of the failure of the liberal experiment had not yet been realized. But if the accomplishments of liberalism had been negative in the main, they had not been entirely unserviceable, for reconstruction ever involves some

---

[1] A. L. Moore in *Lux Mundi*, p. 80.
[2] *The Philosophy of Religion*, p. v.

destruction of the old; and there were not lacking a few enlightened souls who were aware of this:

> I looked and lo! 'mid the decay,
>   The Waster was the Builder too;
> And when the dust-cloud rolled away,
>   I saw the new.

Doubt and uncertainty might be distressing and seem utterly
harmful, but as Keats has reminded us 'a season of mists' may also
be one of 'mellow fruitfulness'. Theology was, indeed, going
through an Autumn period, and there was urgent need for
patience and suspension of judgment in many matters. The flow
of knowledge must neither be dammed up, nor allowed an
uncontrolled course. If some beliefs which seemed an integral
part of the faith were in jeopardy, there was nothing new in such
a circumstance; the thing had happened before, and later ages,
as they looked back, had seen even in the abandonment of some
of them the good hand of their God leading them on to a truer
knowledge of Himself.

So theologians did not 'begin to droop and drowse', but faced
their problems and difficulties with sober confidence and in no
spirit of despair. One of the wisest and most learned of Christian
leaders in modern times, even though not himself a theologian
in the strict sense of the term, could say: 'whatever may be the
features of the present time, we have to seek in them, not
hindrances, but opportunities'.[1] Such problems and difficulties
were, for those who were not bound hand and foot by a stereo-
typed tradition, new occasions for demonstrating the comprehensiveness of the faith and of illuminating fresh aspects of divine
truth. 'It is through difficulties fearlessly met that we are led to
wider knowledge. We condemn ourselves to dead ignorance if
we refuse to take account of them ... difficulties mark the
direction of progress.'[2] A reasoned optimism is the inalienable

---

[1] Creighton, *The Church and the Nation*, p. 24.
[2] Westcott, *Christus Consummator*, p. 100.

birthright of the Christian, for it is founded on the history of the past and the constant teaching of the Scriptures.[1] The frustration of merely human efforts is a call to a deeper reliance on what is superhuman, and a closer union with the divine.

[1] Cf. R. W. Church, *The Gifts of Civilisation*, p. 76, 'it is the peculiarity of the Bible that, whatever may be the aspect of the past and the present, in spite of all glories of what we look back to, and all discouragements in what we see now, it ever claims the future for its own'.

SELECT BIBLIOGRAPHY

To record even a fraction of the innumerable works which appeared during the period, quite apart from later studies dealing with it in whole or in part, would demand an amount of space which cannot here be afforded. The list which follows consists mainly of works which I have myself found particularly useful; many of them, incidentally, include lists of further authorities. Valuable articles with bibliographies, on practically all the subjects considered in the present volume appear in *The Encyclopaedia of Religion and Ethics* (1908 to 1926) and some also in *The Encyclopaedia Britannica*.

Storr, in addition to a general list, provided lists of authorities for the various chapters. I have preferred to arrange them all in a single list under the names of the authors, thus avoiding some needless repetition, for many of the works refer to more than one chapter; at the same time mention has been made in each several chapter of the most important authorities dealing with its special subject or subjects with additional references in the footnotes.

In quoting authorities I have made use of abbreviations, but these will easily be recognized.

ABBOTT AND CAMPBELL. *The Life and Letters of Benjamin Jowett* (1897).
ALBEE, E. *A History of English Utilitarianism* (1902).
ALLEN, A. V. G. *The Continuity of Christian Thought* (1895).
Authority and Archaeology: Sacred and Profane, ed. D. G. Hogarth (1899).
BALFOUR, A. J. *The Foundations of Belief* (1895).
BENSON, A. C. *The Life of E. W. Benson* (1899).
BLACK AND CHRYSTAL. *William Robertson Smith* (1912).
CAIRD, EDWARD. *The Evolution of Religion* (1892).
CAIRD, JOHN. *Introduction to the Philosophy of Religion* (1891).
Cambridge Biblical Essays, ed. H. B. Swete (1909).
Cambridge Theological Essays, ed. H. B. Swete (1905).
CHEYNE, T. K. *The Founders of Old Testament Criticism* (1893).

CHURCH, MARY C. *The Life and Letters of Dean Church* (1897).

CHURCH, R. W. *The Gifts of Civilisation* (1889).

Contentio Veritatis by Six Oxford Tutors (1902).

COOK, S. A. *The Study of Religions* (1914).

CORNISH, F. WARRE. *A History of the English Church in the Nineteenth Century*, Part II (1910).

CREIGHTON, LOUISE. *The Life and Letters of Mandell Creighton* (1904).

CREIGHTON, MANDELL. *The Church and the Nation* (1901).

DALE, A. W. W. *The Life of R. W. Dale of Birmingham* (1898).

DALE, R. W. *The Atonement* (1875).

DARWIN, FRANCIS. *The Life and Letters of Charles Darwin* (1887).

ELLIOTT-BINNS, L. E. *Religion in the Victorian Era* (1936 etc.).

Essays on the Early History of the Church and the Ministry, ed. H. B. Swete (1918).

FAIRBAIRN, A. M. *The Place of Christ in Modern Theology* (1893).

FARRAR, F. W. *The History of Interpretation* (1886).

FRAZER, JAMES. *The Golden Bough* (1890 etc.).

GOOCH, G. P. *History and Historians in the Nineteenth Century* (1913).

GORE, CHARLES. *The Body of Christ* (1901 etc.).

  The Incarnation (1891 etc.).

HARFORD AND MACDONALD. *Bishop Handley Moule* (1922).

HATCH, EDWIN. *The Influence of Greek Ideas and Usages upon the Christian Church* (1890).

  On the Organization of the Church (1881).

HORT, A. F. *The Life and Letters of F. J. A. Hort* (1896).

HORT, F. J. A. *The Christian Ecclesia* (1897).

  The Way, the Truth, the Life (1908).

HOWARD, W. F. *The Fourth Gospel in Recent Research and Criticism* (1931 etc.).

HUNT, J. *Religious Thought in England in the Nineteenth Century* (1896).

HUXLEY, T. H. *Collected Essays* (1898).

ILLINGWORTH, A. L. *The Life of J. R. Illingworth* (1917).

ILLINGWORTH, J. R. *Divine Immanence* (1906).

  Personality: Human and Divine (1907).

INGE, W. R. *Christian Mysticism* (1899).

JACKS, L. P. *The Life and Letters of Stopford Brooke* (1917).

JOHNSTON, J. O. *The Life and Letters of H. P. Liddon* (1904).

JONES, HENRY. *Browning as a Philosophical and Religious Teacher* (1891).

KENYON, F. G. *The Textual Criticism of the New Testament* (1901 etc.).

KINGSLEY, F. E. *Charles Kingsley* (1876).

LANCELOT, J. B. *F. J. Chavasse* (1928).

LIGHTFOOT, J. B. *Essays on 'Supernatural Religion'* (1889).
The Apostolic Fathers (1869–85).
The Christian Ministry (1868).

Lux Mundi, ed. Charles Gore (1889 etc.).

MATHESON, P. E. *The Life of Hastings Rashdall* (1928).

MAURICE, F. *The Life of F. D. Maurice* (1884).

MAURICE, F. D. *Moral and Metaphysical Philosophy* (1861).

MEAD, G. H. *Movements of Thought in the Nineteenth Century* (1936).

MONTEFIORE, C. G. *The Religion of the Ancient Hebrews* (1892).

MORLEY, JOHN. *Recollections* (1917).

MOZLEY, J. B. *Miracles* (1866).

MOZLEY, J. K. *The Doctrine of the Atonement* (1915).
Some Tendencies in British Theology (1951).

MYERS, F. W. H. *Human Personality and Its Survival of Bodily Death* (1903).

NETTLESHIP, R. L. *Memoir of T. H. Green* (1906).

OMAN, JOHN. *Vision and Authority* (1928).

PAGET, STEPHEN. *Henry Scott Holland* (1921).

PFLEIDERER, OTTO. *The Development of Theology in Germany since Kant* etc. (1890).

PRESTIGE, G. L. *The Life of Charles Gore* (1935).

PRINGLE-PATTISON (SETH), A. *The Idea of God in Recent Theology* (1917).

PROTHERO, R. E. *The Life and Letters of Dean Stanley* (1894).

RAMSAY, WILLIAM. *St. Paul the Traveller and the Roman Citizen* (1895).
The Church in the Roman Empire (1893).

RASHDALL, HASTINGS. *Philosophy and Religion* (1915).

RAVEN, C. E. *Science, Religion and the Future* (1943).

ROBINSON, J. ARMITAGE. *The Study of the Gospels* (1902).

SANDAY, W. *Inspiration* (1893 etc.).
The Life of Christ in Recent Research (1907).

SANDFORD, E. G. *Frederick Temple: an Appreciation* (1907).
Memoirs of Frederick Temple, ed. by Sandford (1906).

SCHWEITZER, A. *The Quest of the Historical Jesus* (1910).

Sidgwick, Henry, a Memoir (1906).

SMITH, G. A. *Historical Geography of the Holy Land* (1894 etc.).

SMITH, W. ROBERTSON. *The Old Testament in the Jewish Church* (1881).
  The Prophets of Israel (1882 etc.).
  The Religion of the Semites (1889 etc.).
STORR, V. F. *Development and Divine Purpose* (1906).
  *The Development of English Theology in the Nineteenth Century:
  1800–60* (1913).
STREETER, B. H. *The Four Gospels* (1924).
TENNYSON, HALLAM. *Alfred, Lord Tennyson: a Memoir* (1897).
THACKERAY, H. ST. J. *The Relation of St. Paul to Contemporary Jewish
  Thought* (1900).
TULLOCH, JOHN. *Movements of Religious Thought in Britain during the
  Nineteenth Century* (1885).
WAGGETT, P. N. *Religion and Science* (1904).
WATSON, E. W. *The Life of Bishop John Wordsworth* (1915).
WEBB, C. C. J. *A History of Philosophy* (1915 etc.).
  A Study of Religious Thought in England from 1850 (1933).
WESTCOTT, ARTHUR. *The Life and Letters of B. F. Westcott* (1903).
WESTCOTT, B. F. *Christus Consummator* (1886).
  Religious Thought in the West (1891).
  Social Aspects of Christianity (1887).
  The Gospel of Life (1892).
  The Incarnation and Common Life (1893).
WOOD, ALEX. *In Pursuit of Truth* (1927).
WOOD, H. G. *Belief and Unbelief since 1850* (1955).

INDEX

A

ABAILARD, 248
Abbott, E. A., 23, 161, 162, 318
Acton, Lord, 95f., 111, 114, 119, 173, 250
Adam, James, 84
Agnosticism, 69, 184, 284, 294, 324ff.
Ainger, Canon, 21, 365
Albee, E., 64, 68
Allegorical interpretation, 117, 175, 188f., 201f.
Allen, A. V. G., 55, 187
Allen, E. L., 337
Anselm, St., 247, 249, 362f.
Anthropology, 194ff., 270, 343
Apocryphal writings, 107, 159
Apologetics, 45, 55, 83, 122, 186, 187, 202, 320, 367ff.
Apostolic succession, 267
Aquinas, Thomas, St., 12, 87, 211, 219, 235, 320
Archaeology, 100ff., 146ff., 200
Architecture, 99f.
Aristotle, 76, 154, 273, 296
Arnold, Matthew, 223, 275, 296f., 336;
  religious views, 11f., 224, 299f.;
  literary works, 86, 299, 357
Arnold, Thomas, 111, 287f.
Articles, The Thirty-nine, 23, 210f., 217, 257
Asquith, Lord Oxford and, 66, 69, 126
Athanasian Creed, The, 218
Athanasius, St., 214
Atheism, 24, 324f., 335, 352f.
Atonement, The, 218, 233, 234, 244ff., 314
Augustine, St., 201, 222, 267, 343
Authority, 7, 83f., 212f., 319ff.: see also
  Bible; Church

B

BACON, Francis, 38, 47f.,
Balfour, A. J., 31, 60, 63, 88

Baptism, 268ff.
Barth, Karl, 235
Baur, F. C., 90, 154, 165
Bell, Gertrude, 101
Bengel, 118
Bennett, Arnold, 329
Bennett, W. J. E., 273
Benson, E. W., Archbishop, 134, 168, 363
Bentham, 7, 71, 296
Berenson, B., 342
Bernard, T. D., 181
Bethune-Baker, J. F., 124, 190, 236, 242
Bible, The, 2, 17, 31, 44, 102, 116f., 128, 174ff., 238, 256f., 313, 376; authority of, 18, 44, 51, 82f., 185, 191; neglect of, 48f., 190, 350; Canon, 155; Revised Version, 172
Biblical criticism, 26, 117ff., 217, 282, 308f., 342f.
Bigg, C., 214, 238
Blake, William, 248, 327
Boer War, The, 357f.
Bosanquet, Bernard, 30, 70, 318, 368
Bradley, A. C., 180
Bradley, F. H., 70f., 300, 325
Briggs, C. A., 144
Bright, William, 111, 123, 271
Broad Churchmen, 316f., 332
Brooke, Stopford, 20, 22f., 298
Browning, E. B., 275
Browning, Robert, 296, 298f., 352; views, 225, 232, 253, 295; quoted, 6, 76f., 181, 294
Bryce, Lord, 69f., 99
Buchan, John, 71, 79, 275
Buckle, 27
Burgon, Dean, 170
Burkitt, F. C., 160
Burney, C. F., 144, 152
Butler, Bishop, 54, 82, 197f., 221
Butler, Samuel, 36